WELL-READ LIVES

· ·

WELL-READ LIVES

· ·

How Books Inspired a Generation of American Women

BARBARA SICHERMAN

The University of North Carolina Press · Chapel Hill

Designed by Courtney Leigh Baker and set in Minion by Graphic Composition, Inc. Manufactured in the United States of America. The paper in this book meets the guidelines for permanence and durability of the Committee on Production Guidelines for Book Longevity of the Council on Library Resources. The University of North Carolina Press has been a member of the Green Press Initiative since 2003.

Library of Congress Cataloging-in-Publication Data
Sicherman, Barbara.
Well-read lives : how books inspired a generation of American women / Barbara Sicherman.
p. cm.
Includes bibliographical references and index.
ISBN 978-0-8078-3308-7 (alk. paper)
1. Women—Books and reading—Social aspects—United States—History—19th century. 2. Girls—Books and reading—Social aspects—United States—History—19th century. 3. Women and literature—United States—History—19th century. I. Title.
Z1039.W65S53 2010
028'.9082—dc22
2009039480

Earlier versions of chapter 1 appeared in "Reading *Little Women*: The Many Lives of a Text," in *U.S. History as Women's History: New Feminist Essays*, ed. Linda K. Kerber, Alice Kessler-Harris, and Kathryn Kish Sklar (Chapel Hill: University of North Carolina Press, 1995); of chapter 4, in "Sense and Sensibility: A Case Study of Women's Reading in Late-Victorian America," in *Reading in America: Literature and Social History*, ed. Cathy N. Davidson (Baltimore: Johns Hopkins University Press, 1989); and of chapter 5, in "Reading and Ambition: M. Carey Thomas and Female Heroism," *American Quarterly* 45 (March 1993): 73–103.

Portions of chapter 2 appeared in "Reading and Middle-Class Identity in Victorian America: Cultural Consumption, Conspicuous and Otherwise," in *Reading Acts: U.S. Readers' Interactions with Literature, 1800–1950*, ed. Barbara Ryan and Amy M. Thomas (Knoxville: University of Tennessee Press, 2002), and in "Ideologies and Practices of Reading," in *A History of the Book in America*, vol. 3, *The Industrial Book, 1840–1880*, ed. Scott E. Casper et al. (Chapel Hill: University of North Carolina Press, 2007).

Portions of the epilogue appeared in "Connecting Lives: Women and Reading, Then and Now," in *Women in Print: Essays on the Print Culture of American Women from the Nineteenth and Twentieth Centuries*, ed. James P. Danky and Wayne A. Wiegand (Madison: University of Wisconsin Press, 2006).

14 13 12 11 10   5 4 3 2 1

IN MEMORY OF
Jeannette Bailey Cheek and Janet Wilson James

CONTENTS

ILLUSTRATIONS

WELL-READ LIVES

. . . .

. . . .

Books and Lives

This is a book about women, reading, and the connections between them. More particularly it is about reading in the lives of young women growing up in America's Gilded Age who, in varying degree, broke away from the domestic lives expected of them. Born roughly between 1855 and 1875, they belonged to a generation of women that individually and collectively left an unparalleled record of public achievement—as physicians and scientists, social workers and educators, perhaps most of all as leaders of the social justice wing of the Progressive reform movement of the early twentieth century.[1]

How women maneuvered their way from overprotected childhoods marked by extreme gender stereotyping to lives of adventure is one of the fascinating aspects of this generation's history. Many ingredients fueled the desire of girls and young women for public lives. Chief among them were the exciting new opportunities for higher education and professional employment that came along at the right time; some, like the settlement houses, they created for themselves.

Well-Read Lives examines a less tangible but no less significant factor in women's journeys to public identities: the ways in which reading stirred imaginations and fostered female ambition. It argues both that reading has long been an important vehicle for promoting and sustaining women's aspirations and that it had special resonance for young women in the years after the Civil War.

Literature in general and fiction in particular have been of critical importance in the construction of female identity. Developmental psychologists suggest that stories are so appealing because they relate to issues in readers' lives in emotionally powerful ways. Starting even before they can read, fiction helps boys and girls sort out and control their fears and desires in fantasy; work out their relationships to the world through identification with hero or heroine; gain insight into the meaning of life; and, later, develop analytic thinking.[2]

At all ages girls and women read more fiction than do boys and men. This was true in the late nineteenth century as it is today.[3] The reasons for this predilection have yet to be fully explored; among those advanced are women's socialization to be attentive to the emotions of others and their need to find satisfactions unavailable in other ways. In addition, because of their subordinate position in society and their traditional consignment to the home, women more than men have had to learn about life from books. Given the restrictive norms of Victorian culture, this was never more true than in the late nineteenth century, when the cultural contradictions surrounding gender were considerable. On the one hand, girls were encouraged to develop their minds and even applauded for intellectual precocity. On the other, virtually everything they read and heard, whether emanating from press, pulpit, or academy, equated true womanhood with domesticity.

The scarcity of models for nontraditional womanhood has prompted women more often than men to turn to literature for self-authorization. This is especially true during adolescence (and the years just before and just after), a time of heightened imagination and often intense contemplation of the future. Books provided women not with an exact template or blueprint, but with malleable forms that could be tried on for fit, to be emulated, appropriated, discarded when no longer useful. Men too could find their futures in books, but because they had real-life mentors and models, in general they had less need to do so. Where men were expected to make their way in the world, women struggled to do so.

Ambitious women needed real determination to achieve their goals. There were fathers (and sometimes mothers) to convince that it was worthwhile to educate a daughter; there was outright discrimination in institutions of learning and employment that hindered their quests; there were also conventions of propriety to overcome, including restrictions on socializing with men and on working outside the home after marriage. At a time when motherhood was highly idealized, remaining single was, with few exceptions, a virtual condition for a middle-class woman to have a career. As both a personal resource and a cultural system, reading allowed young women to enter imaginative space that might provide a bridge to their future lives as they navigated difficult terrain.

Women of the comfortable classes grew up in a "culture of reading" that permeated virtually every aspect of family life, leisure activities as well as education. By culture of reading I mean an environment or way of life that fostered intense engagement with literacy in its diverse forms. The Gilded Age was in many respects the high-water mark of literacy in America. Not only was reading sanctified as a means of promoting knowledge, morality, and cultural competence; it was also a popular form of family entertainment, unchallenged by movies, radio, and television. Its dual status, as admired cultural practice and pleasurable entertainment, helps account for reading's unusual impact at the time. Although skills and access to intellectual resources varied, this domestic literary culture was widely diffused among the middle and upper classes, shared by young and old, by boys as well as girls.

Literary accomplishments became important markers of distinction for young women, writing fine letters or reciting poetry signs of superior talent and worth. Eager participants in the family literary culture, they also developed distinctive modes of reading that reinforced its potency. Most important was the collective nature of many of their endeavors. In the broadest sense, all reading is social, and never more so than at this time. Women often read and wrote together, whether in informal reading circles or organized study clubs, each with its own rituals and opportunities for performance. Through reading—and its corollary writing—young women created communities of learning, imagination, and emotional connection. During what was often a period of extended adolescence, their reading communities helped sustain women in their ambitions despite parental resistance or self-doubt.

Contemporary structures of reading intertwined with women's lives in synergistic ways. As an esteemed cultural practice, a frequently intense social ritual, a wellspring of pleasure as well as knowledge, reading had much to offer an ambitious young woman. No wonder so many found in reading a way of apprehending the world that encouraged imaginative freedom and new self-definitions. Vicarious perhaps, but no less potent or real. Young women read and reworked stories for themselves and intimate friends in ways that generated new narratives with which to construct less restrictive lives.[4] By immersing themselves in the alternative worlds opened by books, young women came to recognize previously hidden thoughts and feelings, a necessary stage before acting on them. In such circumstances, reading helped nurture and sustain private dreams that could later be transmuted into public acts. Ostensibly a private activity, reading was thus intimately connected with the public sphere. Although insufficient by itself, reading had much to recommend it as a starting point to any woman discontented with the status quo.[5]

It is the overall pattern of reading in a life that concerns me. In the context of a life, what reading means is more than the sum of the books a person has read. It is more, too, than a matter of interpretations, conscious or not, of particular books and authors or of identifications with favorite characters, although it is these as well. Meanings depend on the interactions among readers, texts, and environments. They are constructed through the practices of communities of readers and refracted through individuals. How one reads as well as what and with whom are of central importance to the enterprise, even to the act of interpretation. As historian Roger Chartier aptly reminds us, "reading is always a practice embodied in acts, spaces, and habits."[6] In Janice Radway's formulation, it is "a complex intervention in the ongoing social life of actual social subjects."[7]

If reading is to be studied as a behavior, it is a behavior with deep symbolic import. To understand the meaning of reading in a life, the "web of significance" spun around it, I have drawn on anthropologist Clifford Geertz's method of thick description. Where he employed the close-up to elicit the symbolic meaning of a Balinese cock fight, I have applied it to the study of reading, surely one of the chief ways in which people make sense of their culture and their own behavior as well.[8]

To capture both the gestural and symbolic significance of reading for historically situated readers, I have organized this book principally around individual reading communities.[9] The case study approach may forfeit the grand generalizations allowed by surveys based on aggregate data or general populations. But the reasons for adopting it seem to me compelling. Probing the significance of reading in a life requires close attention to relationships, not only between readers and texts, reading acts and interpretations, but among readers as well. Understanding of this sort can be attained only by intensive inquiry into readers' lives over time. In understanding the connections between books and lives, case studies allow for a specificity that is often lost when seeking a common denominator. Averaging can flatten out experiences, obscuring the ways in which meanings are made. Blending may result in blurring or distortion rather than in synthesis.

In employing the case study approach, I have been influenced by recent scholarship in the burgeoning field of book history, which has moved the study of reading from one that examines texts or their distribution in the population, to one that foregrounds practices and relationships of reading.[10] A key insight of this work is that meanings derive not just from texts, but from the interaction of readers and texts, what readers bring to and take away from them. Another is that these transactions are influenced by the social context in which they occur. In *Well-Read Lives*, I have attempted to extend these insights to the study of historically situated readers by examining connections between specific reading practices and the long-range meaning of reading in a life. It is an approach that highlights reading's creative possibilities and its capacity to affect behavior.

Use of the close-up foregrounds the emotional impact of reading, a subject often neglected by scholars who treat reading primarily as an intellectual endeavor or as an adjunct to formal education. By contrast, my emphasis is on self-directed or voluntary reading, an approach that permits analysis of the relationships among cognitive development, emotions, and the larger culture that are so important for understanding how reading works in practice and over time. As psychologist Keith Oatley observes, "fictional narrative has its impact primarily through the emotions." When emotional engagement occurs in "contexts of understanding," he suggests, reading can "affect a person's whole identity."[11] Given women's long-standing attraction to fiction and the greater discontinuity of their lives than men's, exploring the connections between women's emotional and intellectual lives helps to unlock the challenging historical question with which this introduction begins: how a generation of women successfully found their way into uncharted territory. This study of women's reading is then also a way of writing women's biography.

WELL-READ LIVES is constructed as theme and variations. If the theme is the significance of reading in young women's lives, the variations are its performances in differently situated communities.

To set the stage and to demonstrate my contextual approach to connecting texts and lives, I begin by examining diverse responses to *Little Women* (1868–69), the paradigmatic text for young women of the era and one in which family literary culture is prominently featured. Although commissioned as a "girls' book" (a new publishing category with a domestic focus that paralleled boys' adventure stories), Louisa May Alcott's classic and her heroine Jo March have appealed to intellectual women, especially prospective writers, well into the twentieth century. The contrast in response of two communities of readers—native-born women of the comfortable classes and Jewish immigrants—points to the importance of aspirations as well as social location in how a book is read.

White women presided over the domestic literary landscape of the Gilded Age. They not only had attained near literacy equality with their male counterparts but had primary responsibility for overseeing literary culture, a newly important marker of middle-class status. Both sexes were socialized into this domestic literary culture, but young women's relationship to it was especially intense. Their distinctive engagement with reading in its cultural, emotional, and social dimensions is elaborated in profiles of Florence Kelley, Alice Stone Blackwell, and Charlotte Perkins Gilman.

The central figures in my story were intellectuals, most of them writers, many of them activists as well. Whether because of unusual talent, drive, opportunity, or all three, they made effective use of their literary culture. The subjects of the first three extended reading profiles were white women from elite families who, despite their privilege and ready access to books, had distinct relationships to literacy and made different uses of it. Each profile foregrounds a different reading modality.

In the case of the extended, mainly female, Hamilton family of Fort Wayne, Indiana, my focus is on the collective reading culture that was central to family identity. The Hamiltons read together, talked incessantly about books, and modeled their own literary efforts after what they read. They also peopled their lives with characters from their wide reading of novels, finding in the porous boundary between fiction and life opportunities for self-creation. Although collective, their reading culture left room for individual expression, as sisters and cousins chose signature books and literary models to suit their temperaments. Two of the women attained unusual distinction: Edith Hamilton, best-selling interpreter of classical civilizations, and her younger sister Alice Hamilton, a physician and social reformer whose studies of industrial poisons took her to Harvard as its first woman professor.

M. Carey Thomas's engagement with literature was more individualistic than that of the Hamiltons: her parents were devout Quakers, a faith that, in theory at least, disallowed fiction, music, and theater, all of which Thomas came to love. Reading became a lifelong passion, at once a pleasure and a temptation that at times she struggled to control. The intensity of this passion was apparent in a journal she kept in early adolescence that registered the connections between her reading and ambitions, which in the early years included attending college and becoming a writer. She later found support from members of a Baltimore feminist literary circle that combined female sociability with radical gender politics and a taste for transgressive authors like Shelley and Swinburne. Thomas never became a writer, but as president of Bryn Mawr College she created the sanctuary for intellectual women she had dreamed of in her teens.

Where Thomas found aesthetic and emotional satisfaction in literature, Jane Addams looked to it for clues about how to live. The answer did not come easily. Even as she engaged some of the major thinkers of her time, among them Matthew Arnold and Leo Tolstoy, her literary enthusiasm was tempered by fear that self-culture would prevent her from making her mark in the world. Despite an ambivalence to reading that was apparent even in her college essays, Addams's cultural studies—and her ability to integrate them with her spiritual and moral concerns—had an important place in the route that led her to found Hull-House, the pioneering Chicago settlement. Addams's success at synthesizing and applying what she read to the gritty world she inhabited helped her become the preeminent interpreter of the settlement movement and one of the foremost intellectuals of the era.

The last third of *Well-Read Lives* examines the efforts of less privileged women to attain expressive literacy, by which I mean the ability to read and write fluently and to use these abilities for self-defined goals. Because their access to traditional education was limited, working-class, immigrant, and African American women often acquired full literacy through alternative routes, ranging from informal venues that fostered self-improvement to institutions like settlement houses and libraries.

When Hull-House opened in 1889, along with child care and assistance in dealing with landlords and the law, residents offered classes—on Robert Browning and George Eliot, as well as basic English and bookkeeping. The majority of participants in the culture classes were young women, among them Hilda Satt Polacheck, an immigrant for whom the experience was life-changing. The classes, and the sociability that accompanied them, not only relieved the boredom of her life as a factory worker but provided skills that enabled her to enter the American middle class. As Addams became better acquainted with her neighbors and learned that most of them desired to be entertained, reading classes gave way to theater, a cultural form that, while literary in part, provided greater opportunity for community building and the cross-class reciprocity Addams sought. The experience suggests that reformers could not succeed with a cultural agenda that did not meet the needs and wishes of the neighborhood.

First-person accounts by African American and immigrant women make it possible to view the process of attaining literacy from the vantage points of seekers rather than providers. For Russian Jewish immigrants, access to books and libraries was often central to their experience of America, symbols of freedom and plenty unknown in their tightly bounded Old World communities. For women, whose access to literacy had been more restricted than men's, these opportunities promised a new gender equality as well. In published autobiographies, some made much of the new identities they found in English-language books (and the libraries and settlements that provided them). Where Rose Cohen, who was unable to attend school, recorded her painful struggle to become more literate, first in Yiddish, then in English, the well-educated Mary Antin celebrated her transformation from a humble Jewish girl into a proud American citizen. Different though their experiences were, their American reading helped both women reimagine and re-create themselves: they not only moved up in social class but forsook religious practices they came to associate with a repressive, patriarchal culture.

For African Americans, claiming expressive literacy was both a matter of enhancing knowledge and of securing their due standing as Americans. As a young teacher in Memphis, Ida B. Wells honed her literary skills, both oral and written, in the sociable environment of an African American lyceum. There she gave recitations (ranging from Shakespeare to dialect poems), challenged racial segregation in railroad cars, and began her career as a journalist. Wells made effective use of her oratorical and literary skills when she launched her courageous campaign against lynching. With middle-class African American women as her strongest supporters, her crusade helped unite a burgeoning club movement into a national forum. Like Wells, who regretted that she had never read "a Negro book" in her youth, many of its leaders were proponents of a "race literature," books by and about African Americans, a genre they thought would promote more positive racial images. African American women's communal literary activities, with their frequently religious foundation, provide a striking contrast to the alienation of many Jewish literary women from their communities and religion.

The experiences of Jewish and African American women underscore one of the central premises of *Well-Read Lives*: that although reading is inflected by class and race as well as gender, it is not confined by these or other identities. Despite barriers and difficulties, some African American and immigrant women found emotional and intellectual sustenance in the books they read and forged new identities from them. As was the case with native-born white women, for those with opportunity and inclination, books had the power to take readers to "the place of elsewhere," sometimes literally as well as figuratively.[12] Members of both groups found in their literary activities a way to claim an identity as cultured American women.

However an individual's literacy was acquired, under the right circumstances reading could be a transformative experience. What these circumstances were for American women in the late nineteenth century is the subject of this book.

PART ONE

YOUNG WOMEN'S READING IN THE GILDED AGE

. . . .

CHAPTER ONE

Reading *Little Women*

All girls are what they read; the whole world is what it reads. Ask any girl whom you have never met before what books she reads and, if she answers truthfully, you will know her, heart and soul.

On a young girl's choice of reading depends the happiness or misery of her entire future. . . . If you wish to be good girls, read good books.

These were not the words of a Victorian sage, but of Rose Pastor, a recent Jewish immigrant from eastern Europe. Writing as "Zelda" for the English page of the *Yiddishes Tageblatt* in July 1903, Pastor admonished her readers to avoid the "'cheap, poisonous stuff' . . . the crazy phantasies from the imbecile brains of Laura Jean Libbey, The Duchess, and others of their ilk!" That is, the authors of the "sensational" romances read by working-class women.[1]

Responding to requests for advice, Pastor later elaborated on what girls should read and thus, presumably, become. Heading the list for girls sixteen and under was Louisa May Alcott, a writer known for her "excellent teachings" and one from whom "discriminating or indiscriminating" readers alike derived pleasure. With the accent on pleasure and the assurance that "good" books need not be "dry," the columnist figured Alcott as a writer with wide, even universal, appeal. Citing a dozen titles, Pastor also commended the story of Alcott's life by Mrs. E. D. Cheney, claiming that "the biographies of some writers are far more interesting, even, than the stories they have written." In her judgments the immigrant journalist echoed more established critics.[2]

By the time Pastor wrote, Alcott's *Little Women* had been prescribed reading for American girls for a full generation. Commissioned to tap into an evolving market for "girls' stories," her tale of growing up female was an immediate "hit," whether judged by sales or by its impact on readers. Published in early October 1868, the first printing (2,000 copies) of *Little Women; or, Meg, Jo, Beth and Amy* sold out within the month. A sequel appeared the following April, with only the designation *Part Second* to differentiate it from the original. By the end of the year some 38,000 copies (of both parts) were in print, with an additional 32,000 in 1870. Nearly 200,000 copies had been printed in the United States by January 1888, two months before Alcott's death.[3] With this book, Alcott established her niche in the expanding market for juvenile literature. She redirected her energies as a writer away from adult fiction—some of it considered sensational and published anonymously or pseudonymously—to become not just a successful author of "juveniles," but one of the most popular writers of the era. A very well paid one, at that.[4]

Even more remarkable than *Little Women*'s initial success has been its longevity. It topped a list of forty books compiled by the Federal Bureau of Education in 1925 that "all children should read before they are sixteen."[5] Two years later, in response to the question "What book has influenced you most?" high school students ranked it first, followed by the Bible and *Pilgrim's Progress*.[6] And on a Bicentennial list of the eleven best American children's books, *Little Women*, *The Adventures of Tom Sawyer*, and *Adventures of Huckleberry Finn* were the only nineteenth-century titles. Like most iconic works, *Little Women* has been transmuted into other media, into song and opera, theater, radio, and film, even a comic strip that surfaced briefly in 1988 in the revamped *Ms.*[7] Not to mention the inevitable commercial spin-offs—dolls, notebooks, and T-shirts.[8] As of May 2008, Barnes and Noble's online database listed seventy editions, not counting foreign language–thesaurus versions, audiocassettes, CDs, paper dolls, and the like.[9] No wonder *Little Women* has been called "the most popular girls' story in American literature."[10]

Polls and statistics do not begin to do justice to the *Little Women* phenomenon. Reading the book has been a rite of passage for generations of adolescent and preadolescent females of the comfortable classes. It still elicits powerful narratives of love and passion.[11] In a 1982 essay on how she became a writer, Cynthia Ozick declared, "I read 'Little Women' a thousand times. Ten thousand. I am no longer incognito, not even to myself. I am Jo in her

Frontispiece, Ednah Dow Cheney, *Louisa May Alcott: The Children's Friend* (1888), lithograph by Lizbeth B. Comins. Courtesy of American Antiquarian Society.

'vortex'; not Jo exactly, but some Jo-of-the-future. I am under an enchantment: Who I truly am must be deferred, waited for and waited for."[12] Ozick's avowal encapsulates recurrent themes in readers' accounts: the deep, almost inexplicable emotions engendered by the novel; the passionate identification with Jo March, the feisty tomboy heroine who publishes stories as a teenager; and—allowing for exaggeration—a pattern of multiple readings.

Running through the testimony of nineteenth- and twentieth-century readers, Ozick's story of deferred desire and suspended identity yields an important insight into *Little Women*'s appeal to young females: its ability to engage them in ways that open up future possibility. As a character readers imagined becoming, Jo promoted self-discovery, revealing hidden potentialities to those in the liminal state between childhood and adulthood. If they were not yet "Jo exactly," through Jo readers could catch glimpses of their future selves. With their own identities still uncertain, they could nevertheless emulate the unconventional heroine who strove so passionately for a future of her own making. For women growing up in the late nineteenth century, having a future outside the family was anything but assured; even well into the twentieth, it could not be taken for granted.

Little Women has been exceptional in its ability to elicit narratives of female fulfillment. As in Ozick's case, these narratives often followed the trajectory of a "quest plot" and not—or not only—the "romance plot" women are assumed to prefer. If, as has been claimed, "books are the dreams we would most like to have," then it is not too much to say that *Little Women* was the primary dream book for American girls of the comfortable classes for more than a century.[13]

Not everyone has the same dreams. Readers bring themselves to texts, the selves they are as well as those they wish to become. Through reading they gain entry into imaginative space that is not the space they currently occupy.[14] Readers can and do appropriate texts and meanings in ways unintended by authors or publishers, or for that matter, parents and teachers. Such imaginative leaps, though constrained by historically conditioned structures of feeling and interpretive conventions, permit the reader to move beyond her everyday circumstances. As Emily Dickinson so memorably observed: "There is no Frigate like a book / To take us Lands away."[15]

Young women in the late nineteenth and early twentieth centuries developed means of transport that allowed them to chart their own directions. For those born in relative privilege, Alcott's story often provided a focal point for elaborating dramas of personal autonomy, even rebellion, scenarios that may have helped them transcend otherwise predictably domestic futures. By contrast, some Russian Jewish immigrants, perhaps even readers of Rose Pastor, found in *Little Women* a model for becoming American and middle class, a way into, rather than out of, bourgeois domesticity. In this case aspiration mattered more than actual social position, so often considered the major determinant of reading practices.

Alcott's classic was a book that enabled both sorts of readers to extend what literary theorist Hans Robert Jauss calls the "horizon of expectations." Claiming that a "new literary work is received and judged against the background of other art forms as well as the background of everyday experience of life," Jauss maintains that "the horizon of expectations of literature . . . not only preserves real experiences but also anticipates unrealized possibilities, widens the limited range of social behavior by new wishes, demands, and goals, and thereby opens avenues for future experience."[16] In other words, reading can have real-life consequences.

Are girls what they read, as Rose Pastor suggested in time-honored fashion in her 1903 column? The evidence from *Little Women* and from studies of reading generally suggests rather that readers interact with texts in multiple and varied ways: what readers bring to their encounters with print is critical to the construction of meaning. Readers are not simply shaped by the texts they read; they help to create them. In the case of *Little Women* this was literally as well as figuratively true.

. . . .

"Verily there is a new era in this country in the literature for children," proclaimed a reviewer in the "Literature" section of the December 1868 *Putnam's Magazine*. "It is not very long since all the juvenile books seemed conducted on the principle of the definition of duty 'doing what you don't want to,' for the books that were interesting were not considered good, and the 'good' ones were certainly not interesting." The prime example of the "different order of things" was *Little Women*, which a twelve-year-old girl of the reviewer's acquaintance, who read it twice in one week, pronounced "just the *nicest* book. I could read it right through three times, and it would be nicer and funnier every time."[17]

Putnam's reviewer was correct in sensing "a new era" in children's literature and in assigning *Little Women* a central place in it. Juvenile literature was entering a new phase in the 1860s, with the appearance of several American classics of the genre, including *Hans Brinker; or, The Silver Skates* (1865) by Mary Mapes Dodge and *The Story of a Bad Boy* (1869) by Thomas Bailey Aldrich; indeed, a 1947 source claims that, together with *Little Women*, these titles "initiated the modern juvenile."[18] This literature was more secular and on the whole less pietistic than its antebellum precursors, the characterizations more apt; children, even "bad boys," might be basically good, whatever mischievous stages they passed through.

An expanding middle class, eager to provide its young with cultural as well as moral training, underwrote the new juvenile market. Greater material well-being and new forms of family organization allowed children of the comfortable classes new opportunities for education and leisure, with literary activities often serving as a bridge between them. So seriously was this literature taken that even magazines that embraced high culture devoted considerable space to reviewing children's fiction; thus the seeming anomaly of a review of Alcott's *Eight Cousins* in the *Nation* by the young Henry James.[19]

Little Women was commissioned because a publisher believed that a market existed for a girls' story, a developing genre defined by both gender and age. The book's success suggests that his conjecture was correct. The novel evolved for the female youth market, readers in the transitional period between childhood and adulthood—variously defined as eight to eighteen or fourteen to twenty—that would soon be labeled adolescence.[20] In fact, there is evidence that people of all ages and both sexes read and enjoyed *Little Women*, a generational crossover that was not unusual at the time: six of the ten best sellers between 1875 and 1895 could be considered books for younger readers.[21]

Still relatively new in the 1860s, the segmentation of juvenile fiction by gender was a sign of the emergence of more polarized gender ideals for men and women as class stratification increased.[22] An exciting adventure literature for boys came first, beginning around 1850, a distinct departure from the overtly religious and didactic stories that enjoined young people of both sexes to be good and domesticated. Enjoying wide popularity in the last third of the century, when female influence was increasing at home and in school, this literature featured escape from domesticity and female authority. Often condemned as "sensational"—a contemporary critic described typical subjects as "hunting, Indian warfare, California desperado life, pirates," the list goes on—books like *The Rifle Rangers* and *Masterman Ready* by authors like Captain Mayne Reid, Frederick Marryat, and G. A. Henty highlighted epic struggles of masculinity, including military conquest and the subjugation of natives.[23]

By contrast, a girls' story was by definition a domestic story. It featured a plot in which the heroine learns to accept many of the culture's prescriptions for appropriate womanly behavior. This formula may account for a staggering irony in the publishing history of *Little Women*: Alcott's initial distaste for the project. When Thomas Niles Jr., literary editor of the respected Boston firm of Roberts Brothers, asked Alcott to write a *"girls' story,"* the author tartly observed in her journal, "I plod away, though I don't enjoy this sort of thing. Never liked girls or knew many, except my sisters, but our queer plays and experiences may prove interesting, though I doubt it."[24] Since Alcott idolized her Concord neighbor Ralph Waldo Emerson, adored Goethe, and loved to run wild, one can understand why she might have been disinclined to write a "domestic story." This reluctance may also help to explain how she managed to write one that transcended the genre even while defining it.

Because of its origins as a domestic story, some recent critics view *Little Women* primarily as a work that disciplined its young female characters, who are coerced into overcoming their personal failings and youthful aspirations as they move from adolescence to young womanhood. Alcott has even been accused of murdering her prime creation, Jo March, by allowing her to be tamed and married.[25] This interpretive line acknowledges only one way of reading the story. There is no evidence that Alcott's contemporaries read the book in this way. Like the reviewer in *Putnam's*, most early critics admired *Little Women*'s spirit; some even found the author transgressive. Henry James, though he praised Alcott's skill as a satirist and thought her "extremely clever," took her to task for her "private understanding with the youngsters she depicts, at the expense of their pastors and masters."[26]

Despite claims that *Little Women* is a disciplinary text—for its readers as well as its characters—a comparison with other girls' stories of the period marks it as a text that opens up new avenues for readers rather than foreclosing them. The contrast with Martha Finley's *Elsie Dinsmore* (1867), a story in which strict obedience is exacted from children—to the point of whipping—is instructive. In this first of many volumes, published just a year before the first volume of *Little Women*, the lachrymose and devoutly religious heroine is put upon by relatives and by her father, who punishes her for refusing to play the piano on the Sabbath. Elsie holds fast to her principles but is otherwise self-abnegating in the extreme: it is difficult to imagine her ever having fun.[27] A comparison between Alcott and Mrs. A. D. T. Whitney, a once-acclaimed writer with whom Alcott was often compared, highlights the differences. *Faith Gartney's Girlhood*, a best seller of 1863, is the story of a girl's emergence into serious and self-affirming womanhood. Written for a female audience between fourteen and twenty to show "what is noblest and truest," the book is more complex than *Elsie Dinsmore*, the tone less charged. But Whitney relies heavily on didactic narrative and does not fully exploit the emotional potential of her plot: the authorial voice is moralistic, the religion conspicuous.[28] Unlike Alcott's books, *Faith Gartney's Girlhood* had a long run in the Sunday-school libraries.

While using John Bunyan's *Pilgrim's Progress* as a framing device, *Little Women* replaces an older Calvinist view that emphasized sin and obedience to the deity with a moral outlook in which self-discipline and doing good to others come first.[29] A reviewer for the *Ladies' Repository* pointedly observed that *Little Women* was "not a Christian book. It is religion without spirituality, and salvation without Christ."[30] Consonant with *Little Women*'s new moral tone, so congenial to an expanding middle class, are its informal style and rollicking scenes. There are lessons for the young, of course, but Marmee teaches her daughters by example and by letting them make their own mistakes.[31]

In many ways, the novel is also a harbinger of modern life, of consumer culture as well as new freedoms and opportunities for middle-class children. The older March girls are forced to take on paid work, but the sisters study art and piano and in other ways seek to acquire cultural capital. Their longings—for riches as well as fame—can be read as a conspicuous declaration of consumer desire. Indeed, *Little Women* opens with the sisters' laments that they cannot buy what they most desire: "pretty things" for Meg; two classic European tales, *Undine* and *Sintram*, for Jo; new music for Beth; and for Amy, a box of Faber erasers. Notwithstanding the family's relative poverty, their individual desires, mainly for cultural commodities that require at least a modicum of leisure, locate the sisters squarely in the middle class.

Influenced by her love of the theater and by her youthful idol, Dickens, Alcott was a skillful painter of dramatic scenes; some, like the death of Beth March, tug at the heart, but many more involve spirited descriptions of games, theatrical productions, and other joyful occasions.[32] Alcott also had an ear for young people's language. Her substitution of dialogue for the long passages of moralizing narrative that characterized most girls' books gave her story a compelling sense of immediacy. So did her use of slang, for which critics often faulted her, but which must have endeared her to young readers. Finally, the beautifully realized portrait of Jo March as tomboy spoke to changing standards of girlhood. Tomboys first became a major literary type in the 1860s. They were not only tolerated, but even admired—up to a point, the point at which girls were expected to become women.[33]

This is the point at which some late-twentieth-century critics deplored Alcott's concessions to bourgeois, heterosexual convention. But it is again instructive to compare Alcott with her contemporaries, in particular the popular Katy books by "Susan Coolidge," which are closest to hers in spirit. Katy Carr, who at twelve is another Jo, an ambitious, harum-scarum, fun-loving girl, is severely punished for disobedience; only after suffering a broken back and several years of painful invalidism does she emerge as a thoughtful girl who will grow into true womanhood—in this case, single womanhood, with responsibility for her widowed father and younger siblings.[34] By contrast, Jo's punishment for not preventing the sister who is her greatest trial—and who has just destroyed her manuscript—from falling through the ice is guilt, a harsh penalty, but not in this instance unduly incapacitating. As for growing up, her punishment is marriage to a man of her own choosing.

This turn of plot—its evolution and its negotiation—is in fact both an unusual feature of *Little Women*'s publication history and an important element in the book's long-term power and appeal. Readers had an unusual say in constructing its plot. Eager to capitalize on Roberts Brothers' foray into girls' fiction, Niles urged Alcott to add a chapter "in which allusions might be made to something in the future."[35] Employing a metaphor well suited to a writer who engaged in theatrical performances most of her life, the volume concludes: "So grouped the curtain falls upon Meg, Jo, Beth and Amy. Whether it ever rises again, depends upon the reception given to the first act of the domestic drama, called 'LITTLE WOMEN.'"[36] Reader response to Alcott's floater was positive but complicated her task. Reluctant to depart from autobiography, Alcott insisted that by rights Jo should remain a "literary spinster." But she felt pressured by readers to imagine a different fate for her heroine. The day she began work on the sequel, she observed, "Girls write to ask who the little women marry, as if that was the only end and aim of a woman's life. I *won't* marry Jo to Laurie to please anyone." To foil her readers, she created a "funny match" for Jo—the middle-aged, bumbling German professor, Friedrich Bhaer.[37]

The aspect of the book that has frustrated generations of readers—the foreclosing of marriage between Jo and Laurie—thus represents a compromise between Alcott and her initial audience. Paradoxically, this seeming misstep has probably been a major factor in the story's enduring success. If Jo had remained a spinster, as Alcott wished, or if she had married the attractive and wealthy hero, as readers hoped, it is unlikely that the book would have had such a long-lasting appeal. Rather, the problematic ending contributed to *Little Women*'s popularity, the lack of satisfying closure helping to keep the story alive, something to ponder, return to, reread, perhaps with the hope of a different resolution. Alcott's refusal of the conventionally happy ending represented by a pairing of Jo and Laurie and her insistence on a "funny match" to the rumpled and much older professor subvert adolescent romantic ideals. The absence of a compelling love plot has also made it easier for generations of readers to ignore the novel's ending when Jo becomes Mother Bhaer and to retain the image of Jo as the questing teenager.[38]

At the same time, an adolescent reader, struggling with a less-than-ideal appearance and unruly impulses while contemplating the burdens of future womanhood, might find it reassuring that her fictional counterpart emerges happily, if not perhaps ideally, from similar circumstances. For Jo is loved. And she has choices. She turns down the charming but erratic Laurie, who consoles himself by marrying her pretty and vain younger sister, Amy. Professor Bhaer is no schoolgirl's hero, but Jo believes he is better suited to her than Laurie. The crucial point is that the choice is hers, its quirkiness another sign of her much-prized individuality.[39] It is true that Jo gives up writing sensation novels because her future husband considers them unworthy, but she makes it clear that she intends to contribute to the support of their future family and hopes to "write a good book yet."[40]

By marrying off the sisters in the second part, Alcott bowed to her readers' interest in romance. The addition of the marriage to the quest plot enabled *Little Women* to touch the essential bases for middle-class female readers. In this regard, it was unusual for its time. In adult fiction, marriage and quest plots were rarely combined; success in the former precluded attainment of the latter.[41] The inclusion of a marriage plot in a book intended for a non-adult audience was also unusual. At least one reviewer judged the sequel "a rather mature book for the little women, but a capital one for their elders."[42] But the conjunction of quest and marriage plots helps to account for *Little Women*'s staying power. It is difficult to imagine large numbers of adolescent females in the twentieth century gravitating to a book in which the heroine remained single.

Little Women took off with the publication of the second part in April 1869. A Concord neighbor called it "the rage in '69 as 'Pinafore' was in '68."[43] A savvy judge of the market, Niles urged Alcott to "'Make hay while the Sun shines'" and did everything he could to keep her name before the public.[44] Shortly after the appearance of *Little Women, Part Second*, Roberts Brothers brought out an augmented edition of her first critical success under the title *Hospital Sketches and Camp and Fireside Stories*, and in succeeding years published *An Old-Fashioned Girl* (1870) and *Little Men* (1871), a sequel to *Little Women*. Niles encouraged publicity about books and author, whom he kept informed about her extensive press coverage while she traveled abroad. Alcott was then at the peak of her popularity; between October 1868 and July 1871 Roberts Brothers sold some 166,000 volumes of her juvenile fiction.[45]

Alcott's realistic subject matter and direct style, together with the well-publicized autobiographical status of *Little Women*, encouraged identification by her early middle-class readers. Reviewers stressed the realism of her characters and scenes; readers recognized themselves in her work. Thirteen-year-old Annie Adams of Fair Haven, Vermont, wrote *St. Nicholas*, the most prestigious of the new children's magazines, that she and her three sisters each resembled one of the March sisters (she was Jo): "So, you see, I was greatly interested in 'Little Women,' as I could appreciate it so well; and it seemed to me as if Miss Alcott must have seen us four girls before she wrote the story."[46] Girls not only read themselves into *Little Women*; they elaborated on it and incorporated the story into their lives. In 1872, the five Lukens sisters from Brinton, Pennsylvania, sent Alcott a copy of their home newspaper, "Little Things," which was modeled after "The Pickwick Portfolio" produced by the March sisters. Alcott responded with encouragement, asked for further details, and subscribed to the paper; subsequently she offered advice about reading, writing, and religion, and even sent a story for publication. She took their aspirations seriously, providing frank, practical advice about magazines, publishers, and authors' fees to these budding literary women.[47]

There was, then, a reciprocal relation between the characters and home life depicted in *Little Women* and the lives of middle-class American girls. An unusual feature of this identification was the perception that author and heroine were interchangeable. From the start, Alcott's work was marketed to encourage the illusion not only that Jo was Alcott but that Alcott was Jo. An early ad called *Little Women* a "history of actual life."[48] When Alcott traveled in Europe in 1870, Niles encouraged her to send for publication "'Jo's Letters from Abroad to the March's [*sic*] at Home'"; the following year he asked her to select "from the million or less letters" some that could be published in a volume entitled "Little Women and Little Men Letters or Letters to 'Jo' by 'Little Women' and 'Little Men.'"[49] Neither book materialized, but *Shawl-Straps*, a humorous account of Alcott's European trip, appeared in 1872 as the second volume in the *Aunt Jo's Scrap-Bag* series. Niles sometimes addressed his leading author as "Jo," "Jo March," or "Aunt Jo." Alcott often substituted the names of the March sisters for her own when she answered fans; on occasion, she inserted them into her journal.[50]

Readers responded in kind. An ad for *Little Women* quotes a letter written by "Nelly" addressed to "Dear Jo, or Miss Alcott": "We have all been reading 'Little Women,' and we liked it so much I could not help wanting to write to you. We think *you* are perfectly splendid; I like you better every time I read it. We were all so disappointed about your not marrying Laurie; I cried over that part,—I could not help it. We all liked Laurie ever so much, and almost killed ourselves laughing over the funny things you and he said." Blurring the lines between author and character, the writer requested a picture, wished the recipient improved health, and invited her to visit.[51] The illusion that she was the youthful and unconventional Jo made Alcott more approachable.

Just as this blurring of boundaries between fiction and life, author and character, made *Little Women* more immediate to its early readers, so Alcott's well-publicized success was exhilarating to aspiring young writers like the Lukens sisters. With the publication of *Little Women, Part Second*, Alcott acquired a kind of celebrity that in more recent times has been reserved for male rock stars. Correspondents demanded her photograph, and autograph seekers descended on her home while she "dodge[d] into the woods *à la* Hawthorne."[52] Customarily shunning the limelight, she was mobbed by fans on her rare public appearances. After a meeting of the Woman's Congress in 1875, she reported, "the stage filled . . . with beaming girls all armed with Albums and cards and begging to speak to Miss A. . . . 'Do put up your veil so we can see how you really look' said one. 'Will you kiss me please,' said another. . . . I finally had to run for my life with more girls all along the way, and Ma's clawing me as I went."[53] Alcott avenged herself with a devastating portrait of celebrity hounds in *Jo's Boys* (1886), the sequel to *Little Men*.

In the 1860s and 1870s authorship was the most respected female vocation—and the best paid. A teenage girl contemplating a literary career could dream of becoming a published author who, like Alcott, might produce a beloved and immortal work. At a time when young women were encouraged, even expected, to take part in the literary activities that suffused middle-class domestic life, such success was not beyond imagining. Readers could learn from encyclopedia and newspaper articles that Alcott began writing for publication at sixteen and, by hard work and perseverance, became self-supporting by her pen as well as famous in her late thirties.[54]

Before the consolidation of the American literary canon at the end of the century, women writers had an acknowledged, though not unchallenged, place in the world of letters. Alcott was well respected as a writer during her lifetime, an era of relatively nonhierarchical definitions of literature that included books for children and other genres that would later be eliminated from the canon. An American literature course at Rockford Female Seminary in 1878–79 covered authors of domestic fiction, Alcott among them.[55] Her reputation transcended the classification. A review of *Little Men* pronounced, "Even thus early in her brief history as a country and a nation, America can boast a long list of classics—Prescott, Irving, Hawthorne, Longfellow—and Time, the great sculptor will one day carve Miss Alcott's name among them."[56] Alcott received nearly a page to Hawthorne's page and a half in James S. Hart's *A Manual of American Literature: A Text-Book for Schools and Colleges* (1873), which listed both authors under the category "Novels and Tales." She was compared with her former neighbor on more than one occasion; a younger Concord resident proclaimed, "In American fiction 'Little Women' holds the next place to the 'Scarlet Letter' and 'Marble Faun.'"[57] Since Hawthorne stood at the pinnacle of American literature, this was high praise indeed.

. . . .

With this kind of literary standing, not to mention the pleasure she brought readers, Alcott was well positioned to reach a wide audience. Reading her works became a necessary ritual for children of the comfortable classes. Growing up at a time and in a class that conferred leisure on its young, children devoted considerable time and energy to literary pursuits. For many, *Little Women* was a way-station en route to more adult books. Alcott was such an accepted part of childhood that even men acknowledged liking her. Theodore Roosevelt, for one, declared, "at the cost of being deemed effeminate," that he "worshiped" *Little Men*, *Little Women*, and *An Old-Fashioned Girl*.[58]

Little Women was also a text that acquired its own cachet. "I have read and re-read 'Little Women' and *it* never seems to grow old," fifteen-year-old Jane Addams confided to a friend in 1876.[59] Addams did not say just why she liked *Little Women*. But her partiality was far from unusual among women of her generation. Readers explained their fondness for Alcott in different ways. Not all of them focused on Jo: each of the sisters was distinct and recognizable. Some viewed the story as a (mainly female) family drama, centering around a strong maternal figure—an unusual feature at a time when fictional mothers were often ill, powerless, or dead.[60] The March family invited favorable comparison with the reader's own. Charlotte Perkins Gilman, who grew up in genteel poverty, liked the fact that in Alcott, as in Whitney, "the heroes and heroines were almost always poor, and good, while the rich people were generally bad."[61] For her part, S. Josephine Baker considered Alcott "the unattainable ideal of a great woman." A tomboy who became a prominent physician and wore ties to downplay her gender, "Jo" Baker claimed Jo March as her "favorite character in all fiction" and pointedly dissociated herself from Elsie Dinsmore.[62]

Jo March fueled the fantasy life and literary aspirations of M. Carey Thomas, one of Alcott's first readers, during the critical years of early adolescence. When Thomas began a journal in 1870 at age thirteen, she did so in Jo's name. Declaring at the outset, "Ain't going to be sentimental / 'No no not for Jo' (not Joe)," she had much in common with Alcott's heroine.[63] Both were "bookworms" and tomboys; both desired independence and had difficulty meeting conventional norms of female decorum. Like Jo, Thomas wished to do something "very splendid."[64] Thomas's ambitions were still diffuse, but they centered on becoming a famous writer, a famous *woman* writer—"Jo (not Joe)." Her life was suffused with literature, with writing as well as reading: in addition to keeping a journal, she wrote poetry, kept a commonplace book, and compiled lists of favorite books and poems, some of them annotated.

At the time Thomas was so engaged with *Little Women*, she was already a feminist. Sensitive to any gender restriction or slight, whether from people she knew or from biblical or scientific authorities, at fifteen she resolved to disprove female inferiority by advancing her own education. Despite its inception as a domestic story, then, Thomas read *Little Women* as a female bildungsroman, as did many women after her. This has been the most influential reading, the one that has made the book such a phenomenon for so many years.

With its secular recasting of *Pilgrim's Progress*, *Little Women* transforms Christian's allegorical search for the Celestial City into the quintessential female quest plot. In a chapter entitled "Castles in the Air," each of the March sisters reveals her deepest ambition. In its loving depictions of the sisters' struggles to attain their goals (Jo to be a famous writer, Amy an artist, and Meg mistress of a lovely house), *Little Women* succeeds in authorizing female vocation and individuality. Nor did Alcott rule out the possibility of future artistic creativity: at the novel's end, although married and managing a large household and school, Jo has not given up her literary dreams (she achieves them in the sequel), nor Amy her artistic ones. Beth, who has no ambition other than "to stay at home safe with father and mother, and help take care of the family," dies because she can find no way of growing up; her mysterious illness may be read as a failure of imagination, her inability to build castles in the air.[65]

In Jo, Alcott constructed a portrait of female creativity customarily beyond a woman's reach:

> Every few weeks she would shut herself up in her room, put on her scribbling suit, and "fall into a vortex," as she expressed it, writing away at her novel with all her heart and soul, for till that was finished she could find no peace. . . .
> She did not think herself a genius by any means; but when the writing fit came on, she gave herself up to it with entire abandon, and led a blissful life, unconscious of want, care, or bad weather, while she sat safe and happy in an imaginary world, full of friends almost as real and dear to her as any in the flesh. Sleep forsook her eyes, meals stood untasted, day and night were all too short to enjoy the happiness which blessed her only at such times, and made these hours worth living, even if they bore no other fruit. The divine afflatus usually

lasted a week or two, and then she emerged from her "vortex" hungry, sleepy, cross, or despondent.[66]

Alcott's portrait of concentrated purpose—which describes her own creative practice—is as far removed as it could be from the ordinary lot of women, at least any adult woman. Jo not only has a room of her own; she also has the leisure—and the license—to remove herself from all obligation to others. Jo was important to young women like Thomas because there were so few of her—in literature or in life. One need only recall the example of Margaret Fuller, a generation older than Alcott, who suffered nightmares and delirium from her hothouse education and often felt isolated as the exceptional woman. By contrast, Jo is enmeshed in a supportive community of women.[67] The trick for any female would be to sustain such a life as adolescence gave way to womanhood. To this end, many ambitious women of Thomas's generation not only chose to remain single but often developed their own institutions, living with other women, sometimes in predominantly female communities.

In this context, Alcott provided counsel on two subjects of growing concern to women of the era: economic opportunities and marriage. She was well qualified to advise on the former because of her long years of struggle in the marketplace. Though portrayed more starkly in *Work* (1873), Alcott's autobiographical novel for the adult market, middle-class women's need to earn a living is a central motif in *Little Women*, as it was in the author's life. At a time when even conservative critics were beginning to concede the point, Alcott's classic can be read as a defining text on this subject. Mr. March's economic setback, like Bronson Alcott's, forces his daughters into the labor market. Their jobs (as governess and companion) are mainly unrewarding, but Jo's literary career is described with loving particularity. As we have seen, to please her readers, Alcott compromised her belief that "liberty [is] a better husband." The March sisters marry, but Marmee, who wishes no greater joy for her daughters than a happy marriage, declares that it is better to remain single than to marry without love. Opportunities for self-respecting singlehood and women's employment went hand in hand, as Alcott knew.[68] In *An Old-Fashioned Girl*, which followed *Little Women* and sold nearly as well, Alcott ventures much further in envisioning a life of singlehood and lovingly depicts a community of self-supporting women artists.

If Alcott articulated issues troubling young women of her era, Jo's continued appeal suggests not only the dearth of later fictional heroines to foster dreams of glory but the continued absence of models in literature or in life.

Perhaps that is why in the early twentieth century Simone de Beauvoir was so attracted to *Little Women*, in which, like Ozick after her, she thought she caught a glimpse of her future self:

> I identified myself passionately with Jo, the intellectual. . . . She wrote: in order to imitate her more completely, I composed two or three short stories. . . . The relationship between Jo and Laurie touched me to the heart. Later, I had no doubt, they would marry one another; so it was possible for maturity to bring the promises made in childhood to fruition instead of denying them: this thought filled me with renewed hope. But the thing that delighted me most of all was the marked partiality which Louisa Alcott manifested for Jo. . . . In *Little Women* Jo was superior to her sisters, who were either more virtuous or more beautiful than she, because of her passion for knowledge and the vigor of her thinking; her superiority was as outstanding as that of certain adults, and guaranteed that she would have an unusual life: she was marked by fate. I, too, felt I was entitled to consider my taste in reading and my scholastic success as tokens of a personal superiority which would be borne out by the future. I became in my own eyes a character out of a novel.[69]

De Beauvoir found in Jo a model of authentic selfhood, someone she could not only emulate in the present but through whom she could read—and invent—her own destiny. It was a future full of possibility, open rather than closed, intellectual and literary rather than domestic. By fictionalizing her own life, de Beauvoir could more readily contemplate a career as a writer and intellectual, no matter how improbable such an outcome seemed to her family. She could also rationalize her sense of superiority to her environment and to her own sister. De Beauvoir later claimed that she first learned from *Little Women* that "marriage was not necessary for me," but she responded to the romance as well as the quest plot and found them compatible. Her conviction that Jo and Laurie would marry some day suggests the power of wish fulfillment and the reader's capacity to create her own text. Her romancing came to an abrupt and reluctant halt a year later when she read part II, which in British editions continued to be published under the title *Good Wives* in the late twentieth century. Although initially "crushed" that Jo did not marry Laurie, de Beauvoir took comfort in her choice of a professor "endowed with the highest qualities," a "superior individual" who understood her.[70]

It is because of similar testimony that Jo has with justice been called "the most influential figure of the independent and creative American woman."[71] This is not the only way of reading *Little Women*, but it constitutes a major interpretive strand, probably the primary one during most of the twentieth century. Testimony on this point began as soon as the book was published and persists today among women who grew up in the 1940s and 1950s (some report reading the book yearly in their teens or earlier and even confess to reading it occasionally as adults). It still draws passionate readers born in the 1960s and 1970s, although probably fewer.[72]

.　.　.　.　.　.　.　.　.　.　.　.　.　.　.　.　.　.　.　.

To read *Little Women* as Thomas and de Beauvoir did, or even as a failed bildungsroman, as do critics who view Jo's marriage as a surrender of autonomy and a capitulation to traditional femininity, assumes an individualistic outlook on the part of readers, a belief that a woman could aspire to and even attain personal success outside the family claim. While adolescents from diverse backgrounds *can* interpret *Little Women* as a search for personal autonomy—and have in fact done so—this is by no means a universal reading. There is no single mode of reading Alcott's text that transcends class, race, ethnicity, and historical era. The female quest plot is inflected by class and culture as well as by gender.

Not everyone has access to the same cultural resources, wishes to engage the same texts, or interprets them in identical ways. Although class is by no means the sole determinant of what or how much is read, it is a critical variable in determining basic literacy and educational levels. These in turn, in conjunction with the aspirations of group, family, or individual, influence reading practices and preferences.

Most of what we know about responses to *Little Women* comes from middle-class readers, the group with greatest access to the text. Given American racial realities, its readers have been of predominantly European ancestry. For African American women, in the nineteenth century at least, class rather than race was the primary determinant of reading practices. Mary Church Terrell, a graduate of Oberlin College, observed that Alcott's books "were received with an acclaim among the young people of this country which has rarely if ever been equaled and never surpassed," while Ida B. Wells, a passionate reader throughout her life, claimed she had formed her ideals on Alcott's stories along with those of Mrs. Whitney, Oliver Optic, Dickens, and Charlotte Brontë. Neither singled out *Little Women*; both seem to have read Alcott as part of the standard fare of an American middle-class childhood.[73]

For mid-twentieth-century African American writer Ann Petry, *Little Women* was much more than that. On the occasion of her induction into the Connecticut Women's Hall of Fame in 1994, she noted her admiration for women writers who had preceded and set the stage for her—"Think of Louisa May Alcott." *Little Women* was the first book Petry "read on her own as a child." Her comments are reminiscent of those of de Beauvoir and other writers: "I couldn't stop reading because I had encountered Jo March. I felt as though I was part of Jo and she was part of me. I, too, was a tomboy and a misfit and kept a secret diary. . . . She said things like 'I wish I was a horse, then I could run for miles in this splendid air and not lose my breath'. I found myself wishing the same thing whenever I ran for the sheer joy of running. She was a would-be writer—and so was I."[74]

Two contrasting responses to *Little Women* from up and down the class ladder suggest the traditionally middle-class and perhaps also middle-brow nature of the book's appeal. Edith Wharton, who drops the names of famous books and authors in an autobiography dominated by upper-class and high-culture values, noted that her mother would not let her read popular American children's books because "the children spoke bad English *without the author's knowing it.*" She claimed that when she was finally permitted to read *Little Women* and *Little Men* because everyone else did, "My ears, trained to the fresh racy English of 'Alice in Wonderland,' 'The Water Babies' and 'The Princess and the Goblin,' were exasperated by the laxities of the great Louisa."[75]

Historical evidence from working-class sources is scarce and often filtered through middle-class observers. What we have suggests that working-class women did not always have access to "the simple, every-day classics that the school-boy and -girl are supposed to have read" and that many had a penchant for less realistic fiction of the sort usually dismissed as escapist.[76] Alcott's juvenile fiction did not appear in the story papers most likely to be found in working-class homes; nor was it available in the Sunday school libraries to which some poor children had access. They might, however, encounter Alcott at libraries, settlements, and other middle-class sites. In the late 1880s, for example, she was one of the three most popular authors at the reading room for "deprived" girls run by the United Workers and Woman's Exchange in Hartford.[77]

Like Wharton, though for different reasons, some working-class women found *Little Women* banal. Dorothy Richardson suggests as much in *The*

Long Day, a journalist's account of life among the working class. In an arresting episode, the narrator mocks the reading preferences of her fellow workers in a paper box factory. The plot of a favorite novel, Laura Jean Libbey's *Little Rosebud's Lovers; or, A Cruel Revenge*, is recounted by one of the workers as a tale of a woman's triumph over all sorts of adversity, including abductions and a false marriage to one of the villains. A worker dismisses the narrator's summary of *Little Women*: "That's no story—that's just everyday happenings. I don't see what's the use of putting things like that in books. I'll bet any money that lady what wrote it knew all them boys and girls. They just sound like real, live people; and when you was telling about them I could just see them as plain as plain could be . . . I suppose farmer folks likes them kind of stories . . . They ain't used to the same styles of anything that us city folks are."[78]

The box makers found the characters in *Little Women* real—an interesting point in itself—but did not care to enter its narrative framework. Though they were not class-conscious in a political sense, awareness of their class position may account at least in part for their disinterest in a story whose heroines not only work at mundane though middle-class jobs but learn to adjust to the day-to-day realities of rather humdrum adult lives. Since *their* "everyday happenings" were exhausting work and low pay, the attraction of fictions about working girls who preserved their virtue and came into great wealth, either through marriage or disclosure of their middle- or upper-class origins, is understandable. To women who rarely earned enough to support themselves and who could anticipate lives of married drudgery, such denouements might well have seemed the most likely way of transcending their class status—certainly no more implausible than a future in a suburban cottage. In the absence, in story or in life, of a female success tradition of moving up the occupational ladder, the "Cinderella tale" of marrying up was the nearest thing to a Horatio Alger story for working-class women.[79] For middle-class women, the situation was just the reverse. With new professional employment becoming available, ambitious women could imagine a life of public achievement and dignity outside the family claim. For them, heterosexual romance would likely put an end to ambition of other than the domestic sort.

Reading practices depend on cultural norms as well as class position, on whom one wishes to become as well as on one's current location. Some Jewish immigrant women, who would be defined as working-class on the basis of family income and occupation, not only enjoyed *Little Women* but found in it a vehicle for envisioning a new and higher status. Unlike the workers in the box factory, these newcomers read it as a fairy tale rather than a story about "real, live people." Jews had not only escaped oppression in Europe, but believed in the possibility of starting over in the new land. For young women, Alcott's classic provided a model for transcending their status as ethnic outsiders and for gaining access to American life and culture. It was a first step into the kind of middle-class domesticity rejected by women like Carey Thomas. For them too, *Little Women* was a source of future possibility—but of a different kind.

In *My Mother and I*, Elizabeth Stern charts the cultural distance a Jewish immigrant woman traveled from Russia and a midwestern urban ghetto to the American mainstream: she graduates from college, studies social work, marries a professional man, and becomes a social worker and writer. *Little Women* occupies a crucial place in the narrative. When she comes across it in a stack of newspapers in a rag shop, the book utterly engrosses her: "I sat in the dim light of the rag shop and read the browned pages of that ragged copy of 'Little Women.' . . . No book I have opened has meant as much to me as did that small volume telling in simple words such as I myself spoke, the story of an American childhood in New England. I had found a new literature, the literature of childhood." She had also found the literature of America: "I no longer read the little paper-bound Yiddish novelettes which father then sold. In the old rag shop loft I devoured the English magazines and newspapers." Of the books her teachers brought her from the public library, she writes:

> Far more marvelous than the fairy stories were to me in the ghetto street the stories of American child life, all the Alcott and the Pepper books. The pretty mothers, the childish ideals, the open gardens, the homes of many rooms were as unreal to me as the fairy stories. But reading of them made my aspirations beautiful.
>
> My books were doors that gave me entrance into another world. Often I think that I did not grow up in the ghetto but in the books I read as a child in the ghetto. The life in Soho passed me by and did not touch me, once I began to read.[80]

Stern's testimony to the importance of reading in reconfiguring aspiration is not unlike de Beauvoir's, although the context is entirely different, as is the nature of the desire elicited. In American books, the ghetto fell away and the protagonist discovered both childhood and beauty. Far from being realistic, as it was to middle- and upper-middle-class, native-born readers, to Jewish immigrants, *Little Women* might be an exotic American fairy tale.

Indeed, some of the narrator's "precocious" thirteen-year-old school friends "scoffingly averred that there were 'no such peoples like Jo and Beth.'" As she climbs the educational ladder, she discovers that such people do exist and that a life of beauty is possible, even for those of humble origin. With its emphasis on middle-class domesticity, *My Mother and I* is a story of Americanization with a female twist.[81]

Unlike the middle-class readers who for the most part took for granted their right to a long and privileged childhood, Jewish women immigrants could assume no such thing. Too many of them had to enter the labor market in their teens or earlier. Nor were those raised in Orthodox Jewish households brought up on an individualistic philosophy. But their school experiences and reading—American books like *Little Women*—made them aware of different standards of decorum and material life that we tend to associate with class, but that are cultural as well. For some of these readers, *Little Women* offered a fascinating glimpse into an American world. Of course, we know, as they did not, that the world Alcott depicted was vanishing even as she wrote. Nevertheless, that fictional world, along with their school encounters, provided a vision of what life, American life, could be.

Cultural mediators, including teachers and librarians, encouraged Jewish immigrants to read what had come to be regarded as *the* American female story. Book and author became enshrined in popular legend, especially after publication of *Louisa May Alcott: Her Life, Letters, and Journals* (1889) the year after the author's death, by her friend Ednah Dow Cheney. Interest in Alcott remained high in the early twentieth century. There was a 1909 biography by Belle Moses and a dramatization in 1912 that received rave reviews and toured the country. Alcott's books were sometimes assigned in public schools.[82] Jews too served as cultural intermediaries between native and immigrant communities, as did the settlement librarian who offered *Little Women* to a recent immigrant as a less taxing vehicle for learning English than Shakespeare, and as Rose Pastor did when she recommended Alcott as a safe and salutary writer.

At least one Jewish immigrant found in Alcott a model for literary success, all the sweeter no doubt because English was not her native language and because there was no prototype for female authorship in Polotzk, where she was born. In *The Promised Land*, her highly acclaimed autobiography, Mary Antin recalled Alcott's as the children's books she "remember[ed] with the greatest delight" (followed by boys' adventure books, especially Alger's). Antin lingered over the biographical entries she found in an encyclopedia and "could not resist the temptation to study out the exact place . . .

where my name would belong. I saw that it would come not far from 'Alcott, Louisa M.'; and I covered my face with my hands, to hide the silly, baseless joy in it."[83] We have come full circle. Ambitious, eager to assimilate, and with a mastery of English that enabled her to shed much of her European past, Antin responded in ways reminiscent of Alcott's early native-born and middle-class readers who admired her success as an author. She too could imagine a successful American career for herself, one for which Alcott was the model.

· · · · · · · · · · · · · · · · · · ·

Can readers do whatever they like with texts? Up to a point. As we have seen, *Little Women* has been read in many ways. It has been read as a romance or as a quest, or both. It has been read as a family drama that validates virtue over wealth. It has been read as a how-to manual by immigrants who wanted to assimilate into American middle-class life and as a means of escaping that life by women who knew its gender constraints only too well. For many, especially in the early years, *Little Women* was read through the life of the author.

Of course particular interpretations, like reading preferences themselves, arise out of life experiences and aspirations: these influence not only how a given work will be read but whether it will be read at all. Social location, aspirations, temperament, the age at which a work is read, whether it speaks to one's needs at a particular moment—all influence responses. The situations in which reading takes place, how it is practiced and with whom it is shared, the physical setting, the form and feel of a book—are integral not just to the existential moment but to the making of meanings. *Little Women* has performed different cultural work for diverse reading communities, based on readers' experiences in living and in reading.[84] The passage of time too influences the reception of a work. Initially praised by readers and reviewers as a realistic story of family life, by the time of its successful stage adaptation in 1912–14, some reviewers found it "quaint."[85]

There have been striking continuities as well. In *Little Women*, Alcott created a classic story of growing up female. Her vivid depictions of the trials and triumphs of female adolescence continue to ring true to many readers—someone, after all, must be reading those seventy editions. Despite the vast changes in the social context of this stage of life since Alcott wrote, it still involves contemplation of unknown futures: whom or whether to marry, how to earn a living, how, altogether, to be in this world, not to mention the ups and downs of daily life in what came to be known as the Sturm und Drang period.[86]

Both the passion *Little Women* has engendered in diverse readers and its ability to survive its era and transcend its genre point to a text of unusual permeability. The compromise Alcott effected with her readers in constructing a more intricate plot than is usual in fiction for the young has enhanced the story's appeal. If it is not exactly a "problem novel," it is a work that lingers in readers' minds in ways that allow for imaginative elaboration. Surviving reader testimony in both the nineteenth and twentieth centuries points to *Little Women* as a text that opens up possibilities rather than foreclosing them. For readers on the threshold of adulthood, the text's authorizing of female ambition has been a significant counterweight to more habitual gender prescriptions.

That one book performed this role for well over a century is evidence not only of its strengths as a literary work but of the continued relevance of its subject for its intended audience. Its longevity points as well to surprising continuities in gender norms from the 1860s at least through the 1960s. *Little Women*'s persistence has also been a consequence of the snaillike pace of change for women—in fiction as in life. The almost predictable frequency with which *Little Women* appears in recollections of girlhood reading for well over a century indicates a scarcity of attractive female models in literature: in this context, Jo March remained, for far too long, unique.[87]

For Alcott's first readers, *Little Women* pointed to new horizons, particularly in its portrait of Jo, an attractive new literary type: the girl as creative intellectual. For those who were middle-class, the novel also depicted a familiar and comforting world: the thrill of recognition was a repeated refrain. Stocked with characters like themselves, the novel reproduced situations from everyday life that were both hilarious and moving. Among them are numerous scenes of reading.[88] Starting with the opening chapter, which frames the novel as a quest variant of *Pilgrim's Progress*, *Little Women* communicates the ways in which the bourgeois culture of the era was in many respects a literary culture. (A secular literary culture, for although the March sisters learn to carry their burdens, as did Christian, the pilgrim of the seventeenth-century allegory, theirs is an earthly quest formulated as a game: "Playing Pilgrims" is the chapter title.) Whether it is the numerous references to particular works of literature (many of them more popular in Alcott's youth, though still read at the time she wrote) or the portraits of family literary activities (the Busy Bee Society, at which Jo reads aloud as she knits, the popular card game "Authors," the Pickwick Literary Club, and the "Pickwick Portfolio," a home newspaper), the novel highlights the degree to which literary activities permeated bourgeois family life. Young women were—and were expected to be—culturally literate. Like the March sisters, many had a great deal of fun in the process. *Little Women* not only reproduced familiar practices but, as the exemplary girls' book of the era, helped to reinforce and legitimate endeavors that often became occasions for building "castles in the air" and, for some, formulating concrete future plans as well.

CHAPTER TWO

Women and the New Cultural Landscape of the Gilded Age

If the literary culture portrayed in *Little Women* resonated powerfully with the book's first readers, it was a culture that would have been virtually unrecognizable at the start of the century. Changes in the practice of literacy, in middle-class family life, in attitudes toward culture, and in women's relationship to all three altered the domestic literary landscape in fundamental ways. Commonly viewed as more culturally sensitive than men, women became primary agents in the transmission of a family-based literary culture that by the late nineteenth century symbolized the claims of an expanding middle class to superior moral status. By that time white women were not only highly literate, but in growing numbers had leisure to read and an expanding supply of reading material from which to choose. A more favorable attitude toward secular culture also emerged, including the home-based literary activities—once considered frivolous if not outright sinful—that gave young women license to read and write for pleasure as well as for spiritual or intellectual profit.

For young women growing up after the Civil War, these changes and the opportunities for higher education and paid employment that accompanied them were critical to their ability to enact nondomestic lives. Jane Addams, Carey Thomas, and the Hamilton sisters were more privileged than average in their access to books as in other ways and more successful in their undertakings. But they emerged from a culture that valorized reading and writing for women as well as for men. That had not always been the case.

.   .   .   .

By midcentury, white women had attained near literacy parity with their male counterparts, erasing a gender gap that had existed at the time of the nation's founding, when women's literacy was significantly lower than that of men. According to the 1850 census, 10 percent of whites over the age of twenty were unable to read and write, men and women in about equal numbers, from which figure a 90 percent *literacy* rate has been extrapolated.[1] That figure is probably exaggerated, but the advance in women's literacy was real and did much to eliminate extreme disparities within a household, such as that between Benjamin Franklin and his wife Deborah, who was nearly illiterate. Even if white female literacy fell short of the 90 percent mark, it was high by the standards of the day; British women's literacy rate has been estimated at 55 percent (compared to 70 percent for men).[2] Despite ongoing debate throughout the century about the unsettling consequences of education for women, there was no serious opposition to white female literacy in the United States as there was in England. An older tradition of Bible literacy linked to America's dissenting Protestant origins joined with the ideology of republican motherhood that presupposed a certain level of female learning in order to produce virtuous male citizens.[3] Only for enslaved African Americans was literacy considered inherently dangerous.

Nothing did so much to equalize literacy between white men and women as the rapid expansion of female education in the years after the American Revolution. By 1860 there were more than 350 female academies and seminaries, not only in New England, where historians expect to find them, but also in the South. Many offered significantly more in the way of education than the images of "finishing" that these schools typically evoke. Often rationalized as establishments designed to fit women for their domestic roles, the best of the all-female institutions provided an education comparable to that received by men. In addition to the decorative and ornamental arts, they taught Latin, natural philosophy, geography, and physiology, often from the same books assigned in men's colleges.[4] Accompanying the expansion of female education was an extraordinary decline in fertility, from an average of 7 children per white mother in 1810 to an average of 3.5 in 1900.[5] One of the most significant developments in nineteenth-century women's history, this change made possible the outpouring of charitable, reform, and other non-domestic activities that were so significant a part of middle-class women's lives. As African American women's educational opportunities improved after the Civil War, their fertility declined as well.[6]

With literacy came economic opportunity. In the paid labor sphere, women with the requisite verbal skills found ready employment as teachers. As public education expanded in the 1830s and 1840s, school boards, eager to hold down costs, began to hire women teachers, often at half the salaries paid their male counterparts. With the accompanying rationale that women's presumed nurturing qualities made them ideal teachers of young children, the feminization of teaching proceeded rapidly, and by 1870 women constituted 59 percent of public school teachers.[7] Freed by industrialization from many domestic chores, spinning chief among them, many young white women taught for a year or two before marriage.

As a market for ladies' magazines and domestic novels emerged, middle-class white women of all ages had opportunities to earn money for work that required little in the way of financial investment and could be done in kitchens or sitting rooms. Like Louisa May Alcott, a literary woman might become the principal support of her family when fathers or husbands faltered. Women attained success as poets and as authors of popular textbooks on history, science, and advice books of many kinds. A flourishing magazine market specializing in subjects presumed to be of interest to women gave editors like Sarah Josepha Hale of *Godey's Lady's Book* influence and power, which they used to endorse female domesticity.[8] But it was as fiction writers that women attained their greatest success. They not only wrote almost three-quarters of the novels published in the United States by 1872, but were among the best-selling authors of the era. Beginning with Susan Warner's *The Wide, Wide World* (1851), many "women's novels" sold more than 100,000 copies. *Uncle Tom's Cabin* (1852), the best-selling novel of the century, sold an estimated 300,000 copies within the first year and half a million in the United States alone by the end of the fifth.[9] Hawthorne's dig at the "damned mob of scribbling women" was not just a manner of speaking, but a pained recognition of women's astonishing popularity—and financial success—in the field of literature.

Women's educational and vocational opportunities expanded exponentially in the second half of the century. With the establishment of women's colleges and the admission of women to formerly all-male colleges and universities after the Civil War (in large part to meet the need for teachers), women became a visible presence on campuses, including the new normal schools set up to train teachers. Only a small minority of Americans of either sex attended institutions of higher education (less than 2 percent of the college-age population in 1870, roughly 4 percent in 1900), but by the end of the century women comprised approximately 40 percent of the postsecondary school population.[10] With their new access to the world of learning, ambitious women were able to establish themselves in a variety of professions, including medicine and science. For the most part they worked in sex-typed occupations or specialties (nursing, home economics) or in sex-segregated institutions (all-female colleges and hospitals).[11] In its cultural and economic aspects, women's successful use of literacy depended on the rhetorically gendered division of labor and a segmented labor market.

So great were the changes in women's public performance of literacy that in the years after the Civil War reading was in important respects gendered female, as were cultural pursuits generally. In the context of men's pursuit of business and the conquest of a continent, the gendered thinking that ascribed to women inherent nurturing traits also assigned them the province of culture, at least those aspects that radiated out from the home or were locally based.[12] As the principal carriers of literacy in middle-class homes, women had long been responsible for teaching children and younger siblings to read. During the last third of the century they helped set the cultural tone as well. The women who sought enrichment in study clubs and home-based educational programs like the Chautauqua Literary and Scientific Circle brought their new learning and the books and magazines connected with it into their homes. These activities spurred a demand for books, then in short supply in rural areas, small towns, and even cities. Beginning on a small scale, often in private spaces, women went on to found numerous libraries across the nation. In this way, private goals became public projects, and homemakers turned into patrons of culture.

. . . .

Literary culture was never more widely admired than in the late nineteenth century. Not only were books considered ennobling, but they came to symbolize the tangible and intangible aspirations of the broad middle class. Whether valued as precious objects, as repositories of wisdom, as conveyors of cultural status, or as wellsprings of personal meaning, books—reading them, talking about them, sometimes owning them—became a marker of middle-class status, for some perhaps *the* critical marker.[13]

For those growing up middle-class in Gilded Age America, a certain proficiency with words was a given, a skill needed to succeed in an increasingly professionalized and bureaucratized society. At the most basic level, literacy skills influenced access to jobs as well as other, less easily measured indicators of status. At a time when nonmanual work had become the principal line demarcating the middle from the working classes, proficiency in reading and writing was essential for employment in the expanding white-collar sector. Entry into the professions required some facility, if not necessarily sophistication, with words. Despite wide salary differentials within the middle class, those who worked with their heads rather than their hands tended to earn larger incomes. They did not as a rule need to rely on the earnings of their wives or children as all but the most skilled manual workers did.[14]

Beyond providing access to more prestigious jobs, literary competence was a culturally valued and in some families even a sacred rite that transcended correct grammar and a fine hand, important though these attainments were. Being clever with words and familiar with the (mainly British) cultural heritage that Americans of the comfortable classes considered their birthright stamped the most proficient with virtual titles of what Pierre Bourdieu has called "cultural nobility."[15] In a world increasingly differentiated by class hierarchy, cultural competence became a badge of distinction, a mark by which members of an expanding middle class could set themselves apart not only from the less well off but from those less personally cultivated as well. The ability to pursue literary activities in a sustained way depended on the increased leisure that also manifested itself in the new popularity of vacations and art. Conversing intelligently about authors and artists, reciting poetry, or demonstrating familiarity with Greek and Latin allusions (knowledge of the original was not required) signaled a degree of sophistication beyond the reach of most Americans. Literary mastery, along with correct pronunciation and spelling, situated a person on the right side of the cultural divide. Not everyone could have said just what the possession of culture signified. Its presence was the important thing, for nothing was thought to differentiate the civilized person from "the savage" so much as the presence (or absence) of literacy.[16]

Books and reading were associated with the gradual elaboration of the middle-class home, a space where women exercised growing authority in the last third of the century. A certain level of income was necessary to maintain a way of life that guaranteed sufficient leisure to pursue literary activity. The emergence of the middle-class domestic ideal, a family unit constituted around a male breadwinner, a housewife, and children freed from long hours of physical labor, made it possible for more people to devote time and energy to literary and aesthetic pursuits formerly the preserve of the rich. Along with parlor organs, pianos, and chromolithographs—and more than any of these—books became tokens of leisure and cultivation. They were nowhere more manifest than in the parlor, in many ways the center of Victorian middle-class intellectual and moral life. The ubiquitous parlor table, complete with "a Bible, recent magazines, a carte-de-visite album, travel books, books of poetry, or a stereoscope and slides," exemplified the material side of that life. The plaster casts of famous authors (Shakespeare, Milton) and scenes immortalized in literature (Miles Standish's courtship) that decorated parlors and the long-lasting popularity of the card game "Authors" further attest to the cultural resonance of literature.[17]

"Everybody wanted culture in the same way that a few years earlier everybody wanted sewing machines," recalled writer Mary Austin of her youth in Carlinville, Illinois, in the late 1870s. Culture "by this time . . . meant for one thing, more than another, the studious reading of books." Writing more than half a century later, when deriding the bourgeoisie was an almost necessary badge of intellectual seriousness, Austin cast a critical eye on her neighbors' "fetishistic use of books," the conspicuous parading of culture that prompted them to discuss and even quote books they had not read. For those seeking to keep up, there was a general consensus "that you did have to read to maintain your pretensions to culture." Austin knew whereof she spoke: she had been as eager a consumer as her neighbors. Despite her mocking tone and elitist disdain for the parvenu, her pride in coming from a family in which "more and better books were read than was usual" pervades her autobiography, *Earth Horizon*, which lovingly records her encounters with print. However deficient it appeared in later years, what passed as culture in Carlinville not only was central to Austin's memories of childhood but also set her on her course as a writer.[18]

Austin stressed the competitive edge to cultural acquisition, observing that it was "the one item in which, without violating any principle of democracy, you could entertain the pleasant consciousness of being superior to your fellows." An arena that required mastery of certain essential skills, culture was a domain that offered unusual scope for women. Men had many avenues in which to prove their superiority—athletics, business, politics, to name a few. But for women of a certain class, direct competition with men was taboo. Widely viewed as a spiritual endeavor outside market forces, culture became a suitable arena for feminine striving, one in which a woman could excel without challenging gender norms.[19] Even as she portrayed women as the cultural movers and shakers in Carlinville, Austin was under no illusion that achievement in this domain was on a par with success in masculine endeavors: "The status of being cultivated was something like the traditional preciousness of women: nothing you could cash in upon, but a shame to you to do without."[20]

Despite the competitive aspect, individuals engaged in cultural pursuits were not to be equated with those who chased the dollar. Indeed, a reverence for books was for some a means of distancing themselves from the crude materialism and conspicuous consumption that gave the Gilded Age its name. In reading's less tangible aspects, cultural and religious strivings were closely linked. Reading had long been associated with spiritual and moral endeavor. The Bible was so central to the Protestant dissenters who settled New England that as early as 1642 Massachusetts Bay Colony passed a law encouraging reading instruction for all children. From primers to the Old and New Testaments, instruction in reading and religion were intertwined. By the 1830s and 1840s, the equation of literacy with morality became a prime justification for establishing public schools. Educator Horace Mann believed that schools would "create a more far-seeing intelligence, and a purer morality, than has ever existed among communities of men."[21] For Unitarian minister William Ellery Channing in the same period, reading was an important vehicle for "self-culture." This he defined as "the care which every man owes to himself, to the unfolding and perfecting of his nature"; he believed it to be within reach of anyone who sought it in a "disinterested" manner, that is, without anticipated material rewards. Since the goal of reading in this scheme of things was cultivating character rather than accumulating information, Channing insisted that good books must "not be skimmed over for amusement, but read with fixed attention and a reverential love of truth."[22]

By the end of the century, the explicitly religious moorings of culture had loosened still further, a development mirrored in the changing definition of "culture" from a term describing a process of intellectual, spiritual, and aesthetic development by an individual or group to one connoting more exclusively "the works and practices of intellectual and especially artistic activity," that is, specific works of literature, music, and theater.[23] In other words, culture came to mean *Hamlet* or a Beethoven symphony rather than the process of self-development prescribed by Channing. With the onslaughts of Darwinism and biblical criticism and the waning of the Calvinist doctrine of predestination, many Americans began to look to this more specialized kind of culture for values, certainties, and possibilities for transcendence they had once found in religion. Austin suggested as much when she observed that the "best people" now seemed "anxious about the state of their culture, where formerly they had been chiefly concerned about their souls."[24]

No one did more to elevate the spiritual dimension of culture than British poet and critic Matthew Arnold. Discerning in culture a core of eternal values and timeless truths, he defined it as "a pursuit of our total perfection by means of getting to know . . . the best which has been thought and said in the world."[25] For a middle class moving away from a tightly bounded evangelical religion, this formulation had wide appeal as something at once ineffable yet knowable. The moral value attached to books in general and to secular works rather than the traditional Protestant texts was one of many signs that reverence for culture was replacing an older religious sensibility. The transformation of *Scribner's Monthly*, a general periodical with an evangelical Christian flavor founded in 1870, into the *Century*, an oracle for secular American culture a few years later, signals the trajectory.[26]

This "sacralization of culture" had broad implications for Americans who embraced the more permissive standards of bourgeois life in the latter part of the century.[27] Previously suspect forms of entertainment, such as theater and even paintings and statues depicting the female nude, became acceptable as "art" to those who had shunned them in their evangelical days. A case in point is Harriet Beecher Stowe, whose father had forbidden all fiction except the novels of Sir Walter Scott. Recording the experiences of her first European trip in a travel book, she meditated freely on art and acknowledged a fondness even for Rubens. She also wrote the text of *Woman in Sacred History* (1873), less a religious than an art book and one that depicted several scantily clad heroines. The transformation of her younger brother Henry Ward Beecher from a young hell-fire preacher into an apostle of culture was emblematic of the changing times. In his 1844 evangelical tract, *Seven Lectures to Young Men*, Beecher condemned fiction, along with theater, gambling, and other temptations of modern life. Following a trip to Europe, where he had been overwhelmed by the beauties of culture, and the move to a well-heeled Brooklyn congregation, he reassessed his wholesale rejection of modernity. He even wrote a novel, published in 1868, that one biographer considers the "death certificate" of New England Calvinism for America's middle class.[28]

Fundamental shifts in the nature and practice of literacy were in fact well under way, in particular the new abundance of reading matter, much of it secular. Where formerly a few "steady sellers," including Bibles, psalm books, and sermons, dominated the literary landscape, a vast array of printed materials circulated after 1850.[29] In addition to works of fiction, travel, history, and biography, the outpouring of print included advice literature on subjects ranging from childrearing, health, and etiquette to building a house. School books were the biggest sellers, followed by fiction. Popular British novels were available in editions that ran the gamut from expensive sets of revered authors to the "cheap books" published in the 1870s and 1880s, which sold for ten or twenty cents. At that price, they were within reach of at least some members of the working class.[30]

The new abundance made it possible to satisfy many reading tastes and markets, some segmented by gender, age, and class. Books, although the most prestigious category, constituted only a fraction of the total output. Newspapers, the least expensive and most popular genre, and the one most favored by the working class, had a preponderantly but by no means exclusively male readership.[31] There was also a flourishing market for periodicals, with 1,200 magazines published in the United States in 1870, up from 700 just five years earlier. The Gilded Age was the great age of the general circulation magazine, of which *Harper's Monthly* and the *Century* were the most prominent exemplars, with estimated peak circulations of 150,000 and 222,000 respectively.[32] Strong on fiction, including serial stories, often handsomely illustrated, and generally without overt political commentary, the genre appealed to an upper-middle-class audience, usually thought to be mainly female. A secular juvenile market (magazines as well as fiction) gained momentum in the 1860s. Indeed, *Youth's Companion*, which had roots in antebellum evangelical culture, was the most popular magazine in the Gilded Age, with a circulation approaching 400,000.[33]

The changing status of fiction was an important sign of the growing approbation of secular culture. The genre had been suspect from the outset, not least because of its appeal to women and to youth of both sexes, the groups deemed most in need of moral supervision. Arbiters of culture feared the power of fiction to stir the imagination and, in consequence, its ability to undermine the established order. These concerns persisted during the Gilded Age in debates about which novels libraries should circulate and in attacks on the "cheap books" that flooded the market, with their depictions of urban vices and seduction from which families sought to shield their sons as well as daughters. But by then "serious" fiction had attained the status of high culture. At issue were rather what and how much fiction to read.

Emblematic of the change was Noah Porter's guide, *Books and Reading; or, What Books Shall I Read and How Shall I Read Them?*, one of many advice books that appeared during the Gilded Age. For Porter, professor of moral philosophy at Yale College and a Congregational minister, "ethical truth is but another name for imagination." While warning that an exclusive diet of novels might turn the reader into "an intellectual voluptuary," he insisted that a really good novel or poem was, like love, a source of "superhuman elevation" and that imaginative literature could aid in self-culture, at once producing "pure and exquisite delight," adding power to the intellect and imparting "grace and finish to the character and life."[34]

Fiction constituted just a portion of an educated person's reading, but its inclusion in the advice literature about how and what to read and even on lists of the 100 "best" books of all time was a boon to young female readers.[35] As the century advanced and women took their place as students and writers, an older image of women as frivolous readers diminished, although it did not disappear altogether.[36] The most earnest readers drew up their own book lists, checking them off as they proceeded. Catalogues of this sort, whether published or personal, were inventories of both aspiration and achievement. For those who judged others by the books they read, they also provided a formula for sorting out the "best people" from those who were not.

Unlike other forms of bourgeois display, however, one's cultural standing did not depend on such crass indicators as the size of a family's bank account. Not all those who were well off economically could be considered cultured, nor was the person who possessed the culture found in books necessarily rich in worldly goods. In a world in flux, reading, the right reading, differentiated not only the middle from the lower classes but the genuinely cultured from the nouveaux riches. One might lose one's money, but one's culture, presumably, was a lifelong possession.

The literary culture described here was prevalent in middle- and upper-class white families, among rural and small-town as well as urban dwellers. It was not unknown among African Americans and less well off whites. Since books did not have to be owned to be enjoyed, reading depended less than other forms of consumption on a rising standard of living. Few families who constituted the broad middle class, as distinct from the wealthiest segments, owned large numbers of books, certainly not enough to satisfy avid readers.[37] The less affluent borrowed books wherever they could: from neighbors, from subscription libraries, and from the new public libraries that were becoming an important feature of urban life. Members of groups with historically limited access to books and schooling could in this way hope to compensate for their deficiencies and benefit from the vogue of self-education that continued throughout the century. Young African Americans found reading material in Sunday school libraries, as, later, Jewish immigrants did in urban settlement houses. As markers of class, then, books designated permeable rather than fixed boundaries and sometimes provided the means of crossing them.

. . . .

Initiation into reading began early for both sexes. Because school attendance was more casual and home instruction more common than they would become in the twentieth century, children often learned to read at home—from ABC blocks, from books like *Reading without Tears*, or by some idiosyncratic method like picking out letters with a pin. Following in a tradition dating back to seventeenth-century New England when women taught children to read (but not write), teachers were usually female: mothers, aunts, an older sister, or friend of the family. Journalist William Allen White was among those who knew the basics before attending school; in his case, the three-lettered words in a "colored linen picture book."[38] Some children exhibited unusual precocity. M. Carey Thomas recalled reading fluently at three, others by four or five, while Meta Lilienthal, daughter of German immigrants, reported, "I was not yet six when I read, unbidden, and learned by heart poems by Henrich Heine from a luxuriously bound and illustrated volume lying on the table in the living room—love poems, that a little girl of the late Victorian era was not supposed to know at all."[39] Whether or not such recollections are altogether accurate, they conjure up the allure of grownup books and the worlds opened by them.

In autobiographical reminiscences, Edith Abbott summoned the family reading culture in which she and her younger sister Grace grew up. Born in the prairie town of Grand Island, Nebraska, both sisters became prominent in social welfare, Edith as a professor at the University of Chicago, Grace as director of the U.S. Children's Bureau. Their mother, a graduate of Rockford Female Seminary and a high school principal before marriage, was a passionate reader whose children teased her about letting the plum jelly cook too long while lost in a favorite Thackeray novel. Her daughters would have welcomed the occasional doll or "gim-crack," but Mrs. Abbott considered books "the only suitable gift." She sacrificed needed household expenditures to buy books—only the "best"—to be read and reread; these she considered an investment rather than an extravagance. The Abbotts also subscribed to the *Century* and the *North American Review*, two of the magazines that enriched the homes of culturally inclined families in Gilded Age America. But the budget could be stretched only so far, and Elizabeth Abbott became "the moving spirit" in the public library. She secured the initial funds from money left over after the defeat of a woman suffrage amendment and served as president and board member for many years. The library, for which Mrs. Abbott ordered choice volumes, gave her children access to books by Louisa May Alcott and Mark Twain.[40]

The Abbotts owned only three children's books—one by the popular illustrator and author Kate Greenaway, James Otis's *Toby Tyler; or, Ten Weeks with a Circus*, and *Huckleberry Finn*—the first two gifts from teachers. But the youngsters read books that passed as such in many homes: *The Old Curiosity Shop, Robinson Crusoe, Gulliver's Travels*, and *Thaddeus of Warsaw* by Jane Porter, a popular early nineteenth-century writer of historical novels. The family also owned "standard" works like *Aesop's Fables, The Arabian Nights*, Anderson's and Grimm's fairy tales, the "old Household Edition of Dickens," novels by Thackeray, poetry by Tennyson, Whittier, Longfellow, and Scott, as well as two illustrated volumes of English history, which fascinated the children, and "a poorly printed, cheap edition" of Dickens's *A Child's History of England*, which did not.[41]

Many features of this literary heritage would have been familiar to any child growing up middle-class in the late nineteenth century. None more so than Elizabeth Abbott's central role in her children's literary education; Othman Abbott, a lawyer who was also a reader, left most of the supervision to his wife.[42] The Abbotts' passion for literature was probably above average, but in character the children's reading was fairly typical for a family with intellectual interests and a middling income. Classic texts ("standard" in the language of the day), early exposure to literature for adults, and an emphasis on English history and fiction were the norm in many families.

Give or take a few titles, the Abbotts' books constituted the foundation of the literary heritage a middle-class child might expect, but not always attain. Sociologist Edward A. Ross, who grew up on farms near Marion, Iowa, was orphaned at ten, and intermittently attended a one-room school, later lamented that he "had never read one of the children's classics. All a boy's cultural heritage—the hero tales, the Greek myths, *Aesop's Fables, Arabian Nights, Robinson Crusoe, Gulliver's Travels, Ivanhoe, B'rer Rabbit*—I read while I was in college!" Ross identifies these books as "a boy's cultural heritage," but as the testimony of Edith Abbott and other women makes clear, they constituted a girl's cultural legacy as well. Since there was not even a district school library nearby, Ross had to content himself with his school texts and "perhaps six books" at home, including a couple of histories and a Bible dictionary, as well as two weekly papers. On Sundays, after rereading the books "for the hundredth time," he sometimes resorted to a *Report on*

Hog Cholera Experiments for the U.S. Department of Agriculture, although he found it "repulsive fare."[43] For his part, writer Hamlin Garland relied on occasional poems about domestic or rural nature to relieve the "dry prose" of a farmer's almanac or state agricultural report.[44]

As Ross's account suggests, farm children were at a particular disadvantage in obtaining books. Those growing up in less isolated environments were more fortunate. With the spread of public libraries in the second half of the century, even in small towns like Grand Island, Nebraska, young readers had access to the new secular children's fiction and other books that families could rarely afford to buy. Osage, Iowa, a town of 2,000 in 1890, had, in addition to the public library founded in the 1870s, reading rooms or libraries connected with the Masons, the Woman's Christian Temperance Union (WCTU), and various Sunday schools.[45] By contrast, Broken Bow, Nebraska, where Grace Abbott taught school as a young woman, had only a small WCTU reading room.[46] Children and young adults in cities with public libraries thrilled at the range of books they could borrow with library cards of their own.

Beginning with fables and fairy tales and other works that appealed to the imagination, like *Robinson Crusoe* and *The Arabian Nights*, the family literary canon went on to include more realistic fiction, history, and, later, belles lettres and a range of secular works from Plutarch to Emerson often considered inspirational. These joined the classic texts of Protestantism as required reading in many families. The Bible remained the most frequently owned book, but, with the waning of evangelicalism in the last third of the century, some families now approached it as literature rather than as revelation.[47] *Pilgrim's Progress* still loomed large in the lives of children, even for those who found Bunyan's allegory boring rather than frightening. Some parents made little of it, among them Othman Abbott, who belonged to no church and believed in evolution. Nevertheless, this standby of Protestant culture remained a lifelong reference point for Grace Abbott, as it did for many Americans, probably the last generation for which this was the case.[48] In families where faith played a larger part, devotional and other forms of religious literature remained important, often as the only acceptable form of Sunday reading. Sacred and secular sometimes coexisted uneasily. William Allen White's mother, a devout Congregationalist convert from Catholicism who was an avid reader of books, including some of dubious standing, was shocked when her twelve-year-old son "went stark mad over Mark Twain" because of the writer's reputation as an atheist.[49]

Despite the era's heightened gender consciousness and the marketing of books for young readers according to sex, the overlap in boys' and girls' reading was considerable. Recent library studies support descriptions of childhood reading in diaries and memoirs on this point. The most comprehensive, Christine Pawley's survey of an Iowa town during the last three decades of the century, reveals substantial overlap in the books charged out by male and female public library patrons between the ages of ten and twenty. There were some gender preferences—the boys' favorite was adventure-story writer "Oliver Optic" (William Taylor Adams), while girls preferred "Pansy" (Isabella Alden), a writer with an evangelical Christian message—but a majority of the most popular books (including these) turned up on the most frequently borrowed lists of both sexes. Of course, the person who charges out a book is not necessarily the person who reads it, but the finding is suggestive.[50]

So ingrained is the association of "girls' books" with "what girls read" that critics have often conflated the two to the point that girls' stated preferences for other kinds of literature have been discounted. The author of an 1886 survey of "What Girls Read" in *The Nineteenth Century* considered it so improbable that 1,000 English schoolgirls between the ages of eleven and nineteen ranked Dickens as their favorite author, with Scott second, and Charles Kingsley tied for third with Charlotte Mary Yonge (an English writer whose large output included popular girls' stories), that he wondered whether they had been frank in stating their preferences. It evidently did not occur to him that girls in secondary schools, as many of them were, might have left Alcott and other authors of girls' books behind.[51]

In fact, it is likely that middle-class boys and girls of this era had greater access to each others' stories, both materially and psychologically, than did later generations. As a highly valued family activity, reading provided a point of overlapping, though not identical, interests between genders and generations.[52] Just as young people often read adult books at early ages, adults enjoyed books written for "children of all ages." At a time when middle-class youth were expected to be familiar with certain authors and reading aloud was widely practiced, boys often read—or listened to—their sisters' books and sometimes acknowledged liking them.[53] Moreover, young people's magazines like *St. Nicholas* published both types of stories, in contrast to the gender-segmented content and readerships of twentieth-century publications like *Boys' Magazine*, which featured athletics, and *Seventeen*.[54]

The overlap does not mean that boys and girls read in identical ways, but it suggests a need to consider the effects of crossover reading and to question the traditional assumptions that reading domestic fiction "tamed" girls by forcing them to give up worldly ambition for marriage and mother-hood. This was a message prevalent everywhere—at home, school, church, virtually any place they turned—but, as in the case of *Little Women*, the role of girls' books in reinforcing it is less certain. The fact that girls read boys' books as well as those written for adults must be factored into any estimation of how reading worked, either for individuals or for a community of readers. Reading takes place on a continuum, of years as well as genres.

Learning to appreciate the right books and do the right things with them were important aspects of a child's socialization into middle-class life. Adults encouraged the reading habit, not only by giving books as gifts, but by assigning their children literary tasks. Some went so far as to offer monetary rewards for successful performance. Mary Austin collected $5.00 from her grandfather as the first grandchild to read the Bible "*all through.*"[55] Perhaps the most frequent assignment was memorizing and reciting poetry, a practice that mirrored formal educational practices. Not only was elocution the focal point of reading instruction throughout the nineteenth century, but poetry recitations remained a required part of public school curricula in all grades throughout the United States well into the twentieth.[56]

A "reading child" no doubt participated in these endeavors with greater enthusiasm than one who was a "reluctant reader," but it was the rare child in such families who did not feel the pull of print culture: to be a member in good standing one had to take part. Edith Abbott recalled her mother's expectation that the children "'read good books,' and we all read diligently and learned to enjoy it." As she put it, "We just accepted the fact that we ought to want books and so we did our best to get the books that we knew we ought to want to read. And read them we did." Abbott's sly rendering hints at the coercive side of family reading practices. Children sometimes rebelled when they reached their limits: the young Abbotts found the serialized stories in genteel magazines dull and implored their parents to postpone reading William Dean Howells's *The Rise of Silas Lapham* until they had gone to bed.[57]

Parental pressure notwithstanding, for many this sort of reading culture was an essential component of family well-being and youthful pleasure, enjoyed by young and old alike. Middle-class homes were suffused with literary activities, boisterous as well as meditative, collective as well as private. In the Abbott family, both parents read aloud evenings, often poetry: their father, Longfellow's "Hiawatha"; their mother, Tennyson. Othman Abbott also favored Dickens, Darwin, and Civil War books, especially General Grant's *Memoirs*, which he read and discussed with his children, reworking the Vicksburg campaign on the dining room table.[58] In addition to reading aloud and storytelling, families often entertained themselves with exuberant word games and with poetry, both humorous and sentimental, written to order for special occasions. As in *Little Women*, home theatricals and newspapers as well as heroic outdoor battles, sometimes inspired by the *Iliad* or tales of Robin Hood, afforded the younger generation opportunities for vigorous and self-determining play.

Literary activities not only permeated daily life; they did so in ways that were at once participatory and collaborative.[59] From early ages, middle-class boys and girls were expected to produce written work. In addition to school essays, there were poems written to order for family celebrations as well as word games, like writing nonsense verses in alternate lines, all of which required verbal facility. These circumstances were of singular importance for women.

By the late nineteenth century, diary and letter writing had become predominantly female arts. If women did not monopolize them, they were thought to have special talents or responsibilities for their performance. Once a common spiritual exercise for both sexes, diary keeping had evolved into something of a calling for female adolescents of the comfortable classes. Often presented by parents as gifts to girls in their early teens, diaries were sanctioned as a technique for promoting discipline and character, a practice that might aid in the transition from sometimes ornery adolescence to more pliant womanhood. In their pages, girls recorded, sometimes painfully, their struggles to "be good," to settle gnawing religious doubts, to subdue their pride or resentment at parental authority. Whatever the intent of adults, by fostering exploration of inner lives, diaries often promoted self-reflection of an individualistic sort in ways that allowed for a more assertive female subjectivity. In their (presumably) secret pages, girls could express anger and try out a variety of identities, some of them at least mildly subversive. Perhaps critics were right to consider diaries sufficiently dangerous to warn against them, as some did in the 1870s.[60]

Diaries assumed their greatest importance during adolescence, but women of all ages were often prodigious letter writers. As those charged with the emotional well-being of extended as well as nuclear families, women kept in touch with absent members and distant relatives. The pattern began in youth: boys might be expected to write letters, but their lapses were more readily tolerated than those of their sisters. In a mobile society that detached people from their points of origin, women's letters often constituted the primary means of communication between family members. As the principal letter writers, women not only demonstrated their vaunted verbal facility but gained authority in negotiating family matters.[61]

Diary keeping and letter writing originated in gendered obligations. But they were often so much more. In addition to any personal satisfaction they brought, these genres enhanced powers of observation and self-reflection. Self-conscious about their letters, which they knew would be read aloud or passed around among family members, young women labored over their literary productions. Observant correspondents like Alice Hamilton became vivid storytellers who set their scenes with care, created characters out of themselves and the people they met, and adjusted their narratives to fit their intended audience.[62] Earlier in the century, in just this manner, letter writing proved to be an important training ground for Harriet Beecher Stowe, who incorporated techniques she had perfected in her correspondence into her domestic fiction.[63] In creating themselves in and through their diaries and letters (that is, both for themselves and for others), women often drew on models available to them from literature. In this way reading and writing converged.

Poetry held a special place in women's early literary endeavors: here reading and writing shaded into performance. Building on gendered assumptions, some critics suggested that poetry, because it "presupposes a nicety of eye, a reflecting habit, and, above all, a delicacy of feeling," had greater appeal to girls and women than to their male counterparts, especially at youthful ages.[64] Girls in fact often delighted in memorizing "miles" of poetry, which they recited for family and friends.[65] Longfellow, Scott, Thomas Babington Macaulay, Elizabeth Barrett Browning, Tennyson most of all were favorite choices for the set pieces girls declaimed. Tennyson's "The May Queen" was the favorite of Mary Church Terrell, while Grace Abbott chose the poet's "Lady Clara Vere de Vere" and "Come into the Garden, Maud." Not all signature poems originated at the level of high culture. Charlotte Perkins Gilman included Rose Hartwick Thorpe's melodramatic "Curfew Must Not Ring Tonight" in her repertoire, as did Mary Austin, who was also partial to old ballads and to Longfellow's "Tales."[66] Young girls were lapped about with praise for their public performances, many of them precocious by twentieth-first-century standards. At a time when maxims about women's silence pervaded public discourse, girls relished these ceremonial opportunities for self-display. Perhaps that is why women recalled their youthful performances so vividly in their autobiographical writings.

In addition to reciting the works of others, girls wrote their own poems and stories, a habit encouraged by the do-it-yourself ethos of producing occasional poetry. The new children's magazines, with their serial stories and special features, including puzzles and letters to the editor, did much to foster literary ambitions. Mary Church Terrell was thrilled to see her name appear in *St. Nicholas* for solving a puzzle, while Mary Austin claims she first learned from the magazine that one could get paid for writing.[67] Girls sometimes experienced early literary success, and not only in *St. Nicholas*. Some of Austin's verses appeared anonymously in the *Union Signal*, journal of the WCTU; they had evidently been sent by Frances Willard without consulting the author, whose mother was active in the organization. And two poems by Alice Stone Blackwell materialized in print when she was in her early teens, one in the *Woman's Journal*, edited by her mother, Lucy Stone, the other in *Our Young Folks*, a short-lived but influential children's magazine whose editor her mother most likely knew.[68] These examples indicate not only that girls often had parental backing but that, then as now, well-placed intermediaries enhanced their chances of breaking into print. Even if few succeeded, the fact that adolescent girls sent off their poems and stories, some even to general circulation magazines, suggests they had a sufficiently well developed sense of self and of their literary abilities to put their work forward in this way. The tradition of female authorship that lasted through the century encouraged such boldness, as did the authority women gained from the valorized cultural heritage that began at home.

WOMEN OF THE Progressive generation were the first to write themselves into history in significant numbers. This was literally the case, since many of them wrote autobiographies. Jane Addams, Alice Hamilton, Rose Cohen, Mary Antin, and Ida B. Wells were among those who wrote their life stories for public consumption. The ability of labor leaders, social workers, physicians, and others not known primarily as writers to do so suggests that their early literary pursuits had a lasting impact. Many wrote lovingly of their childhood reading, no doubt in part to establish their intellectual and literary credentials, but also to reconnect with pleasurable aspects of the past. Above all, the autobiographical act provided an opportunity to reflect on their lives, on what they and their cohort had achieved, on their hopes for the future, perhaps also to justify the way they had lived. Like men of their generation, women autobiographers wrote mainly about their work, subordinating their personal to their public lives.[69]

That so many women could conceive of themselves as worthy figures for public instruction is nothing short of remarkable. Self-advertisement, not necessarily a virtue even for men of this generation, was altogether out of bounds for women. For a woman to write about herself in this way flew in the face of traditional norms of female modesty and renunciation of ambition of a nondomestic sort. Such conspicuous self-presentation required a conviction that the writer had accomplished something worth bringing to public attention. In view of women's socialization into domesticity, such an individualistic subjectivity was far from assured. But individualism was the authorizing ideology of their class, and insofar as bourgeois women partook of that class privilege, they were not only exposed to the ideology but often absorbed it as well. In some respects, then, assumptions based on their class privilege helped to undermine traditional patterns of gender socialization. Yet because of that socialization, many also retained an identification with their sex that enabled them to work not only for personal advancement but for that of other women as well.

Differences in motivation and temperament, as well as in family resources and cultural receptivity, played a part in women's ability to acquire new and more public identities. So did their associations with like-minded women, some of them originating in youthful literary friendships. The uses women made of their literary culture contributed significantly to their ability to seize the historical moment. Together young women not only cultivated their literary skills but worked and reworked the stories that engaged them. Many of these featured quest plots, stories of individual achievement—traditionally coded male—that challenged women's socialization into domesticity. If women's intense engagement with literature promoted dreams of worldly success, the support of peers helped to authorize and sustain female ambition, providing a launching point from which to move out of parlors and into public places. Of course, not everyone had the leisure or inclination to devote to literary pursuits. But their gendered class position enabled some young women of the comfortable classes simultaneously to fulfill and subvert the bourgeois culture of reading in which they grew up.[70]

. . . .

CHAPTER THREE

Young Women's Ways of Reading

Growing up with books together, men and women of the comfortable classes could draw on the mental and emotional substrate of ideas and images reading offered. To the extent that they read the same books, they can be said to have shared a common language and culture. They often knew the same literary allusions and gossip, enjoyed tales of adventure in common, laughed at similar absurdities, shed tears at the same deathbed scenes. But this considerable overlap did not mean they had identical imaginative lives or frames of meaning. Given their greater investment in reading, it is not surprising that young women developed an especially complex and elaborated relation to it. Because literature was in some respects women's province, some became more adept in its ways than their brothers. Because, too, domestic literary culture was participatory, a culture of writing as well as of reading, contemporary structures of reading intertwined with women's lives in synergistic ways. At once study and play, a source of knowledge and pleasure, public performance and private dreaming, reading opened up space unlike any other. As an esteemed cultural practice, a wellspring of aspiration, and a gratifying social ritual performed with members of their own sex, reading assumed a central place in young women's lives in ways that were less true for men. In this instance, female socialization and opportunity went hand in hand. That these opportunities were partly compensatory does not gainsay their significance.

. . . .

Many of those growing up in reading families considered their interactions with books basic to who they were and who they wished to become. Cultural proficiency originated in class relationships, but it was not something that could be conferred by birth alone. Genuine culture demanded effort—one reason why its possession meant so much to women. It helped to define them as valuable persons in their own right and therefore entitled to take their place with their male counterparts—at least in the family circle.

One of those who went to great lengths to establish her cultural credentials was Florence Kelley, daughter of a prominent Republican congressman from Philadelphia who supported Radical Reconstruction of the South and herself a leading progressive reformer and major architect of the campaign against child labor. In autobiographical reflections she depicts her youthful reading as a solemn cultural project marked by moral earnestness and self-imposed duty. Educated at home, in a household marked by the deaths of five of her seven siblings and her mother's perpetual melancholy, Kelley attributes the heroic undertaking of working her way through her father's vast library to being "a very lonely child deeply ashamed of having no school experience."[1]

At the heart of Kelley's story is her father's extensive library, which she recalls as "my great resource." Beginning "in good earnest" on her tenth birthday, she claims she read through its entire contents by the time she left for Cornell seven years later. Working her way from top to bottom, she started with the "modestly bound, small volumes of the Family Library." She "understood almost nothing in these books of so-called Natural Science"—which had no illustrations—but from them she learned the names of prominent scientists, whom she "revered indiscriminately, classing them all with Dr. [Joseph] Priestley, who was a friend of Benjamin Franklin and . . . a hero of the family." She moved on to the works of Sir Walter Scott in "nine large volumes of bad print . . . [which] saw me well along through the year of my twelfth birthday." (For other novelists—"Dickens and Thackeray, along with Miss Alcott and Horatio Alger"—she relied on the Library of Congress, to which she had recourse when Congress was in session.) "At home there was little poetry beyond Shakespeare, Milton, Byron, Goldsmith and several anthologies dear to my memory. But there were long shelves of history. Full sets of the writings of President Madison, and Daniel Webster's orations, and the histories of Bancroft, Prescott and Francis Parkman, alone must have weighed hundreds of pounds." Essays by Emerson, sermons by Channing, the works of Burke, Carlyle, Godwin, and Herbert Spencer, she observed, were "fortunately for me . . . near the floor, and I was nearly fifteen when I arrived at them." Later she tried "the tall, soberly bound volume" of Restoration plays, so "hopelessly beyond" her that she abandoned it.

Kelley presents her encounters with the weighty and sober sets and series in her father's library as a "huge, indigestible, intellectual meal" that brought neither joy nor enlightenment. Except for her references to the poetry anthologies, "dear to my memory," the tone is cold, a far cry from the accounts of the many female readers who found pleasure and freedom in books. In the absence of contemporary evidence, one can only speculate about Kelley's responses at the time of these early intellectual forays. Strong in political economy and U.S. history and deficient in novels and poetry, William Darrah Kelley's library was coded male; perhaps the gendered nature of his books dampened his daughter's enthusiasm.

Kelley's narrative of youthful folly has a larger moral: it is a critique of inherited cultural privilege at one with her adult commitment to socialism and labor reform. The contrast between her privileged childhood and that of the maimed working children "with crooked legs, and splay feet" depicted in "a terrible little book" from which her father taught her to read underscores the message. But despite her disavowal, Kelley's quest for knowledge was of a piece with the ambition that took her to college. Entering Cornell as one of the first women students was "an almost sacramental experience." With so little formal education, she had to cram for admission, but since she acknowledged having "an excellent verbal memory," it is likely that some residue of her solitary travels through her father's library remained.[2] Her later career, including her interest in political and economic theory—she translated Friedrich Engels's *The Condition of the Working Class in England in 1844* from the German—further suggests that her childhood reading may have been less futile, if no more pleasurable, than she intimates.

From a twenty-first-century perspective, when girls are often pressed to cultivate their bodies rather than their minds, Kelley's undertaking is astounding. Even then it was unusual in its scope, in its apparently solitary nature, and in the ready availability of books. But at a time when school attendance was erratically enforced and education itself often equated with having the run of a good library, girls often set themselves ambitious intellectual tasks—and felt entitled to do so. Where Kelley's scheme was based on the spatial arrangement of books, her future Hull-House colleague Jane Addams devised one based on "some fantastic notion of chronological order and early legendary form."[3] Addams too found her earlier ardor misplaced, a view, like Kelley's, consonant with her adult political outlook. Both women took on themselves the entire onus for their prodigious undertakings, but as children they were surely aware of the cultural value of their fathers' bookshelves. Cultural aspiration began at home. It was an essential part of a child's socialization in certain kinds of families.

. . . .

Beyond reading's value as a cultural resource, young women often found it an irresistible temptation. Freed from many household tasks—but not from obligations of family care—girls growing up in the Gilded Age had more time to read than those of earlier generations. But the passionate, even obsessive, reading that characterized adolescence was more than a matter of opportunity. It was more too than the dutiful pursuit of culture devised by Florence Kelley. One of the few approved arenas for female pleasure, reading was both a source of desire and a system of social relations that could be critically important in the formation of female subjectivity. For some, books elicited feelings so intense that they alarmed parents—and even at times youthful readers themselves; so did their literary choices.

A journal kept by Alice Stone Blackwell between the ages of fourteen and sixteen reveals something of the character and intensity of female adolescent reading. It points as well to dynamic aspects of reading on both an individual and a family level. Blackwell was the only child of prominent abolitionists and feminists Lucy Stone and Henry Blackwell, a lineage that placed her in a rarified subculture, one more common in Boston than elsewhere. Growing up in suburban Dorchester, Alice checked out books on weekly or biweekly trips to the Boston Public Library and the Boston Athenaeum. She had access as well to periodicals received at the office of the *Woman's Journal*, which her parents edited. During the twenty-seven months in which she kept the journal, she mentioned 130 books, magazines, and newspapers, as well as numerous poems, and commented on many of them.[4]

A voracious reader, in early adolescence Alice gravitated to all kinds of fiction. She read almost all the novels of Henry Kingsley, a minor writer of improbable romances. Other favorites were George MacDonald, author of rather somber novels on religious themes as well as the fantasies for which he is still remembered, and Margaret Oliphant, who wrote domestic fiction about English provincial life that Blackwell found "pleasant." At fourteen, she had a penchant for the dramatic, even the melodramatic, and her most pointed comments were reserved for works that were gender neutral or typically viewed as boys' books. A rare remark on a girls' story, Mrs. Whitney's *Real Folks* (1872), reveals that she considered it realistic: "her people *are* real; I have seen several of them, and I am one myself." Perhaps that is why she gave the book as an anniversary present to her parents, who laughed "over the inscription (To my Revered Parents), followed by an apology for my lack of reverence."[5] Recognition was one thing, absorption and excitement another.

Blackwell's highest encomium went to Charles Kingsley's *Westward Ho!* (1855): "I think that will always be the story of stories for me, as John Brown is the song." When a book she was reading made her "nervous," she proclaimed, "I must read . . . Amyas Leigh [hero of *Westward Ho!*] to compose myself. That will do it if anything can."[6] A tale of adventure on the high seas set in Elizabethan times, Kingsley's novel mixed romance with bloody battles, imperialist striving, and anti-Catholicism. What drew Blackwell and the book's many other female admirers (it was also the favorite of girls in the 1886 British survey)? Was it identification with the hero who underwent so many trials, including blindness, before marrying an Indian princess (actually the daughter of an English explorer)—or fascination with him? Was it the romance? The fierce sea battles culminating in the defeat of the Spanish Armada? The overthrow of Papist villains by Protestants, as the association with the evangelical antislavery crusader John Brown might suggest? Or was it several or all of the above, in various admixtures, enhanced by being served up in a rousing adventure yarn? It is not possible to pinpoint Blackwell's reading strategies precisely, but when taken together with similar choices, it is clear that she relished the drama and excitement of the story apart from any messages she found there.

At this time Blackwell read both as an adolescent girl interested in romance (at least at the safe distance afforded by a novel) and as a feminist, approaches that sometimes clashed. Her response to Thomas Hughes's *Tom Brown at Oxford*, the nearest boys' equivalent of a girls' story, indicates an attraction to male authors and characters:

> felt so delighted I squirmed all over, and laughed, and would have liked to hug Tom Hughes. T. B. at Rugby would make me want to do that anyway. What he says meets my views just—especially what he says about wild oats—and about all sorts of things too. What he says is so good and true and brave, and he says it so well and bravely and truly that I feel braver and better for it even when it does not especially apply to me.[7]

Here Blackwell acknowledges her warm and possibly erotic feelings for the author, and most likely also for the hero, the author's stand-in. The novel provided entertainment—she liked it so much that she reread it along with "a whole armful of Thomas Hughes" less than two months later—as well as a satisfying moral.[8] As the daughter of feminists, Alice read with a practiced ideological eye and approved the novel's heavy-handed emphasis on reforming male behavior through abstinence from alcohol and control of sexuality, common themes in feminist circles. In *Tom Brown at Oxford*, pleasure, ideology, and romance worked together for her. This was not always the case. On one occasion, she picked up a volume by James Fenimore Cooper, "being attracted by a picture of a romantic looking pirate, who had just climbed in at a window, and was holding a moonlit conversation with a lady; but found afterward to my disgust that he disapproved Womans [sic] Rights and called Queen Bess a Monster because she was strong minded."[9] Then as now, reading was a complicated enterprise.

Like other teenagers, Blackwell read in many moods and for many reasons. Some books excited her, others made her cry, some enraged her, some made her nervous, others she found calming, still others inspiring. Whatever the case, reading was essential to her well-being. As an only child, shy, moody, and by her own account possessed of a temper, reading provided a safe haven, a way of smoothing herself out, perhaps of stabilizing the wayward feelings and emotional turbulence of adolescence. In addition to the fiction that enthralled her during the two years she kept the journal, she also read, memorized, and wrote poetry and shared books with friends. She read and reread favorite authors, including a local minister on whom she seems to have had a crush and whose works she turned to whenever she needed to be lifted out of a "slough of despond," which was fairly often. Altogether, Blackwell spent a great deal of time absorbed in literary activity, only a fraction of which involved schoolwork.

Despite Blackwell's penchant for moralizing, as exemplified by her comment about wild oats in the Tom Brown books and her condemnation of Byron's poem *Don Juan* for treating "ugly things . . . jokingly," her reading concerned her parents.[10] Given the power to ennoble or debase then attributed to books, it is not surprising that parents scrutinized their children's intake, that of sons as well as daughters. Both the perceived threat and degree of oversight diverged by gender. For boys, dime novels represented the greatest danger. Middle-class parents associated the dimes' freewheeling depictions of smoking, drinking, gambling, and crime with the lower orders, who also constituted the principal audience for the genre. Of his youthful passion for reading Beadle "half-dime" novels, Robert Morss Lovett, professor of English at the University of Chicago, recalled that "such reading was a major vice . . . and could only be indulged out-of-doors or in school behind a geography."[11] Despite parental concern, boys seem to have had little difficulty in gaining access to the dimes. By buying and trading them with schoolmates and farmworkers, writer Hamlin Garland read nearly one hundred during a year spent on a farm.[12] Boys not only had more pocket money than girls with which to buy forbidden (and other) items, but were less subject to parental (which by this time meant mainly maternal) supervision.

No longer afraid that reading novels about seduction would make a young female reader more likely to succumb to a cad, parents in the late nineteenth century worried about their daughters' fondness for fiction and the intensity with which they read it. *The New Novel*, Winslow Homer's well-known 1877 portrait of a young woman stretched out dreamily on the grass, exemplifies the image of the entranced female reader. What to twenty-first-century observers conveys a positive air of freedom had negative connotations to adults at the time. So did the vision conjured up by M. Carey Thomas, who advocated "lounging away the afternoon, as all hot Sunday afternoons ought to be lounged away, with a novel on the bed."[13] To cultural authorities and parents, this kind of reading conveyed a disturbing lack of discipline, even license. Negotiated solutions ranged from parental insistence that serious works be interspersed with lighter fare to keeping overheated books like *Jane Eyre* out of their daughters' hands until they reached the "appropriate" age (fifteen in Thomas's case). One family banned novels during daytime, which was reserved for "serious reading and study," a restriction reminiscent of conventions for alcohol consumption.[14] Often considered an addiction, reading became a site of struggle for girls in ways it usually did not for boys.

Alarmed by her daughter's interest in "trashy" serial stories, Lucy Stone tried to curtail Alice's reading of the *New York Ledger* and sometimes disposed of copies sent to the office of the *Woman's Journal*. In adolescence Alice reserved some of her most passionate comments for the *Ledger*, a weekly story paper that had not shaken off its earlier suspect reputation even though by 1872 it published Longfellow, Henry Ward Beecher, and other respected writers. During a fourteen-month period, Blackwell mentioned it more than two dozen times, with comments like "*no Ledger*!!!" and "I felt that to wait till night for my Ledger meant insanity." She was outraged when her mother said she "never meant to let another [*Ledger*] come into the house. . . . To stop me off right in the midst of Mark Heber's Luck! I straightway went off to bed mad, with tears in my eyes."[15] The story that absorbed Blackwell—she mentioned it on four occasions—was a western Horatio Alger tale of the heroic deeds of an orphan who overcomes Indians and assorted villains and succeeds by following his father's formula that "honesty, industry,

Winslow Homer, *The New Novel*, 1877. The Horace P. Wright Collection, Michele and Donald D'Amour Museum of Fine Arts, Springfield, Massachusetts. Photography by David Stansbury.

perseverance and uprightness bring luck."[16] Despite frequent battles with her mother, Alice managed to read the *Ledger* fairly regularly during this period, after which she either lost interest or no longer felt the need to comment. She moved on to the publications of moral reform societies engaged in rescuing prostitutes, one of her mother's causes, a change that may suggest a new level of maturity or interest in a different kind of formulaic story, one that might have been even more titillating to an adolescent than anything a story paper had to offer.[17]

Henry Blackwell's interventions were of a more didactic kind. Most evenings he read aloud to his wife and daughter, mainly acknowledged masterpieces of nineteenth-century British literature—*Ivanhoe*, *Nicholas Nickleby*, *Middlemarch*, as well as an occasional work written for a youthful audience, such as *The Story of a Bad Boy* by Thomas Bailey Aldrich. The sessions, at which Alice often sewed, were relaxed; in hot weather, the family adjourned to the roof, where on occasion she chased her father. But Alice found them tame, even boring. When her father read a book on the geography of the sea, she observed: "I tried to seem interested, though I hardly heard what he said."[18] She craved exciting stories and on another occasion was in agonies of suspense after being called away from *Les Misérables*: "just as my favorite Enyolras had put a pistol to the head of Le Cabuc and given him one minute to say his prayers, Papa made me stop to listen to that stupid biography of Scott. I went to bed with the white cold face and flying hair of that young executioner before my eyes."[19]

The evening reading sessions were times of family conviviality and socialization into a (mainly) high literary canon rather than occasions for emotional intensity. Only Thackeray's *The Newcomes* elicited spirited diary entries from Alice, but nothing like those accorded her favorites, *Westward Ho!* or Henry Kingsley's *Ravenshoe*, which left her "crying too hard to see the words. Henry Kingsley will certainly make an end of me sooner or later."[20] Not to mention "Mark Heber's Luck." Like other fathers, Henry Blackwell wanted his daughter to read serious literature and less of the light fiction that typically engaged her. On one occasion Alice observed, not without irony: "Papa sat with his feet on the top of the stove, saturated with laziness, and rated me for enjoying stories, and formed plans to give me a taste for instructive literature, and ended by making me bring Plutarch's Lives, and beginning to read them aloud."[21]

Henry Blackwell was not the only father who tried to steer a reluctant daughter away from fiction to history. Young women did not always warm to this paternal instruction and sometimes expressed a disinterest in or distaste for history and a preference for fiction.[22] Alice Stone Blackwell found some of her history lessons "perfectly dreadful" and failed the subject twice. (By contrast, she received prizes for her imaginative writing.) After dreaming she was General Burgoyne "and doing the wrong events," she declared, "I wish History was at the bottom of the sea." Despite this aversion, many of the books she liked qualify as historical novels.[23] Novelist Gene Stratton-Porter, too, preferred to get her history by reading fiction: "I . . . get my pictures of ancient Florence from *Romola*, of revolution from Hugo, of art from Bulwer, of incident from Dumas. All the histories I ever read never gave me such an idea of Scotland and her hero Wallace as does Jane Porter's *Scottish Chiefs*."[24] History was most real and therefore most instructive when packaged as literature. It goes without saying that it was more pleasurable as well.

If other young women viewed history as Blackwell did—"facts related in the order they occurred"—their aversion to the subject is not difficult to understand.[25] Defined so flatly, history lacked the rudiments of a good story, the kind that kept one interested by virtue of the twists and turns in plot or by the authentic sense of atmosphere and character that a fine novelist can convey more convincingly than most historians. Novels also conveyed romance and excitement, qualities found more unequivocally in books than in young women's lives. In addition to being bored by history, some young women may have felt excluded from a past that highlighted wars and politics. That kind of history might even haunt one's dreams: as General Burgoyne, Blackwell found herself "doing the wrong events." History was not only male, it had already happened. Complete unto itself, with heroes and villains well established at the outset, history might be difficult for a woman to read herself into.

Critic Mikhail Bakhtin provides a way of understanding women's long-standing penchant for fiction. Although innocent of gender analysis, his important inquiry into the novel suggests why the genre had much to offer women in the way of plot, setting, and character. In contrasting the novel with the epic, Bakhtin maintains, "From the very beginning the novel was structured not in the distanced image of the absolute past but in the zone of direct contact with inconclusive present-day reality. At its core lay personal experience and free creative imagination." The realistic novel in particular takes place in the present, in the space of parlors and salons rather than in castles and other locations identified with the past. Unlike epics and other "distanced genres," such as history, novels are about everyday events, about imperfect and incomplete heroes. As a result, Bakhtin maintains, "We can experience these adventures, identify with these heroes; such novels almost become a substitute for our own lives." Novels are about individual growth and change rather than heroes who are perfect from the outset: "A crucial tension develops between the external and the internal man, and as a result the subjectivity of the individual becomes an object of experimentation and representation . . . In a novel the individual acquires the ideological and linguistic initiative necessary to change the nature of his own image."[26]

Bakhtin helps us understand why many women found fiction compelling, both in itself and in contrast to more distanced genres like history. Novels depict worlds women can enter, in ways women can enter them. Women's lives exemplify the quotidian, the here and now: the parlor is their territory. The presence of highly individualized characters promotes the process of identification, of experiencing their adventures as the reader's own. Socialized to cultivate feelings and to assume responsibility for personal relations, women may also have found it easier than men to enter the lives of others, including those of fictional characters—even male characters. Reading fiction, particularly when it is done with intensity, unlocks the potential for individual transformation. The "personal experience and free creative imagination" that Bakhtin discerns at the core of the novel were also at the heart of many readers' encounters with books. Central to these encounters was the reader's capacity to "change the nature of his own image"—in this case, her own image.[27]

Philosophers, psychologists, and psychoanalysts maintain that fiction can play an important role in reconfiguring consciousness, particularly during the preadolescent and adolescent years. These are years, Erik Erikson tells us, when imagination plays a crucial role in the formation of identity. Imagination is at its peak in childhood, when individuals identify "more or less experimentally, with real or fictitious people of either sex and with habits, traits, occupations, and ideas," while adolescents endeavor to "define, overdefine, and redefine themselves."[28] Erikson was generalizing about mid-twentieth-century adolescents, but the conditions that foster a more fluid trying on of identities were in place for middle-class youth almost a century earlier: longer and more protected childhoods exempt from formal labor; greater occupational choice; and the deferred maturity dictated by longer years of professional training prior to marriage.[29] Available evidence suggests that, then as now, reading was at a peak during a person's younger years.[30]

Literature offers the possibility of constructing new self-images to both men and women. But for women, reading has more often provided a fundamental source of identity than it has for men: the need was greater, the alternative routes to self-development fewer. Especially in the preadolescent and adolescent years, when a sense of personal deficiency among girls is so common, reading provided opportunities to enlarge their experience of life, explore the meaning of problematic or conflictual concerns (romance, religion), and try on diverse identities, many of which they could not entertain in real life. On a more mundane level, girls' passionate reading provided relief from boredom or unpleasantness and an occasion for expressing normally repressed emotions—or just giving vent to emotional highs and lows—in the relatively safe space of a book.

Although not entirely free of conflict, reading enabled girls and young women to enter a zone as near to unalloyed and self-determining pleasure as the culture allowed members of their sex. It was by and large an approved pleasure, yet one that could carry the reader into uncharted territory. Mary Austin, a passionate nature writer, recalled her youthful reading of Hugh Miller's *The Old Red Sandstone* as a transcendent experience that gave meaning to both present and future. Reading this volume gave her "the feel of the author behind the book, the feel of the purposeful earth," and a "sense of the unfolding earth [that] never left her."[31] Reading was, moreover, a pleasure enhanced by being shared with friends. In a culture that did not encourage individualism in women, the self-expression afforded by reading—in its diverse forms—was of considerable consequence, as young women shaped and reshaped the images of who they were and who they wished to become. It was a journey they often made with one another.

For women growing up in the Gilded Age, reading looked outward as well as inward. From the informal occasions when two or more girls read together, to the joint wordplay, writing ventures, and informal reading circles of schoolmates or friends, to the more formal study clubs popular with adult women at that time, many of women's most significant literary experiences were collaborative. Perhaps this aspect of women's reading culture was what most differentiated it from men's.

Young men also engaged in joint cultural activities. They joined college literary and debating societies and read or attended lectures at lyceums, mercantile libraries, and other public places.[32] But, in a society that encouraged individualism in men, these activities were often competitive, notably so in the case of debating. Even when boys and young men read in the company of others, they usually did so silently, while for adult men, reading aloud occurred mainly in domestic settings, during courtship or, after marriage, with wives and children.[33]

By contrast, books and reading were central to the web of female friendship. Girls and young women read to one another for fun and frolic, for romance, as a soothing ritual to comfort an invalid or cure a headache, or to be together while sewing or brushing one's hair. Young women's reading culture also connected them to a more public world that fostered hopes for futures different than those of their mothers. Disadvantaged in attaining goals that did not center on domestic life, women needed one another for mental stimulation, personal sustenance, and affection: intellectual growth and emotional well-being went hand in hand.[34] Intellectual inquiry, exploration of normally forbidden topics, practical help in sharpening one's ideas and literary style—all coexisted with absolute loyalty and understanding that was attainable nowhere else. Even when mothers were supportive, as they often were, those who bore children in the 1860s and 1870s were rarely able to be of much intellectual help. Additionally, in an era when extreme awkwardness characterized relations between men and women of marriageable age, young women necessarily looked to one another for intellectual openness as well as emotional intimacy. Gender relationships were so formal in some circles that men had to ask permission to initiate a correspondence, and individuals who had known each other since childhood began to address one another as Miss and Mr.

The literary activities of several young women who came of age in Providence in the late 1870s and early 1880s reveal the potential of collaborative endeavor. They came from some of New England's most intellectually distinguished families: Channings, Beechers, and several connected with Brown University. None seems to have taken advantage of the formal opportunities for advanced education newly available to their sex. The best known, Charlotte Perkins Gilman, was the great niece of Harriet Beecher Stowe and Catharine Beecher, but her formal education was neglected, primarily because of deteriorating financial circumstances after her father abandoned his wife and children. In later years, following a severe breakdown, Gilman claimed that libraries were "an appalling weariness just to look at," but she described herself as a voracious reader between the ages of five and fifteen, a girl for whom a library was "as a confectioner's shop."[35]

A champion of the disciplined life, in her midteens Gilman undertook a rigorous program of mental, physical, and spiritual improvement. She studied Latin and natural philosophy and read contemporary works on history and science recommended by her father. Frederic Beecher Perkins was well qualified to advise his daughter on the subject of books: he was a prominent librarian and author of *The Best Reading: Hints on the Selection of Books; On the Formation of Libraries, Public and Private;* and *On Courses of Reading, Etc.*, a standard reference work in its fourth edition in 1877. Charlotte also enrolled in the Rhode Island School of Design and took courses through the Society to Encourage Studies at Home, a Boston-based program in which women corresponded with teachers about books they read on self-designed topics, ancient history in her case.[36]

In shifting pairs and clusters, members of the Providence circle engaged in overlapping literary activities.[37] In her late teens, Gilman belonged to an "Essay Club" with several female friends. Little is known about the group, but the meetings appear to have been lighthearted and eclectic: there were discussions, songs, and readings (including one by Gilman of "my Valentine"). Of one occasion, she observed in her diary, "Morning at Essay Club. Very pleasant. Quite distinguish myself in discussion"; of another, "Essay Club. Nothing original." She thought well enough of her fellow "Clubbists" to propose reestablishing the group two years later: "Look here. Some sort of club—a society we must have. . . . Somewhat like that Essay Club, only *in earnest* we that can meet to tell all to write, and all to help each other."[38]

During this period, members of the group kept on writing—often together. A "triangular" literary society included Gilman and her closest friend, Martha Luther, who on her own also edited and published an amateur newspaper, the *Hillside Register*.[39] Bound together by literary interests and intimate ties of affection, they read and commented on one another's stories and poems and engaged in high-spirited literary play. In "The One Word Game," participants built a story by contributing one word at a time—often to hilarious effect. Here was the ultimate collaboration, the whole more than the sum of the parts: "It touches combinations impossible to any single thought-process."[40] With two other friends, Grace Channing and Grace's sister, Gilman wrote "partnership novels," while Luther and another friend together rewrote the endings of novels. At least some of their literary efforts were seriously intended: Luther sent a story to *Harper's* (it was rejected), while Gilman's first poem appeared in the *New England Journal of Education*, her father acting as intermediary.[41]

These collaborative activities were in a real sense rehearsals for future literary attainment. One of the leading feminists of her era, Gilman became a prolific writer of stories, poems, and social criticism; despite recurrent periods of depression, she supported herself by writing and lecturing. Most of the others also found their way into print. Caroline Hazard, who became president of Wellesley College, published poetry as well as books on education and Rhode Island history, in which her family had played an important part. Grace Channing, who later collaborated on plays with Gilman, wrote throughout her life and had several stories and poems published. Martha (Luther) Lane wrote and edited textbooks and community publications and collaborated on at least one work with Mabel Hill, another member of the circle, who taught history at Lowell State Normal School. Their text for elementary school students, *American History in Literature* (1905), a collection of prose and poetry, told the history of the United States from the days of exploration right down through the recent acquisition of the Philippines. Featuring selections by prominent writers like Washington Irving and Hawthorne, the volume included a story about Pocahontas by Martha Lane. Its rationale—that "every intelligent teacher of history makes more or less use of literature to give reality and vividness to persons, events, or conditions under consideration in the classroom"—would have resonated with the women of their generation who preferred their history in literary dress.[42]

The family connections of the Providence women undoubtedly smoothed the way to authorship, but the activities in which they engaged as teenagers were not uncommon. Some groups had more formal arrangements, but in joining sociability with intellectual stimulation, the Essay Club met the essential components of the women's literary societies and study groups that proliferated in the last third of the century. So did its members' enthusiasm for self-improvement.

The most famous venture in self-culture, the Chautauqua Literary and Scientific Circle (CLSC), was an adult education program that offered a fixed course of study to men and women organized in local circles at a yearly cost of $7.00 (reading materials included). In a given year, members might concentrate on England, the United States, Europe, or classical civilizations (interspersed with readings on other subjects); the estimated 10 to 12 percent who completed a four-year cycle received diplomas. Like its parent body, the Chautauqua Society, a movement that originated in a summer school for Sunday school teachers, the CLSC brought culture to a middle-class Protestant population.[43]

Of the 225,000 individuals reached by the CLSC between 1878 and 1894, approximately four-fifths were women. By 1900 there were over 10,000 circles, an estimated three-quarters of them in communities of 3,500 or less, many of them lacking a public library. In practice, the CLSC brought a semblance of a college education to women who could not otherwise have attained it. To encourage participation by every member, the organization directed circle leaders to ask each in turn to give "an interesting fact noted in connection with the reading" until everyone had five opportunities to do so; only then were they to proceed to recitations and drills. Despite its religious origins, by 1894 the CLSC had eliminated theology from its required readings. By then there was a "Jewish branch" that included reading courses on Jewish history and literature and a well-organized Catholic Educational Union, complete with its own journal.[44]

Even more popular than the CLSC were the literary or study clubs in communities across the country, from Cambridge, Massachusetts, to Morrilton, Arkansas, to Leadville, Colorado. With names like the Saturday Morning Club, Friends in Council, and Over the Teacups, many of them evolved from informal reading circles; some are still going strong in the twenty-first century. Beginning in the late 1860s and peaking in the 1890s, the clubs allowed middle-class Protestant women, most of them married, to expand their intellectual horizons, a particular challenge to those living in small towns. In 1890 local clubs formed the General Federation of Women's Clubs, an organization that had over a million members by World War I. Excluded from membership, African American women established their own clubs and in 1896 joined together in the National Association of Colored Women. About the same time, Jewish, Catholic, and working-class women's groups also organized around reading.[45]

The clubs cultivated rituals that promoted personal growth, sociability, and collective identity. Less centralized and structured than the CLSC, clubs often began meetings with a roll call, to which everyone responded with a "memory gem"—usually a quotation from the assigned author or topic of the day. In the early years especially, when women hesitated to speak in public, practices of this sort ensured that even the most reserved would participate. Clubs typically concentrated on a mutually agreed upon subject for the year, often some aspect of literature, history, or art, with leeway for stray topics. British, western European, and American subjects of the high-culture variety predominated: Shakespeare alone accounted for one-half of the programs of Texas reading groups in 1902–3.[46] Taking turns presenting papers, members might be followed by an official critic or monitored by a person who corrected pronunciation (most homes lacked dictionaries), activities often leavened by refreshments and sometimes by musical entertainments. Some groups supplemented regular meetings with debates; others wrote or adapted plays, which they performed publicly. Variable in quality and depth, these activities were the nearest many members came to a higher education.[47]

Women took their clubs seriously. From the beginning they gave their organizations a public face by constructing an official record and a history. They wrote and adopted constitutions and bylaws, kept minutes, and produced printed yearbooks; some published newspapers as well. Documents of this kind, along with adherence to parliamentary procedure, gave members a sense of the importance of their enterprise that promoted confidence and cohesion. The organizational framework of the clubs, along with rituals requiring participation and mandatory voting on even the smallest expenditure, suggest democratic internal procedures that provide a striking contrast with the exclusionary class and racial basis around which most of them organized. The knowledge of political processes acquired through these collective activities encouraged women, who began as students of culture unfamiliar with public life, to pursue more controversial undertakings that qualified them as semi-public or even public bodies.[48] Meeting initially in parlors for the most part, as membership increased some clubs moved to public meeting spaces. In Michigan and elsewhere, clubs raised funds to construct their own buildings, thereby creating a visible and permanent public presence. They also turned to subjects of more immediate political concern—suffrage, immigration, and urban improvement projects like kindergartens and juvenile courts, major concerns of women at the time. The social activism of white women's clubs developed gradually, but by the early twentieth century, many had moved on from culture to social reform. For African American women, what literary historian Elizabeth McHenry calls "public literacy" prevailed from the start.[49]

One of the clubs' most important public services was bringing books to their communities. Frustrated by the shortage of reading material, members tried a variety of remedies, from sharing books to setting up their own subscription libraries, often in a member's home. Women's clubs established public libraries in cities and towns across the nation—an estimated 75 percent of the total, according to a 1933 American Library Association report—and traveling libraries in rural areas. They may have been most effective in the West and the South, where the public library movement lagged: in Texas, for example, women founded an estimated 85 percent of the libraries. But their reach was nationwide.[50]

Collectively the clubs did much to keep women's literary work alive. They did so on a continuing basis by reading and discussing books written by women. Most visibly, they displayed women's writing at the 1893 World's Columbian Exposition in Chicago commemorating (a year late) the 400th anniversary of Columbus's arrival in the Americas. The Woman's Building featured arts, crafts, and music by women, but its centerpiece was a library housing 7,000 books, 4,000 of them by Americans. The New York exhibit included 2,400 volumes by state authors as well as "a showing of" work by seventy-five literary clubs and classes, each with a bound volume containing the constitution, bylaws, membership list, club history, and four representative papers. Massachusetts clubs sent many fewer books, but catalogued 2,000 titles by state residents, while Connecticut spotlighted Harriet Beecher Stowe with a bookcase containing a complete set of her works and forty-two copies of *Uncle Tom's Cabin* in translation. It was an impressive display of female literary talent.[51]

Significantly, at this landmark event art and imagination were represented as female, science as male, visual depictions that symbolized contemporary understanding of the gendered division of intellectual labor. If women's representation at the Exposition is any indication, that division permitted white women—African Americans were for the most part excluded from participation—to carve out a public presence for themselves, a presence that built on understandings of the sort that writer and literary impresario Thomas Wentworth Higginson put forward more than a decade earlier, when he asserted, "it may fairly be assumed that the women's clubs have become to some extent the popular custodians of literature in America."[52]

Despite some initial ridicule and disapproval directed at women's study clubs, to the extent that their endeavors belonged to the voluntary realm, they posed little threat to male leaders or institutions. By the end of the century, however, women had made sufficient inroads into neutral or male turf to invite negative reaction. Sparked by fear of competition and a desire to avoid the taint of feminization, professional men sometimes resorted to the strident hyper-masculinity in vogue in the 1890s, a decade marked by martial rhetoric and imperialist expansion.[53] As male writers and artists sought to upgrade the status of their fields and their own place within them, they offered new definitions of excellence that often marginalized women. Among artists, for example, opportunities afforded women in the Gilded Age decreased around the turn of the century, as competition for jobs, new marketing structures that tended to exclude women, and a more "masculine" rhetoric of individual achievement replaced that of cultural refinement. Art once valued as "refined," whether produced by men or women, became relegated to a lower category of the "feminine."[54] Developments such as these suggest that earlier, gender-based understandings of the division of cultural labor had in some ways worked in women's favor, at least at the rhetorical level.

BY 1893, CHARLOTTE PERKINS GILMAN, M. Carey Thomas, Florence Kelley, Jane Addams, and Ida B. Wells were well launched on public careers. (Edith and Alice Hamilton were still preparing for theirs, while immigrants Mary Antin, Rose Cohen, and Hilda Satt Polacheck, all younger, had just arrived or were about to do so.) Thomas, the oldest, was the predominant intellectual and administrative force at Bryn Mawr College and would be appointed president the following year. Gilman, recently separated from her husband, had begun a precarious career as a lecturer and writer. The year before, she had published "The Yellow Wallpaper," a chilling story based on her emotional breakdown following the birth of her daughter, and in the fall of 1893 her first volume of poetry appeared in print. Living in California, she was the only one of the five who did not attend the Exposition, but she served on an "Advisory Council of the Woman's Branch" and sent "a short powerful paper" on "The Sex Question Answered" for one of the congresses called to coincide with the event.[55] Kelley, who had three children and had also left her husband, was living at Hull-House, where she had recently directed a pioneering survey documenting the substandard living and working conditions of the neighborhood. The survey paved the way for passage of a state bill that regulated sweatshop industries, limited hours of work for women and girls, and prohibited child labor; Kelley's appointment as chief factory inspector for Illinois followed. In her early thirties, Addams was already an important person in Chicago reform circles and a nationally recognized leader of the settlement movement. She delivered a talk on "Domestic Service and the Family Claim" at the World's Congress of Representative Women, which she later incorporated into her first book. Wells, who launched her campaign against lynching in 1892, had recently returned from a tour of England where her lectures had been favorably received. Bold in temperament and already a seasoned activist, the thirty-one-year-old journalist organized a protest against the Exposition's exclusion of African Americans and took the lead in compiling a pamphlet calling attention to this omission as well as to African Americans' many contributions to American culture.

On the cusp of a new century, women seemed poised for major triumphs. With new educational and professional opportunities, outlets for their artistic and literary work, and a growing voice in public affairs, they had reason to believe they would soon attain their rightful place in American life. Even the dormant movement to gain voting rights showed new signs of life with the recent coming together of the two major suffrage organizations, a move led by Alice Stone Blackwell. So when Frances E. W. Harper, a distinguished African American writer and activist, declared at the World's Congress of Representative Women that "we stand on the threshold of woman's era," there was every reason to believe her.[56]

PART TWO

PRIVILEGED READERS

· ·

. . . .

CHAPTER FOUR

(Reading as) A Family Affair

The Hamiltons of Fort Wayne

"I wish people did not think us quite so terribly bookish," Edith Hamilton exclaimed to her cousin Jessie.[1] The future best-selling author, then in her twenties, might well have saved her breath. The identities of at least three generations of Hamiltons were closely bound up with books. Older members of this large and self-consciously literary family treasured and collected them, donated them for public use, and made sure their children appreciated them. In this they succeeded admirably: the lives and happiness of the mainly female third generation—Edith and Jessie's—depended on them. As Jessie's younger sister Agnes put it: "What could I do if I did not have books."[2]

The Hamiltons' ability to create a world in which books were central—even their desire to do so—originated in class privilege. Daughters of one of Fort Wayne's most elite families, the young women had easy access to books and the leisure to enjoy them. Eager to acquire cultural credentials that did credit to the family, they read widely—history, biography, essays, fiction, and more besides—even as they took care with their own literary productions. Except for more formal instruction in Latin, Greek, and modern languages, much of their early education was self-directed.

Class standing, while it gave the Hamiltons unusual access to books and opportunities to use them, did not account for all that reading meant to them. The young women found romance in books, though not the traditional kind. At once study and play, discipline and release, reading provided intellectual and spiritual nourishment, inspiration for living and models of style, as well as the delicious pleasure of losing oneself in a book or sharing it with beloved members of the family. For the Hamiltons, reading was a cultural style, an elaborate system of rituals and exchanges central to the fabric of everyday life.

Their interactions with books helped shape family identity as well as individual self-consciousness to an unusual degree. Psychologists tell us that storytelling is essential for children to envision their own place in the world.[3] In this regard, as in others, the Hamiltons were exceptionally well endowed. Through the narratives they read and re-created, they constructed stories of themselves in the world. The Hamiltons constituted their own interpretive community, a group of like-minded readers who privileged certain texts and understood them according to its own codes. Within this common framework, individuals singled out books to which they attached special meaning.

By providing a frame around which the young people could spin their dreams and a common language in which to share them, reading stimulated the reciprocal interplay between books and lives. The Hamiltons' playful mode of interacting with books, the characters in them, and the authors who wrote them spurred youthful imagination and provided a catalyst for self-creation. Whether in the form of resonant personal or family narratives, reading brought opportunities for invention and exchange. In conjunction with the strong antimarriage ethic of the women, the family's reading culture encouraged dreams of personal agency rather than domestic bliss. Proud of their intellectual attainments, the Hamilton women looked down on women of their class whose ambitions ran to social success and expedient marriages. They hoped to make their mark in more public ways—as scholars, artists, and physicians—when to do so women needed unusual determination, perhaps those of the upper classes most of all.

One of the most distinctive aspects of the Hamiltons' reading was the degree to which it was collective. Their romance with books was a family affair. When the Hamiltons thought of each other, they thought of each other reading. Edith away at school wished she could be transported to Jessie's room to watch her cousin reading (Sunday books on Sunday), while Jessie recalled Edith at thirteen reading a book in Greek as she combed her hair.[4] Despite Edith's disclaimer, this shared passion was among the characteristics that marked the Hamiltons as "a tribe"—to themselves as well as to others.[5]

Edith and Jessie Hamilton were granddaughters of Allen Hamilton, a Scots-Irish immigrant from County Tyrone, Ireland, who came to the frontier village of Fort Wayne, Indiana, in 1823 following a decline in the family's fortunes. Through shrewd business judgment and well-placed connections, he became prosperous in the fur and Indian trade, retail merchandising, banking, and especially land speculation. His wealth, combined with the requisite civic-mindedness, lifted him into the city's elite and made it possible for his five surviving children and eighteen grandchildren to enjoy the accouterments of the good life: elegant houses, travel, education, and easy access to books. After his death, both sons lived on the family estate, as did his widow and unmarried daughter; his two married daughters lived nearby.[6]

His oldest grandchildren, seven women and one man all born between 1862 and 1873, belonged to three nuclear families; in childhood the cousins were each others' only playmates. Two of them attained international renown: Edith Hamilton, oldest daughter of the second son, who wrote best-selling interpretations of classical civilizations after she retired as headmistress of the Bryn Mawr School of Baltimore, and her sister Alice Hamilton, a pioneer in industrial medicine and long-term resident of Hull-House, who became Harvard's first woman professor. Margaret followed Edith first to Bryn Mawr College and then to the Bryn Mawr School, where she taught science and headed the primary department, while Norah, the youngest sister, was an artist who did bold etchings, lithographs, and drawings of urban life (some of them illustrate Alice's and Jane Addams's autobiographies) and taught art classes for underprivileged children at Hull-House and in New York. Their female cousins did not realize their goals to the same extent, but in youth all had serious aspirations. Katherine, a gifted student of languages, hoped to be a professor; Jessie, the most beloved of the cousins, was a serious student of art who in later years worked mainly in etchings and oils; and Agnes studied architecture and painting before going on to a long career at the Lighthouse, a religious settlement in Philadelphia. Allen Hamilton Williams, a graduate of Harvard College, became a physician. He was the only one to marry.[7]

The family's literary tradition derived from their paternal grandmother, Emerine Jane (Holman) Hamilton, who came from a prominent political family in southern Indiana. Her father, Jesse Lynch Holman, was a state and later a federal judge, and her brother, William Steele Holman, a sixteen-term Democratic member of the U.S. House of Representatives. Jesse Holman, a devout Baptist, leader in the national and regional Sunday school

The Hamilton cousins of Fort Wayne, ca. 1885–92. Left to right: Norah, Margaret, Edith, Jessie, Taber, Katherine, Allen Williams, Alice, Agnes, Allen Hamilton, Creighton Williams. Hamilton Family Papers, The Schlesinger Library, Radcliffe Institute, Harvard University.

movements, and a founder of a Baptist college in Franklin, became an ordained clergyman later in life. A man of broad public spirit, he also promoted a public library and school system in Aurora, where he lived.[8]

Emerine came by her literary interests honestly: she was named for the heroine of *The Prisoners of Niagara; or, Errors of Education*, a sentimental novel written by her father and published in 1810, the year of her birth.[9] After her marriage to Allen Hamilton, she became a pillar of the First Presbyterian Church of Fort Wayne, which her husband helped organize and where he led a successful move to grant women the right to vote in church affairs. Emerine was known locally for her generosity to Fort Wayne's poorer citizens, including African Americans, who came to the door to pay their respects during her final illness. A woman of strong and independent character, she supported temperance and woman suffrage and remembered both Lucy Stone and Susan B. Anthony in her will.[10]

Emerine's love of reading made a strong impression on her granddaughters. To Alice she was a fascinating if somewhat remote presence, a woman who "lost herself" in books: "She loved reading passionately. I can remember often seeing her in the library of the Old House, crouched over the fireplace where the soft-coal fire had gone out without her knowing it, so deep had she been in her book." For her part, Agnes envied her grandmother's ability to extricate herself from disagreeable people by immersing herself in a book. In addition to carving out psychic space by reading, Emerine enthralled her grandchildren with Sir Walter Scott's poems, which she rendered mainly in prose, sometimes dropping into poetry.[11]

The Hamiltons surrounded themselves with books. At a time when most Americans owned few if any, four of Allen and Emerine's five children were among Fort Wayne's largest collectors.[12] The oldest son, A. Holman Hamilton, a graduate of Wabash College who studied at Harvard Law School and in Germany and served two terms as a Democratic member of the U.S. House of Representatives, had the largest private library in the city. Variously estimated at between 6,000 and 8,000 volumes, the collection contained over 600 books on folklore (Irish and Scottish especially) and many on witchcraft. These interests were already evident in his 1855 graduation address on "Books of Childhood," which commended goblin and fairy tales, old ballads and legends, and other imaginative works for the very young. Holman's collection ranged from Bibles, rare medieval manuscripts, and books on dialects, to Beadle's Dime Series and an occasional tale of "low life," along with standard volumes of essays, history, and fiction and numerous magazines. It also reflected the interests of his daughters, Katherine, Jessie, and Agnes—*Dotty Dimple's Flyaway* and *The Girls of the Bible* when they were young, and books and magazines on art and architecture that corresponded with their later interests.[13]

Holman's younger brother and protégé, Montgomery Hamilton, craved books from an early age. Subscribing to Holman's "Magazine" out of his "coffee money" when he was eleven, Montgomery commanded, "I want you to have some stories that I like to read." At the same age, the future father of Edith and Alice spent $2.25 on a set by popular writer T. S. Arthur (with titles like *Making Haste to Be Rich* and *Keeping up Appearances*) before moving on to adventure stories by Mayne Reid, local humor, a biography of revolutionary war hero Francis Marion, and Washington Irving's *Crayon Miscellany*.[14] Montgomery attended Princeton and, like his brother, studied in Germany and at Harvard Law School. He still required a steady supply of novels for his happiness and, in romantic pursuit, looked to fiction for heroic models. He married the woman in question, Gertrude Pond Hamilton, whose knowledge of modern fiction and languages impressed him.[15] Settling down as a partner in a wholesale grocery store, Montgomery built up a mainly reference library of about 1,000 books, which included numerous works of theology and ethnology as well as bound magazines (among them the complete *Punch* of 1841–70).[16] Prominent in local Democratic politics as a young man, he served several terms as an alderman. In later years, like his brother, he retreated into his library—well stocked with port and cigars as well as with books.

Everyone in this family read passionately, but, like their female counterparts across the land, it was the women who extended reading from a private pleasure into an occasion for public service. With her three daughters, Mary Williams, Ellen Wagenhals, and Margaret Vance Hamilton, Emerine Hamilton established a Free Reading Room for Women in 1887. The collection of 400 volumes, including magazines, newspapers, and reference books, featured works of "general literature and art and the best fiction," past and present. Renamed the Emerine J. Hamilton Library following the matriarch's death two years later, the reading room became a circulating library with an enlarged collection that included history and biography as well as books for children; the founder's granddaughters, who took turns assisting the librarian, were among its most eager patrons. In 1896 the library, by then numbering more than 4,000 volumes, went to the new YWCA (Agnes Hamilton was president). The transfer followed the founding of the Fort Wayne Public Library, an outgrowth of efforts by the Woman's Club League.[17]

Emerine's youngest daughter, Margaret, was a leader in the league's drive to establish the public library and after its founding in 1894 served on its selection committee. She had a significant collection of her own, estimated at 2,000 or more volumes, including many on art and Italian history and literature (in Italian as well as English), subjects of considerable interest to her.[18] Less than a decade older than her oldest niece, she was an indulgent aunt who took her siblings' children to bookstores and to artists' studios in New York and rented a farmhouse in Farmington, Connecticut, so she and her nieces could keep in touch with their boarding school friends. She also bankrolled some of their Fort Wayne projects, remodeling her carriage house in 1892 into a studio that became the nucleus of an art school; Jessie, Agnes, and Norah not only studied and exhibited there, but taught classes when more experienced teachers could not be lured to Fort Wayne.[19]

The Hamiltons' fortunes suffered during the depression of the 1890s and their presence in Fort Wayne diminished. Holman died in 1895, and Margaret Vance Hamilton, unable to maintain the family homestead, eventually moved to her mother's ancestral home in Aurora, Indiana. Holman's oldest son, the second Allen Hamilton, stayed on, practicing medicine and carrying on the family literary tradition. Montgomery's four daughters and

Agnes left Fort Wayne to pursue their vocations. The economic downturn also brought to the surface cracks that had begun to disrupt family harmony after Emerine's death in 1889. The cousins weathered these economic and family storms and remained close. In later years, four of them became near neighbors in Connecticut, Alice and Margaret in Hadlyme, Jessie and Agnes in Deep River.

.   .   .   .

Stories were woven into the fabric of a Hamilton's life virtually from the moment of birth. Children gathered around the nursery fire to hear grown-ups read and listened as well to older siblings tell scary stories in a tree they called "the Frightful." Living in close proximity, shifting groups of young-sters read and played word games together, not to mention outdoor enter-tainments based on literary models, like the siege of Troy and King Arthur. As they matured, they took their places in informal family reading circles. They had little choice. Alice later claimed that she and Norah were "reluc-tant" readers, but that "family pressure made us too into bookworms finally." Not all the pressure came from the grown-ups. On obligatory daily walks, Edith, a "passionate reader" and "natural story teller," left off her summaries of favorite stories at climactic moments in order to induce Alice, younger by only eighteen months, to read them on her own instead of the childish books she still favored—evidently with little success.[20]

The Hamiltons had access to an unusually wide range of children's litera-ture, including bound periodicals like the *Wide Awake*. According to Alice, early favorites included Jacob Abbott's antebellum "Franconia" series, nos-talgic tales of growing up in small-town and rural America that conveyed practical information as well as gentle moral lessons, and Sophie May's con-temporary "Susy and Prudy" stories that carried young sisters and cousins through many volumes. They also read Susan Coolidge's popular "Katy" books, the adventures of a fun-loving and mainly female family in which Katy Carr, an ambitious and absent-minded tomboy, learns consideration for others without losing her individuality; Alice claimed that the Hamil-tons preferred them to Louisa May Alcott's. More complex works followed, including novels by Charlotte Mary Yonge, a prolific English writer and fol-lower of the Anglo-Catholic Oxford movement whose domestic fiction ap-pealed across religious lines. In her seventies, Alice observed that Yonge's May and Underwood families "are still more vivid to me than any real people I met in those years."[21] These retrospective comments attest to fiction's com-pelling hold on youthful imaginations, a tendency no doubt intensified by the family's inwardness: except when they attended church, the Hamiltons rarely interacted with "outsiders."

Moving on to more adult fare meant first and foremost Sir Walter Scott, a favorite with three generations, with Emerine and Montgomery—who affixed the name "Sir Walter Scott('s admirer.)" to a college essay on "Heroines"—as well as Edith and Jessie. For the older generations at least, the family's Scots-Irish origins likely enhanced the appeal of the novelist whose popularity moved Scottish lore and history to a central place in British letters. They passed on the tradition by requiring their children to memorize Scott's poems and by showering them with gifts: in her early teens Agnes received a Scott novel every vacation.[22]

The preeminent novelist in Great Britain and the United States during the first half of the century—and in evangelical circles often the only acceptable one—Scott was second only to Shakespeare in the eyes of some critics. After 1860 or so, he fell out of critical favor except as a writer for younger readers. He still held an honored place in many families, but often as transitional fare en route to more grown-up books.[23] His poetry and ballads, with their romantic retellings of Scottish legends and history, remained set pieces for training young people in memory and elocution. Often considered a founder of the historical novel, Scott was widely credited with opening up the imaginative possibilities of the past. Following a path well-worn by American tourists, Margaret Vance Hamilton acted on this belief on a trip to Lake Kitrine in the Scottish Highlands, the setting of Scott's long narrative poem, *The Lady of the Lake*. There she visited Ellen's Isle, becoming, if only for a moment, Ellen Douglas, the poem's heroine.[24]

Beyond Scott, the young Hamiltons enjoyed the full range of books Victorians designated "the best."[25] These included numerous histories and biographies—Knight's as well as Macaulay's history of England, but not the American historians Bancroft or Hildreth. Novels too played an indispensable part in their upbringing. The young people enjoyed the standard British authors, not only Dickens, George Eliot, and Thackeray, but also those they considered "old novelish," like Maria Edgeworth.[26] There were personal favorites too: Agnes claimed she read Jane Austen's *Persuasion* four times each year and the rest of the writer's corpus once.[27] Where solemn individuals still insisted that it would be better to read the Bible than novels, Jessie agreed with the view that "sometimes other things make you appreciate the serious more."[28] Sunday was reserved for the serious ones, including religious novels and devotional works like *The Imitation of Christ* by Thomas à Kempis and

F. W. Farrar's *The Life and Work of St. Paul.* Agnes gravitated to reading of this kind, as she did to Jane Austen.[29]

British fiction and belles lettres dominated the American literary scene until the 1890s, but the Hamiltons represented something of an extreme, particularly in their bypassing of the New England literary tradition then gaining influence in American letters. Among American writers, only Hawthorne and Poe seem to have penetrated family reading circles. Montgomery Hamilton had no interest in American literature and history; with his passion for "clarity and definiteness," he favored Macaulay, Froude, Addison, and Pope to the "woolgathering of the New England school."[30] It is likely that other Hamiltons, good Democrats and Presbyterians that they were, also disdained Emerson's romantic individualism.[31] The young women were, however, avid readers of the handsomely illustrated magazines of Gilded Age America, of which *Harper's* and the *Century* were particular favorites. Less esteemed than books, magazines offered women of the comfortable classes pleasurable opportunities for reading, gossiping, and dreaming. Jessie, who enjoyed illustrations and stories about artists, sometimes looked over several issues as they lay scattered about her on the floor.[32]

Although steeped in high culture, the Hamiltons also indulged in an array of now-forgotten books read mainly for diversion. Some they considered "trash," a designation that included overwrought and excessively sentimental as well as lurid works.[33] While recognizing the category, they did not always agree on its boundaries: one person's trash was another's sensibility. Thus Edith remarked of a book a younger sister's college friends considered trashy: "It seems to me an earnest, thoughtful book, with a high tone through it all. I do like it very much."[34] Supervision seems to have been minimal in Edith and Alice's family, but a few racy items fell into the category of "forbidden" books, of which Alice recalled only *The Decameron*, the *Heptaméron* of Marguerite of Navarre, and Eugène Sue's *The Wandering Jew*.[35] The cousins encountered greater restriction, and Agnes at nineteen was careful not to take home a novel by popular German romance writer E. Marlitt, a book she had read years before.[36]

Questionable categories aside, reading constituted the core of the Hamiltons' education, indeed, was barely distinguished from it. Despite the preponderance of female offspring in the third generation, there was nothing traditionally feminine about their education. Committed to an ideal of genteel learning that defined an educated person as one who knew ancient and modern languages, history, the classics of Western culture, and of course the

Bible, the Hamiltons held their daughters to the highest standards. Edith, Alice, and their younger sisters were educated entirely at home until age seventeen or so. They learned by reading on their own for the most part, but received instruction in French and German (which they had earlier heard spoken by their mother and the servants, respectively). Their father taught them Latin and oversaw their education.[37]

A frustrated classicist whose grocery business failed when Edith and Alice were in their teens, Montgomery Hamilton proceeded by having them read his favorites and by setting them research tasks in his ample reference library. He read them Macaulay's *Lays of Ancient Rome* and Scott's poems and required Edith and Alice to memorize all of *The Lady of the Lake* and recite a few lines each evening. (Memorizing this poem was a convention in the cousins' family as well.) Montgomery also gave them a page of the *Spectator* to "read over three times" and then write out from memory. In addition, they learned the Bible, which Alice claimed she knew better than any other book. Religion was a serious matter in this family, especially for the women, who attended the First Presbyterian Church and taught Sabbath school. But Montgomery Hamilton, more interested in theology than devotional practice, taught religious texts like any others: he had Edith and Alice search the Bible for proof of the doctrine of the Trinity—he thought it originated elsewhere—and learn the Westminster Catechism.[38]

This method of learning—reading, memorizing, and reciting—was by no means unique to the Hamiltons: it dominated formal schooling throughout the century, fostering a rich oral tradition that included storytelling at home and dramatic public oratory. Montgomery Hamilton's pedagogy conformed as well to the widespread belief that an acknowledged stylist like Joseph Addison, who edited and wrote for the influential early eighteenth-century periodical, the *Spectator*, would promote distinction in a reader's literary style. Admonished too that inferior prose might result from reading worthless stories, young Hamiltons sometimes attributed a mundane or scattered letter to a late night with a trashy novel.[39]

Exposure to classic male authors, Scott in particular, connected the women to an important tradition of historical writing that took the novel beyond its familiar domestic origins. (Some even considered his works accurate sources of history, a view Edith ridiculed a few years later.)[40] Addison explicitly sought to bring philosophical discourse to the "tea-tables," that is, to women, but did so very much within traditional domestic boundaries. At fourteen, Edith made fun of the *Spectator* assignment, even as she used it to model a literary vocation. "Don't be astonished, Jeddie, at the finished &

elegant diction of my letters," she forewarned her cousin. "I flatter myself my style is getting quite Addisonian. I hope you keep all my letters; some day, you know, they will be all treasured up as the works of 'Miss Hamilton, the American Addison, Scott & Shakespeare'!"[41] In another letter of the same period, Edith chided her cousin for writing in a non-Addisonian vein and went on to demonstrate her own skill in a parody that captured the substance as well as the style of her model: "And remember, Jessie dear, that foolish, ignorant girls seldom get husbands, and rarely find means for settling down to a happy, domestic life, which should be every woman's highest ambition."[42] Even as she ridiculed the domestic ideal, the self-mocking tone with which Edith referred to her literary aspirations must have offered a measure of protection against feelings of inadequacy that haunted her for years—to the point that she dreaded writing to a friend whose letters she thought "fit to be printed."[43] If in youth Edith Hamilton separated the medium from the message, in her early sixties she made good on her half-jesting declarations when, starting with *The Greek Way* (1930), she began writing the interpretative studies of ancient civilizations that catapulted her to fame. Widely acclaimed for their style, the books found a large readership.

Following a tradition begun by their aunts, the cousins continued their education at Miss Porter's School in Farmington, Connecticut, an institution that attracted mainly well-off families of Congregationalist and Presbyterian persuasion. Sarah Porter, a devout Congregationalist, encouraged the acquisition of Christian character and liberal culture, placing the latter at the center of the curriculum, as did her brother Noah Porter at Yale. Free to select their classes, the Hamiltons chose ancient and modern languages, English literature, drawing, art history, and music—all subjects familiar to them—as well as moral and mental philosophy and, less frequently, entomology and geometry. Some were so far advanced that they received private instruction, as Katherine did in Greek from a retired professor from Western Reserve University whom she revered, as did all the Hamiltons who followed. (Not all the teaching was so inspired.) At the center of it all was Miss Porter with her deep hold over students. To Alice she embodied "the best of the New England tradition—integrity, self-control, no weakness or sentimentality, love of beauty, respect for the intellectual, clear thinking, no nonsense." Miss Porter did not, however, encourage careers. On that score, the Hamiltons would have looked to her example rather than her precepts. The school was in many ways an extension of the home environment—reverence for learning and books, strict observance of the Sabbath, plenty of outdoor exercise, and social rituals that included Miss Porter's nightly bedtime readings. For the Hamiltons, the school's main impact may well have been social: in addition to making lifelong friends, their common attendance was a further family bond.[44]

When they returned to Fort Wayne in their late teens or early twenties, the Hamiltons engaged in the voluntary activities expected of young women of their class: they joined Shakespeare, sketch, and German clubs, taught Sunday school, and undertook charitable work for the poor. Some supervised the education of younger siblings or cousins, listening to Latin and other recitations. Unlike most of their female contemporaries, they also embarked on ambitious programs of study—now mostly linked to career objectives— that included lessons with local teachers. Edith and Katherine took Greek and Latin, subjects required for college entrance (Edith attended, Katherine did not); Alice studied chemistry and later science at a Fort Wayne medical college before leaving for the University of Michigan Medical School; Jessie worked with local artists; and Agnes, preparing at the time for a career in architecture, took a home study course, read classics by Ruskin and Viollet-le-Duc, and worked in the office of a local practitioner. By this time the young women had acquired considerable cultural capital. Their knowledge of ancient and modern languages and familiarity with history and literature gave them a secure intellectual foundation, linguistic skills, and—notwithstanding the self-doubt that sometimes surfaced in this as in other talented families—the confidence to move forward with their vocational goals.

The years after Miss Porter's also provided the Hamilton women with what Erik Erikson calls a period of "*psychosocial moratorium*," a time of experimentation between adolescence and adulthood during which they sought to find their places in the world.[45] Even as they prepared for careers, they continued to engage in the literary play that had bound them together as children, knowing they could count on each other's unqualified support.

. . . .

What the Hamiltons read formed an important substrate of their mental landscape. How they read provides insight into the connections between reading and behavior, between books and lives. Beyond the sum total of volumes read, beyond even the cultural level at which they aimed, reading was an integral part of a system of family relations that bound the Hamiltons together even as it allowed for individual variation. All reading is socially based, but the Hamiltons developed reading's social potential into a fine art. Their interactions around books and the easy passage between serious and light reading encouraged imaginative play and the collective elaboration of stories.[46] The social character of their reading was central to its impact on youthful family members.

This is nowhere more evident than in the long-lasting hold of signature books, especially those read in childhood. Read, reread, and often elaborated collectively, these continued to occupy a place in the Hamiltons' psyches well past the years of latency and early adolescence when literary preoccupations are, in recent times at least, thought to be at their peak.

The practice of rereading, more common in the nineteenth century than today, satisfies a number of needs. There are some books, Matei Calinescu tells us, that have "strong if often mysterious claims over our memory, attention, and imagination," books that "haunt" the reader and "urge us to reread them, to make them present to our mind again and again."[47] Such books, by virtue of their manifest or latent content, their characters or atmosphere, venture into territory of particular relevance to the reader, unresolved conflicts perhaps, goals to aspire to, or validation or re-creation of a way of life. Above and beyond the pull of particular books, what Janice Radway calls "deep reading" can foster "an inextinguishable desire to experience a particular kind of fusion with a book," including those that evoke the security of childhood.[48] Perhaps it is because reading experiences of this kind provide such an intimate connection with characters or authors that they often seem more real than life. Rather than presupposing a straightforward evolution of reading tastes, then, reading may more aptly be viewed as a layered process, somewhat akin to an archeological site, in which older interests and meanings persist, perhaps in altered form, even as new ones emerge. In a psychoanalytic vein, rereading is a way of drawing an individual's psychic past into current reality.[49]

The Hamiltons were much given to "pouring over our few favorites," often books first encountered in childhood.[50] None more so than Agnes. Although she had undertaken a rigorous program of self-study in languages and history the year before, during her first year at Miss Porter's Agnes requested several favorites from home, including *The Mice at Play* and *Johnnykin and the Goblins*. Responding with mild ridicule, Jessie exclaimed: "What extraordinary developments you are making in your taste for literature . . . Wouldn't you like me to put in Dick and his Cat too?"[51] Much like eating comfort food, rereading fulfilled deep-seated emotional needs for Agnes and other Hamiltons, preserving the warmth and security of childhood as they ventured forth in the world. Later readings of familiar books provided both a defense against homesickness and, by recovering memories of past encounters, another way to reaffirm family bonds. Favorite characters, defined as old friends, provided similar reassurance; years later, Agnes explained that when she really liked a novel, "I get a homesicky feeling if I cannot get hold of the book not for anything especially fine in it but just for the people."[52]

Some signature books of childhood and youth acquired intense meaning for the Hamiltons and continued to be the stuff of family life well into adulthood, generating emotionally resonant models—for writing as well as for living. One such book was *The Children of Abbotsmuir Manse* by Louisa M. Gray. In his early twenties, Allen Williams claimed the Abbotsmuir children as fictional characters who "seem to belong especially to us."[53] It is easy to see why. The six young Maitlands bear a striking resemblance to the Hamiltons. Schooled mainly in their Scottish home by their father, a Presbyterian minister, the children grew up "all eager for books and writing." The oldest, all girls, were engaged in a long-term project of creating a collective and ongoing story, "the Families," set in the time of the Wars of the Roses. One sister was writing a family narrative of her own, describing "The Future Fortunes of the Maitland Family," as well as a historical novel prompted by the group's reading of John Lothrop Motley's *The Rise of the Dutch Republic* (a book in which Alice Hamilton later claimed she and her sisters were "steeped"). Isabel, the oldest and also the principal storyteller, concludes that "every one has a story in their lives . . . or, perhaps, it would be better to say, a novel or a poem," before stating what must have been obvious to her sisters all along: "We are all our own heroines, of course."[54] Even as the book taught the inevitable moral lessons (learning consideration for a less fortunate neighbor and experiencing the exhilaration of genuine Christian faith), it celebrated the individual and collective joys of growing up in a literary family.

In reading *The Children of Abbotsmuir Manse*, the Hamiltons might have been reading about themselves. The similarity made for an easy interchange between characters and readers in ways that invited comparison and emulation. Even where correspondences were less exact, family narratives constituted favorite reading in childhood and youth, not only the tales of well-known writers like Charlotte Yonge and Mrs. (Juliana) Ewing, another Hamilton favorite, but also Elizabeth Rundle Charles's *Chronicles of the Schönberg-Cotta Family*, the story of a German family that followed Martin Luther out of the Catholic Church. Told in multiple voices in the form of journal entries by family members, the novel follows individuals and the entire family for nearly half a century. The strong Protestant thrust of the story no doubt mattered in a family that viewed the Roman and even the Episcopal Churches with distrust. It is likely too that the mix of individual and family stories, of difference within likeness, had special appeal to a family as closely knit as the Hamiltons.[55] A comment by Agnes on Robert Louis Stevenson's *A Child's Garden of Verses* years later suggests as much. She found the book "perfectly charming, full of child-thought so that we were deliciously carried back not to our common childhood but to our individual child-thought, to our untold childish ideas and plays by each carried on alone."[56] Revisiting the family's past was one of the great pleasures of reading.

After years of elaborating on the family narratives they read, it is not surprising that the Hamiltons discerned in their own lives stories that warranted literary treatment, whether in the form of history, fiction, or memorials to individuals.

The fullest expression of the memorializing impulse came from Agnes. Even at thirteen she took on the role of family chronicler, answering queries about family members in the form of a newspaper—"The H. family"—which she signed "EDITORESS Agnes Hamilton."[57] In her late teens, she conceived a grander undertaking. "I am going to write your life and call it Memoirs of a Sister," she informed Jessie. The project had a direct literary antecedent, for it followed Agnes's reading of *Memorials of a Quiet Life*, a work based on the diaries and letters of Maria Leycester Hare, a woman whose Christian faith, thoughtful deeds, and gentle English breeding made her Agnes's "ideal . . . in every way." Grateful for her sister's home letters, which she considered "really too splendid to be lost," Agnes decided "that there is not a person in the family who can equal you in that line," a judgment with which Alice concurred. A volume of life and letters—then a popular genre—would fulfill several purposes, Agnes wrote: "Your letters will be published, a Farmington girl's life will be told, and at last our family will be thoroughly written up."[58] Agnes's grand vision united her sister's epistolary prowess, the family's ties to Miss Porter's, and the exemplary nature of both Jessie and the family.[59]

Allen Williams seems to have flirted more seriously with a literary career; while a student at Harvard Medical School he served as an editor of a short-lived Boston-based magazine, the *Mahogany Tree*, for which he also wrote. He took a playful approach to family narrative, which he variously proposed writing as history or fiction. He jested about embarking on "that great novel of Fort Wayne," promising to reserve Agnes for "the heroine of another book." After becoming engaged, he wrote a long letter in the form of a story, "the Adventures of two children," which he thought might "be rewritten and sometime find its way into Vol. II. of the Family Archives." (He and Agnes may have contemplated a joint literary venture, for a short time before he had proposed that "the second part of our book" be devoted to the much younger Wagenhals cousins.)[60] In Allen's rendering, family history and fiction had become interchangeable. Either way, the stories of each others' lives were to be taken seriously: as records of an elite family and its individual members and as prospective opportunities for authorship. It matters less that neither Agnes nor Allen made good on their literary goals than that their projects aimed at according the family a literary place—as subjects and as authors.

The Hamiltons' playful and pleasurable literary pursuits continued as they matured and planned for the future, although in altered form. At times they shared their own literary productions, as when a group of "literaries"—Katherine, Jessie, Edith, Allen Williams, and a rare outsider, the librarian at the Reading Room—met to read stories and poems they had written.[61] More often, group endeavors centered on reading aloud. Although often originating in familial obligation (older siblings read to younger ones, adult daughters to mothers, women of all ages to invalids), reading aloud remained a pleasurable and lifelong custom for the Hamiltons. For several years in their late teens and early twenties, the young women and Allen Williams joined their aunts in overlapping reading circles. Agnes described "a sort of a reading club" where, in the spring of 1885, "every Saturday in Aunt Marge's room, we read [Thackeray's] Henry Esmond and while one reads the rest of us do our mending or other sewing."[62] The group progressed to Andrew Lang's Letters to Dead Authors (1886) and Charles Lamb's essays and the following year to history classics by Edward Gibbon and Thomas Carlyle, about which Jessie informed Agnes (away at Miss Porter's) in richly detailed letters. Daily at half past four, the Hamilton cousins "went over to Gibbon" (also known as "Gibbonhour") at their Aunt Mary Williams's.

You don't know what fun it is to go into her rooms where the dark red curtains are pulled across the windows and the lamps and wax candles are lit and spend an hour reading. Gibbon is becoming quite interesting[;] it is no longer an effort to listen. After dinner at seven we went to Aunt Marg's room to read Carlyle's French Revolution, it is splendidly written and wonderfully powerful when you can tell exactly what he is driving at. Of course the mind was not the only part refreshed, the fruit, oranges, bananas, green, purple and pink grapes made a lovely picture in a straw basket. And what do you think we did there, something that seemed to make one of my dreams suddenly to become substance—we hemmed the dish towels for the Farmington House.[63]

Returning to the subject of Carlyle two weeks later, Jessie observed even more pointedly, "the whole was so jumbled up that as I look back at it I have not a single clear idea. I remember much better how the candied cherries and the wafers tasted."[64]

Despite the emphasis on weighty historical texts, group reading practices were flexible. When someone was absent, participants took up *A Bachelor's Blunder*, a contemporary novel by William Edward Norris, of which Jessie observed, "I read parts of it aloud to mamma and though it is not anything you care about as you do Thackeray or George Eliot still it is very interesting." On another occasion, *A Bachelor's Blunder* followed *King Lear*.[65] Carlyle was resumed the following winter, but Jessie reported that on one occasion "somehow it did not work and we rambled off to other things."[66] The reading club continued at least sporadically until early 1889, after which it seems to have come to a halt.[67]

In their depiction of family reading, the letters suggest that for Jessie, the aspiring artist, the aesthetic and sensuous aspects of the group sessions were central to her enjoyment—the physical accompaniments, the food, the alluring rooms with their beauty and hint of mystery. A range of family business was transacted at the sessions, including sewing (in this case for the cottage in Farmington that Margaret Vance Hamilton was fixing up to entertain her nieces and their friends), planning their vocational futures, and gossiping about absent members. Altogether there is a fluidity about this reading circle: several books are kept going at the same time, there is no rush to finish, at times the sessions break down. Jessie's comments further suggest a receptive attitude to all sorts of books and a lack of self-consciousness in this very proper family about reading "light" fiction. Although differentiated from the classics, *A Bachelor's Blunder* is mentioned in the same breath with Carlyle and Shakespeare and deemed an acceptable substitute. Jessie's description of social reading reveals the playful side of Hamilton family life, a quality seen as well in their love of word games. It is a kind of playfulness perhaps best afforded by those seriously committed to literature and secure in their position as members of a cultured class.

.   .   .   .

Whether in intellectual or social mode, the Hamiltons' reading culture influenced their understandings of the world and interactions with one another. In a family that protected its young and cultivated self-restraint to an unusual degree, books opened up avenues for experience and emotional expressiveness. Stimulated by the intensity with which they read and the collective nature of their play, the Hamiltons incorporated their imaginative renderings of books into their lives in ways that at once heightened and blended with everyday experience. With such porous boundaries between fiction and life, characters melded with authors and both became stand-ins for people in the real world. In such liminal spaces arose possibilities for the creation of new kinds of subjectivity. Self-chosen personae had ample opportunity to flourish during the prolonged period of family play.

At the most basic level, books gave the Hamiltons a way of ordering—and understanding—their lives. They provided a common language and a medium of intellectual and social exchange that helped the women define themselves and formulate responses to the larger world. The process started early. When Jessie went off to Miss Porter's, seven younger Hamiltons ranging in age from fourteen to six contributed to a joint letter addressed to "Dear boarding school girl." Agnes and Alice, thirteen and twelve respectively, elaborated: "Do you find boarding school as nice as it was in 'Gypsy's Year at the Golden Crescent', or in 'What Katy Did at School'? or are you homesick like the story Mrs. Stanton told in one of the 'Bessie's'?" Here the Hamiltons are not only relating life to fiction, but behaving like fictional characters: the boarding school story, a staple of preadolescent fiction, often included letters from at-home relatives.[68] In this case fiction provided a rehearsal for future experience for those who had not yet gone away to school.

Reading equipped the Hamiltons with a symbolic code and a shorthand for experience that continued throughout their lives. When sisters or cousins were geographically distant, a literary allusion captured an encounter in just a few words. Thus Alice could describe a rector as "a delicious mixture of Trollope and Mrs. Oliphant and Miss Yonge" and expect to be understood precisely.[69] Only occasionally did literature fail, as when Edith had difficulty in fathoming Bonté Sheldon Amos, an audacious and intriguing Englishwoman who belonged to the avant-garde Bertrand Russell set: "She is a kind of girl I have never even read of before." They took these comparisons seriously. Edith reread a novel whose heroine had been suggested as a possible model for Miss Amos but thought the parallel inexact.[70]

As the boarding school letter indicates, reading did not foreclose experience for the Hamiltons but offered them a range of possible responses. When Agnes began her diary shortly after her fifteenth birthday, she cited three fictional models from which to choose: "There are so many different ways of commencing journals that I did not know how to commence mine, whether to do as Else did and commence by telling about every member of the family or as Kate in Stepping Heavenward did and describe myself, but I think I will do as Olive Drayton and go right into the middle of it with out any commencement."[71] Such explicit formulation of the possibility of choice suggests both the open-ended quality of reading in this family and the degree to which literature provided alternatives from which to choose.

The Hamiltons' world was peopled with fictional characters. It was not just that as readers they were "admitted into the company and present at the conversation."[72] The fictional company was very real to them. Allen Williams in his early twenties exclaimed, "I never can get over a feeling of personal injury in never having known the Abbotsmuir children: don't you think that, after Ellen Daly and Norah, they and Polly and Reginald seem to belong especially to us?"[73] At times fictional characters became interchangeable with family members; during a long stay abroad, Margaret Vance Hamilton wrote Agnes: "I felt a very great longing for you and for Elizabeth Bennet and sat down to tell you so, but it seems foolish now to say anything about it, because you know I want to see you and you don't care whether I miss Elizabeth or Anne or Jane or any of the others or not." Here Agnes is conflated with the heroines of *Pride and Prejudice* (Elizabeth Bennet) and *Persuasion* (Anne Elliot) and with the author she most admired.[74]

For the Hamiltons, then, there was a reciprocal relation—a continuum—between fiction and life. If fiction was a referent for people they encountered in real life, life also cast light on fiction: Alice claimed she understood William Dean Howells's women "much better" through knowing a real-life stand-in.[75] In view of such fluid boundaries it is not surprising that the Hamiltons fictionalized their own lives and those of their friends. After being absorbed for weeks in the story of a romance between the art teacher and a student at Miss Porter's, Edith wrote Jessie: "Don't you feel as if you had got into a story book? And with Susy Sage of all people for the heroine."[76]

The tendency to fictionalize their lives was most evident at the time Allen Williams informed Agnes and Alice, his closest cousins—they were known as "the three As"—of his (still secret) engagement. Agnes thought his letters read "like a continued story . . . and I am as eager and as interested as I ever was for one in Harper's or Century far more so, for, aside from its being Allen, it is so naturally written, so deliciously written."[77] Allen's fiancée, Marian Walker, a Radcliffe student preparing for a medical career, reminded him not only of Alice and Agnes, but of the heroines of two novels beloved by the young Hamiltons, Nora Nixon in *Quits* (1857) by Baroness Tautphoeus (née Jemima Montgomery), a distant relative who was born in Donegal but lived and set her novels in Germany, and Ellen Daly in Annie Keary's *Castle*

Daly (1875). As Allen informed Agnes, Marian "is very fond of Quits! I have told her she cannot meet any of the family until she has read Castle Daly. Can you forgive her for not having done that?" While to Alice he exclaimed, "Of course she is like Nora, otherwise I could not have fallen in love. And of course *Quits* is one of her favorite books."[78] The use of such preferences as a means of establishing boundaries for group membership may strike us as quintessentially adolescent, but Allen was in his late twenties at the time.

Although professing greater maturity, Alice responded in kind: "And it just warms my heart and fills me with gladness to have the boy turning into the sort of a man that I wanted him to be, to have him doing an impulsive, unpractical, youthful thing. . . . Why he talks like the heroes in [William] Black's novels, like Willy Fitzgerald and George Brand and Frank King. I am so glad. . . . Agnes it mustn't pass over, it is too sweet and dear and fresh and cunning. . . . Would anybody believe that that introspective, slightly cynical, critical, over-cultured fellow could be so naive, so unconsciously trite, so deliciously young!"[79]

Alice Hamilton cast Allen as a hero, but there is no evidence—then or later—that she was interested in the marriage plot for herself. Allen called her an "unconscious hypocrite" for suggesting that Marian give up her medical career, since he believed his cousin cared only for her work.[80] At forty-nine Alice still gushed about a book in words similar to those she had deployed for Allen's romance more than two decades earlier: "It is just as cunning as can be and so romantic, you can't believe any hero could be so noble."[81] But her life history, like those of her sisters and cousins, makes it clear that she preferred her heroes in books rather than at firsthand; in this case at least, the boundaries between fiction and life remained fixed. Given the assumption of ambitious women of the era that they must choose between marriage and career, heroes between the covers of books were safer than men encountered in life. The Hamiltons took this common view of the matter to an extreme: of the eleven women of the third generation, only the youngest married; a full generation younger than her oldest cousins, she did so as an act of rebellion.[82]

The Hamiltons' experiences of reading suggest a need to reconsider the conventional assumption that women respond to fiction principally through the mechanism of identification with heroines of romantic plots. It was the Hamilton men rather than the women who seem to have been most fascinated by romantic heroines as models of womanhood. Montgomery wrote an essay on the subject for the Princeton literary magazine in the 1860s, and when he fell in love, like his nephew Allen Williams thirty years later, he

"The three As": Alice Hamilton, Allen Hamilton Williams, and Agnes Hamilton. Hamilton Family Papers, The Schlesinger Library, Radcliffe Institute, Harvard University.

alluded to *Quits* as well as *The Initials* (1850), another Tautphoeus novel—this one with a protagonist named Hamilton. Envisioning himself as a hero in an Edward Bulwer-Lytton novel, one who was "a faithful, but disappointed lover," he contemplated writing up his story for a magazine.[83]

It was other sorts of plots, plots of adventure and social responsibility, that appealed to the Hamilton women. Favorite novels—even those that end with an impending marriage—provided models of independent and socially minded womanhood. In *Quits* it is likely that the women responded more to the character of Nora Nixon than to her romantic fate. An unaffected and generous heroine, Nora is a great reader who loves the outdoors and orders her life rationally. She does what she pleases and deploys her newly acquired fortune for socially useful ends on her travels in Bavaria. Active, worldly, and independent, she provides a striking contrast to the stereotype of the submissive and domestic "true woman." Ellen Daly, the exuberant Irish heroine of *Castle Daly* whose family has come on hard times, is less able to control her surroundings than Nora, but she too is generous, unself-conscious, and independent. Like Nora, she serves the people around her and follows her beloved single aunt in distributing relief to Irish tenants at the time of the famine. In this novel about the Irish-English conflict, the marriage plot is even less central than it is in *Quits*.[84] Both novels take place outside formal society and play out amid a contrast of nationalities.

An interest in socially conscious heroines, real as well as fictional, was by no means unique to the Hamiltons; the desire to be socially useful pervades the autobiographies of women growing up in the late nineteenth century. If this goal originated in the prevailing belief in women's moral superiority (and the responsibilities presumed to ensue), it often evolved into something much more complex. The literature of the era was conducive to dreams of female heroism outside family life. As Martha Vicinus has observed, the downplaying of sexuality in Victorian literature and the lesser concentration on the marriage plot encouraged girls to fantasize about other sources of fulfillment. Florence Nightingale appears in biographies for girls as a heroic and religiously inspired woman whose early interest in healing is transformed into a mission to reform society. In contrast to this exemplary figure, mid-twentieth-century biographies not only emphasized family conflict as a motivating force, but constructed Nightingale as a "failed romantic heroine"—an unattractive choice in an era that celebrated marriage and domesticity.[85]

In fiction, too, opportunities for service to humanity or the deity provided a legitimate springboard for action that transcended the family claim. Novels like Charlotte Yonge's popular *The Daisy Chain* (1856), while telling stories about the taming of tomboys, nevertheless afforded scope for female agency, albeit within a separate, feminine sphere. Much like Jo March in *Little Women*, Ethel May is transformed from a helter-skelter tomboy and prospective bluestocking into a thoughtful and family-centered woman, in this case her family of origin. She also fulfills a public mission by founding a church in a poor neighborhood, an action that had a counterpoint in the Hamiltons' involvement in "Nebraska," a poor section of Fort Wayne where the women and some of the men taught Sabbath school.

Of all the Hamilton women, the narrative of service, more specifically Christian service, touched Agnes most deeply: it was she who persuaded the First Presbyterian Church to set up a mission in Nebraska. The diary she kept between the ages of fifteen and twenty-eight registers her struggles to live a life that fully reflected her religious commitment. It also records the abundant interactions with books that marked her as a passionate reader: whether joyful or sorrowful, fleeting or lingering, solitary or social, her responses were typically intense. As a Hamilton, she aspired to intellectual self-improvement and reproached herself for any deficiencies she detected in this regard. She also took to heart Miss Porter's injunction that books helped in determining "our true aim" in life and looked to them for spiritual sustenance and guidance.[86] Perhaps most of all she read to discover who she might become.

For Agnes reading was a complex and sometimes fraught activity and one she struggled to control. The most morally earnest of the Hamiltons, she worried about her "insane passion" for novels; they "are my opium," she confided to a friend. After an alarming binge in her late teens, she resolved not to read another novel for a week at least.[87] There was little danger that she would give them up for long: reading was too great a refuge, an anodyne for pain for which nothing worked like "a dose of Miss Austen." While reading, she was "completely lost to all outside life, no matter what trouble or worry or necessary work I may have," a trait she thought she shared with her grandmother.[88] (In her early twenties, the troubles included the life-threatening illness of her sister Katherine and her father's refusal to let her become an architect.) The practice of removing oneself in this way from unpleasant situations is often considered escapism. But escape is a complex phenomenon and one that can have significant impact on the daily lives of readers. Since reading took Agnes to the place of elsewhere, where she experienced "a change of air," it might more aptly be considered a self-protective and self-sustaining activity that helped her persevere in the tasks at hand.[89]

Even as she sought to live a more spiritual life and to meet family obligations with better grace in the years after Miss Porter's, reading allowed Agnes to live expansively in imagination: "I live in the world of novels all the time[.] Half the time I am in Europe, half in different parts of America; I am sober and sensible, gay and frivolous, happy or sorrowful just as my present heroine happens to be or rather as the tone of the book happens to be. I never heard of a person more easily influenced."[90] Twenty-one at the time, Agnes articulated the varieties of experience—and possibilities—she found in fiction's imagined worlds. In addition to whatever solace or pleasure she found there, these encounters also allowed Agnes, standoffish and "snubby" as she tended to be, unaccustomed freedom, including a chance to read a novel populated by "the nastiest people I should not speak to in real life."[91]

In the diary entry describing her literary travels, Agnes represents herself as entirely subject to an author's whims, but the very next passage finds her in deep communion with a favorite novel: "Sunday I read Stepping Heavenward. I had not read it for years and for two weeks I could not keep it out of my mind."[92] A spiritual manual in diary form, Elizabeth Payson Prentiss's *Stepping Heavenward* (1869) charts the spiritual progression of Kate Mortimer, a heedless and self-centered sixteen-year-old at the outset, into a woman who not only lives a sanctified life but helps others do so as well. She has reached this goal by prayer and by dedicating herself to God and then only after extreme suffering that included grave illness and the death of a child. In recounting the heroine's step-by-step progress toward the desired goal, the novel reinterprets traditional Calvinism by holding up daily obligation rather than conversion as the paradigm of religious practice. Agnes knew this milieu intimately—Thomas à Kempis, the sermons, the prayers. Her identification with the heroine is of a piece with her desire to become a better Christian: the novel reminded her of the importance of finding a "higher Spiritual Life" and of her negligence for not impressing this imperative on her Sunday school students.[93] Deliberative, reflective reading of this kind that connected with her life was in fact Agnes's preferred practice. "Usually when I read a splendid novel," she wrote Jessie, "I don't touch another for months so that I go all over it again in my mind."[94]

For all of Agnes's anguish about novels, the emotional intensity with which she read them and her ability to identify with heroines—that is, her capacity for deep reading—may well have prepared her for the transition to biography and her subsequent investment in that genre. In her late teens, she found Mrs. (Elizabeth) Gaskell's *Life of Charlotte Brontë* (1857) "as interesting as any novel" and later explained the appeal of both genres in remarkably similar terms, observing of novels, "I think it is getting into another life," and of biography, "it is the people, the characters that I care for."[95] In her early twenties, while struggling to integrate her religious beliefs with her daily life and to find a way to do her "share of the work in this world," she found inspiration in the "lives of splendid people," principally Christian women who were "well-bred" and lived virtuous and mainly private lives; these included her grandmother, whose life she thought "would be a true Stepping Heavenward."[96] Looking to books to enlighten her way, she observed, "biographies of great Christians are of very great aid. They help one to form a world of one's own, a world of books."[97] That is, a world of possibility.

The "splendid people" Agnes admired were not those rare individuals who altered history but those like Maria Leycester Hare, who, her nephew and adopted son observed, "had always tried to make the simple experience of her own quiet life as useful to others as it might be." Agnes revered Maria Hare, even though she found it difficult to conceive how she and her husband could carry "that same noble spirit with them" in their everyday lives. She found similar virtues in Sara Coleridge, the invalid daughter of the poet and a writer in her own right. Although Coleridge "hid herself under a bushel as far as her wonderful mind was concerned, except to her family and intimate friends," she had accomplished laudable work. Agnes, who often spoke of these women as friends, also admired them for their love of family, as she did the otherwise very different Brontë sisters.[98]

Agnes's veneration of women like Maria Hare may have helped her shape earlier heroic aspirations into more realistic proportions. As girls, she and Alice "mourned over the martyr days which would never come again . . . the glory of the world was gone; it had grown prosaically good and no one would burn us."[99] By 1896, when she recalled this youthful lament, Agnes had found more prosaic ways of making religion count—as a leader in Christian women's activities in Fort Wayne. In addition to her success in persuading the Presbyterian Church to establish the church on the other side of the tracks and later heading the Christian Endeavor society there, she served as first president of the local YWCA and was active in its Noon Rest program for working-class women. There was a strong element of noblesse oblige in these activities, as her admiration for well-bred people suggests, but Agnes worked hard at moving out of her narrow and protected circle. In addition to reading prominent British and American social theorists, including Frederick Maurice Denison, Charles Kingsley, and Richard Ely, for insights on contemporary social disparities, she sought advice from Florence Kelley, who was leading a campaign to ban sweatshop labor. Freed by her father's death to make her own choices and reassured that she was not neglecting family duties, Agnes studied art with Jessie in Philadelphia before becoming a resident of the Lighthouse, a Christian settlement in that city where she lived for three decades.

The model of Christian womanhood Agnes admired seems conventional and even self-sacrificing, but it enabled her to leave Fort Wayne, while her older sisters stayed behind to care for their ageing mother. It was a choice she made among several alternatives and one shaped in part by her own efforts to re-create herself in the image of the models she found in "a world of books." Agnes's reading trajectory suggests the ways in which an individual with a conventional religious and moral outlook used traditional values for her own purposes. Reading was not the "cause" of her behavior in any simple way. Her desire to fashion herself after women of unquestioning faith and good works influenced both her choice of books and the manner in which she read them. If she eventually chose a more public life than women like Maria Hare, it was a life in the shadow of the settlement's head resident; perhaps, in the spirit of resignation and humility she and her heroines cultivated, she needed to admire a heroine rather than to become one herself.

If Agnes tested and judged herself against heroines (both real and fictional), not all the Hamilton women engaged with literature in the same way. The traditional emphasis of critics on identification with one character is far too restrictive an approach to an experience as complex as reading.[100] More varied interactions between readers and texts are possible, even likely, including multiple identifications with a novel's characters (heroes as well as heroines). Individuals may also have characteristic reactions to texts based on deep-seated psychological traits or needs, or they may respond to the interaction of characters or even to the "tone" (or mood) of a book, as Agnes did.[101]

For the Hamiltons, the continuum between literature and life gave considerable play to the imagination. Reading provided both the occasion for self-creation and at times the narrative form from which they might reconstruct themselves. Given the way they peopled their lives with fictional characters and the intensity of their interactions with books, they were quite capable of reading themselves into fiction or other forms of adventure without a strong identification with a particular heroine.

Alice Hamilton offers a striking example in claiming a literary inspiration for her decision to become a physician: "I meant to be a medical missionary to Teheran, having been fascinated by the description of Persia in [Edmond] O'Donovan's *The Merv Oasis*. I doubted if I could ever be good enough to be a real missionary; but if I could care for the sick, that would do instead, and it would enable me to explore far countries and meet strange people."[102] Since *The Merv Oasis* (1882) is a work of travels and adventure, over 1,000 pages in length, and with no discernible missionary focus, Alice must have come to it with a mind prepared. The message she found is consistent with her early preferences in novels, among them Charlotte Yonge's, which highlight conflicts between individual achievement and the family claim. Like any retrospective memory, this one may be faulty, but the conflict troubled her deeply as a young woman, and she resolved it only when she found work that enabled her to combine science and service, thereby effecting a balance between individualism and self-sacrifice, as she saw it. She struggled for many years before she found her true calling in industrial toxicology, a field that permitted her to use her scientific knowledge in the service of humanity.[103]

For all of Alice's commitment to service and her admiration for her precocious older sister, it was she—the self-described "reluctant reader"—rather than Edith who wrote an autobiography. Like other models of the genre by Progressive men and women, *Exploring the Dangerous Trades* (1943) centers on work rather than on personal life. But it captures with charm the early family saga, so far removed from the story of workers' health and political activism at the center of the book—and from the daily concerns of its initial readers in the midst of World War II. Alice Hamilton is not remembered primarily as a writer, but her vivid letters and crisp political analysis, along with the autobiography, make it clear that she too had absorbed the literary lessons of her youth.

Edith's aspirations and literary preferences were of a different kind. There is no mention in her letters of doing good, a frequent theme of Alice's and Agnes's; rather there is a longing to "live" and to do great things. Where Agnes looked for inspiration to unassuming Christian heroines, Edith from an early age stood in awe of the Greeks. Less reverent and self-sacrificing than her cousin, Edith chose the discipline of study rather than perfection of character. Before she became the first woman in the family to attend college, she admired the Greek language and sometimes, even on vacation, read "a little Odyssey before breakfast." After attending a production of *Electra*, she observed: "I have been in ancient Greece to-day, I have been through one of the experiences of a Greek of the time of Pericles."[104] It was this kind of imaginative leap—into the presumed minds and souls of the ancients—that she later re-created for her readers.[105]

For Edith, often moody as a young woman, reading was a lifeline, a way of getting out of herself. At sixteen her favorites were Scott's *Rob Roy* (1818) and *Lorna Doone: A Romance of Exmoor* (1869) by R. D. Blackmore.[106] The heroine of *Rob Roy*, Diana Vernon, is one of Scott's most appealing—she is an outdoorswoman, well-read, outspoken, fearless, and untutored in the feminine graces. But the characterization of the heroine is unlikely to account for the novel's appeal. (Diana fades away, becoming first an obedient daughter and, in a hastily contrived ending, wife.) Edith may have been intrigued by the sympathetic Robin Hood figures in both novels and the ambiguous rather than stringent treatment of their dubious morality. It is even more likely that she responded to the settings and plots: her favorites are tales of derring-do in historical settings and wild places (the Scottish highlands, the Devonshire moors), landscapes having much in common with the rugged Maine coast where she later spent her summers. They might well have cast a spell on one who was herself "a natural storyteller" even in her youth and who later captured the imagination of millions with her retellings of classic myths and her romantic vision of ancient Greece.

.   .   .   .

Though built on a foundation of class privilege, the Hamiltons' reading culture and the aspirations that went with it differentiated them from members of their own class whose inclinations ran to personal display and social success. Agnes's depiction of an afternoon outing on Mackinac Island, where the family summered for many years, vividly captures these differences. The cousins "were all torn and dilapidated and were lying, reading on the beach" when they encountered "daintily dressed" boat passengers from the gaudy resort hotel they disdained. The gear of the two parties marked the differences: "Their traps were boxes of candy and silver flasks, ours, baskets, coffee machine, sketching bags, shawls, books, mackintoshes." Agnes, who regretted that the other passengers did not speak to them during the long boat ride home, concluded that the family's tendency to sit apart made them appear too "self-sufficient."[107]

The Hamiltons' bookishness no doubt reinforced their tendency to keep to themselves. Their reading was at times self-protective, a retreat from family troubles, or a substitute, a default, for more immediate kinds of experience. On learning of her Uncle Holman's death, for example, Edith felt as if she were reading about it in a book.[108] This was the kind of remoteness from lived experience that Jane Addams later condemned as a negative consequence of excessive immersion in literary culture. The isolating tendency was particularly marked among the Hamilton men, who, with the exception of Allen Williams, the women considered demanding and peculiar.

The young women's sense of difference propelled them forward in their efforts to make their mark in the world and carried them through periods of self-doubt and discouragement. With all their advantages, they could not take advanced study for granted. Careers for women were still an experiment, and not all the Hamilton elders thought their female offspring should undertake them. Indeed, the persistence of Edith and her sisters in pursuing their educational goals was a major source of the tension that surfaced in the extended family in the 1890s. With the failure of their father's business, their need to support themselves was greater than that of their cousins, but their success depended on the unwavering encouragement of their mother, Gertrude Pond Hamilton, who braved the disapproval of her in-laws by her independence.[109] At times the cousins articulated diverging views, with Agnes upholding loyalty to the family, "the most sacred thing on earth," and Edith proclaiming a woman's right "to give up her family and devote herself to improving herself and her own individuality," a debate Agnes characterized as one between socialism and individualism.[110]

Whatever their later differences, the Hamiltons' reading practices reinforced a family culture that promoted female aspiration. The older generations fostered daughters' intellectual development even if they did not always encourage pursuit of careers. In the face of such mixed messages, the young people's collective reading culture—at once so serious and so playful—not only encouraged the women to imagine new possibilities for themselves, but helped sustain them as they formulated and reformulated vocational plans.

The Hamiltons' experiences of reading were the sort that encouraged them to extend the range of the possible. Psychologists maintain that this is a characteristic of reading generally, particularly in its connection to play.[111] How much more so in a family like the Hamiltons, where reading was such a collective and emotionally resonant activity. By stimulating fantasy and imaginative play, reading provided space—literal, temporal, and psychological—that enabled the women to exempt themselves from many traditional gender obligations, whether imposed by the rituals of formal society or by family. In a world full of social constraints, the Hamiltons associated reading with freedom and possibility. As Edith observed on a beautiful summer day: "Alice and I are out of humour, because at four o'clock we must get into something stiff and go down to Mrs. Brown's to meet some people and drink some tea. What I want to do, is to take *Wuthering Heights* and go and sit down on the shore below Arch Rock. I can feel how sweet and still and cool it would be there, how smooth and misty and pale blue the water would be, and how the little ripples would break at my feet with a soft splash."[112]

The sentiments Edith articulated so poetically here—her preference for reading a book (a wild and romantic one at that), out of doors, and in the company of her favorite sister, over a formal social encounter—capture the pleasure and freedom the Hamiltons found in reading. (The unadorned beauty of the writing accords as well with her view that the essence of Greek poetry was its spareness.) Given the Hamiltons' penchant for reading, it is hardly surprising that others considered them bookish. Edith may have chafed at the label, but she was not ashamed of the condition. Reading, in addition to being so distinctive a family marker, was so great a joy, how could she be?

. . . .

CHAPTER FIVE

Reading and Ambition

M. Carey Thomas and Female Heroism

"The fact is," fourteen-year-old Minnie Thomas declared in 1871, "I don't care much for any thing except dreaming about being grand & noble & famous but that I can never be." She did become famous—as M. Carey Thomas, feminist president of Bryn Mawr College, where she provided a model and an environment that promoted ambition in other female dreamers. In her early teens she hoped to show "that the woman who has fought all the battles of olden time over again whilest reading the spirited pages of Homer Vergil Heroditus . . . been carried away by Carlyle & 'mildly enchanted by Emerson' . . . is not any less like what God really intended a woman to be than the trifling ballroom butterfly than the ignorant wax doll baby which *they* admire." The passage reveals persistent themes of Thomas's adolescence: her passionate absorption in books, the possibilities for female heroism she found in classic texts, a feminist outlook that sought to erase rather than highlight sexual difference, and a belief that intellectual endeavor, even the sort usually gendered male, need not unsex a woman. It also demonstrates a reciprocal relation between Thomas's reading and her ambition, continuing, "my greatest hope & ambition is to be an author an essayist an historian to write hearty earnest true books that may do their part towards elevating the human race."[1]

To a remarkable degree, books provided fodder for Thomas's youthful dreams, transporting her to "the place of elsewhere," a site more conducive to heroic endeavor than a present she considered prosaic and that she understood from an early age placed severe limits on female aspiration.[2] She knew as well that reading by itself could not serve her larger goals, intimating, as it did to many, daydreaming and lack of purpose.[3] For Thomas was not simply fighting the battles of olden time. She was a frontline warrior in a stirring contemporary contest: securing for women an education equal to that of men. Even as she yearned to be "grand & noble & famous" like the authors whose names she recorded, her journals "vibrated" with an overwhelming longing to attend college.[4] With her bachelor's degree in hand but uncertain what to do next, she turned for intellectual and emotional support to members of a Baltimore literary circle who shared her delight in casting off the sacred creeds of bourgeois Victorians. It was this group—"the Friday Night"—that became Thomas's critical reference point, as the family was for the Hamiltons.

Satisfying as Thomas found the affiliation, she realized that the single-minded pursuit of culture could not bring personal and financial independence. As she attempted to move from adolescent dreaming to grown-up resolve, she found it necessary to rein in her passion for "roving through literature," a source of pleasure and imaginative stimulus associated with an earlier era of her life that could not survive the onset of adult obligations intact.[5]

. . . .

Thomas was born in 1857, the oldest of the eight surviving children of James Carey Thomas and Mary Whitall Thomas.[6] Her parents were orthodox Quakers active in the Baltimore Society of Friends, her father as a lay minister, her mother as clerk of the Women's Meeting; both conducted Bible classes. Despite their expanding family size (and though often short of funds), the Thomases were reasonably well-off: James was a prominent physician, and Mary's parents were wealthy. But they were not typical bourgeois consumers of culture: their religion forbade such worldly pursuits as theater, novels, popular music, as well as ostentation of any kind. The Society of Friends permitted poetry, however, and "a complete set of 'British Poets'" launched Carey Thomas on a lifelong love of verse. Although religion came first in this family, Thomas's parents were not personally severe and sometimes bent the rules: they evidently concealed their piano when Grandmother Whitall visited.[7]

Thomas's life took a decisive turn shortly after her seventh birthday when a kitchen accident engulfed her in flames and burned her so severely that her family feared for her life. Even after the immediate danger passed, the pain immobilized her for months and was so intense that she had to be carried in a basket specially designed for the purpose. While still convalescing, an attack of typhoid fever again threatened her life. The protracted invalidism, by forcing her to live so much in her imagination, heightened her susceptibility to literary impressions.[8] The stories and poems her mother and aunts read and recited provided a lifeline, *The Arabian Nights* in particular, which Thomas insisted that her mother read over and over again. She also began her first journal, dictating her thoughts to her mother, who rarely left her side and was the only one allowed to dress the painful leg wound that would not heal.[9]

In autobiographical notes and reminiscences, Thomas linked her reading to her evolving sense of self. With recovery, came freedom: "After 18 months of enforced quiet, listening to reading & to the talk of my mother & her sisters and friends . . . and being read to all day long, I got up a Romantic Victorian. I think the change would have come in any case but probably more slowly. . . . And then I began to read for myself and my education began and changed my childish world."[10] Thomas here identifies herself with a literature and mode of reading that fostered self-discovery. The Romantic poets' emphasis on the ego and self-creation appealed to one eager to find new ways for women to live. Shelley, the exemplar of the misunderstood intellectual and rebel against society, was a particular favorite; his work would help sustain her in difficult moments.

Thomas did her best to make up for lost time. She led her younger siblings in acting out games from literature, including *Gulliver's Travels*, *Pilgrim's Progress*, and *Uncle Tom's Cabin*.[11] With several cousins she formed a secret society dedicated to having fun, intellectual fun included. Whatever she did, she did at fever pitch, whether it was climbing trees and skating, or conducting laboratory experiments, collecting bugs, and dissecting a mouse (at fourteen she wanted to be a doctor and chafed at being considered unladylike).[12] Retrospectively at least, it was her literary activities that stood out. "School was an aside," she recalled, claiming that she had read continuously from the time she recovered until she departed for boarding school at fifteen.[13] During the two years before she left home, she started a journal, kept a commonplace book, and compiled lists of favorite poems and of books she had read. She also wrote poems and short stories and sent one of each to *Harper's*; both were "Respectfully returned."[14]

Like other conscientious parents, the Thomases monitored their precocious daughter's reading.[15] Retrospectively she highlighted parental constraints, a posture consistent with her self-presentation as a rebel. Once, when Mrs. Thomas observed Minnie's "wildly excited" appearance while listening to her husband read Macaulay's "Ivry"—almost as if she were on the battlefield with Henry of Navarre—she admonished her daughter to remember that "it is nothing but poetry." On another occasion, as Thomas tells it, her father "snatched" a copy of Byron's *Don Juan* out of her hands; he "threw it in the fire & stayed to see it burn which took a long time."[16]

Religious scruples and oversight notwithstanding, Thomas's parents allowed their daughter considerable freedom in her choice of books as in other matters. She had the run of a neighboring uncle's "good old fashioned library" where she had access to "all the English prose classics."[17] She also haunted Baltimore's Mercantile Library, a subscription library whose holdings ran the gamut from *The Green Mountain Girls*, which Thomas at thirteen labeled "the most trashy immoral miserable Yankey bad book," to the "4 great big volumes" of Flavius Josephus's history of the Jews, which Mary Thomas selected one day when Minnie wasn't looking. (They compromised on Rev. J. H. Ingraham's *The Prince of the House of David*, a novel about the ministry of Jesus.) By this time Thomas was already an impassioned reader with a taste for books at all cultural levels—"Ruskin on arcutecture," Thomas Hughes's *Tom Brown at Oxford*, and the genre to which she consigned *The Green Mountain Girls*. She had recently begun to study Greek, an unusual pursuit for a girl.[18]

For all her bravado in latency and adolescence—alone among her classmates she professed to admire Napoleon—Thomas's grand if still diffuse ambitions alternated with fear that she would be found wanting. Commenting on a mournful essay, her teacher noted "all the *intensity* of feeling & unsatisfied desire."[19] And a diary in Mrs. Gaskell's novel *Cranford*, in which characters first listed what they had wanted to do and then what they had done, elicited the comment, "What a sad one mine would be." Better to have lived in the age of chivalry, "when there would at least [have] been the satisfaction of dying in the Crusades & living to some purpose."[20] A sense of having been saved for some higher goal may help to account for both the intensity of the longing and the fear of falling short. That life was precarious she knew from her own experience and from the sudden death in 1872 of Frank Whitall Smith, the beloved first cousin with whom she shared books and dreams. He was buried on his eighteenth birthday.[21]

A literary encounter two years later highlights Thomas's intensity as a reader. The book was Baron Friedrich de La Motte Fouqué's *Sintram and His Companions* (1814), a popular tale of a Christian knight who is tested by his sometime companions, Sin and Death.[22] Thomas had refused to let an aunt read it to her during her convalescence because "it excited me so fearfully that I could never bear to have her finish it lest he should fail at last." Longing to be carried out of herself, she finally gave herself up to it one November evening when she was seventeen.

> As I wandered over the hills with Sintram & his strange companions Sin & Death & felt the fearful power of his roiled passionate nature breaking out again & again I could understand why I had to leave it unfinished. When the book was ended I lay back & sobbed & cried. I could not help it—it is a wild sweet story & such a type of the endless struggle of man to subdue Sin & his nature so that he can commune with his Parent. Death is indeed a gentle longed for friend for many a Sintram.[23]

The story centers on Sintram's struggle to conquer the "roiled passionate nature" that prompts him to evil thoughts and deeds. A hard case, he eventually succeeds in his quest and becomes a model knight, unlike his father who never overcame his own fierce nature. Thomas's charged response to the hero's fate not only marks her as a passionately involved reader, but suggests as well the lingering impact of her own early brush with death. In a household in which Satan was a real presence and prayers for her soul a daily occurrence, it is likely that religious anxiety was at the core of Thomas's dread.[24] Her sobbing response after years of pent-up anxiety indicates relief for herself as well as for the hero.

Thomas's experience reading *Sintram* speaks to the questions of how a literary work becomes lodged in an individual's psyche—in the particular case, even before it was read—and how it can influence thought as well as feeling. Engaging *Sintram* at a moment of her own choosing, Thomas experienced painful emotions from the past at a safe distance, even as she moved beyond her own subjective experience, an outcome psychologists consider one of the most powerful effects of reading fiction. Thomas, an analytic as well as an emotional reader, explained how *Sintram* became a part of her: "An account, whether true or not, if *truly* portrayed—whether it is of some fearful struggle or of some passionate love—becomes a type of all succeeding—on this rests the secret of Sintram's power to move—of Shakespeare's—& more wonderful than all, so intermingled is the material & the spiritual, that any objective circumstance has its counterpart in the subjective life of man."[25]

In reading this tale of knighthood, she was able "to relive some patterns of experience, and at the same time . . . to think about its implications."[26] Altogether, the encounter reveals Thomas's unusual sensitivity to literary impressions and their importance in her subjective life.

.   .   .   .

The links between Thomas's ambition and her mode of reading can be traced in her responses to two favorites in early adolescence, *Little Women* and Carlyle's *On Heroes, Hero-Worship, and the Heroic in History* (1841). They seem an unlikely pairing, but in Thomas's feminist readings, both promoted dreams of glory, especially literary glory. We have seen that when Thomas began her journal in 1870, she did so in the persona of Jo March: "Ain't going to be sentimental / 'No no not for Jo' (not Joe)." Imitating a literary character was a common practice among young diarists as they attempted to establish their own identities. There were compelling reasons for Thomas to choose Jo. In the first half of the novel, Jo rejects sentimentality and traditional femininity, as did Thomas; in the opening entry she referred sarcastically to being a "*young lady*," a state she was resisting despite her father's admonitions. Jo was a "bookworm" and ambitious: like Thomas, she wanted to do something "splendid." Perhaps most important, she was a successful author who was paid for her writing. Alcott's heroine appealed because as "Jo (not Joe)" she demonstrated that a woman could be a writer and aspire in other ways as well.[27]

Thomas's emulation of Jo exemplifies the ways in which reading enabled women to act out fantasies of achievement, first in early adolescent role-playing, later, given the right circumstances, in life. For two years *Little Women* loomed large in her relations with her closest childhood friends, Frank Smith and Bessie King, a distant cousin. Thomas assumed the persona of "Jo" in 1868, the year Alcott's heroine first flashed across the literary landscape; Frank took the part of "Laurie." These sobriquets coexisted for a time with earlier literary nicknames, Minnehaha and Hiawatha. Thomas's incarnation as Longfellow's Indian maiden was more a play on her childhood name—Minnie—than a serious persona. It was different with Jo March. King, who had evidently accepted the secondary role of Owanee in the earlier fantasy, made an unsuccessful bid to become Jo, the only acceptable heroine of *Little Women* in this circle. Frank wrote Minnie that Bessie must decide what "she *would* like to be called, if she won't be Jo 2., or Meg, or Beth, or Amy; or Daisy, or anybody besides Jo 1. since *thou will* be the latter." Rather than play second fiddle, Bessie chose Polly, the appealing heroine of *An Old-Fashioned Girl*, Alcott's latest.[28]

Although *Little Women* combines romance and quest plots, it was the quest plot that most engaged Thomas. Jo's declaration that "I want to do something splendid . . . something heroic, or wonderful . . . I think I shall write books, and get rich and famous" prefigures the manifesto by Thomas with which this chapter begins.[29] Years later, as Thomas started graduate study in Germany in 1879, King acknowledged the importance of their childhood play: "Somehow today I went back to those early days when our horizon was so limited yet so full of light & our path lay as plain before us. It all came of reading over Miss Alcott's books now the quintescence [*sic*] of Philistinism then a Bible. . . . Doesn't thee remember when to turn out a 'Jo' was the height of ambition"?[30] With *Little Women*, then, we are dealing with a key text in the formation of Thomas's subjectivity and with a fantasy that was shared rather than private.

In her early teens Thomas also had a penchant for romancing that *Little Women* could not satisfy. These grander visions were of the sort traditionally enacted by male heroes. Thomas read herself into male as well as female plots, into nonfictional as well as fictional characters, and into the lives of authors as well. The quest tales of knighthood (which she and Frank Smith invoked in their dreams of the future), the classics, and Carlyle's *On Heroes* all provided Thomas with material for her daydreams. At fourteen, she declared that *On Heroes* "has interested me more than any book I ever read almost." In a copybook dated 1871–72, quotations from Carlyle predominate under "Selections from Prose Writers." Years later, Bessie King sent her a copy of James Anthony Froude's life of Carlyle, "for the sake of old times when he was a prophet to us—thee must spare time to look over it."[31]

Carlyle's cranky rhetoric makes for difficult reading today, but it stirred his contemporaries and remained a favorite of young men and women well into the century.[32] From its ringing opening declaration—"Universal History, the history of what man has accomplished in this world, is at bottom the History of the Great Men who have worked here"—*On Heroes* endorses individual action in ways calculated to inspire idealistic young people not only to admire but also to cultivate heroic genius. The influence of Carlyle, for whom the "Man-of-Letters Hero . . . [is] our most important modern person. . . . What he teaches, the whole world will do and make," is apparent in Thomas's desire, at the peak of adolescent romanticism, to write "hearty earnest true books that may do their part towards elevating the human race." Long after Carlyle had ceased to be a prophet, his prose echoes in Thomas's assertion, at twenty-four: "Hero worship, or rather genius worship is one manifestation of the religious insti[n]ct in wh[ich] one can pour heart & soul."[33]

Carlyle's models—the hero as divinity, prophet, poet, priest, man of letters, and king—are all male. Why then did they appeal to Thomas? By the time she read *On Heroes*, she was already a feminist determined to prove women the intellectual equals of men, a project she later fulfilled at Bryn Mawr: "How *unjust*—how *narrow-minded*—how *utterly uncomprehensible* to deny that women ought to be educated & worse than all to deny that they have equal powers of mind. If I ever live & grow up my *one* aim & consentrated [*sic*] purpose *shall* be & is to show that a woman *can learn can reason can compete* with man in the grand fields of literature & science & conjecture that opens before the 19th century that a woman can be a woman & a *true* one with out having all her time engrossed by dress & society." Given such an outlook, Thomas would not have made a prophet of Carlyle if she had read him as excluding her.[34] Instead, she inserted herself into the text, reading the generic masculine as inclusive rather than exclusive, in accord with a stirring feminist passage from *Jane Eyre* in her copybook: "women feel just as men feel . . . they suffer from too rigid a restraint, too absolute a stagnation, precisely as men would suffer."[35]

Diverse critics have assumed that women read themselves only into female parts or that reading "as a man" is invariably harmful, or both. Such a perspective unduly restricts women readers to passive roles or at best to that of a sprightly female heroine.[36] Given the imaginative possibilities opened up by reading, it is much too limited an approach. Critic Cora Kaplan is on sounder ground in suggesting that literature can provide the reader with multiple and shifting points of entry and the possibility of identification with heroes as well as heroines, without occupying a fixed subject position.[37] Kaplan focuses on romantic fantasies, but, as in the case of *Sintram*, women like Thomas were adept at reading themselves into heroic and ostensibly nonromantic parts. (Tales of knighthood had particular appeal for female questers.) The lesser self-consciousness of a pre-Freudian era no doubt encouraged such generic readings, as did the new tolerance for tomboys—at least until the age of seventeen or so, when girls were expected to put aside activities typically gendered as male.[38]

As for the fictional heroines available to them, many of Thomas's contemporaries found them wanting in the requisite qualities of heroism, or else too good to be true. A young friend of Jane Addams observed of the heroine of *Bleak House*, "Esther was a character to forever be admired and extolled, *but are* there any such?"[39] And as a Wellesley College senior, Katharine Lee

Bates, author of "America the Beautiful," wrote of the heroine of William Dean Howells's *The Lady of the Aroostook*, "We deny that Lydia Blood is a sample of our best national girlhood, much less the boasted American heroine, for the predominant stamp of heroism must be activity, visible or invisible, and this girl is as passive as a wooden angel, or a wax rose, with neither thorns nor fragrance."[40] Women writers offered more promising models, and young women admired, read, and read about Elizabeth Barrett Browning and George Eliot; they also read about queens and reformers of various stripes. For those seeking adventure, male heroes, fictional and real, offered intriguing possibilities if not exclusive models.

There was even some cultural encouragement for young women to read the generic "he" as inclusive. About the time Thomas was reading Carlyle, Victoria Woodhull and other feminists were claiming that because women were "persons" they were already enfranchised under the terms of the Fourteenth and Fifteenth Amendments.[41] Some Victorian writers explicitly made room for women within their definitions of heroism. And, although Carlyle's heroes were all male, as were Emerson's "representative men," the era's pervasive worship of genius extended to both sexes. In a college essay on "Some of the Representative Men of the Present Time," Thomas unself-consciously proclaimed George Eliot the representative novelist.[42]

Three years earlier, at the age of fifteen, Thomas had acted out a fantasy of female literary achievement with Bessie King. The focal point was "a library with all the splendid books[,] with a bright wood fire always burning[,] dark crimson curtains & furniture, great big easy chairs where we could sit lost in books for days together." Far from being idle dreamers, the companions were authors and laboratory scientists of whom people would say, "Their example arouses me, their books enoble [*sic*] me, their deeds inspire me & behold they are women!" Thus did Thomas transform the image of reading as a passive activity of schoolgirl dependence into one of adult purposefulness. Gender symbolism permeates this vision: the masculine accouterments of the library accompanied the appropriation of names that were masculine or androgynous. Thomas and King were, respectively, Rush and Rex, the latter a play on King's name, which, Thomas explained, meant "Queen." Here, as elsewhere in her role-playing, Thomas seems to have regendered the male hero as female; she also imagined a future that transcended gender.[43]

The fantasy prefigured Thomas's life at Bryn Mawr: the decor, the intellectual ethos, and the feminist life ventures with women. Here the fifteen-year-old was able to "write her own life in advance of living it," in Carolyn Heilbrun's telling phrase. It was a life in which Thomas was to inspire other women by her ideals and example and to ennoble them by her books. It is less important that she did not gain fame as a writer than that books were the touchstone for a fantasy—again a shared one—in which Thomas imagined herself a (female) Carlylean hero.[44] Perhaps these early dreams came to mind a decade later when she informed her mother of her triumph in receiving her Ph.D. summa cum laude from the University of Zurich: "Hail the conquering hero comes."[45]

Thomas's youthful dreams may have been more grandiose than some, her expression of them more exuberant. But her lofty ambitions and passion for reading were common among white, middle- and upper-middle-class women growing up in Gilded Age America, many of them also keen to "make something of themselves." Far from being idle dreamers, some grew up to attain distinction in academe, in science and medicine, in social welfare and reform. A self-conscious vanguard, members of the Progressive generation often thought of themselves collectively as the "first" generation of college women; they were, in Jane Addams's view, "this special generation"; in literary scholar Vida Scudder's, women who could "make ourselves significant if we will." For privileged women of Thomas's generation, dreams of glory often came from books.[46] Under the right circumstances, dreams could be transmuted into realities.[47]

In the process of articulating desires and appropriating meanings, Thomas's contemporaries tried out a variety of selves, some of them at odds with the "true women" they were expected to become. Jane Addams, for example, confessed to a fondness for a character representing a new, and freer, persona. Claiming that her favorite childhood story was *Undine*, Addams compared the water sprite to Scott's White Lady in *The Monastery* (1820), who "has a peculiar attraction for me, there is some-thing glorious to me in the idea of being without a soul, doing what you please without being responsible to yourself." The idea of Addams without a soul is arresting, for it was her soulfulness that most struck those who knew her as an adult; even as a child she was known for her solemnity. For Addams, the persona was self-consciously playful, a momentary diversion. But books also offered models against which to measure oneself, as in the case of Agnes Hamilton. Emily Greene Balch, a socially minded economist and Nobel Peace Prize winner, recalled with pleasure the stories of Maria Edgeworth and Charlotte Yonge, which "were largely built around a heroine who had a mission."[48]

Thomas was not alone in expressing greater interest in quest than romance plots and in female heroism than traditional heroines or prince charmings.[49] Mary White Ovington, in the opening passage of her memoir, suggests multiple origins for her later career as a leader of the NAACP: "Every imaginative child who has access to books or hears tales of a romantic past—and the past grows romantic in the telling—has a gallery of heroes upon which he loves to brood." Her heroes included Robert Bruce and Erling the Bold; "but the pictures that stirred me most and that I turned to oftenest were those of fugitive slaves. I saw Eliza crossing the ice on the last lap in her course to freedom . . . Anthony Burns incredibly escaping to Boston to be incredibly returned to slavery; and Frederick Douglass—most dramatic because he wrote his own story."[50] Here Ovington, who was white, mixes real heroes, black and white, with a fictional heroine—Eliza of *Uncle Tom's Cabin*—in a way that suggests the capaciousness of imagination. For Ovington, as for Thomas, the quest plot *was* romantic.

Playacting of this kind opened up imaginative space that permitted women to bracket at least some of the conventions of Victorian life and enter a world of their own choosing and subject to their own control. The term "escapism," with its connotations of uselessness or worse, is inadequate for understanding the process. For aspiring female adolescents of the Progressive generation, reading offered escape *to* as well as escape *from*: in their (day)dreams began possibilities.

Cognitive psychologists who study the relationships among reading, daydreaming, and fantasy suggest how reading stimulates personal choice. To Jerome Singer, daydreaming is "conscious fantasy behavior" and thus a cognitive skill rather than a sign of social inadequacy or repressed libido. Along with other stimuli of fantasy like books and movies, daydreaming is a form of internalized play that encourages "a more flexible and *playful* approach to one's own thought processes," thereby promoting growth and self-mastery. In this view, fantasy-prone individuals are often highly creative and self-directing rather than the starry-eyed, impractical characters they are often taken for. Because daydreaming permits the individual to pay attention to inner processes, "to produce images, to rework the unpleasant, or to contemplate the future in the complete privacy of one's mind," Singer claims that it is of special importance during adolescence, a time of doubt about achievement, the future, and sexuality.[51]

Paradoxically, it is the reader's status as spectator that helps to account for reading's intensity. With attention shifted away from the self and freed from the need to act, the reader is carried "off into other worlds," sometimes with a concentration so intense that reading may be said to "transfigur[e] both book and reader." Far from being a condition of detached aloofness, reading theorists maintain, the spectator role stimulates desire rather than pacifying it and in this way can alter consciousness. Something happens that is imperative for readers to understand. By permitting them to remove themselves temporarily from the necessity to act, it enables them to use this freedom "to *evaluate* more broadly, more amply," and thus to "modify categories according to 'the way [one] feel[s] about things."'[52] The heightened imaginative capacity and sense of vicarious participation associated with reading can help individuals to evaluate, clarify, and alter feelings.

Reading then is not so much a cause of female ambition as a vehicle for articulating and, consequently, intensifying desires. Thomas again proved to be a thoughtful observer, noting the excitement (and fear) she experienced on seeing her own thoughts expressed by someone else: "Sometimes when I have been reading a book . . . that has made a difference in me, whether it lie in me or in the book or poem I can never tell[.] (I think perhaps it is a habit of th[ough]t which blindly works on behind a veil until some sentence on the pages of a book or in the mouth of a person rends it & with a passion of appropriation the thought is mine.)" The passage suggests both a reciprocal relationship between reader and text and the reader's ability to make her own meaning. Seeing a thought on the printed page enables the reader to perceive what until then had existed only "blindly . . . behind a veil." The articulation of a half-formed thought or hidden desire, its exposure to consciousness, makes it available for further reflection and elaboration and thus for the development of even more novel thoughts.[53]

Books could not create a desire for female heroism where no tendency existed in the reader. Class position, family support, and expanding vocational opportunities all fostered ambition and also put some women in a favorable position to *realize* their goals. But, in conjunction with a supportive family culture and a network of friends that encouraged female aspiration, reading could *stimulate* worldly ambition by providing the occasion for perceiving one's inmost needs and wants—desires that might later be acted on. Particularly during the impressionable preadolescent and adolescent years, reading opened up in imagination a range of possibilities otherwise not available to women. By encouraging one another to pursue in life at least some of their dreams, ambitious women, Thomas among them, collectively developed a new sense of female destiny.

. . . .

It was one thing to dream of a heroic future, another for a woman in Gilded Age America to construct a future worthy to be told. Thomas staked her all on education and, despite her father's initial hesitation, graduated from

Cornell University in 1877 after two years in residence. Before leaving for graduate study in Europe two years later, she struggled with issues that often plague ambitious women (what work to choose, the likelihood of gender discrimination, how marriage might affect a career) as well as those particular to her own situation (growing religious doubt). During this difficult period, she found authorization for her dreams from members of a Baltimore literary circle who shared her intellectual passions and feminist outlook. Formed in the winter of 1877–78, "the Friday Night" combined self-conscious literary intellectualism and radical gender politics with friendship, love, and female sociability of a more traditional sort. In addition to Bessie King, the group included Mary E. Garrett, whose father's position as president of the Baltimore and Ohio Railroad opened doors for his daughter to meet luminaries like Herbert Spencer and Robert Browning; Julia Rogers, Garrett's intimate friend; and Mamie Gwinn, the youngest and most intellectually daring. Their fathers were Baltimore influentials: John Work Garrett, Charles Gwinn, Francis T. King, and James Carey Thomas were all trustees of Johns Hopkins University, which opened in 1876. King and Thomas were also founding members of the Quaker college for women that would become Bryn Mawr.

When the group began meeting, Carey Thomas was a graduate student at Johns Hopkins. Although the trustees had rejected coeducation, she was admitted under a special arrangement that allowed her to study with Basil Gildersleeve, professor of classics, but barred her from attending seminars—the lynchpin of the Hopkins system.[54] The only college graduate in her circle, Thomas was also the only one who needed to earn a living. But the others had ambitions of their own. King had decided "to risk all on *art*."[55] Garrett and Rogers were studying for the Harvard entrance examinations, not because they hoped to attend—Harvard did not admit women until late in the next century, and its female "annex," Radcliffe College, opened only in 1894—but to test their educational attainments. (Rogers later studied at Newnham College, Cambridge.) Gwinn marched to her own drummer without fixed career plans or an apparent need for external validation.[56]

The women were drawn together by their mutual literary interests and their sense of being modern women. These qualities were evident even in their teens, when Garrett, King, Rogers, and Thomas insisted on studying Greek, the ultimate (male) marker of intellectual standing. At sixteen Garrett talked back to John Ruskin who, in his popular essay "Lilies," subtitled "Of Queens' Gardens," maintained that although women should be educated in "nearly" the same way as men, they should not study as deeply. Garrett

"The Friday Night," Baltimore feminist literary circle, ca. 1878–79. Left to right: Carey Thomas, Julia Rogers, Mamie Gwinn, Mary Garrett, Bessie King. Courtesy of the Bryn Mawr College Library.

pronounced the essay "perfectly beautiful," but repudiated Ruskin's admonition "that woman's knowledge of higher subjects should merely be elementary . . . just so that she may be able to help her husband . . . No! 'Knowledge . . . is power' and I, for one, am going to do my best to gain it."[57]

In their early twenties, members of the Friday Night were aspiring intellectuals and writers who felt "mortified" by a gap in literary knowledge. They met fortnightly at one of their homes and, according to Thomas, wrote "2 chapt[ers] of a novel & an essay or two each night." Their shared dreams of literary glory culminated in a collective novel, with members writing alternating chapters; several, including Thomas and Gwinn, embarked on novels of their own.[58] In addition to their formal activities, members engaged in joint study: two or three read German or studied Greek together. All kept up with the latest English and American literary magazines and talked and wrote endlessly about books that moved them. (These were mainly British and later French; except for Henry James, they expressed little enthusiasm for American authors, and not always for him.) Some of the reading rituals indulged in by members seem more congruent with traditional female roles than with their image as an avant-garde: reading was also an occasion of love and healing—they read poetry to one another to cure a headache.[59] Through their literary activities and personal friendships, the group forged a collective identity that valorized female intellect and independence.

The Friday Night constituted a forum for exploring avant-garde ideas on virtually every subject. Determined "to go to the bottom of things," the women, all of them "brought up in the most carefully guarded homes," not only questioned the validity of Christianity and the sacredness of marriage, but championed art for art's sake, political radicalism (if only for a time), and in more lasting fashion, a feminist agenda that encompassed both private and public life.[60] Rejecting anything that smacked of "philistinism" in art and literature, they had a shared disdain for the ordinary, including the common lot of women. Garrett, although she found "a great deal of kindness & goodness" in many characters in Jane Austen's *Emma*, was dismayed that not one of them had "the slightest desire . . . to rise above or out of the dull commonplace of their daily life."[61]

Gravitating to transgressive writers, the women considered themselves an advanced set, "our chosen few," in King's words, "*nous autres*" in Thomas's.[62] Thomas was drawn to Shelley from an early age and as a teenager encountered his "infidel views" with "half distressed delight."[63] Under Gwinn's influence, she now claimed William Godwin, Shelley's father-in-law and a philosophical anarchist, as a mentor. Godwin's *An Enquiry concerning Political*

Justice (1793) was a powerful critique of inequality and of the institutions that promoted it, including government, religion, private property, and marriage. (Notwithstanding, he married Mary Wollstonecraft, whose early feminist treatise, *A Vindication of the Rights of Women* (1792), challenged patriarchy.) In a society organized more rationally and without such impediments, Godwin believed, the natural benevolence of humanity would flourish and individuals come nearer the perfectibility and happiness of which they were capable.[64] Thomas later credited Shelley "and through him Godwin, for almost all the light[s?] I walk by."[65]

Thomas also expressed extravagant admiration for the contemporary poet Algernon Charles Swinburne, a latter-day Romantic whose innovative meters, lyrical power, and bold subject matter appealed to rebellious youth of her generation. Like Shelley, Swinburne was a republican and atheist who challenged conventional political and religious norms. By celebrating same-sex love and sadomasochism, he crossed sexual boundaries as well. The poet's scandalous reputation had abated among literary critics by the mid-1870s when Thomas encountered him, but she still felt compelled to defend him at times. She was carried away by the "rapture & fire" of his poetry—literally it seems. "It was dancing & Swinburne that did it," she breezily exclaimed of a "true type of a 'Literary smash'" with a female friend at Cornell that commenced when they read *Atalanta in Calydon* (1865).[66] With Swinburne as her guide to literary and artistic trends, she and her friends were drawn to aestheticism, to Gabriel Dante Rossetti and other pre-Raphaelite friends of the poet, and to French writers like Théophile Gautier who made it a point to *épater les bourgeois*. Even as they enlisted under the banner of "art for art's sake" and enjoyed shocking others by admitting that they read French novels, the young women sometimes justified their conduct on the grounds of improving their French; to her mother, Thomas suggested that familiarity with the seamy side of life would in the long run help a young woman defend against its dangers.[67]

If the women rejected orthodox Christianity and endorsed the radical artistic currents of the day, their attitudes toward sexuality were in some respects more traditional than modern. Like most well-born young women with limited experience of life, their understanding of the world was shaped in large measure by their reading. Thomas claimed that her eyes had been opened "to the great world of passion" by a professor's reading of Tennyson's "Maud." Not very wide, as it turned out.[68] Despite the women's desire to shock, all but Gwinn rejected Godwin's endorsement of free love, which Thomas believed would degrade women.[69] And when—evidently for the first time—members of the group read up on the facts of life in her father's medical books and *What Women Should Know* (1873) by social purity reformer Eliza Duffey, Thomas "went to bed sick, absolutely." She was twenty-one. Influenced by admonitions from her mother and her aunt Hannah Whitall Smith, leaders in the Maryland WCTU and social purity movements, respectively, Thomas retained a deeply Victorian suspicion of male sexuality and a belief in female purity and moral superiority. These essential components of the paradigm of "passionlessness" ran counter to her stated commitment to gender equality.[70] But the young women's belief in voracious male sexuality and female passionlessness fed their conviction that marriage would undermine their ambitions.

Above all, members of the Friday Night admired and cultivated female independence. In King's view, "There is no doubt that the feeling which is silently growing among women for independent life, apart from their relations to men[,] is the motive power for the revolution we hope for." Endlessly debating "the woman question," the women considered it difficult if not impossible for a married woman to fulfill her potential and kept a close watch whenever a prospective suitor appeared. Thomas, who considered family life hampering to male as well as female genius, did not rule out marriage in theory and urged a recently engaged friend to stick with her work. Nevertheless, during this period she avoided a prospective suitor she thought she loved.[71] "If it were only possible for women to elect women as well as men for a '[life's] love,'" she wrote her mother, "all reason for an intellectual woman[']s marriage w[oul]d be gone." Throughout her life, Thomas was attracted to women and what was an *if* became a reality: she lived with Mamie Gwinn and, after Gwinn's marriage in 1904, with Mary Garrett.[72]

Taken together, the activities of the Friday Night reveal the multiple possibilities of reading in promoting female agency. In particular, the social nature of their reading, with its potent blend of intellectual challenge and emotional sustenance, provided a setting in which vocational plans flourished. Meeting at a critical time, when women's ambitions often fell victim to marriage, illness, or the care of ailing relatives, the Friday Night demonstrated the importance of like-minded peers in helping women sustain an often precarious vision.

Even a strong-minded woman like Thomas found it difficult to settle on a realistic course of action. Echoing the desire she expressed so confidently at fourteen, she could still assert, "I do not care for anything except to try for the realization of some of my dreams." The problem was that in her early twenties her dreams led in different—and conflicting—directions. On the one hand, the life of culture opened to her by her worldly new friends enthralled her. She was "carried away" when, in a decisive departure from Quaker tradition, she attended her first play shortly after her twenty-first birthday. Her newly awakened love of beauty and dedication to culture inspired the hope that she might fulfill her "dream of dreams" and become a poet; writing, she sometimes claimed, was the only goal worth having. Despite doubts about her talent, she allowed herself to hope that she could produce something of lasting value.[73]

On the other hand, single-minded pursuit of culture conflicted with her desire to free herself from financial dependence on her parents and to become an active player in the world. In this frame of mind, she proclaimed, "Study . . . & influence are the two things I care about."[74] In truth, neither her studies nor the process of becoming a scholar satisfied her romantic sensibility, one manifestation of which was boundless admiration for Greek—her "Holy of Holies." Nothing, she claimed, was like "the feeling of passionate beauty that comes over me when a Greek tragedy is mentioned. . . . A possession that comes when I open the pages."[75] By contrast, study of the language was not only "lifeless," but to master it, she would have to forgo "the noblest literatures" for years.[76] Then too, her anomalous situation at Hopkins was becoming more and more frustrating.

As Thomas struggled with issues of career choice and professional training, intimacy and independence, spiritual doubt and family conflict, not to mention lingering uncertainty about having given up the suitor, her life spun out of control. The determined teenager who staked her all on attending college gave way to the irresolute and anguished young woman who felt possessed by contending forces. Her depressed mental state during the spring and summer of 1878 is recorded in the pages of her journal. When she read it seven years later, at the start of her Bryn Mawr career, she declared it "a mortifying record of avocations, not vocations—esp. of emotional disturbances."[77]

Matters came to a head during the spring and summer of 1878, the latter spent mainly at the vacation home of her devout maternal grandmother. Deprived of companions her own age, even more than usual her life revolved around books in their infinite variety: Greek and German for study; "solid" books for illumination on matters of faith; and novels, which she craved and alternately denied herself and feasted on. Her conflicting desires played themselves out around her reading.

Thomas looked to contemporary intellectuals for answers to her growing doubt about the tenets of Christianity. Her slide toward unbelief—which she still resisted—was poisoning relations with her parents, and she longed for the certainty she had not attained despite years of reading. Matthew Arnold's *Literature and Dogma* (1873), which she read at the end of May, helped, for it expressed what she had "been coming to for the last 5 years." Arnold upheld the core validity of Christianity, while disclaiming supernatural "extra beliefs" like the resurrection and virgin birth for which no scientific evidence existed. Thomas agreed that Jesus "had more thirst for righteousness, more attainment of it than any other man." But "He was misunderstood. His disciples made him, forced him to be a god." Reading the book for the third time, she observed: "For the first time I feel beyond the possibility of a faith in the divinity of [Christ]." Although comforted by the thought that this conclusion need not lead to atheism, she feared it would promote relativism. The best that could be hoped for was the conclusion reached earlier by the Friday Night that without faith in traditional Christianity, moral judgments must be based on reason, a proposition that later prompted the observation that "Godwin may give hope." Thomas needed hope, for although Arnold was the first writer to pour "oil upon the troubled waters," in the end he brought the "calmness of despair rather than the peace wh[ich] passeth all understanding."[78]

Like many men and women of her generation, Thomas turned to science for ultimate answers—about religion as in other matters. Such was her faith that she could exclaim, "What does it all mean—this unhappiness? I will read Spencer & try to find out." In his grand evolutionary synthesis of human history, *The Principles of Sociology*, Herbert Spencer drew on a wealth of anthropological and sociological data to demonstrate the primitive origins of modern customs and ideas, belief in God and immortality included. Thomas read the first volume "almost choking with anger" and wanted to shoot the author who "tears down with the most contemptuous sarcasm the Jehovah of the Hebrews & the glorious old Greek gods who have been to me inspiration & joy." But finding "no flaw in his logic," she felt compelled to accept his analysis: "It is unreasonable to think ideas of immortality & god arose from any other than sleep & dreams . . . if it can be shown that they are now arising among savages in that way."[79] But even Spencer did not allay her emotional distress. After reading Swinburne's "Hymn of Man" with Mamie Gwinn later in the summer, Thomas observed: "It is a paean of triumph over the vanishing of the Xian [Christian] religion. To Mamie it was elixir[,] to me poison; though I could not help the bewildering beauty of it carrying me away."[80]

Stripped of her former beliefs but with nothing to replace them, Thomas's life seemed "a horrible blank." Toward the end of the summer she experienced a momentary impulse to commit suicide by upsetting her rowboat.

> . . . no god to pray to, no shrine of Apollo to go to. . . . Suddenly, as suddenly as a possession, came over me the temptation to upset this boat. . . . I came so near doing it, I tremble to think of it. "Sudden thy shadow fell on me." There seemed to come as a stealing melody some use & beauty into life. All the old fighting to believe died away. I lay behind me a cast off garment I have been striving to put on . . . All religions are "part of the hunger & thirst of the heart[,]" good and noble so long as they do not shackle; but only notes in the chorus. Godwinism—its core, the heavenly secret of Shelley "to fear himself & love all human kind" the secret of Christ "a dying daily—self renunciation," are all one. It is worth working for worth living to work out that. . . . I am happier than I have been for a long time. I will try to be good & work out that—Ah God, if I had genius to dedicate to it.[81]

In her dramatic telling, Thomas appears to have been saved by a literary epiphany. The "old fighting to believe" died away and was replaced by a vision that reconciled practical Christianity with the secular humanism of Shelley and Godwin and insisted on the commonalities of all religions. She drew not only on her old heroes, but also on her reading of Spencer, whose views she echoed when she wrote Garrett about the incident: "All religions, as all other things take their place in the grand chorus of progress."[82] Yet even as Thomas discarded religious belief—like "a cast off garment"—she invoked a central tenet of Protestantism: that in order to be sanctified, individuals must struggle mightily (the "dying daily") to live out the gospel and overcome sin. (Contemporary liberal Protestants were infusing this notion with an ethical twist by suggesting that believers "must die daily by giving up a bit of themselves for the sake of others.")[83] Although Thomas remained haunted by uncertainty about her future, by enabling her to apply a religious concept to secular goals, this integrative moment helped her move on with her life.

Thomas's call for sacrifice for a higher purpose was no passing fancy. But she seems to have had in mind personal rather than broad humanitarian goals. Even before her redemptive moment, she had announced a new "theory" to Garrett: "Just as the young knight renounced so many things as he received the acolade [sic], as Christ said the life of his followers must be a 'dying daily,' so a thought life requires many renunciations & crucifixions. Novels & lounging & daydreaming before sunsets . . . are inexpressibly pleasant, but if we girls are to accomplish anything we must give them up."[84]

She had in fact sworn off novels at the beginning of the summer in order to concentrate on Greek. It was a severe test, for she had recently declared, "Every thing seems secondary to my desire to read, it has come as I imagine possession of some demoniacal force came upon those old seers in the wilderness."[85] Her resolution lasted less than a month. About the time she was reading Spencer, the desire became uncontrollable: "such a longing for a novel . . . came over me. I would see the names of some I saw at a circulating library here dancing before me. I got Pascarel & lost sight of my miseries for the rest of the day—A novel is a true draught of Lethe to me & it is such a temptation." The following evening, "without meaning to" she took out a second novel, which she "read by the light of a candle till 12. I am frightened to see how I care about them when I try to stop; before I never tried & so never knew. A great deal of my time has been wasted in them & yet they are a rest."[86]

This extraordinary passage is more than a classic description of reading as escape from unbearable perplexity, although it is that too. It is a tale of seduction in which the protagonist lacks willpower and agency, almost as if hypnotized. Other young female readers might have recognized themselves in the scene, but most likely they would have done so at younger ages. For in describing her desire to read in the language of possession and suggesting that she was overcome by an outside force, Thomas sounds more like a teenager than an ambitious college graduate who had recently attained her majority. Her tale of libidinous desire and compulsive behavior suggests a breaking through of repressed emotions, the pleasure principle she associated with youth and passion. Desultory reading of this kind—and her passion for it—had become a threat rather than a stimulus to ambition, as had other pleasures. Aware that the prohibition increased the desire, in later years she meted out her pleasures more wisely and, even while concentrating on her graduate studies, allowed herself the occasional "debauch."

Thomas's strenuous efforts to control her reading in her early twenties came at a difficult moment. But, taken together with subsequent comments and those of her friends, her struggles suggest that there is something of a natural life cycle to women's reading, at least in its most intense phase. Thomas linked emotionally overpowering reading experiences to youth. At the advanced age of twenty-three, she was surprised that Robert Browning's drama, *A Blot in the 'Scutcheon*, took her breath away, as Keats and Shelley had in the "*Sturm & Drang Periode*." She hoped the Friday Night "w[oul]d . . . be reborn," but thought it unlikely once members began to pursue their interests: "It is much easier to meet when each has an untried enthusiasm." It is likely that reading, whether individual or social, has its greatest significance during a period of prolonged adolescence.[87] A time of dreaming and planning, of untried enthusiasms, it is a stage of life when reading retains an intensity less often found among adults, for whom, presumably, doing replaces dreaming.

Thomas's intuition that the Friday Night would not meet again proved accurate. But each of its members found ways to fulfill at least some of her enthusiasms. All supported feminist causes. During her long career at Bryn Mawr College, Thomas opened a new chapter in the history of women's higher education in the United States. Mamie Gwinn, who attained a Ph.D. from Bryn Mawr and later taught there, helped Thomas establish the college's rigorous intellectual standards; Elizabeth King (Ellicott) became a leader in the women's club and suffrage movements in Maryland; Julia Rogers published articles on cultural topics in the *Atlantic Monthly* and the *Nation*, was active in volunteer activities in Baltimore, particularly those promoting women's higher education, and bequeathed half a million dollars to Goucher College; and Mary Garrett became a prominent suffragist and philanthropist. Before they fell out in the 1890s, the women created two lasting legacies. They founded the Bryn Mawr School in Baltimore (1885), a rigorous college preparatory school for girls that sent many graduates to its collegiate namesake. Led by Thomas and Garrett, they also secured the admission of women to the Johns Hopkins University Medical School, at its opening in 1893 the premier medical institution in the United States. This stunning achievement depended not only on the connections of several of the women's fathers to the University Hospital and Medical School, but on a brilliant national fund-raising campaign among women—and on Garrett's sizable fortune. These triumphal ventures also exemplify the collective nature of feminist endeavor, which, in this case, began in the private and collective dreams of five young women seeking to fulfill the potential of their sex, dreams reinforced by their encounters with print.[88]

. . . .

Thomas resigned from Hopkins in October 1878, stating that she had not received the assistance she required. After another dispirited year at home, she left for graduate study in Germany the following August, accompanied by Mamie Gwinn. She spent three years at the University of Leipzig, where she studied philology, and then moved on to the University of Zurich when it became clear that no German university would grant her a degree. In addition to a thesis comparing the fourteenth-century English poem *Sir*

Gawayne and the Green Knight with French poems of the previous century, she completed in short order the required paper on an English author—she chose Swinburne—and a three-hour oral exam in which she triumphed.[89]

Despite the promising start, both before and after receiving her degree Thomas expressed ambivalence about her pursuit of scholarship—"hack work" she called it—when "to have written one poem . . . or if not that—to have spent one's life in sympathizing with such things is far nobler." Viewing writing as an act of inspired genius, she considered it a "profanation" to attempt it "in cold blood."[90] Her idealized views on literary creativity reveal the extent to which faith in culture had replaced her discarded religion—as well as the continued pull of Romanticism. Still hoping to become a writer in the high culture tradition, in her early twenties she projected a "lyrical love drama" in blank verse—set "in Venice, of course"—an ambitious literary form associated with Shelley and Swinburne.[91]

How serious Thomas was about this project, and about writing in general, is difficult to say. But in seeking to emulate her heroes, she was not only choosing a notoriously difficult literary form but claiming a moral license that could only be treacherous for a woman of her class, especially one who hoped to advance the cause of women. She daringly asserted that her love drama will "try to express a moment I have never seen treated—it is perilously near immorality & yet moral to the core."[92] Even apart from its bravado, the claim was at odds with contemporary imperatives for female respectability, as Thomas well knew. Only a short time before, when she asked her parents to forward an article she had written to *Harper's*, they objected because of "indelicate" allusions to the models' "naked female backs & thighs & knees."[93]

Thomas was in fact pursuing a more realistic prospect: a position at Bryn Mawr College. She angled for it with all the resources at her disposal, which were considerable: in addition to her own credentials, her father, Francis King, and her mother's brother were all trustees. Despite her unsound views on religion (which she played down), when the college opened in 1885, the board appointed Thomas dean and professor of literature (but not president, as she had boldly proposed). As she prepared to take up the position, she proclaimed it "an aside, like the Ph.D. degree." But her visits to women's colleges reminded her of "the curse of belonging to an unfree race," and she became fired up by the prospect of building an institution that would demonstrate women's intellectual potential.[94] Here was an opportunity to realize another of her adolescent dreams: to prove women the intellectual equals of men.

As a professor, Thomas remained true to her youthful literary heroes. In her two-year survey of English language and literature required of all Bryn Mawr College students, she hoped to lead girls "to the study and love of the best literature."[95] To that end she lavished praise not only on Shelley but on the pre-Raphaelites and Swinburne long after they had fallen out of favor. And although the Carlylean view of literature as a source of moral influence had been undermined by the aesthetic movement, his *On Heroes* remained required reading at the Bryn Mawr School.

Even before she became president in 1894, Thomas was the dominant intellectual force at Bryn Mawr. Determined to make the college a showcase for women's higher education, she introduced European standards of scholarship, making it unusual among American institutions of higher learning, and not only among women's colleges. She hired male and female professors with outstanding scholarly credentials (the men often left for major universities) and established the first graduate program at a woman's college. An elitist in intellectual matters—she believed that the few women and men of creative genius in any generation should join in service to humanity—she was also an unapologetic defender of white class privilege: Bryn Mawr excluded African Americans and restricted the number of Jews, with Thomas leading the way on both fronts.[96]

Thomas proved an effective champion of women's higher education. In speeches and articles she challenged the negative assessments of women's intellectual capacities by Harvard president Charles W. Eliot and other naysayers and cogently set forth her ideas on liberal education. But she never became a scholar or a writer. She did not even complete the autobiography she began after retiring in 1922, although she lived another thirteen years. Since many women of her generation wrote their life stories, Thomas's inability to do so is noteworthy. Characteristically, she attributed this failure to her love of reading: "Reading has remained the supreme delight of my life and never more so than now. Even at seventy five years of age I find it difficult to make myself write my memoir because reading is so great a temptation."[97] Although more muted in tone, this depiction of reading as a temptation recalls the vivid image of book titles dancing before her more than half a century earlier.

Was it only the pleasure of reading that kept Thomas from completing her autobiography? She worked at it, certainly, leaving behind multiple drafts and mountains of notes, not only on her childhood and ancestry, but on favorite authors and the autobiographies of contemporaries.[98] She did not mention that she had become accustomed to the good life. With access to Mary Garrett's fortune, both before and after the latter's death, Thomas could indulge her taste for high living, including extended periods of travel, accompanied by a retinue and trunks full of books. In the struggle between pleasure and discipline, pleasure won out: the days of renunciation were over.

The many lists and uncompleted drafts also suggest that she had trouble finding a way into her subject: the shape and meaning of her life. Outwardly, it was a life of considerable achievement: she had not only made Bryn Mawr a monument to women's higher education, but was arguably the most prominent woman educator of her generation as well as a leader in the woman suffrage movement and other public causes. For one who had dreamed of scaling the heights, perhaps no achievement would have been enough. Years before, as she prepared to take up her duties at Bryn Mawr, she sounded the theme of unfulfilled ambition that had haunted her in her teens, fearing that she would have many of "Rossetti's 'Lost days,' 'each one a murdered self'' to mourn for."[99]

Whatever regrets Thomas may have harbored about her life or concerns about the telling of it, books never let her down.[100] She claimed she found them more satisfying than people. She never expressed this passion more tellingly than at the end of the tumultuous summer of 1878, when she signaled her intense delight at her renewed access to books: "I feel intoxicated with joy. When I came from the Adirondacks I went in 4 days & read all day in the Mercantile library & the hours were seconds. I was thirsty with an unquenchable thirst. It was like treading on air. It is the purest happiness— the one thing wh[ich] no man taketh from you."[101] Here Thomas suggests not only that reading never disappoints, but that it is an activity, perhaps the only one, within the reader's possession—most of the time at least. This sense of control may help explain why women—whose lives have so often been fragmented—have been the principal readers of fiction.

If during adolescence reading can be a spur to ambition, for adults it is often a time-out, perhaps a refuge from life's unfinished business or from loneliness. But even in old age, as Thomas continued reading to advance the "thought life" she valued so much, she may still have been entering new territory rather than marking time. As she put it many years before: "As one grows older . . . [books and thoughts] become the real life, and reaching thus horizon after horizon the land becomes in time a *new* land upon whose possession we must enter."[102] Of M. Carey Thomas it may be said that she both possessed and was possessed by what she read.

. . . .

CHAPTER SIX

Working Her Way through Culture

Jane Addams and Literature's Dual Legacy

For Jane Addams, as for other intellectual young women, literature was a primary source of experience. This was not just a matter of exploring in imagination pleasures or sorrows as yet unknown or of absorbing the feel of other times and places. Some degree of cultural competence was expected of daughters of the comfortable classes, but Addams went beyond her peers in the range and seriousness of her intellectual interests. Her reflections on what and how she read and on reading as a cultural system provide insight into how women of her class, raised in a society that did not expect them to become active agents in the world, negotiated their way into public life.

Like so much of her best work, Addams's views on culture were written out of her own experience. More than any of her contemporaries, she articulated the complexities of women's relationship to literature: its perils and its possibilities. She looked to literary culture, then still defined broadly to include virtually every field of knowledge, for clues about how to live and act in the world—the very thing culture was supposed to provide, according to proponents like Matthew Arnold.[1] Attracted to some of the major thinkers of her time, she struggled to define herself and her relationship to the world through them.

This was no easy matter for an ambitious young woman growing up in Gilded Age America. As she wrestled with the philosophical and moral questions addressed by writers as diverse as Arnold, Carlyle, Ruskin, Tolstoy, George Eliot, and Thomas De Quincey, Addams had to contend not only with a multiplicity of intellectual paradigms but with the gendered assumptions embedded in them. The books she read presented confusing models, as they might have done to a man of her generation. But she faced a challenge not encountered by her male counterparts: how was a woman, still subject to "the family claim," to pursue her goals in the face of family opposition, restrictive gender norms, and spiritual and psychological doubt?

In the early years, the knowledge of life gained from reading sufficed. But as Addams matured, it seemed at best derivative, something that mediated between the reader and real life. Indeed, Carlyle and Emerson, the Romantic writers who influenced her most during her college years, suggested as much when they insisted on the superiority of nature over books as a source of experience. Even then Addams expressed ambivalence about her reliance on what others said. Later, while demonstrating her own mastery of literary culture—and its continuing hold on her—she offered a devastating critique of its power to ensnare men and especially women of the upper classes into lives of safe and unthinking comfort. By immersing themselves in literature, the privileged insulated themselves from the world around them, the world of poverty and hardship. Her passion on the subject suggests the degree to which she was writing about and for herself.

Addams did not find a way to fulfill her large ambition until 1889, when, shortly after her twenty-ninth birthday, she and her college friend Ellen Gates Starr founded Hull-House, one of the first American settlement houses. She had initially framed her aspirations on the romantic model of heroic individualism that also attracted Carey Thomas, but when faced with decisions about what to do with her life, Addams found it debilitating. Although she later rejected that standard, she still looked to literature to define her goals, finding in writers like George Eliot and Tolstoy models for human connection more commensurate with her temperament—and with contemporary gender norms.

Her wide reading of visual as well as literary culture prepared the way for this resolution. No doubt her frustration with leading a life devoted exclusively to family sharpened her desire to make the move and an independent income made it possible. But she committed herself to a course of action only after she found a practical way to draw on her cultural studies for her own purposes and to transform them into a satisfying guide for living. Given the vehemence with which she criticized cultural immersion, it was an ironic outcome. If her experience was mediated by her reading, it was not rigidly determined by it: both what she read and how enabled Addams to move beyond the cultural givens with which she grew up.

For all her criticism, Addams never rejected literary culture. How could she, when it provided ideas and a vocabulary with which to develop her own insights into class divisions, democracy, and the role of art and literature in human experience? Understanding that literature satisfied some of the deepest human longings—for emotional connection with one's fellows and truer understanding of them—she viewed it as one of the most powerful means of fostering association among diverse people, affinities she hoped would extend beyond the printed page. In that sense, literature might actually prepare an individual for entering a wider life. From this perspective, culture was not a luxury but something to be cultivated in every human being of whatever class or origin.

Reading and writing remained central to the construction of Addams's subjectivity, as they did, ultimately, to her politics. Along with her uncommon vision and democratic style of leadership, her skill as a writer helps account for her own preeminence and that of her settlement, which attracted a cadre of unusually creative, mainly female, residents.[2] Her retrospective critique in some ways obscures her complex relation to culture and the way she redefined it. It also makes light of the intellectual seriousness with which she attempted to work her way through it—and her success in articulating solutions with broad appeal to her contemporaries. Gendered in some though not all respects, her resolution helped to create new opportunities for women of her class.

. . . .

In her classic 1910 autobiography, *Twenty Years at Hull-House*, Addams took devastating aim at the literary culture in which she grew up. In this, her best-known work, the founder of America's most famous settlement constructs herself as a consumer of culture so absorbed in self-reflexive pursuits that she cannot respond adequately to human misery. "The Snare of Preparation," the pivotal chapter in the narrative of her progress from illness and futility to vitality and purposefulness that came with the founding of Hull-House, is a virtual object lesson on the point: too great immersion in culture leads to paralysis. In making this critique, Addams drew on her own life story: the eight years of ill health, depression, and spiritual striving following her graduation from Rockford Female Seminary in 1881, years given over to the pursuit of culture and, though she does not mention them, to family obligations.[3]

In a haunting episode, Addams describes her first visit to "outcast London" in the fall of 1883. With a party of tourists, she surveyed "two huge masses of ill-clad people clamoring around two hucksters' carts" as they bid on decaying vegetables and fruit. Witnessing "myriads of hands, empty, pathetic, nerveless and workworn, showing white in the uncertain light of the street, and clutching forward for food which was already unfit to eat," her eyes came to rest on a man who, upon catching the cabbage he had bid on, "instantly sat down on the curb, tore it with his teeth, and hastily devoured it, unwashed and uncooked as it was."[4] It was a scene straight out of Dickens. Unsettled by this disturbing exposure to poverty and by her inability to do anything about it, she recalls, "No comfort came to me then from any source, and the painful impression was increased because at the very moment of looking down the East London street from the top of the omnibus, I had been sharply and painfully reminded of 'The Vision of Sudden Death' which had confronted [Thomas] De Quincey one summer's night as he was being driven through rural England on a high mail coach." Addams summarizes the writer's efforts to warn two absorbed lovers in an oncoming carriage who are about to be crushed to death by the mail coach in which he is riding:

> De Quincey tries to send them a warning shout, but finds himself unable to make a sound because his mind is hopelessly entangled in an endeavor to recall the exact lines from the "Iliad" which describe the great cry with which Achilles alarmed all Asia militant. Only after his memory responds is his will released from its momentary paralysis, and he rides on through the fragrant night with the horror of the escaped calamity thick upon him, but he also bears with him the consciousness that he had given himself over so many years to classic learning—that when suddenly called upon for a quick decision in the world of life and death, he had been able to act only through a literary suggestion.

Addams's version is in fact something of a misreading. De Quincey, author of *Confessions of an English Opium-Eater* (1822) and a habitual dreamer whose mind was numbed by laudanum at the time, points to a different moral: "Strange it is, and to a mere auditor of the tale might seem laughable, that I should need a suggestion from the 'Iliad' to prompt the sole resource that remained. Yet so it was. Suddenly I remembered the shout of Achilles, and its effect." Far from *trying* to recall the Homeric passage, only when the literary image came to him unbidden was De Quincey able to act. His warning succeeds because of the heroic last-minute efforts of the oncoming driver. It is the near miss rather than the defects of classical learning that preoccupy him. In a larger sense, though, Addams has taken the author's meaning. "The Vision of Sudden Death" is a sustained reflection on the horror of failing to meet the ultimate test of moral responsibility when it is in one's hands, especially if one has not risen to the moment. In dreams, De Quincey observed, everyone "has a bait offered to the infirm places of his own individual will; once again a snare is presented for tempting him into captivity to a luxury of ruin; once again, as in aboriginal Paradise, the man falls by his own choice."[5]

What was for De Quincey an occasion for philosophic reflection on human frailty roused Addams to a critical appraisal not only of herself but of the misplaced values of her class and of intellectuals more generally. His warning shout became her wake-up call:

> This is what we were all doing, lumbering our minds with literature that only served to cloud the really vital situation spread before our eyes. It seemed to me too preposterous that in my first view of the horror of East London I should have recalled De Quincey's literary description of the literary suggestion which had once paralyzed him. In my disgust it all appeared a hateful vicious circle which even the apostles of culture themselves admitted, for had not one of the greatest among the moderns plainly said that "conduct, and not culture, is three fourths of human life."

By invoking Matthew Arnold, even without attribution, Addams drew on one of culture's most fervent advocates to buttress a central point of her autobiography: that genuine culture would result in admirable conduct. She was also displaying her command of the very culture she denounced.[6]

There is no way of knowing whether De Quincey's near miss came to mind at the exact moment Addams surveyed the East London scene from the top of the bus. In a sense it doesn't matter: like all autobiographical retrospections, this one makes the didactic point necessary for the author's purposes.[7] We do know that the scene and the "Dickens neighborhood" in which she found herself unsettled her: a few days later she informed her brother, "It was simply an outside superficial survey of the misery & wretchedness, but it was enough to make one thoroughly sad and perplexed."[8] Whether literally accurate or not, the De Quincey allusion is consistent with Addams's youthful fascination with the author, a fascination compounded of attraction and admonition. In her college essays and notebook, she fashioned "the brilliant English opium-eater lost in a maze of beautiful incomplete dreams" into a symbol of the pleasures of the imagination, but also of its dangers, the chief of which were irresolution and inaction. Those overly tempted by imagination, Addams declared in a college essay, would lose sight of the fact "'That the end of life, is an action not a thought, were that of the noblest.'"[9] De Quincey remained a touchstone for Addams, the frightening embodiment of her own mental paralysis.[10] Sixteen months after the East London episode, she invoked "The Vision of Sudden Death" as a symbol of "the will paralyzed by the very multiplicity of ideas and perceptions."[11] De Quincey's example—and his literary rendition of the division between thought and action—haunted her for years.

This division, Addams believed, was the peculiar predicament of the overly cultivated, those who, while indulging themselves in pleasurable and even self-improving activities, did nothing to make the world better. If De Quincey's temptation was to lose himself in dreams induced by drugs, Addams's was to immerse herself in books and other forms of "self-culture." In this way she linked the division between thought and action to the self-absorption of men and women of the privileged classes who blinded themselves to the basic human needs of the overworked and impoverished city dwellers she encountered in Europe. Before she was done, Addams uncoupled culture from class and redefined the cultivated person as one with broadly human interests rather than superior cultural attainments, a person who left behind exclusive associations to become a citizen of the world. In the process she also provided a rationale for harnessing women's untapped energies.

.   .   .   .

Most of what we know about Jane Addams's early reading comes from *Twenty Years at Hull-House.* As she tells the story, her youthful associations with books, like her other memories of childhood, were closely bound up with her father.[12] John Huy Addams, who migrated to Cedarville, Illinois, in 1844 from Pennsylvania, was the village's most prominent and prosperous citizen. He was an entrepreneur who started out as a mill owner in the pioneering community, later diversifying into insurance, banking, real estate, and railroads, which he helped attract to the region. A Republican from the party's founding in 1854, he served eight consecutive terms in the state senate. The death of his wife in 1863, when Jane was just over two, strengthened the bond between Addams and his youngest daughter.[13]

Jane Addams's world rose and set by her father, after whom she modeled herself at every turn. As a child she sometimes awakened at 3:00 A.M., the hour her father rose as a young man to take his turn at the mill: "I imagined him in the early dawn in my uncle's old mill reading through the entire village library, book after book, beginning with the lives of the signers of the Declaration of Independence." Attempting to "understand life as he did," she resolved to read all the books in the house, a project akin to that of her future colleague Florence Kelley.[14] This was no small task, since the Addams homestead was the site of the Cedar Creek Union Library Company.[15] As Addams tells it, "Caught by some fantastic notion of chronological order and early legendary form," she started with "Pope's translation of the 'Iliad,' . . . followed by Dryden's 'Virgil' . . . [but] finally gave them up for a thick book entitled 'The History of the World' as affording a shorter and an easier path."[16] She presents her grand scheme as an instance of youthful folly, but it may have offered the motherless child relief from a deep loneliness, as it did Kelley.

Addams's father provided direction by encouraging her to read books that were the birthright of the educated classes. He "insisted upon a certain amount of historic reading ever since he had paid me, as a little girl, five cents a 'Life,' for each Plutarch hero I could intelligently report to him, and twenty-five cents for every volume of Irving's 'Life of Washington.'"[17] John Addams presumably encouraged his daughter to read what he valued most. Plutarch's exemplary moral tales of ancient Greek statesmen had been standard reading in educated households for centuries: next to the Bible, Plutarch's *Parallel Lives* was the most widely read ancient text in early America. Leaders of the revolutionary generation in particular found models of statesmanship in these stories and greatly admired them.[18] John Addams in turn revered the founding fathers, and his library contained numerous volumes by and about heroes of that generation and the next. No doubt he shared the prevailing view that biographies were not only instructive but provided readers with heroic models for emulation.[19]

John Addams supplemented these venerable ancient heroes with more modern exemplars, notably Abraham Lincoln and Giuseppe Mazzini. Jane Addams devoted an entire chapter of her autobiography to the American president whom her father had known personally and over whose death he wept. He considered Lincoln "the greatest man in the world," a greatness his daughter attributed to the president's understanding that the "'common people'" were the most important resource of the nation. Highlighting the war heroes who sacrificed their lives in order to free the slaves, she noted that her father had helped recruit a regiment for the Union Army—the "Addams Guard."[20] The martyred president was a hero to many Americans, but the Mazzini connection was idiosyncratic. When Jane was eleven her father made his grief at the death of the Italian patriot and revolutionary into an object lesson "of the genuine relationship which may exist between men who share large hopes and like desire, even though they differ in nationality, language, and creed; that those things count for absolutely nothing between groups of men who are trying to abolish slavery in America or to throw off Habsburg oppression in Italy."[21] Thus did the autobiographer establish her connection to the European as well as the American republican tradition and accent the oneness of humanity. In her early years at Hull-House Addams authenticated the democratic credentials of the settlement by explicitly drawing on the legacies of both men.[22]

One wonders whether John Addams ever thought his lessons in republican citizenship odd for a girl slated for domesticity. His youngest, who quoted Elizabeth Barrett Browning's *Aurora Leigh* in connection with the Mazzini story, seems to have had at least retrospective doubts: "He wrapt me in his large / Man's doublet, careless did it fit or no."[23] In view of Addams's otherwise total idolization of her father, this passage can only be seen as a rebuke, however mild. The father's efforts to guide and the daughter's to "try to understand life as he did" were to make for a sometimes problematic "fit." Not only were the proffered models all male; they were larger-than-life heroic figures. Fascinated by their clarity of purpose and resolve, Addams praised leaders of this type in college. But ultimately they did not serve. Not for a woman whose primary parent was an idealized father with traditional gender expectations: the former miller required each daughter to bake him a satisfactory loaf of wheat bread on her twelfth birthday. Nor were they useful for a woman, who, like other early college graduates, struggled to detach herself from exclusively family ties to find a public purpose.

Contemporary sources suggest more varied cultural influences than does the autobiography. Encouraged by her entire family in her efforts to become culturally literate, Addams belonged to a "Littery Society" at the age of ten. Two years later she sent John Greenleaf Whittier what the poet considered a "generous appreciation" of his work; he assured her of the authenticity of Barbara Frietchie, the eponymous elderly heroine of a poem who insisted on raising the Union flag as Confederate troops marched by.[24] The arrival of a stepmother a few years earlier brought a new level of cultural aspiration to the previously rather spartan Addams household. A passionate reader and proficient musician, Anna Haldeman Addams sang while accompanying herself on the guitar and read Shakespeare aloud to Jane and her son George Haldeman when they were in their teens, "taking the characters turn about."[25]

A diary Addams kept for six months at the age of fourteen reveals an absorption in literary activities typical for her age and gender. As a teenager she was a great reader of novels: Dickens's *The Pickwick Papers* with George, which she initially found disappointing, and *The Old Curiosity Shop*, which she "like[d] . . . every [sic] so much, I think Nell is just perfect"; and Elizabeth Phelps's *The Gates Ajar* ("there is not much in the story itself but there is a good deal in the book"). She also memorized poems, including Longfellow's "The Day Is Done," which she thought was "perfectly beautiful," and wrote them as well.[26]

If John Addams, portrayed by his daughter as a man of such integrity that he was never even *offered* a bribe, paid her to read about heroic historical figures, he may have thought it necessary.[27] Although Jane Addams later proclaimed a "genuine interest" in history, at fifteen she confided to a friend that she tended to "over do" reading her favorite, Dickens, but still had "not been 'worked' to that fine and appreciative point" of liking history: "I now have an arrangement with Pa, that I am to read a certain amount of history first, and the rest of the day can read 'standard' that is a little more interesting."[28] The following year, she further confessed: "You spoke of reading Scott. I have 'never partaken very freely of his great genius.' I suppose of *course* I shall enjoy him, but as a rule (dreadful to relate) 'instructive novels' are to me a bore."[29] It was evidently more difficult to appreciate the reading and models offered by her father than Addams suggested in *Twenty Years*.

. . . .

Jane Addams the intellectual comes into view at Rockford Female Seminary, which she attended from 1877 to 1881. She later highlighted the deficiencies of her education, her dislike of the religiosity of the headmistress, Anna P. Sill, and her resistance to efforts to recruit her as a missionary.[30] But she flourished there and left an impressive record. Star student and debater, she was an officer in many organizations (although not the missionary societies), including the Castalian (a literary society), class president, and in her senior year editor-in-chief of the *Rockford Seminary Magazine* and valedictorian. Despite her retrospective criticisms, in her twenties she thought well enough of Rockford to contribute $1,000 for the purchase of scientific books and to serve as a trustee.

Founded in 1849 by Presbyterian and Congregational ministers with the goal of educating young ladies, Rockford Seminary in the late 1870s was in the process of becoming a full-fledged college. Addams took the collegiate course, with an academic program that included ten courses in Latin and Greek, five each in math and science, six in Bible and Bible history, and one on "Evidences of Christianity." She also took courses in literature (including Shakespeare and American literature, the latter something of a novelty at the time), rhetoric, ancient and modern history, civil government, mental philosophy, and eight classes in German, as well as the capstone senior course in moral philosophy. In 1882, a year after her graduation, she received a bachelor's degree, the first time Rockford awarded that degree.[31]

Addams attended college at a time of transition in higher education, when the older emphasis on piety was giving way to more varied curricular approaches. A telling sign of change was the diminished role of moral philosophy, a course designed to reinforce Christian beliefs and principles that was gradually disappearing from the college curriculum.[32] As taught by Miss Sill, moral philosophy at Rockford would have remained true to its original mission. But Addams was also exposed to newer intellectual trends: she took courses in botany, astronomy, geology, and chemistry, specialized subjects that were replacing more general offerings in natural history. Her science teacher accepted Darwin's theory of evolution even if Miss Sill did not.[33]

In line with the new contemporary emphasis on liberal culture, literature courses encouraged cultivation of imagination and breadth of learning rather than memory or the acquisition of information.[34] Students read and reflected on "the best," beginning with Homer and Shakespeare. A bookish young woman who experienced the religious doubt that troubled so many of the post-Darwinian generation, Addams probed literature as a source of moral authority and guide for action. With Matthew Arnold, she believed that literary culture was "a moral endeavor to constantly learn more of the universal order so that we may conform ourselves and others to it, may be in harmony and 'make reason and the kingdom of God prevail.'"[35] Like many other seekers, she was working out a "salvation by establishing relations with spiritual truths embodied in sacred texts."[36]

For Addams, as for Carey Thomas, the most sacred of these derived from the language and culture of ancient Greece.[37] Knowledge of Greek had long been the mark of an educated person, but Arnold and others now viewed the classics as a source of spiritual values as well. Themes from Greek mythology inspired two of Addams's major public addresses at Rockford.[38] But she also claimed that her nearest approximation "to a faint realization of

Jane Addams, ca. 1880. Courtesy
of Jane Addams Papers Project,
Fayetteville, North Carolina.

the 'beauty of holiness'" took place on Sunday mornings when she read the
Greek testament with a teacher.[39]

Her reverence for the language is apparent in a series of ardent pro-
nouncements her junior year. "It will be a week always memorable to me
because I began Homer in it," she informed her stepmother. "I have never
enjoyed the beginning and anticipation of anything as much as I have of
that." The normally reserved Addams apologized for the "extravagance" of
her words, but repeated them soon after. As she wrote her sister: "I would
be willing to study Greek for ten years, even peg along in Crosby's grammar
all that time if I could have the fun of reading Homer in the end."[40] When
she dropped Greek the following year, she observed, "I would sooner part
with anything else I have gained in school than the Homer I have read."[41] The
contrast between her extravagant admiration of Greek and her later critique
of the paralyzing effects of the classics on De Quincey is striking.[42]

Addams's intellectual development can be traced in her carefully preserved college essays. She was in many respects already a writer in training,
crafting and rewriting papers on themes that ranged from the lofty ("The
Element of Hopefulness in Human Nature") to the mundane ("Dress"). A
few appeared in the *Rockford Seminary Magazine*, including an essay on
Macbeth that still impressed Ellen Gates Starr several years later.[43] In view of

Addams's six courses on the subject, the scarcity of biblical topics and allusions is noteworthy. Her essays are filled with references to literary figures and to historical subjects, many of them immortalized in literature. The language is the language of culture. Comments by her writing instructor on an essay Addams wrote in her junior year set the standard: "*Brood* upon these four men, *fill* yourself with the facts of their lives, with the momentous occasions which called them out, seek the meaning of events[,] then after some months rewrite."[44]

Addams was drawn to subjects that explored the nature of human achievement. With titles like "'Follow Thou Thy Star'" and "The *Magnificence* of Character" and maxims like "true character is born not written," her essays endorsed a heroic model of genius and creativity.[45] Only toward the end of her college career, as the contradictions between the grand achievements she admired and the possibilities available to her as a woman became apparent, did she explore how women might take part in the life of their times.

Bearing the stamp of Emerson and Carlyle, for the most part her essays gave allegiance to an individualistic creed far removed from the empathic politics of her later years.[46] At eighteen she rhapsodized, "Carlyle has a way of saying things once in a while that strike, as it were my key-notes, just exactly what I have been hunting for."[47] She later disavowed the Victorian sage, but in college, she accepted Carlyle's view that history was made by great men.[48] On completing a biography of Michelangelo, which she enjoyed more than anything she had read since Carlyle's *On Heroes*, she observed: "there is the definite impression it has left upon my mind of the breadth, of the greatness of man, and that all great men are intrinsically the same."[49]

Her essays explored the meaning of such greatness. In a class by himself was Goethe, a man "great & free in himself," whose work Carlyle had translated and introduced to the English-speaking world. Addams's essays on Goethe drew heavily on Emerson, not only in a certain closeness of phrasing, but in their insistence on the superiority of nature over books and theories, a frequent refrain in her writing at the time. She portrayed Goethe as a man who appeared "when all Germany was over-civilized, entangled in a morbid feeling of oppression, [when] original talent was weighed down under the load of books and modern philosophies, [and] the finer nature of man had withered under the breath of doubt." Feeling deeply the weight of his times and possessed of a strong sense of destiny, Goethe gave voice to the pain of his era. By studying "the unity and simplicity of nature," Addams maintained, he created harmony and reverence out of discord and skepticism, opening a new era in German literature and civilization in the process.[50]

Describing a very different sort of leader, the fifteenth-century Florentine monk Savonarola, Addams drew on George Eliot's historical novel *Romola*, a signature book that would figure importantly in her life. Both men engaged fully with their times, Goethe in sadness, Savonarola in indignation. If Goethe was a genius who changed the direction of his life to meet the needs of his times, Savonarola was "a man of rare sincerity . . . [who] deviated not an inch from his destined course." Drawn to the monk's efforts to purify the Church, as she would be to other religious movements that favored unpretentious forms of worship over ritual, Addams viewed him as a "true leader" who tried to save his city from the "abominations" of the age and to remodel it according to his own unswerving principles of virtue. For a time "it seemed almost possible to change the nature of men at his bidding," yet in the end, with only himself to fall back on, he had to recognize that the people's enthusiasm for his policies was but an echo of his own, and he died a martyr's death. While recognizing his failings, Addams admired the monk's force of character as well as his goals. Where most lives are indistinct, with their powers "locked up" and "robbed of our true selves," Savonarola was "'an *incarnate idea*,'" a man who could bring people "into contact with truth itself."[51] In later years she found these qualities less appealing. Rereading *Romola* when she visited his cell a few years later, she observed that the monk had "confuse[d] God's cause with Florentine government," George Eliot's view of the matter.[52] Tellingly, Addams's philosophy in maturity was as far from Savonarola's as it could be: learning from the experiences of daily life rather than imposing a predetermined order on it, she eschewed fanaticism and unyielding certainty of any kind.

Beyond such conspicuous examples of greatness, in college Addams believed that the desire for heroic achievement was universal, often quoting Carlyle to that effect: "it is not to taste sweet things, but to do noble and true things . . . that the poorest son of Adam dimly longs." Realization of this goal, however, was precarious. If an individual could "but determine his life-purpose . . . he should *then* strike the key-note of his existence, come into sympathy with nature, and harmony with mankind." But if one's faculties were "locked up" and powers "paralyzed" when the moment of realizing one's ideal self came, "the happiest, noblest and best part" of a life might pass forever.[53] In the grip of Romanticism in her Carlylean and Emersonian phase, Addams also expressed here something of the idealism and grandiosity of youth for whom life is an all-or-nothing, now-or-never affair. She intellectualized the problem as the difficulty of being thoroughly one's self and following an individual course in the modern world, where the tendency is to "bury ourselves that much deeper under a mass of books and other men's thoughts."[54] But the language of these essays, the contrast between Savonarola's unwavering determination and the "indistinct" lives of the majority, the references to locked-up faculties and paralyzed powers, betray De Quinceyan anxieties and anticipate the years of futility and doubt she experienced following graduation. Her concern with missing out on one's best self also suggests an awareness of the problematic nature of heroic achievement.

The problem was—although she did not articulate it fully at the time—how was a woman to fit herself into such a heroic conception of greatness? On the occasions when she wrote about female destiny in college, Addams stressed what she called "force of character," the "common human force, which we know we all possess, but cannot carry out." This force was personified in Meg Merrilies, the gypsy queen in Sir Walter Scott's novel *Guy Mannering*, who, although wild and destructive, "works out . . . her own life purpose, resents all sham & pretence as something foreign to her very nature," remaining "sincere & true to herself." Accepting a widely held view that Gypsies came "nearest to the original type of man's character," and drawing as well on Carlyle's view that a hero was "simply a god-created man true to his soul," she proclaimed Meg, like all Gypsies, a genuine heroine. Although Addams considered brute force appalling, she maintained that when this force was "united to a strong will & a vigorous intellect & the whole directed to one main & definite object, we have the primary condition of greatness."[55] George Sand, too, Addams argued in debate, embodied force of character, as the first woman to speak out with the power of a man. Sand attacked the marriage system that oppressed her, expressing the longings of other women to move out of their narrow orbits. For all her superior intellect, genius, and force, Addams insisted, Sand's "soul and brain were exuberantly and splendidly feminine."[56] In the safety of essays and debates Addams could play with improbable role models. But her choice of female subjects reveals the impossibility of female heroism of this kind: her fictional and real-life examples were well outside the boundaries of respectable society. Neither was an appropriate model for an upper-middle-class Victorian woman, any more than Goethe or Savonarola.

As a student Addams seems to have accepted the generic male pronoun as a universal signifier that included her. But as the move from school to life approached, the fit between male models and female destiny became more problematic. She gave the subject serious attention in two public addresses. Delivering the opening address at Rockford's first Junior Exhibition, she attempted to join traditional female aspirations with those befitting modern college students. Women's ambition had changed in the previous half century, she observed, "from accomplishments and the arts of pleasing to the development of . . . intellectual force, and capabilities for direct labor." She reassured her audience that she and her classmates wished not to be men, or like men, but as modern women claimed "the same right to independent thought and action." The miller's daughter also urged her classmates to remain bread-givers throughout their lives: in the belief that "in labor alone is happiness, and that the only true and honorable life is one filled with good works and honest toil, we will strive to idealize our labor and thus happily fulfill woman's noblest mission."[57] Without challenging the status quo, this formulation opened the door to good works outside the home.

Addams made a bolder bid for female authority in a graduation address crafted around a Homeric subject, Cassandra, the prophetic daughter of the Trojan king who predicted the destruction of her native city by the Greeks. With "no logic to convince," Cassandra represented "pure intuition," her "tragic fate . . . always to be in the right, and always to be disbelieved and rejected." In contrasting female intuition and male knowledge, Addams publicly subscribed to the gender polarities of the era, an endorsement absent from her private writings. But "Cassandra" was no run-of-the-mill analysis. In urging that intuition be taken as seriously as its masculine counterpart, knowledge, Addams hoped to provide gifted women with a way to "make themselves intelligible." For "an intuitive mind . . . [to] attain her *auethoritas*," the right of the speaker to make herself heard, she proposed that every woman study at least one branch of physical science. Men would then see that "the intuitive seeing of Truth" is even higher than the inductive and "all that subtle force among women which is now dreaming fancy, might be changed into creative genius."[58]

Addams went on to suggest that women would be the ones to develop a larger vision: "The actual Justice must be established in the world by trained intelligence . . . only an intuitive mind has a grasp comprehensive enough to embrace the opposing facts and forces." With a woman's newly gained accuracy and "her sympathies . . . so enlarged that she can weep as easily over a famine in India as a pale child at her door, then she can face social ills and social problems as tenderly and as intuitively as she can now care for and understand a crippled factory child." In thus linking general and distant misfortunes with those that were local and known, Addams countered a belief then widely shared by both sexes that women responded only to the personal emotional appeal.[59] With this humanitarian vision, she also moved away from the harsh social Darwinism of an earlier essay, a rare offering on a contemporary subject, in which she had condemned tramps as a group that "render themselves abject & mean and merit . . . universal contempt."[60]

If Addams the student fulfilled the goals of liberal culture by drawing on an ancient story to point a moral for her own time, Addams the future activist was proposing a strategy to give women a public mission, enabling them, like men, "to do noble and true things," though not necessarily the same things. Not yet twenty-one, in 1881 she laid the basis for "trained intelligence" and for a politics of empathy, both of which would characterize women's social commitments in the Progressive era. She did not seem aware of any possible contradictions between trained intelligence and empathy, but then neither did many of her colleagues two decades later. Indeed, Addams seemed to be arguing that an intuition grounded in science could provide the synthesis that would incorporate both thesis and antithesis.

Addams's suggestion that studying science would enhance women's authority may strike us as odd, but it paralleled a growing interest in the subject that peaked during her senior year. Encouraged by her stepbrother, she was preparing for a career in medicine, one of the few professions then open to women.[61] She was impressed too with the view of T. H. Huxley and other scientists that observation of the natural world enabled humans to see "things exactly as they are" and to improve their "capacities as thinking beings to the uttermost."[62] In this way, her interest in scientific training was linked to her doubts about the value of reading.[63] Although she still hoped to be "in contact with *genius* in any form it may present itself," in her new scientific mood she mocked her earlier zeal for Carlylean hero worship, proclaiming to Ellen Starr a few months before graduation: "Don't flatter yourself that I agree with you in your latent vein of hero-worship, I don't, I would rather get my inspiration from a dodecahedral crystal than even [from] a genius because it would take a stronger mind to see a principle embodied by cohesion than embodied by vital personal force."[64]

A similar emphasis on original discovery came into her disparagement of book learning. She could be positively fierce on the subject: "I am sort of disgusted with general reading, it seems to me it weakens, you read a great many things you would find out yourself, if you would take it . . . and wait, my admiration for a well-read person is mingled with just a little bit of contempt that he had to *read* to find out all about it."[65] Most pathetic were the "compilers" (among whom she included ancient priests, medieval monks, Confucian scholars, as well as the contemporary "high priests of Science"), individuals who began with the hope of adding to knowledge but who lost their creativity and produced nothing.[66] In an editorial in the *Rockford Seminary Magazine* published shortly before graduation, she reminded her classmates of Emerson's description of the brilliant college men who "promise such great things" but who fail later in life: "they show a brilliancy not their own, mingling for four years with the best of books and cultured people, they acquire an enthusiasm and force not their's . . . they possess not individual silent resources."[67] Addams's preoccupation with this subject suggests not only the extent of her ambition but her fear of failure. In none of her essays or letters did she exempt herself because of her gender.

Whatever criticisms she made of literary culture, as a sheltered young woman of her era Addams had few other places to turn for experience. An aspiring intellectual for whom the classroom and formal study were only starting points, she read widely and kept up with the latest intellectual debates, including the respective merits of the scientific and cultural approaches to education represented by Huxley and Arnold.[68] She later mocked her "serious not to say priggish tendency," but she earned singular respect from faculty as well as students for her intellect and her reflective nature.[69]

As if to establish her credentials as an adult, Addams turned away from the reading pleasures of her youth, gender-marked pleasures that her father tried to hold in check. Disposed to take the literary high ground, she looked to the arbiters of culture who equated reading with self-improvement. She apologized for beginning a biography with the "sordid" purpose of clearing up the mystery of the Medici and in an editorial in the *Rockford Seminary Magazine* urged her schoolmates to avoid reading "trash." When she acknowledged that she enjoyed an occasional novel some years later, she seemed to consider it a "weakness."[70]

Addams's struggle with the cultural self-absorption she later condemned was already marked in college. She contrasted genuine culture with self-culture, a term that for many carried positive connotations of self-improvement, but one she seems to have used only pejoratively. Normally unresponsive to "the evangelical appeal," Addams was impressed by the cultural breadth of a missionary who addressed Rockford students in 1879 on "The relation between true culture & the missionary work":

But the idea that impressed me most was the breadth it [culture] gave you, just think . . . of having expansiveness of soul enough to pray, actually pray for a South African, a man barbarous & brutal you never expect to see him, he speaks a different language from your own, coarse & uncouth, he seems like an animal and yet you can honestly pray for him, you will be great, cultured in a free sense, it sort of opens to me a possibility that I never thought of before.

She feared that "praying for that man seems a[n] utter impossibility ... I think I am doomed to reach on toward self culture."[71]

The racial and cultural stereotyping of the passage is probably what most strikes the modern reader. Beyond the blatant racism, Addams's wish that she could "actually pray" for the "barbarous & brutal" man demonstrates a concern for the inadequacy of her own response rather than for the South African as an individual, let alone for the salvation of his soul. Yet the pressing desire to move beyond her own limitations was exceptional for a privileged young white woman of her era. Her lament suggests that for Addams genuine culture required "expansiveness of soul" and a breadth of concern for all humanity far removed from the sort of culture that turned a person in on oneself, of which she accused herself. But she did not see a way of reaching it at the time.[72]

Except for the Cassandra address, during her college years Addams held for the most part to an individualistic model of achievement, a paradigm of spectacular greatness. But she identified more mundane sources of strength in humbler souls as well as in individuals like King Arthur and Leonardo da Vinci. Neither hero nor genius, she believed, each man possessed a certain "magnificence of character" extracted "from the experience and thought which most men already possess." Unlike those who are threats to society, each "illuminates & beautifys [sic] the things around him until the world has a new value in the eyes of all who study him." The hearts of such individuals, she wrote, "lay wide open to take in strength & cheer from a hundred connections, they seem kindled with the blaze of active world wide emotions, there is no need to them to cherish faded flowers or expend their love on fancies or ideals; things livelier hold their souls, they look in the face of each man as if a community of feeling lay between."[73] Addams's use of feminine-coded rhetoric (faded flowers, fancies, emotions) for these men of magnificent character is suggestive. So is her emphasis on the community of feeling they engendered. This formulation hints at the path she later carved out for herself. So does her suggestion to a schoolmate of her "idea of the power of *being* great—and good without doing striking things."[74] Just as she was to leave self-culture behind, when she entered history, she found her own way of doing so.

The story of Addams's postcollege years has been told many times, never better than by Addams herself. In reviewing her early life, she focused on the debilitating effect of her single-minded pursuit of culture. In the vignettes and parables that were her literary trademark, she constructed a compelling narrative of her triumph over uncertainty and despair that came with the decision to found Hull-House.[75] Extrapolating from her own situation to that of other women of her class, Addams analyzed the inability of educated young women to find an honorable public sphere of action. She believed that many daughters, propelled by "the social claim," felt accountable to society at large, while their families still expected them to discharge the traditional obligations of "the family claim."[76] It was one of her most compelling insights.

Addams's personal narrative and her analysis of the dilemma facing her female contemporaries were both closely bound up with her critique of the literary culture in which she grew up. In *Twenty Years at Hull-House* she convincingly conveyed the desultory quality of the life of a privileged young woman whose only responsibility was cultivation of the self. That sort of life was self-destructive, she believed: an exclusive diet of culture was like eating "a sweet dessert the first thing in the morning."[77] Pointing to this period of her life as one of both surfeit (of culture and privilege) and deficit (of purposeful activity), Addams's critique of culture is at one with her larger analysis of the core problem of modern urban life: the division of classes into haves and have-nots and the lack of connection between them. Her analysis was thus a critique of contemporary class as well as gender arrangements. Those with leisure, men as well as women, too often acquired a sense of their own superiority by virtue of their cultural attainments and kept aloof from those they deemed deficient in this as in other regards. Believing that many felt a need to connect to a broader humanity, as she did, Addams offered them a way to do so through her settlement.

In fact, Addams's cultural studies played an important part in her route to Hull-House. If they seemed to perpetuate the troubling division between thought and action, she eventually found a way to integrate them into a rich vision of community, first in imagination, then in life. As the heroes and geniuses of her schoolgirl essays ceased to answer, she sought other models of how to be in the world. Culture was the ground on which she worked out her search for personal effectiveness. In its pursuit, she discovered poverty: the contrast between her own situation and that of the poor provided a major impetus for what became her life's work.

Addams's life changed dramatically two months after graduation when her father died without warning. She had looked to him for her moral purpose, and without him she felt painfully adrift. The following spring her vocation too vanished—with no evident regret—when she dropped out of the Woman's Medical College of Pennsylvania because of "the development of the spinal difficulty which had shadowed [her] from childhood" (probably tuberculosis). Following a surgical procedure and several months of recuperation, when she was "literally bound to a bed," she spent nearly two years in Europe, a remedy prescribed by her doctor.[78] Anticipating negative consequences, she wrote Starr: "I quite feel as if I were not 'following the call of my genius' when I propose to devote two years['] time to travel in search of a good time and this general idea of culture which some way never commanded my full respect. People complain of losing spiritual life when abroad. I imagine it will be quite as hard to hold to full earnestness of purpose."[79] Despite the self-mocking reference to her genius, her palpable anxiety about her spiritual life and goals indicates that the stakes were high.

For all her disapproval of general culture, Addams had two lengthy stays in Europe punctuated by self-improving activities in the States. On the first European trip—a grand tour that lasted nearly two years (1883–85)—her party took in Scotland, England, Holland, Italy, Switzerland, Greece, and France, settling down for two months in Berlin, where they studied German and also some French. They were not the first or last tourists to discover that travel was hard work. Loaded with tour guides and art books, they "read up" on the places they visited. Acknowledging that she sometimes found it difficult to get into the spirit of a place, Addams informed her sister, "There is no use in going to see things until you have a little previous knowledge."[80] The party followed a fairly conventional itinerary, visiting the homes of prominent writers and the places made famous by them, taking in museums and galleries, castles and cathedrals, attending lectures and operas. Addams bought reproductions of favorite works of art.

Along with the standard tourist sights and the thrill of seeing such iconic works of art as the Elgin marbles and Raphael's Sistine Madonna, Addams's European travels brought her face to face with extreme poverty, something she had not previously encountered except in books. There was plenty of poverty in the United States, but as an upper-middle-class young woman who had grown up in the village of Cedarville, she had been largely sheltered from it. Poverty was harder to miss in Europe's large cities, although many travelers undoubtedly turned away from its uglier manifestations. But

Addams was a keen observer, and her letters interspersed anxious comments about "appalling" ragged children in London and beggars in Italy with the more conventional accounts of a cultural tourist.

One of the most disturbing encounters took place in Saxe-Coburg, Bavaria, three months after the East London market episode that prompted her meditations on De Quincey. From her hotel, she observed a file of women carrying heavy vats of hot beer on their backs, their faces and hands scarred from the overflow: for fourteen hours a day at this work they received just 37½ cents. Addams later claimed that she tried (and failed) to move the brewery owner out of his indifference; at the time she observed that "it became positively painful and we were glad to get away." Disillusioned because Saxe-Coburg was the birthplace of Britain's philanthropically inclined Prince Albert, she recorded in her diary that she was "impressed with the powerlessness of *one* man to do anything. Prince Albert tried so hard [yet?] here was all this misery and hopeless work." Her dismay at the inability of even a prince to effect change suggests Addams's continued preoccupation with how to make her own life count.[81]

If Addams hoped to intervene in the present, she also needed to establish a direct connection with the past (or with a work of art she was viewing), to take from it not just "the best" but something that would be a useful guide. In getting to know each city, she and her companions began with the "great man" approach, initially focusing on "three or four men, or at least in a generation or two." And then there was Rome. Addams initially felt oppressed by "the amount of history and wickedness that every spot holds . . . & every thing is in the great *Past*."[82] But the vast and deep historical canvas before her produced a sense of finitude that, somewhat paradoxically, strengthened her desire to move beyond exclusive ties to connect with a broader humanity. As she wrote her Latin and Greek teacher:

Rome was like the history of the world itself, no one man was of sufficient account to have made any difference, and each spot of ground had been lived over four or five times and was covered with at least three layers of ruins. It was at first confusing and depressing, but a little familiarity . . . produced an affection and proprietorship as I haven't felt anywhere since I left home. Maybe it is because you see that the ground even can not belong long to any one association, that you feel your broader relationship with the human race as you never were in circumstances to see it before. It makes an impression—

a difference in my own life—as any history I had ever read before never did.[83]

This was a sharp departure from Carlylean individualism and hero worship.

In trying to connect to all that was human, past as well as present, Addams sounded themes advanced by Auguste Comte, the founder of Positivism. Comte's all-encompassing theory of society and history highlighted science and empirical knowledge but also pointed the way to a more humane future in which what he called the "Religion of Humanity" would replace traditional forms of worship and when reason, feeling, and action would be in harmony. Two central premises permeated this religion without a deity: the solidarity (and interdependence) of humanity and the continuity of human life past, present, and future. Comte's ideas influenced many British intellectuals, some of whom even set up a Positivist Church—two of them in fact, since adherents disagreed about liturgy.[84] Addams later noted her interest in Positivism during her European years, specifically in connection with her second trip (December 1887–June 1888). But her comments on establishing a broader relationship with humanity suggest that she had an earlier acquaintance with these ideas, which were widely debated in England, her spiritual home.[85]

George Eliot was one of the British intellectuals most influenced by Comte. Although she did not accept his system of worship, she incorporated many of his ideas into her fiction, often quite self-consciously. While preparing for her Florentine novel, *Romola*, she read the section on the Middle Ages in Comte's *Cours de Philosophie Positive*, of which she wrote: "few chapters can be fuller of luminous ideas."[86] *Romola* has been interpreted as a Positivist allegory in which the heroine moves from egoism to altruism, through the three historical stages posited by Comte, represented by ancient polytheism, medieval Catholicism, and finally the Religion of Humanity, when Romola appears as a madonna-like figure who ministers to the poor and outcast during a raging epidemic.[87]

When Addams in Rome expressed her desire to connect with a broader humanity, she had just reread *Romola*. Whether or not she read it as an explicitly Positivist allegory, its message affected her deeply.[88] She began the book in Florence, she informed Starr, "for the identification of the places but after all the story is the main and absorbing interest and the moral comes with more force than ever that 'ties are not to be disregarded.'"[89] The novel's heroine struggled with this issue: loyalty to a corrupt and deceitful husband? to Savonarola, whom Addams once called "an *incarnate idea*" and whose unyielding approach threatened the separation of spiritual and temporal endeavors? to humanity in need? The ties Addams had in mind would have included those to the blended Addams and Haldeman families that proved so draining during these years.[90] But there were also the broader ties to humanity sanctioned by George Eliot, the ties that Addams later called "the social claim." When Addams observed some months later that George Eliot's books "give me more *motive* power than any other books I read," it is likely she had in mind the incentive they gave her to act on this larger claim.[91]

Addams's growing need for the kind of human connection personified by George Eliot's heroine may cast light on her critical appraisal of Michelangelo's "Night and Day" at the Tomb of the Medici in Florence. Where once she had been awed by the artist's genius (and considered all genius the same), she now questioned the value of this massive, unfinished sculpture. She recognized the power of the figures, but found them "perfectly incomprehensible" and therefore not attractive: "The amount of *mind* that a master spirit or genius I suppose Michael Angelo was, can put into a figure of marble so that it constantly emanates and expresses always makes you wonder and speculate. Although of course the amount of use and good accomplished by the same is another question."[92] Seeing no moral in this work and applying similar criteria of utility to the artist's creation as to her own life, Addams's assessment pointed toward a view of culture later endorsed by Pragmatist philosophers, one to which she contributed.

Despite the hard work and intensity of foreign travel, Addams held up well. More difficult was the time in the United States, where family crises loomed and her own lack of purpose became apparent. Between European trips she and her stepmother spent two winters in Baltimore, where George Haldeman was studying biology at Johns Hopkins University. There Addams had her first introduction to "society," with ladies calling who wore hats and gloves; she also encountered southern views on slavery and disapproval of women's higher education. Taking up the expected cultural pursuits, during the first Baltimore winter she took French lessons, attended "about a lecture a day," and read Ruskin's *Modern Painters* and other substantial works.[93] The second winter, in addition to belonging to "sort of a little German club" that read novels and an art club in which she acquired a reputation for knowing more than she thought she did, she attended Dante readings, a lecture series on evolution by Alfred Wallace, co-discoverer of evolution, and another on Roman archaeology.[94] She also took "a definite course of reading" on United Italy, a movement associated with Mazzini (and thus her father). Guided by a lecturer at Johns Hopkins, she claimed in *Twenty Years* that it "was a source of great comfort to me," despite her disillusionment "at this time as to the effect of intellectual pursuits upon moral development."[95]

Addams called the winters in Baltimore "the nadir of my nervous depression and sense of maladjustment," a judgment supported by contemporary evidence.[96] During the first winter, she declared in a De Quinceyan vein, "I am filled with shame that with all my apparent leisure I do nothing at all. . . . Since I have been in Baltimore, I have found my faculties, memory[,] receptive faculties and all, perfectly inaccessible[,] locked up away from me."[97] The second winter was better: she enjoyed volunteer work at "an orphan asylum for colored little girls," her interest in religion took a more serious turn, and she left Baltimore and her stepfamily early.[98]

There remained the troubling issue of what she and other educated women were to do with their lives. In a dispirited talk she delivered at Rockford College in October 1887 on "Our debts; and how shall we pay them," Addams feared that women of her generation were on "the verge of insolvency" because they had undertaken tasks beyond their means. She offered various explanations, among them taking "our long withheld classics and mathematics too seriously" and becoming "a trifle morbid" in conscience and "a little over zealous for action" in trying to live up to Carlyle's admonition "to do 'noble and true things.'" Intellectual life was difficult, she observed: "It is said that Goethe was the only modern who wielded his immense panoply of learning with ease. It may also require absolute *genius* . . . to satisfy the demands of the enlightened & cultivated conscience." She feared that women would be "overwhelmed & paralyzed by the enormity of our debt, if we continue to cultivate our sense of responsibility, our perception of duty. Imagine the chagrin of the knight who was defeated because his armor was too heavy."[99] Struggling to find a way to act on her conscience, Addams still drew on the rhetoric of individualism, genius, and heroes.

Less than three months later she was back in Europe on a trip that included visits to numerous Christian sites. In a rare solitary excursion around New Year's Day 1888, Addams stopped off at a large Gothic cathedral in Ulm in southern Germany. She later visited others in France and England, as well as Germany, some of which moved her greatly.[100] But at Ulm she had an epiphany. In the inspiring vision of common humanity she experienced there and in subsequent reflections, she arrived at a creative synthesis of her cultural studies with her moral and religious concerns. It was a Positivist vision, a synthesis of past and present and of diverse tiers of humanity that was based on her readings of art and architecture.

A passionate eleven-page letter to a childhood friend from the usually guarded Addams bears witness to the event. It was in fact her second attempt to communicate the experience—the first she considered "exaggerated" and had not sent—and it would be her last: she would "never write the Cathedral again." She was at once awed by the cathedral's external grandeur and heartened by the deep humanity of its interior wooden statues, among them St. Christopher under the tabernacle, portrayed as a "big blundering man, with a fatherly solicitude for the tiny baby on his shoulder," and, in the choir stalls, an "exceptionally fine head of Cicero" and "Socrates with his poor nose, (how do you suppose a poor Swabian artist . . . knew about them").[101]

She was most delighted with the choir stall carvings, the heads of Greek and Roman philosophers on the chairs, above the stalls "the men of the old Testament and still above the apostles and men of the new." On the other side were the women, "and it was something for the early Germans to give so much place to 'die Frauen.'" These included several striking wooden sibyls (female prophets) as well as women of the Old and New Testaments. Addams, who was correct in judging the presence of so many women unusual, was pleased that, with an occasional hint from her guide, she recognized all the biblical women. Writing about the experience in *Twenty Years*, she observed: "The religious history carved on the choir stalls at Ulm contained Greek philosophers as well as Hebrew prophets, and among the disciples and saints stood the discoverer of music and a builder of pagan temples."[102] In other words, Christians and pagans, the sacred and the secular, the New Testament and the Old, women as well as men—all united in one place of worship. The cathedral bore witness to the history of the German Reformation as well, for it included a representation of Luther offering his protest at Wittenberg. This at first surprised her—she had forgotten it was a Protestant church—but in the end

[it] did not seem incongruous, it was part of the same church history. After all the saints are but the embodiment of *fine* action, the history so to speak of the inner church of the Holy Ghost, which we eagerly seize upon wherever it appears and perpetuate in stone and glass, anything that will *last*. There is no doubt that *that* is what we are all trying to do, and curiously enough Matthew Arnold's idea of culture came to me so often, only that this criticism of life was contained in stone and wood rather than literature.[103]

She later claimed that her vision of unity was influenced by the Positivist view that medieval cathedrals offered the final synthesis before the Religion

of Humanity, indeed that she had come to Ulm looking for just such a revelation. Characteristically, she mocked the enthusiasm that had prompted her
to record in her "smug notebook" many "ill-digested phrases from Comte,"
among them "my hope for a 'cathedral of humanity,' which would be 'capa-
cious enough to house a fellowship of common purpose' and which should
be 'beautiful enough to persuade men to hold fast to the vision of human
solidarity.'"[104] Her retrospective dismissal scarcely does justice to the creative
insight she experienced at Ulm.

The rapturous experience did not end in the cathedral but carried over
into passionate reflections recorded in the same letter in which she reworked
the heroic theme that once preoccupied her. After noting that she and Starr
had been admiring Albrecht Dürer's drawings, Addams exclaimed:

> I *believe* that Tolstoi is right, that the *Right* never accomplishes itself
> spectacularly, that it was due to people like Dürer rather than Luther,
> than the Reformation that the turning back to the good came about.
> You know the German proverb that the good is the greatest enemy of
> the best. I think that Luther, Erasmus and the rest of them were *good*
> but that the best was being done quietly, and is always being done in
> that way, not often so clearly as Dürer makes it. His knights are not
> fighting and look as if they realized how useless it was—that it must
> come in another way, and they are ready to try it . . . with an insight
> that they have the truth.

Addams, too, at this moment of cultural integration, arrived at a truth that
would permit her to accomplish good in her own way. It was a way that, like
Dürer's knights and Tolstoy's renunciation of coercive force, would be neither spectacular nor heroic, but quiet and nonconfrontational. This was true
not only of her work for social justice but of her adherence to pacifism, most
notably in her opposition to the Spanish-American War and to the United
States' entry into World War I.

By the time she visited Ulm, Addams was already an attentive reader of
Tolstoy's nonfiction. She had admired *My Religion*, a work that elucidated
the author's literal interpretation of the New Testament, beginning with his
conviction that when Jesus said, "That ye resist not evil," he meant this absolutely. The message she took from it was so deeply etched in her psyche that
twenty-three years later, in language echoing that of the Ulm letter, Addams
identified *My Religion* as the book that had convinced her "once for all . . .
that the Right will not accomplish itself spectacularly, but must be the sum

of all men's poor little efforts to do right, accomplished, for the most part, in the chill of self-distrust."[105] When she visited Ulm, she may have read Tolstoy's *What to Do Then*, a book that also bears on her epiphany—and on her settlement work—in its rejection of traditional attempts to alleviate poverty in Russia in favor of efforts to enter into genuine and sustained relationships with the poor. Recognizing the futility of his charitable efforts, Tolstoy concluded that he must change his own life if he wanted to eliminate the barriers between himself and others. Years later, in an article entitled "A Book That Changed My Life," Addams wrote of her "vivid religious reaction" to *What to Do Then*, a statement, she observed, equally as true of *My Religion*.[106]

Her appreciation of Dürer reflects a growing interest in art following her first European trip, in particular the influence of John Ruskin's *Modern Painters*, which she read in the winter of 1886. The following summer, she referred to Ruskin's discussion of "Dürer's connection with the Reformation and the two kinds of religious despair" in the late fifteenth century, when people began to question their faith.[107] Ruskin contrasted the "gross and terrible" representations of the Calabrian artist Salvator Rosa with the "patient hope" Dürer offered in the face of the disturbances of the time (including a prevalent fear of death), which he attributed to the "quaint domesticity" of Nuremberg, the artist's home city.[108] Addams's belief that Dürer did more good than his younger contemporary, Luther, suggests her preference for gentler solutions to social problems—his knights were not fighting—over Luther's confrontational approach. It is possible, too, that she was intimating that art might have a powerful role in changing consciousness, a view she later advanced with great force.

Addams's creative synthesis of her cultural studies with her moral and religious concerns in her illumination at Ulm and immediately after produced the harmony and insight Matthew Arnold believed culture should bring. If the road to this moment was arduous, the resolution was brilliant—a sign of how fruitful reading could be to the mind prepared. It was also an act of personal integration that foretold not only her commitment to pacifism but the nature of her own future leadership. Altogether it was a solution close to her earlier "idea of the power of *being* great—and good without doing striking things," that is, an acceptable and understated "woman's" way of being.

Addams remained in Europe another six months. She visited many Christian sites, including Byzantine mosaics in Ravenna, catacombs in Rome, more Gothic cathedrals, as well as the Italian parliament in Rome (where she made a point of observing the "bread riots") and a bullfight in Spain.[109]

Toward the end of her stay, she visited Toynbee Hall, the pioneering settlement in London's East End, where she observed the efforts of upper-class men to bridge class barriers by living among the poor. Eighteen months after returning to the United States, she and Ellen Gates Starr established Hull-House. The words in which Addams explained their mission signaled both a coming together of her life and a first step into history, quiet perhaps, but with long and deep reverberations. If her approach did not make her into a heroic figure in the Carlylean vein, she had found a way to fulfill her large ambition, even to become a heroine worthy of emulation.

PART THREE

READING WITHOUT PRIVILEGE

· ·

· ·

CHAPTER SEVEN

Hull-House as a Cultural Space

When Jane Addams and Ellen Gates Starr took up residence at 335 Halsted Street in Chicago in September 1889, they hoped that by sharing their lives with their mainly immigrant neighbors they would find ways to help bridge the gulf between the city's haves and have-nots. That gulf was wide: just three years earlier the Haymarket Affair (which began as a rally for the eight-hour day, spiraled out of control when a bomb killed several policemen, and ended with the execution of several anarchists) frightened Chicagoans into visions of apocalyptic class warfare. The women's initiative in founding one of the first settlement houses proved to be a harbinger of one of the great social movements of the age: by 1900, there were more than 100 settlements in the United States.

As they established themselves in their new home in a deteriorating neighborhood on Chicago's West Side, the founders built on ideas and programs developed at Toynbee Hall, where British university men sought to establish closer connections with the local population. The guiding principle was that only through personal example could those who were well-off have an impact on the disadvantaged; the prevailing method was educational.[1] To the British model, Hull-House gave a decidedly feminine turn. Where Toynbee Hall residents were all men (many of them clerics and civil servants), most residents of Hull-House were women who, initially at least, lacked specific vocations. The distinction between a Hall and a House was more than semantic. Toynbee Hall, with its formal connotations and classroom for 300, presented an imposing public face suggestive of a British university. Headed by two women rather than a clergyman, freestanding rather than university-connected, Hull-House hinted at cozier arrangements. Addams took great pleasure in restoring and furnishing the dilapidated mansion: "Probably no young matron ever placed her own things in her own house with more pleasure than that with which we first furnished Hull-House."[2] The new abode, like the way of life it augured, suited her: she remained there until her death in 1935.

Under Addams's leadership, Hull-House became the nation's foremost settlement, famous for its campaigns against sweatshops, child labor, and industrial diseases that began in the neighborhood and often spread to city, state, and nation. Historians have recently recognized the importance of women's contributions to progressive reform, but their cultural and educational work has been largely overlooked.[3] Yet the cultural mission of Hull-House was enshrined in its charter and fit Addams's belief in women's special responsibility in these matters as well.[4]

Like other institutions with a mission to improve the lives of the underprivileged, Hull-House became a sponsor of culture, a term used here to include educational and cultural ventures designed to extend the intellectual and social horizons of local inhabitants.[5] The expansion of the original mansion to thirteen buildings occupying a full city block gave visual testimony to the settlement's cultural reach. At its peak it encompassed three formal theater groups, art and music schools, a women's symphony orchestra, a chorus of 500 "working people," and clubs of every description, not to mention girls' and boys' basketball teams.

The founders initially took great pride in the adult education classes devoted to Shakespeare, Robert Browning, and other writers they admired. Good Arnoldian that she was, Addams was a firm believer in culture's uplifting, universalizing, and ultimately humanizing powers.[6] Exposure to culture, by enlarging emotional and aesthetic sensibilities, bringing a person's entire resources into play, could help individuals transcend the limits of their immediate circumstances. Although Addams rarely said so explicitly, this view was rooted in the assumption that culture could incorporate the underprivileged, whether native-born or immigrant, into a framework that was middle-class in values if not in material possessions.

Addams began with a commitment to the democratic distribution of culture, often quoting Mazzini: "Education is not merely a necessity of true life by which the individual renews his vital force in the vital force of humanity; it is a Holy Communion with generations of dead and living, by which he fecundates all his faculties." In contrast to those who assumed that the Italian peasant, like others without formal training, was "like a beast of the field" and who thought it "absurd" or even "immoral" to offer instruction, Addams believed that everyone could benefit by "participation in the best of the past"—and deserved to do so.[7] Convinced too that the American working class suffered more severely from spiritual than from economic desolation, she held that the harmony produced by beautiful pictures on the walls, the pleasures and benefits of exercising one's mental faculties, the broadening of social outlook beyond self and family would provide solace and imaginative stimulus.[8]

Addams included men and especially women of privilege as beneficiaries of the settlement's cultural programs. The relationship, like the benefits, was to be reciprocal. Modern urban life damaged those at both ends of the social spectrum, and if the handicaps of the poor were glaringly obvious, she knew from her own experience that educated men and especially women too often led "unnourished, over-sensitive lives" devoid of useful purpose. The goal, in either case, was "to make life more worth living."[9] Institutionally, the settlement provided a structured means by which the culturally advantaged could share their knowledge and enthusiasm with those lacking in opportunity. In the neighborly context of settlement life, leading a literary club or teaching classes on Shakespeare, like those on basic English, became a means of bridging the gulf between rich and poor just as surely as inspecting factories and making sure the garbage was collected.

How did such an ambitious and idealistic program work in practice? Cross-class ventures carry opportunities for misunderstanding as well as for fellowship, particularly in view of likely differences in goals and expectations and the disparities in power between giver and receiver. In view of the scarcity of recorded working-class responses and their frequent filtering through middle-class mediators, it is impossible to reconstruct these cultural interchanges definitively. But despite gaps in the historical record, we do know something about the activities that drew people, thanks to the formal notices, bulletins, and yearbooks published by the settlement over the years, as well as Addams's writings, observations by other residents, and occasional firsthand accounts by visitors from the neighborhood.[10]

Addams was the keenest observer of all. Despite her vested interest in the outcome, she tended to play down the settlement's achievements rather than boast about them. To keep herself honest, she made a point of taking a local inhabitant with her when she spoke in Chicago. A woman of broad intellect and keen observational powers, she brought exceptional empathy to the task

Jane Addams, ca. 1888–92. Jane
Addams Collection, Swarthmore
College Peace Collection.

at hand. Even as she became world famous, she worked hard at keeping alive
the personal, neighborly touch that had been her starting point. What she
observed prompted her to change her mind about the kind of culture the
settlement offered, but she never doubted its importance.

.   .   .   .

The founders hoped for much from their small beginning. With characteristic American optimism, and perhaps too a certain womanly awareness of the
improvisational nature of so many social interactions, Addams believed that
she and Starr would discover what needed to be done by being on the spot.
They and the mainly female residents who joined them began by performing
simple acts of neighborly kindness, such as delivering the baby of an unmarried mother shunned by her acquaintances. More formal programs emerged
with amazing rapidity. The first success was a kindergarten that began when
mothers dropped off their children on the way to work. Within a month
of the settlement's founding, a volunteer arrived to supervise the endeavor
which was attended by twenty-four children, "about half of them Italians,
and the others poor children whose mothers 'work out' most of the day"; a
waiting list of seventy attested to the need.[11] Other early ventures included
boys' clubs (Addams and Starr each took one), girls' clubs, a women's club,
a social science club for men featuring lectures on controversial economic
and political topics, a drawing class taught by a paid instructor, a mandolin

club, concerts, and lectures on Arnold Toynbee, Giotto, and insects, among other subjects. There were also regular evening receptions for Germans and Italians at which educated young women could make use of their language skills—a particular interest of Starr's.

Many activities had a literary slant. In the first few weeks, a volunteer organized a Home Library Association based on a Boston plan, "with ten books and ten children in a circle"; an entry in Addams's diary suggests that the circle readers were "Little Girls."[12] The founders loaned out books, a practice that evolved into a small library maintained by the city's public system; in time its reading room served as a congregating place for foreign-born men eager to read newspapers and periodicals in their native tongues.[13] An elderly woman who had lived at Brook Farm gave talks on the utopian community and on Hawthorne during the month she stayed at the house. Public readings, including a series from *Julius Caesar*, proved popular. A group of "Shakespeare boys" met regularly.

Of the first year's culture programs, the one nearest the hearts of the founders was the "*Romola* class" (sometimes "club"), an informal reading group organized around George Eliot's difficult historical novel set in Renaissance Florence. As is all too common in the case of historical subjects who leave no paper trail, there is no firsthand information about what the young women who attended the sessions thought about them. Addams's diary and her retrospective account in *Twenty Years at Hull-House* provide intriguing hints even as they raise absorbing questions. Responding to an initiative by Starr, a group of young women from the neighborhood "met as guests of the residents" between November and May, on a weekly or biweekly basis.[14] Some historians have assumed that the guests were women from southern Italy who presumably listened to the novel in Italian translation.[15] The evidence suggests otherwise. Insofar as Addams recorded them, the names of the unmarried and most likely young women who listened to *Romola* suggest predominantly old American or Irish American origins: the Misses Proser, Kerr, Duffy, Sullivan, Anderson, and "two Miss Scannones." Their names identify them as "Old Settlers," the early residents of the neighborhood who were beginning to leave as Italians, Russian Jews, Greeks, and Bulgarians pressed in upon them.

The class gave the founders an opportunity to offer cultural enrichment in an informal setting to young women with little access to "the higher life." Sessions centered on Starr's reading aloud. Other kinds of performances occasionally supplemented the readings, including a talk in late January by a Mrs. Mariotti. Addams reported a "beautiful social spirit" at a session at which a Miss Rhea sang. The group addressed substantive issues on at least one occasion, when it "discussed Geo. Eliot's marriage"—the only subject mentioned in Addams's diary. Was it the author's brief marriage to a much younger man shortly before her death or her long liaison with critic G. H. Lewes that engaged them? The record is silent.[16]

There was more to the *Romola* evenings than the sessions themselves, which took place in a "little upstairs dining room." According to Addams, "two members of the club came to dinner each week, not only that they might be received as guests, but that they might help us wash the dishes afterward and so make the table ready for the stacks of Florentine photographs."[17] This passage raises difficult questions about cross-class interactions and their potential for awkwardness and manipulation. With its oriental rugs, stately furniture, fine etchings, and watercolors, Hull-House was an imposing setting for young women whose families may have been on the edge of genteel poverty or below. Did the dish-washing dinner guests view the arrangement as a fair exchange of services or as relegation to the category of "help"? Did they consider the opportunity to dine in elegant surroundings a treat or feel constrained by class hierarchies, however politely invoked? Did they feel welcomed or discomfited by the proffered intimacy of the founders, whose cultural and class superiority would not have escaped them? In other contexts, accounts by working-class members of the Women's Trade Union League and by immigrant writer Anzia Yezierska, who resented being steered into domestic science by patrons when she wanted to be a writer, suggest that working-class women often felt ill at ease with their would-be patrons.[18]

Although the historical record is silent about the reactions of the women who attended, other testimony indicates that neighborhood visitors often found their associations with Addams and Starr friendly, at times even inspiring. Years after she first came to Hull-House as a young factory worker, Hilda Satt Polacheck observed, "Jane Addams was never condescending to anyone. She never made one feel that she was a 'lady bountiful.' She never made one feel that she was doling out charity. When she did something for you, you felt she owed it to you or that she was making a loan that you could pay back." Although some Hull-House residents described Addams as "impersonal"—an intended compliment—Polacheck, who was Jewish and initially feared attending a Christmas party at the settlement, experienced her support as decidedly empathic. She reminisced about an occasion when "Miss Addams, with her infinite patience, sat there holding my hand. I know she was living through my thoughts."[19]

Starr, outspoken where Addams was restrained, may have been more accessible to working-class neighbors. Abraham Bisno, a Jewish union leader and a socialist, recalled his private lessons in reading, writing, and arithmetic with Starr several hours a week as well as their heated discussions of the labor movement and politics: "She was a great comrade, very sensitively honest, wonderfully well bred, and as true as they make them." The tough-minded immigrant was astounded by his experiences with residents in the 1890s: "My acquaintance with the people at Hull House was an eye-opener to me. People who did not belong to our class took an interest in our lot in life. This was very new to me."[20]

It is even more difficult to conjecture what members of the first reading group thought of the novel than how they might have responded to their hosts. Addams later claimed that the reading party "was attended by a group of young women who followed the wonderful tale with unflagging interest."[21] Can we be sure? Addams's pocket diary includes brief comments like "good" and "very nice Romola evening." Not every evening went so well. At least one session was cancelled because of rain. Only two guests showed up on one occasion, on another, the *Romola* evening seems to have "[failed?] because of 'beau night.'"[22] Generally considered one of George Eliot's most difficult works, *Romola* is set in 1490s Florence, a time of turmoil brought about by the efforts of the religious reformer Savonarola to bring moral regeneration to the city. Henry James called it "a splendid mausoleum," while another reviewer observed, "As a novel, 'Romola' cannot be called entertaining: it requires sustained attention, and it is by no means light reading."[23] Saturated with philosophical discourse and details of political intrigue, the novel is a far cry from the popular romances of Laura Jean Libbey that working-class women favored. In devising a disastrous marriage from which the heroine ultimately flees to take up a life of service to humanity, *Romola* also defies the conventionally happy ending anticipated by young novel readers. It is not a work women from the neighborhood would have chosen on their own; most likely they had never heard of it.

Still, difficulty and lack of familiarity need not have prevented enjoyment. Even if they had never before listened to a long, let alone difficult, novel read aloud, the visitors might well have responded to the excitement of the story, with the harrowing twists and turns of a plot that included betrayals, adultery, and burning at the stake. (Starr must have skipped and summarized judiciously.) Moreover, whatever their initial level of interest or comprehension, they were in the presence of a vivid personality and dramatic reader: Starr elicited powerful emotional responses that marked some of her students for life. A Scottish immigrant active in the Woman's Club, recalling her encounters with Starr, first in the Shakespeare class ("I just felt all the evening that I must find some way to hear you again"), and then in Browning, observed: "My life would look bare indeed if the memory of those evenings spent with you were taken out of it."[24]

Whatever they thought of *Romola*, it is unlikely that listeners' reactions depended solely on their appreciation of the story—or lack thereof. Taking into consideration the gracious dining, the unaccustomed surroundings, and the attentions of two women from another station in life, one of them something of a spellbinder—not to mention the opportunity to spend an evening away from home in the company of friends—the *Romola* evenings may been memorable for the guests, although not necessarily for the reasons the founders intended. The young women may well have enjoyed the ambience above and beyond what they took from the novel, much as Jessie Hamilton took pleasure in family readings of *The French Revolution*, even though she was not enamored of Carlyle.

If the choice of *Romola* seemed odd to the young visitors, the selection of this signature work, like the ritual of the reading party itself, reaffirmed the bonds between the two young women as they launched their "untried experiment." For Addams, the heroine's ability to leave a bad marriage and devote herself to aiding the poor and the sick in a city besieged by pestilence would have resonated with her own efforts to move beyond the family claim. Like Romola, she found "the highest happiness" in giving primacy to the claims of humanity that came with founding Hull-House.

. . . .

The *Romola* experiment lived on in the settlement's adult education program. Taught mainly by college men and women, the College Extension Classes started in the fall of 1891. Predating the University of Chicago's extension program, which began the following year, it accented the "humanities" rather than the vocationally useful offerings available in evening schools and business colleges.[25] For fifty cents, a student could take a ten-week class with a volunteer, who might be a recent graduate or a professor at the University of Chicago. The culture classes proved popular, drawing some 200–250 students a term.[26] By the 1894 winter term there were seven literary offerings, including two reading parties, one on the *Odyssey* led by Starr, the other designated simply "Reading in English Literature."[27]

The founders set the tone. Addams offered several reading parties between the fall of 1890 and the summer of 1892, after which her rising national reputation often took her away from Chicago. She taught three novels about social issues: *Les Misérables*, Victor Hugo's powerful indictment of poverty and injustice; George Eliot's *Felix Holt, the Radical*, a novel set in the aftermath of the Reform Act of 1832; and Charles Kingsley's labor novel, *Alton Locke*. *The Marble Faun*, Hawthorne's rather obscure novel about artists and art, makes an odd pairing.[28] Addams had been ambivalent about the book when she read it a decade earlier, but by the time she moved to Hull-House she held the author in such high regard that she used her sister's birthday check to buy "the Hawthorne set as we had planned."[29] Like the Florentine photographs and the pictures in Addams's office, the choice proclaimed the cultural intentions of the founders.

Starr was the mainstay of the settlement's culture program. She not only directed it for a time but kept it going for two decades. Each term she taught a class called the History of Art, specializing in a different period, most often some aspect of Italian art.[30] She taught a second class or reading party (a Shakespeare play in the early years) and, on occasion, three or even four.[31] Some students signed up for her courses term after term as she led them through Dante and Robert Browning's poems, which enthusiasts could read for years without duplication. Other favorites were John Ruskin and William Morris, major influences on Starr's growing interest in the social uses of art. At times, she also taught *Faust*, the *Iliad*, and the Bible. She thought well enough of the *Romola* class to repeat it in the fall and winter of 1892.[32] The policy of cultural immersion had already evolved by then: in addition to the photographic aids, talks on Florentine history were part of the settlement's general lecture series, which were pegged to the classes.

Other residents took their cues from the founders. Most of the offerings were resolutely high culture: Emerson, George Eliot, Carlyle, and Hawthorne each had several go-rounds with different instructors, some concentrating on single works, among them Carlyle's *On Heroes*. There were also classes or reading parties on Charles Lamb and Elizabeth Gaskell, on Elizabeth Barrett Browning's *Aurora Leigh*, and on James Russell Lowell's *Biglow Papers*. In an era when the idea of general culture still held sway, there were also reading parties on Plato's *Dialogues*, James Bryce's *American Commonwealth*, biologist T. H. Huxley's *Lay Sermons*, and "Town Geology" (with specimens and reading aloud from Charles Kingsley).

Beyond reading parties and classes, reading infused Hull-House activities, celebratory and mundane, political as well as cultural. Numerous clubs featured reading and games for boys and girls of various ages, including the Alcott Club for twelve-year-old girls who often sewed while one member read aloud. Young adult social clubs often featured literary evenings or dramatic productions (by the late 1890s they were expected to include such activities). The Hull-House Woman's Club heard lectures on "What Shall Our Children Read?" and a series of "Talks on the Poets." A reading circle for trade union women and their friends met at the settlement and was led by a resident; members of the Jane Club, young working women who lived cooperatively in a settlement-owned building, had a librarian and a reading circle of their own. And the centennial celebration of Mazzini's birth in 1905–6 featured "two little circles" to read *The Duties of Man* as well as several lectures in Italian and one in English by Addams.[33]

To some critics of Hull-House, the attention to literary culture in a neighborhood where many inhabitants lacked basic literacy has seemed remiss, an evasion of more pressing existential problems like inadequate housing, high rates of disease, and young children working in factories. Others have found it patronizing, an attempt to impose elite culture on those who did not seek or want it and, presumably, were incapable of appreciating it. Of course, this assumption carries its own kind of condescension.

For Addams, the key to the cultural program was the social atmosphere in which it was disseminated. This shared literary activity was to be a means of cementing bonds between hosts and guests and of opening opportunities for everyone. In bringing reading to Hull-House, Addams and Starr were adapting a practice customarily performed in private settings to their "public household."[34] The reading party drew on everyday practices of middle-class women that provided pleasurable occasions for intellectual growth, for planning the future, and for personal and social intimacy, just as they did in home parlors.[35]

If the settlement's reading parties and clubs represented a moving out from traditional home spaces, the modified structure of the class imposed changes in social relationships. In the process of adapting an institution developed in middle- and upper-class homes to a public setting, a measure of equality and informality was likely lost. In home reading sessions (at least those of girls and young women if not necessarily of families), everyone started at roughly the same social and educational level. Home-based reading groups (and many of those at schools) were often occasions of mutual self-education, with young women taking turns writing and reading papers, perhaps even writing collectively, as M. Carey Thomas and her circle did. Calling the sessions "classes" signified a formal instructional aspect, one adapted from the founders' college experience rather than their home lives. Perhaps this was one reason for the "reading party" designation.

At Hull-House, initially at least, there were leaders and led, readers and listeners, dispensers and recipients of culture. In the long run, however, there was more give and take and less hierarchy than this dualistic model suggests. Addams considered the settlement "a protest against a restricted view of education . . . [which] makes it possible for every educated man or woman with a teaching faculty to find out those who are ready to be taught."[36] When things went well, students and teachers could relate to one another as guests and hosts, with the teacher as guide and friend rather than as authority. Sharing a beloved literary work with the uninitiated was an act of exchange in which pleasure was both given and received, a reward of teaching at its best. In such face-to-face encounters, teachers became students, learning to see individuals behind the ethnic stereotypes, frayed clothing, and ungainly accents of those initially perceived as "others."[37]

In time the line between students and teachers became less sharply defined. Addams claimed that those who came year after year "feel the responsibility of old friends of the house to new guests." They often tutored one another, and some stayed on to become teachers in their own right. Some clubs lasted for years, and at least one held meetings for children of the original members. Though customarily elite in the culture it dispensed, Hull-House provided an atmosphere in which personal growth and the acquisition of skills could be attained in an enjoyable social setting. As Addams put it, "the educational effort . . . always has been . . . subordinate to its social life, and, as it were, a part of it."[38]

Hilda Satt Polacheck was one of the young neighbors for whom Hull-House worked as intended. Her posthumously published autobiography, *I Came a Stranger: The Story of a Hull-House Girl*, suggests the possibilities the settlement afforded an individual who wanted more from life than her job or home provided. The settlement was at the center of her story of progress from immigrant outsider to the American middle class, from factory to white-collar work and then to domesticity, from pupil to teacher and writer.[39]

Polacheck came to Chicago from Russian Poland in 1892 at the age of ten. Unlike in most immigrant families, her father's wages as a skilled tombstone carver were sufficient to support his large family (twelve children, of whom eight survived) without sending any of them out to work. The family also had indoor plumbing in a neighborhood where outdoor privies were the norm. In her autobiography, Polacheck recalls the pleasure of learning English— including proper pronunciation—at the nearby Jewish Training School. She did well enough there to win a book prize for earning the highest marks in a six-month period. Her father's death when she was twelve changed everything. Her mother became a peddler, and Hilda soon joined her older sister in a knitting factory. She had completed fourth or fifth grade and thought her education at an end. Some years later, "after a particularly boring day at the factory"—she was making cuffs for shirtwaists—she walked the three blocks from her home to Hull-House. It was, she later wrote, "an oasis in a desert of disease and monotony" (63, 73).

Polacheck claims that the settlement filled her need for books, music, and arts and crafts, while also providing the social stimulus of people her own age. A Hull-House regular from 1900 to 1910, she participated in a wide range of activities, from political lectures to dancing classes. Residents seem to have taken an interest in this talented young woman almost from the start, and she in them. The first day Addams directed her to the new Labor Museum that housed a permanent exhibit that depicted stages of women's work and featured weekly demonstrations by skilled spinners and weavers from the neighborhood. She wove "a small Navaho-style blanket" and felt "privileged" to embroider a cross-stitch strip for Addams's bedspread (64–65).[40] Despite her fear that the food might not be kosher, she appreciated an invitation to eat with the head of the museum.

In the winter of 1901, Polacheck took "a reading class" taught by resident Clara Landsberg, a Jewish graduate of Bryn Mawr College who taught German at the University School for Girls. The class, which met once a week, "opened new vistas in reading." In addition to the works assigned, Polacheck read "every book I could borrow. Dickens, Scott, Thackeray, Louisa May Alcott, Victor Hugo, Alexander Dumas, and many others now became my friends." (In her presettlement days, she had access to a different type of book—those by "Bertha M. Clay," a pseudonym for several authors of sensational novels, which she borrowed from a fellow worker but quickly outgrew.) The monotony of making cuffs "was eased by thinking of these books and looking forward to evenings at Hull-House." Polacheck relished the personal connection with her teacher and cherished Landsberg's Christmas present, a copy of Elizabeth Barrett Browning's *Sonnets from the Portuguese* (66–67).

She joined the Shakespeare Club at Landsberg's suggestion and subsequently, on Addams's invitation, a class in English composition taught by Henry Porter Chandler, secretary of the president of the University of Chicago and an instructor in English composition there. She did so well on her first composition, "The Ghetto Market," that Addams and Chandler arranged for her to study at the University of Chicago as a special student. She attended for a term on scholarship in 1904, with Addams lending her the money to make up for lost earnings. Polacheck passed Elementary German and the English Composition course taught by Chandler, but failed English Literature: "The jump from the fifth grade in the grammar school to Chaucer was a little too much for me." Nevertheless, she credited the class with endowing her with "an everlasting desire to read and study" and enabling her to attract the educated American-born man she later married (88).

The experience emboldened her to volunteer to teach English to adult immigrants the following summer. She later thought this "presumptuous" on her part, but she did well enough to keep on with the class during regular terms for several years (96). She prided herself on her ability to teach correct English—some of her students learned to speak without an accent—and on using the Declaration of Independence to teach adults (including a Greek professor) instead of materials of the "cat, rat, mat" variety. Seeing her name listed as a teacher in the *Hull-House Year Book* was an experience equaled only by the offer to study at the University of Chicago (89–91).[41]

Polacheck also participated in the Ariadne Club, a social and literary club for young men and women, of which she became vice president. The group, which held a dance one week and a study session the next, approached its literary mission broadly: students wrote on many subjects, mainly economic and political, in Polacheck's recollection. On literary nights, a member who had been assigned to write a paper on a subject like "the collection of garbage, grand opera, clean streets, single tax, trade unionism" read it to the group. Experimenting with the format, the club also held debates and tried book reviewing. In the latter phase, members read their reviews of classics like *David Copperfield, Ivanhoe, The Count of Monte Cristo*, or currently popular works like *When Knighthood Was in Flower*. Polacheck's review of *Uncle Tom's Cabin* provoked so much discussion that it continued the following week, replacing the planned evening of dancing. In addition to establishing her cultural credentials, she presents the episode as a lesson in Americanization: "I thought of all the racial hatreds in Poland, Germany, and Russia, and I was thankful that I was being cured of this disease of intolerance" (94–95).[42]

By this time Polacheck had moved on to white-collar work at A. C. McClurg and Company, a publishing house and bookstore. Her literary apprenticeship at Hull-House and the University of Chicago prepared her for the shift. It also enabled her to heed "a persistent urge to write" by following up on a suggestion that she dramatize *The Walking Delegate*, a labor novel by former Hull-House resident Leroy Scott. A theater buff, Polacheck attended melodramas and vaudeville in nearby theaters when she could afford tickets and immersed herself in Hull-House's dramatics program. She appeared in *The Dumb-Belle*, a three-act farce, among other productions. Addams arranged for her to wait on tables at a summer settlement camp, where the paths and hills had inspiring names like Browning, Ruskin, Tolstoy, and Lincoln. Between shifts, Polacheck completed the dramatization (which she later revised with the help of the director of the Hull-House Players); she also became engaged. In her case, the fusion of settlement activities, literary achievement, and personal happiness was complete: the performance of *The Walking Delegate* took place on her wedding night.[43]

During her Hull-House years, Polacheck published articles on ethnic and charitable subjects for local papers. After her marriage, she wrote drama criticism for the Socialist *Milwaukee Leader* and worked for the Folklore Project of the WPA Writers' Project following her husband's death; she also wrote her autobiography. In judging the impact of the settlement, it is well to recall that Polacheck had advantages others did not. Prior to her father's death, she lived in greater comfort than most immigrants. Her arrival in the United States before her teens also enabled her to learn English fluently enough to speak and write with ease. But in view of the family's changed circumstances following her father's death and her mother's limited literacy—she evidently could not read and never learned to speak English—it is unlikely that Hilda Satt Polacheck could have acquired the skills to pursue a modest literary life in middle-class comfort if she had not walked the three long blocks to the settlement.[44]

.   .   .   .

Polacheck was unusual in the degree to which she threw herself into Hull-House activities, modeled herself after her mentors, and produced a written narrative—a story of Americanization, class mobility, and the acquisition of expressive literacy. Her demographic profile was more typical. Young women constituted the majority of students enrolled in culture classes and almost all of those attending the six-week summer sessions held at Rockford College during the settlement's first decade.[45] A male former resident recalled this gender imbalance when he wrote Starr nearly half a century after their first encounter: "And how you did teach Dante, so that it has been a treasure to me ever since! Did any young college boy ever have such a post-graduate course with such a wonderful faculty, even if it was a ladies' seminary, so far as mere males were concerned!"[46]

The female preponderance in the settlement's culture courses was not unusual. Women gravitated to the humanities in colleges and universities—to the dismay of male administrators and faculty.[47] No doubt there were reasons for the strong female patronage of Hull-House classes besides an interest in culture. Addams and Starr believed that visitors considered themselves "guests as well as students" and that many who signed up for classes there were unlikely to do so at evening schools because they were "attracted and refreshed by the social atmosphere."[48] Immigrants' typically negative assessments of night school instruction suggests that there was truth to this claim. Young women most likely welcomed their association with an institution in which members of their own sex were so clearly in charge and in which they felt warmly received. Hull-House's growing reputation as a neighborhood center was likely also a draw. Most students lived within six blocks of the settlement, a consideration for young women who might have been reluctant to venture far from home after dark—or whose parents might not have let them.

Students were by no means all poor or foreign-born. There were teachers, typists, and cashiers as well as factory workers. Indeed, it is likely that most students in the culture classes came not from the working-class poor, but from those who were lower-middle-class or somewhat above, as Polacheck was before her father's death. Like Polacheck, too, most were American-born or fluent in English. No one goal animated students who came to the settlement. For young women forced to leave school to support themselves or their families, Hull-House offered opportunities to pursue otherwise unavailable educational or cultural interests, including art and music. Some enrolled term after term; at fifty cents a class, the cost was reasonable, although probably beyond the reach of the poorest. Culture courses could also have vocational resonances. Clerical work and sales, like teaching, had become female occupations and, for daughters of immigrants, a prime way of attaining respectable (though not well-paid) employment; women with limited schooling could hone their language skills, while others learned bookkeeping.[49]

As with the *Romola* class, the historical record is too slim to permit generalizations about the reception of classes and reading parties. Only the Shakespeare class left more than minimal traces. These make it clear that the study of the paramount icon of English literature took on a life of its own. They also suggest that students had a hand in shaping their own education and that the boundary between classes and clubs was permeable. Initiated by Starr in the settlement's second year, the Shakespeare class transformed itself into an ongoing club and back again, continuing in its varied incarnations for two decades. Despite shifting labels and personnel and modifications in format, the group retained a sense of continuity and history that suggests its importance in the lives of participants.

Starr first taught Shakespeare in the fall of 1890. In the next several years, she worked her way through the major tragedies. She read aloud; students may have taken turns as well. They presumably came prepared to discuss the questions on her printed syllabus, which for *King Lear* included: "What is the nature of the wrong-doing in this play?" and "Try to account for Shakespeare's not permitting Cordelia to survive." Starr also suggested that they compare Shakespeare's theory of punishment with Dante's in the *Inferno*, urged "close study" of the Fool (a character "too subtle to 'anatomize'"), and encouraged attention to Shakespeare's landscape and historical sources. It is not clear whether Starr assigned papers, but her general approach was not unlike those employed at colleges at the time.[50]

The Shakespeare class reorganized as a club in 1895, and Starr went on to concentrate on the artistic and literary subjects that then engaged her. Officers and directors rotated frequently. Most members and all the officers were women, some of them married. Yearly celebrations of Shakespeare's birthday and annual receptions for past and current members point to a robust group spirit. On the occasion of the club's eleventh anniversary, the secretary read a history of the group, followed by toasts and speeches recalling incidents from the early days. The popular actress Julia Marlowe, an honorary member, sometimes met with the club when she visited Chicago.[51]

In the club format, the group continued to work its way through the bard's corpus. Activities broadened to include outside lecturers, many from the University of Chicago, but also Harriet Monroe (a former Hull-House teacher and later editor of *Poetry*, a major modernist publication), and attendance at Shakespeare plays. The weekly sessions initially consisted of reading scenes from a play, a paper or two or sometimes a debate, and discussion of set topics. Club members took turns writing papers, with subjects and authors regularly announced in settlement publications. As with those in the *Romola* class, most of the members seem to have been of Irish or old American descent, with the addition of some Jews. Relatively few of the club's approximately forty members wrote papers. Of the authors named between January 1896 and the fall of 1904, only three were men; one was the club's director at the time, the other two were Jewish, judging by their names. Topics included "Violation of the Unities in the Play" (*Cymbeline*), "The Weak Men of Shakespeare" (*The Tempest*), "Brutus and Mazzini" (*Julius Caesar*), and "Shakespeare's Debt to Plutarch." Questions distributed for *Othello* in 1904 included several on race: "What use is made of race differences in bringing on the tragic conclusion of the play?" "Is there anything unnatural in Desdemona's love for a Moor?" "Does Othello show race peculiarities?" One wonders how Miss Bertha Tatch, secretary and treasurer of the club and the assigned discussant, argued these questions.[52]

In the early years of the new century, the club began to study works by other authors, ranging from *The Alchemist* by Shakespeare's contemporary, Ben Jonson, to the poems of the contemporary writer George Moore. Under Henry Porter Chandler's direction, there was a move away from the paper format, which had become "something of a burden."[53] Then in 1910, after thirteen years, the club returned to class status. The *Hull-House Year Book* attributed the move to the many new members who "regarded the class form of association as it obtained at Hull-House, with regular but light dues, as preferable to a club with its more uncertain obligations." Chandler continued as leader and, according to the *Year Book*, "the character of the work was not changed"; in its first year as a class, the group "read in detail" *Othello* and *Midsummer Night's Dream*. A modern note entered with *A Doll's House* and a guest reading of George Bernard Shaw's "woman suffrage play, *Press Cuttings*." But the move back to a class suggests that the group was played out, and it soon disappeared from the record.[54]

Twenty years was a long run for Shakespeare on Chicago's West Side. Occurring at an institution in which clubs and classes came and went, its longevity is remarkable.[55] Did individuals join the Shakespeare Club because they had a passion for Shakespeare and perhaps for theater as well? In order to enhance their cultural credentials? To enjoy the camaraderie? For several or all of these reasons? We don't know for sure, but the fate of Shakespeare at Hull-House suggests that he remained popular with nonelite audiences well into the twentieth century and was by no means the exclusive province of the upper classes.[56] Acquiring a taste for Shakespeare may have been a step toward becoming American and moving up the class ladder. The director of *The Merry Wives of Windsor*, staged by the all-Jewish membership of the Lincoln Club, went so far as to claim that "Shakespeare is a fetich among the Jews." Her observation that club members hailed from "the established and respectable element" of the community rather than from the sweatshops—the girls worked in offices or their fathers' stores, the boys in wholesale houses—suggests that Shakespeare, like the culture classes generally, appealed primarily to those who were interested in Americanizing and on the way up.[57]

Evidence from the North Bennet Street Industrial School in Boston's North End confirms the potential of literary activities in promoting mobility and

Americanization. Beginning as a story hour in 1899, the Saturday Evening Girls Club expanded into eight library clubs that met for weekly discussions of literature, art, and politics for nearly two decades. By the mid-1910s, the clubs, with a combined membership of almost 250, published a newspaper and operated their own pottery. Participants, many of them American-born daughters of Russian Jewish and Italian immigrants, graduated from high school and went on for postsecondary education in greater numbers than their peers; some became librarians, teachers, and social workers. A number of them continued meeting on and off for years and attended a reunion in 1954.[58] The story of the Saturday Evening Girls, like that of Hilda Satt Polacheck, suggests the need to consider aspiration and motivation in cultural receptivity, including whether an individual wishes to engage with a work or a body of literature at all. SEG girls may have been drawn to these activities, as Polacheck was to Hull-House, to find support for aspirations and intellectual interests otherwise not easy to come by. The linking of desire and response again suggests the interactive rather than one-dimensional nature of literary reception.

. . . .

By the end of the first decade, Addams concluded that the settlement's culture classes did not reach enough people. She called those who came for history and literature "the transfigured few ... who are capable of abstract mental effort, and who have more or less of the scholar's mental instinct." A few of them went on to college and left the neighborhood. But for the majority, college-type classes were "usually bookish and remote," the subjects too far removed from their lives.[59] Nor did the traditional classroom suit working-class men and women who found regular attendance difficult in any case and had an "irresistible desire for recreation and distraction" in their few leisure hours.[60] Where Addams once thought that "you cannot have too much of learning," she now concluded that "the number of those who like to read, has been greatly overestimated."[61] Accordingly, the settlement developed programs more likely to satisfy the cultural preferences of its neighbors. In the process, Addams gained a new understanding of culture that took her far from the youthful presuppositions garnered from books.

Addams's reassessment coincided with changes in the ethnic composition of the neighborhood as the Irish and other native English-speakers who had formed the backbone of the culture classes moved away.[62] In response, the settlement stepped up its English language classes, offering from five to ten per term between 1899 and 1910. Although there were still occasional offerings on rhetoric, poetry, or Shakespeare, as well as a reading club, the number of "technical classes" (manual training, millinery, cooking, and the like) grew.[63] By 1913 Starr was nearly alone in offering culture courses, and even she was pressed into service teaching English II.[64]

The settlement offered two new lines of cultural activity: a reorientation to more popular art forms, theater in particular, and an innovative educational program, the Labor Museum, designed to help workers understand the impact of the historical transformation of work on their lives and give immigrants an opportunity to demonstrate their skills in traditional crafts with a view to bridging the gap between European parents and American children. By reversing the roles of teacher and student, both ventures drew on the knowledge and experiences of local people, providing "opportunities for self-expression."[65] In so doing they offered more likely occasions for community building than had classes on Browning and George Eliot.

In endorsing theater, Addams hoped both to capitalize on its enormous popularity among the working class and to transform it: "The theater is a strong force in the life of the ordinary working boy, and has its influence upon all members of the social class of which he is a part."[66] Working-class youth flocked to the theater and movies, she explained in *The Spirit of Youth and the City Streets* (1909), to fulfill a need for adventure and imaginative sustenance that transcended the straitened circumstances of their daily lives, the same impulse that others satisfied by reading Homer and Robert Louis Stevenson. She hoped to wean young people from the "poisonous" commercial theater, with its unrealistic romances and antisocial revenge plots, by harnessing the craving for heroism and a higher life at the root of their fascination with drama for socially constructive purposes.[67] "Unless you entertain the people," she concluded, "they will not profit by coming, nor carry away a lesson."[68] Addams's educational goals were never far from the surface. The lessons she had in mind included improved English, the self-discipline required to mount a production, and the bonding experience—so crucial for wholesome adolescent development in her view—that came from cooperating in an exciting and demanding enterprise.

To foster these goals, Hull-House developed an impressive theater program, especially after the appointment of a drama director in 1896 and completion of its auditorium in November 1899. The program centered on the many children's and young people's clubs, which—no doubt encouraged by leaders eager to raise the taste of their protégés—often performed classic fare, including Longfellow's *The Golden Legend* and Robert Southey's *Wat Tyler*, in addition to Shakespeare. Dramatic clubs that began with very young children in some cases kept together for decades, encouraging the bonding and imaginative play Addams had in mind.[69] So, in a different vein, did the Hull-House Dramatic Association (later the Hull-House Players), a group established at the turn of the century with a permanent director and about a dozen talented—but nonprofessional—club members, among them a cigar maker, a stereotyper, a restaurant owner, a schoolteacher, office workers, and housewives. This troop of untrained actors made a mark beyond the settlement for its skilled performances and innovative repertoire. Best known for productions of realistic drama by Ibsen, Galsworthy, and Shaw, the Hull-House Players attained semi-professional status and was one of the first "little theater" groups in the United States.[70]

In line with Addams's desire to provide opportunities for self-expression and to promote ties with immigrant neighbors, Hull-House also encouraged performances by local ethnic groups. For a successful adaptation of a Greek play, "actors were drawn from the street vendors and tenement-house population of the neighborhood." The director of *The Return of Odysseus* and *The Ajax of Sophocles* viewed these ventures as "a connecting link" between Hull-House and the Greek population of Chicago that lasted beyond the production. It was also an opportunity for Americans to have a "truer knowledge of the intelligence and ability of the large Greek colony."[71] The high cultural status of the Greek language and playwrights gave these offerings special cachet, but plays were also performed in Yiddish, Italian, Russian, and Lithuanian. These productions seem to have broken the ice, at least with the Greek community, which began to use the settlement as a community center.[72]

If the settlement's theater program embraced popular cultural forms, the Labor Museum inclined toward idealizing the past and enshrining ancient arts. Influenced by the ideas of John Ruskin and William Morris on the alienating nature of modern factory work, the Labor Museum highlighted the long historic process that transferred work from craft to machine. Inspired as well by John Dewey's view of education as a "continual reconstruction of experience," it adopted an interactive and multimedia approach. The textile room, which opened in November 1900, depicted the evolution of spinning and weaving through 4,000 years by featuring looms and other artifacts from many places and periods, as well as historical charts, lithographs, and photographs. Every Saturday night, Irish, Italian, Syrian, and other women from the neighborhood demonstrated spinning techniques from their native lands. Lectures on the Industrial Revolution that examined the social dislocations brought about by technological changes, as well as trade unions and factory laws, supplemented the exhibits. A collection of folk songs connected with industry included a "sweatshop song" by the Yiddish poet Morris Rosenfeld, which was set to music by the head of the Hull-House Music School, and a song with which a Mrs. Annunziata accompanied her spinning.[73]

The textile room received the most publicity, but women and men also demonstrated their skills in the pottery, metal, grains, wood, and bookbinding rooms, in some cases teaching them to youngsters who sold their handmade wares to visitors.[74] Insofar as possible, the Labor Museum's work was integrated with the settlement's classes on carpentry, basket making, and the like. In moving beyond traditional modes of teaching and learning, the Labor Museum attempted to develop methods more suited to Hull-House's changing clientele. Overall, both the subject matter—work—and the interactive approach of the Labor Museum were exceptionally innovative for the time. Its emphasis on preserving immigrant cultures sought to counteract the more relentless forces of assimilation prevalent in American society.

Addams expected much from the Labor Museum. Like Dewey and other reformers alarmed by the deterioration of working conditions that accompanied industrialization, Addams looked for ways to make work more meaningful.[75] She hoped that by making young people more conscious of their place in the historic process by which machines had replaced hand production they would gain a better understanding of their own work. Older immigrants would be given a chance, however fleeting, to gain respect, especially from their children. Indeed, the aspect of the museum's work that most excited Addams was its potential for reducing the cultural gap between immigrants and their American-born offspring: she made much of poignant but ultimately heartening incidents in which children, once ashamed of their parents' Old World ways, treated them with new respect after seeing them honored for their skills at the Labor Museum.[76]

This was a different sort of cultural gap than the one that concerned her at the time of Hull-House's founding, although by making immigrants teachers, rather than simply recipients, of culture, the Labor Museum also addressed the gulf between the classes that had been her starting point. Of course, the kind of culture they taught—and that Addams had in mind— was more akin to the anthropologist's definition than to the literary culture she had at first envisioned, a change in her thinking that resulted from her years in the neighborhood. This culture was not restricted to the high arts. As the very concept of the Labor Museum suggested, she now held "that culture is an understanding of the long-established occupations and thoughts of men, of the arts into which they have solaced their toil, of the poesy into which they have poured their aspirations; that the human is not of necessity the cultivated, but it is that which has been much beloved and long tried by the generations."[77]

The Labor Museum's efforts to increase respect for manual work, its celebration of crafts, and its emphasis on understanding the dislocations that came with changed methods of production differentiated it from contemporary programs that trained members of underprivileged groups for a permanent place in the underclass. Its educational agenda had more to do with John Dewey's approach to manual training as a means of integrating intellectual and physical activity than with contemporary business-led programs on industrial education.[78] But as critics point out, the ultimate goal of the Labor Museum was not to challenge the capitalist system in any fundamental way but to make it more bearable.[79]

Did the program succeed in its goals? We know little about its long-range impact. But even if the spinners who demonstrated bygone skills or the workers who watched them gained a better understanding of their place in the labor chain, as Addams hoped, it is unlikely that this knowledge affected their relationship to their work or made them more contented in it. If this feature of the plan seems exceptionally naive, there may have been benefits of a less intellectual kind. For persons displaced from their native cultures, the opportunity to demonstrate their skills and tell their life stories to American visitors may have provided moments of unaccustomed pleasure, even an enhanced sense of self-worth. If as a result they felt less alienated from their Americanized children, as Addams believed they did, that would have been no small achievement. Such efforts to halt the erosion of immigrant cultures, and the values attached to them, could not stem the pressures of Americanization, whether internal or external, but for some they may have made life more livable. In that respect, the achievements of the Labor Museum may not have been so different from those of the literary classes.

. . . .

When she placed her life before the public in her 1910 autobiography, *Twenty Years at Hull-House*, Addams made much of her own culpability in mistaking cultivation for quality. Writing as a reformer and social critic, she highlighted the distance she had traveled from the cultural ideals of her youth, at least those expressed in the motto that hung on the wall of the chess club at Rockford Female Seminary: "There is the same difference between the learned and the unlearned as there is between the living and the dead."[80] In making this mea culpa, Addams was not rejecting literary culture—only its equation with merit and moral character. Far from renouncing culture, she viewed it as potentially transformative. Art was not an escape, it was a vehicle for social connection. The problem, as she saw it, was how best to stimulate the imaginative potential of every human being in socially constructive directions. She had concluded that for most people in the neighborhood, theater and other forms of entertainment that did not depend on formal education achieved this best. But for those of her own class, she still considered reading a powerful stimulus to social regeneration.

At its best, she observed, art could free individuals from their emotional isolation and help build bridges between people of different classes. Drawing on Tolstoy's view of art as infection, Addams stressed its emotional power: "Art makes us understand and feel what might be incomprehensible and inexpressible in the form of an argument."[81] Through its capacity to move, art could lift people out of themselves, allowing them to imagine the experiences of others. Novels in particular, by permitting readers "to see farther, to know all sorts of men, in an indefinite way," countenanced "a wide reading of human life" that enabled individuals to "find in ourselves a new affinity for all men." Such imaginative engagement was, she believed, a first step toward an aroused public conscience and thus to finding remedies for social ills: "We have learned as common knowledge that much of the insensibility and hardness of the world is due to the lack of imagination which prevents a realization of the experiences of other people."[82]

For Addams, then, literature was—or at least could be—a kind of experience rather than a substitute for it. In this view culture was no longer a matter of erudition but a form of "extended experience," and reading books a way "to get over the differences raised by barriers and traditions, that really we may be fair-minded and may know people as they really are."[83] Once having read *Children of the Ghetto* by Anglo-Jewish writer Israel Zangwill, she observed, "No one . . . can afterwards walk through the Jewish quarter of any great city without a quickening of the blood as he passes. . . . Without Zangwill's illumination we would have to accumulate much more experience."[84] Literature, though best supplemented by personal knowledge, could thus shortcut the process of learning about alien peoples. The writers who did this best, Dickens and Zola in addition to Zangwill, appealed to readers' sensibilities by writing books "dealing with life as a whole and presenting people as they are, simply and truly."[85]

With her emphasis on engaging readers on behalf of the outcast and on the importance of interpreting their experiences, Addams could be describing her own goals and literary practice. With her new understandings of

Jane Addams with a young girl, ca. 1930. Jane Addams Memorial Collection
(JAMC_0000_0030_1722), Special Collections, University of Illinois at Chicago Library.
Photograph by Wallace Kirkland.

culture and cultivation, she used her own formidable literary skills to interpret for her middle-class readers the experiences of those among whom she had cast her lot.[86] It might be said that she used Culture to interpret culture.

Like the novelists of urban life she admired, Addams situated herself among people shunned or ignored by most of her class when she went to live in a blighted neighborhood on Chicago's West Side. Drawing on her own experiences, she attempted to interpret for her educated audience the needs and outlooks of her neighbors, many of them immigrants intimately acquainted with poverty and despair. By attempting to portray "life as a whole" and people "as they are," she invited the imaginative engagement of her readers, a practice that differed from that of traditional charity workers, who distanced themselves from the objects of their help.[87] In so doing, Addams made the experiences of those who started out as "others" seem rational and even necessary, however misguided they might initially appear to her readers. Her narrative is full of homely and pathetic stories: the girl who stole clothes because her parents kept all her earnings; the skilled craftsman from Bohemia obliged to shovel coal in America who turned violent during bouts of drinking, but whose "'restless fits'" could be staved off if he had some metal to work. Many of the vignettes are stories of her own haplessness in her first years in the neighborhood, where she had gone full of preconceptions about the people she would find. In one of the most striking, she suggests that her attempts to adhere to "scientific methods" of charity hastened a man's death, from which she learned that "life cannot be administered by definite rules and regulations; that wisdom to deal with a man's difficulties comes only through some knowledge of his life and habits as a whole."[88]

Addams had earlier defined a settlement as "an attempt to express the meaning of life in terms of life itself, in forms of activity."[89] The definition is ambiguous, but it attests to her conviction that social usefulness must be central to ethical theory. Applauding efforts that served basic human needs, Addams rejected ideological purity (whether doctrinal orthodoxy at Rockford Female Seminary in the 1870s or socialism and "Tolstoyism" in the 1890s) and celebrated experience over ideology, pragmatic need over intellectual consistency.[90] Indeed, this is the central theme, as well as method, of *Twenty Years*. Her critique of theory and her emphasis on experience link her to the efforts of pragmatist social theorists to bring theory out of the ivory tower and make it central to everyday life. Enlightened observation rather than precept was to form the basis of social knowledge. More than the male philosophers and social scientists with whom she was connected, however, Addams's rendering of pragmatic ideals joined the revolt against pure knowledge to a critique of contemporary class and gender arrangements, in particular the social separation of the classes into the over- and the underprivileged and the underemployment of female talent.

Although committed from the outset to the primacy of experience, Addams's formulations took a decisive turn through her friendship with John Dewey, a central figure in American pragmatism who taught at the University of Chicago and was a Hull-House volunteer and trustee in the 1890s. The influence was reciprocal. Addams and Hull-House inspired some of Dewey's major ethical and educational theories and their implementation at the University of Chicago Laboratory School, which he headed.[91] Of Addams's essay "A Modern Lear," Dewey wrote, it was "one of the greatest things I ever read both as to its form and its ethical philosophy."[92] In it she compared Shakespeare's arbitrary king to George Pullman, founder of the Pullman Company, whose inability to understand his workers precipitated a harsh and costly strike of national proportion. "A Modern Lear," like *Twenty Years at Hull-House*, makes a strong case for the necessity of empathy in politics, especially on the part of the privileged.[93] It was to be an informed empathy, the sort she had envisioned in her graduation address on "Cassandra" and to which she could now lay claim.

It is a tribute to Addams's capacities as an intellectual and writer that she not only reached a wide public audience but succeeded in influencing her male peers. What of those she wrote about? For individuals like Hilda Satt Polacheck and Philip Davis, a young Jewish immigrant who, with the assistance of mentors, attended Harvard and became a social worker, Hull-House undoubtedly made all the difference in their ability to fulfill some version of the American dream. Others, like Dorothy Mittelman Sigel, who each Saturday attended the Marionette Club, a young people's theater group, absorbed new linguistic patterns and standards of decorum that made it easier to enter the American middle class. Many more enjoyed the opportunity to play basketball or study dance, activities that helped make their lives more livable, one of Addams's animating goals from the outset.[94]

After Addams recognized that her initial cultural goals were out of reach for most of her neighbors, who lacked the education, linguistic skills, leisure, or perhaps desire to partake of them, Hull-House developed programs more likely to foster community. Theater especially promised several kinds of cohesion, among club members, actors, and audiences, and between residents and neighbors. But Addams's vision of the arts, tailor-made for a local community, could not withstand the challenge of movies, dance halls, amusement parks, and other forms of commercial entertainment to which young women and men flocked for pleasure in the early years of the twentieth century. Paradoxically, it was the movies, a medium that conveyed messages of self-seeking that she deplored, that most nearly embodied her vision of the arts as a binding social force. Addams recognized the importance of pleasure in working-class entertainments, but she overestimated the capacity of a settlement—or other social agencies—to compete with mass entertainment.

Whatever its limitations, the cultural space that was Hull-House provided opportunities for those inclined to take them—especially those children of immigrants who found there reinforcement for their own desire to become part of a new culture. Beyond the opportunities for mobility and other kinds of satisfactions that Hull-House offered the underprivileged, the cross-class exchanges had tremendous impact on settlement residents who acquired a sense of immediacy about the needs of their neighbors they could have achieved in no other way. Their leadership in the Progressive movement for social justice attests to that influence. Encounters with cultures other than their own helped to reshape the mind-set of some of the privileged. Addams may have been right after all when she spoke of the reciprocal influence of one class on the other in the context of settlement life.

. . . .

CHAPTER EIGHT

New Books, New Lives

Jewish Immigrant Women, Reading, and Identity

For Russian Jewish immigrants and their children, access to books and libraries was often central to their experience of America, symbols of freedom and plenty unknown in the Old World. Members of both generations, including prominent writers like Philip Roth and Alfred Kazin, have portrayed a youthful encounter with the library as a transcendent experience, the possession of a personal library card as the height of worldly riches. To discover books and libraries was to discover America—and the key to becoming American.

In celebrating the joys of reading, immigrants of both sexes marveled at the contrast between their formerly circumscribed lives and the freedoms they found in America. It was not just that books were in short supply or that the tsarist government censored materials it deemed subversive. There were also constraints in the Jewish community, among them rabbinical strictures against secular reading (not always enforced) and the limited range of available books. Given traditional restrictions on female literacy, Jewish women had special reason to believe that the bounty of America turned on the availability of books—and the ability and opportunity to read them. Books and libraries became symbols not just of freedom, as they were for men, but of a doubled equality—as females and as Jews.

In the early twentieth century, Jewish women autobiographers wrote lovingly of their encounters with print as a source of both solace and inspiration. They looked to books to remove themselves from the harsh conditions of ghetto life, if only for a time, to discover new and less restricting identities, and to find clues about how to become writers themselves. Their stories of reading underscore the importance of access, motivation, and encouragement in determining the difficulty or ease of their journeys—to English literacy, American selfhood, and authorship. Rose Gollup Cohen, who came to the United States at the age of twelve with uncertain literacy skills and without formal schooling, recorded her painful struggle to become literate in *Out of the Shadow* (1918), a memoir that required almost superhuman effort to produce. Despite her father's opposition, she received support for her burning desire to learn and grow from Lillian Wald and Leonora O'Reilly of the Henry Street Settlement at a time when settlements and libraries often provided immigrants with the best opportunities for acquiring an education. Mary Antin, who arrived at about the same age, studied English in elementary school and, with support from her father and influential patrons, became a published writer in her teens. Her iconic *The Promised Land* (1912) is a celebratory account of the transformation of a humble Jewish girl into an American citizen. For her part, Bella Spewack, who came to the United States as a very young child, found American life less stressful than Cohen or Antin, who each experienced ill health and alienation from what they considered a patriarchal culture. Different though these women's experiences were, their English-language reading helped them reimagine and re-create themselves: as they Americanized, they moved up in social class (precariously, in Cohen's case) and found ways to fulfill a pressing desire to tell their own stories.

. . . .

The story of Jewish women's relationship to the word begins in the Old World. For the majority of those coming to the United States that meant the Russian Empire, where most Jews lived in the prescribed area known as the Pale of Settlement. There women's acquisition of literacy is a tale of official disregard, punctuated by a number of strategies, mainly informal, to educate daughters. Most of all, it is a story of contrasts: a haphazard approach to women's literacy that diverged sharply from the value placed on educating men.[1]

The importance of literacy in the lives of Jewish men is one of the defining facts of modern Jewish history. The highest ideal to which a man could aspire was deep knowledge of the ancient Jewish texts, the Torah and the Talmud. This was not only a religious duty, but the path to holiness: all else paled beside it. Boys entered elementary religious schools (heders) at an early age. There they learned to read Hebrew, beginning with the prayer book and moving on to Torah and then to Talmud study. But heders were costly and often inadequate, and few students gained the proficiency needed to attain the desired ideal. Most left around age thirteen to enter the workforce or begin an apprenticeship, with limited knowledge of the Hebrew prayer book. Only the most gifted went on to advanced study; those who married into wealthy families might gain the freedom to spend their days in communal study of the sacred texts.[2]

Sacred knowledge was never an ideal for women. Authorities considered it dangerous and often cited Rabbi Eliezer's famous maxim to support their claim: "He who teaches his daughter Torah is teaching her promiscuity."[3] Exempt from the religious obligations of Jewish men and excluded from Torah study, women rarely learned Hebrew. Even if they knew the alphabet and could follow the prayers in synagogue, they were unlikely to understand them.[4]

For women, the language of literacy was Yiddish. Based on the Hebrew alphabet, but a separate language, Yiddish was the vernacular for both sexes. For women it was the principal route to spirituality as well. With Yiddish, a woman could read *tkhines*, the devotional prayers designed to help her fulfill her religious obligations, and the *Tsenerene*, a compilation of Bible stories, legends, and ethical maxims arranged around the weekly Torah portion. First published around 1600, the *Tsenerene* went through numerous editions and by the nineteenth century was known as "the women's Torah."[5] Like the *tkhines*, it was an instrument of piety rather than learning and was traditionally read at home on the afternoon of the Sabbath, either silently or aloud to family and neighbors. By contrast, men's religious rituals were mandatory and communal.

By the end of the century, as women's access to education increased, a growing number became literate, mainly in Yiddish, although some, particularly in urban areas, could also read Russian or Polish. Scholars have attributed the increased emphasis on female education to the Haskalah (Jewish Enlightenment). But Jewish women's central role as breadwinners was also a factor, since knowledge of written Yiddish or the local language helped in the conduct of business.[6] As might be expected, women's education was off-hand, dependent on the availability of schools and the whims and finances of parents. In the absence of free public education, literacy was acquired mainly in private religious schools or at home. Not surprisingly, fewer girls than boys attended religious schools, at best a ratio of one to eight among the youngest pupils, according to one historian's generous estimate.[7]

After 1860, some girls also attended private secular schools, most of them sex-segregated. They generally came from the wealthiest families, mainly those who lived in large cities and prided themselves on being modern. Despite the high cost of tuition, the gender disparity in attendance was considerably less than at the heders: in 1899 girls constituted about one-third of those attending these schools in Russia.[8] Few Jews—male or female—attended advanced public schools. Russian policy after 1887 restricted the proportion of Jewish students admitted to secondary schools and universities; the "percentage norm"—mentioned with some bitterness in immigrant women's oral histories—ranged from 10 percent inside the Pale of Settlement to 3 percent in St. Petersburg and Moscow.[9]

In view of the restrictions on formal education, the majority of literate Jewish women probably learned to read and write at home from parents or, more likely, from private teachers. Only a few tutors offered much beyond basic skills.[10] In Rose Pesotta's case, a woman studying for her university entrance examinations taught an exciting array of subjects that included Jewish and Russian history, the history of civilization, and the classic Russian writers.[11] Pesotta's family was well-off and committed to educating daughters, but for most women education was a patchwork thing.

Paradoxically, the devaluation of female literacy allowed women greater access to secular learning than men.[12] In some families, daughters studied Russian or French while sons steeped themselves in Hebrew. From such openings came the female participants in the Socialist and Zionist movements and in revolutionary reading circles, secret societies that read clandestine literature smuggled in from western Europe. In addition to her formal lessons, Rose Pesotta read the literature of the Russian underground and later joined a revolutionary reading circle.[13] Deprived of a specifically Jewish education, women evidently found it easier to break their ties to a religious tradition that consigned them to second-class status.

Women had greater freedom of access to other types of reading as well. The presumptive readers of story books since the appearance of prose romances in the sixteenth century, women provided the core readership of the secular Jewish fiction that emerged in the mid-nineteenth century.[14] To broaden their audience, storytellers A. M. Dik and Shomer (N. M. Shaikevitch), both proponents of the Haskalah, switched from Hebrew to Yiddish. They did so apologetically since Yiddish, then known as jargon, was considered a debased and female language. These writers sometimes explicitly addressed themselves to "Dear lady readers," but men, too, read Yiddish fiction, often secretly, since secular reading was not sanctioned for them.[15] Given their opportunity to read Yiddish, some women may have been qualitatively more literate in the language of everyday life than their otherwise more learned husbands and brothers.

Despite women's relative literary license, the disparity in value accorded male and female learning ultimately had negative consequences in the form of an alarming gender gap in literacy. Statistics on literacy are at best problematic. They are especially complicated in the case of Jews because several languages are involved. But the gap was high in every survey. According to the Russian census of 1897, 64.6 percent of the Jewish male and 36.6 percent of the Jewish female population over ten could read some language. Reported literacy rates were higher overall among Jewish men and women who immigrated to the United States between 1908 and 1912 (roughly 80 percent and 63 percent respectively). That still meant that almost twice as many immigrating women as men were illiterate, defined as lacking the ability to read and write.[16] Most startling perhaps, a report of the New York State Commission on Immigration for 1908 indicated that Jews had a higher gender gap in literacy than other immigrants from eastern Europe.[17]

What inferences can be drawn from this disparity? On the one hand, the surveys reveal that Jewish women, particularly young women, were far more literate than stereotype has it. In view of the uncommon emphasis on male learning and the lack of public education, the fact that nearly two-thirds of the Jewish women from eastern Europe who entered the United States in the early twentieth century could read and write is a considerable achievement. But in a culture that placed such a high value on male learning, women's lesser literacy took on a significance it did not have in adjacent peasant societies. Jewish women, even those who could neither read nor write, would have understood the symbolic importance of literacy as well as its more practical uses. Perhaps this helps to account for their often noted enthusiasm for education in the New World.[18]

Jewish men and women were then both differently and unequally literate, many of the former in Hebrew as well as in Yiddish, the latter principally in Yiddish, although some also read Russian or other non-Jewish languages. With Hebrew an esteemed and Yiddish a devalued language, the differences in literacies were invidious. Women's inability to read sacred texts in the original and their relegation to an "inferior" language rankled as emblems of their subordinate status. Resenting the privileges accorded men, the most ambitious rejected the view that all a girl needed was "to be able to sign her name, do enough arithmetic to keep the family accounts, and read the Bible, which of course meant only the Old Testament in Yiddish translation."[19] The fundamental disparity in literacy helps to explain why first-generation Jewish women immigrants were far more likely than their Slavic or Italian counterparts to perceive gender discrimination in their parents' treatment of their brothers and themselves, as 95 percent of those interviewed did in a Pittsburgh study.[20]

The move to the United States marked a turning point for Russian Jewish women in access to literacy as in other ways. In the New World, inhospitable in so many ways to the preservation of traditional Jewish religion and culture, the weakening of communal ties and the diminished relevance of Hebrew study lessened the disparity in status between the sexes and strengthened women's position vis-à-vis men.[21] The availability of free primary schools also gave women assured access to literacy for the first time. Families still tended to keep sons in school longer than daughters, but in the early years at least, girls no longer had to take a back seat to their brothers. With the decline of patriarchal structures, some women were able to pursue their own goals even in the absence of family approval. Their efforts were often aided by American institutions, notably schools, settlements, and libraries.

Relatively few Jewish immigrant women acquired the linguistic skill to express themselves easily in a new language. For those who were past school age or forced to go right to work, literacy in English was often acquired with great difficulty. That some Jewish immigrants, including those with little formal education, wrote autobiographies and had them published is testimony not only to their skill and persistence, but to the liberating possibilities of the new land. With the new language came a new sense of self.

· ·

Rose Gollup Cohen was one of the women for whom America signified freedom and enlightenment. Her 1918 autobiography, *Out of the Shadow*, is the moving story of a young immigrant's efforts to navigate the cultural distance from the Russian countryside to the tenements of the Lower East Side. A central theme of the narrative is the author's struggle to attain expressive literacy, that is, the ability to read and write with ease and to use these skills for self-defined goals.[22] Cohen's is a nonlinear story, full of stops and starts, of her journey from marginal literacy in her native language, Yiddish, to the linguistic accomplishment needed to write in English, a language she came to only in her late teens. Given the obstacles, it is something of a miracle that

Portrait of Rose Cohen, ca. 1918–20. Photograph by Underwood & Underwood Studio. Courtesy of Amy Hyman and Thomas Dublin.

she became a published author. But educational deficits, limited access to books, and paternal disapproval of her literary interests were countered by her need to read and write.

Published in her late thirties, when Cohen was unknown, *Out of the Shadow* is an introspective narrative that conveys with admirable immediacy the author's evolving and painfully acquired literacy and its multiple meanings.[23] Like native-born women, but in a vastly different context, she found reading not only a source of pleasure and of mainly female sociability, but the catalyst to a new and more "modern" identity. Impressive as the story of one woman's experience, Cohen's narrative puts a human face on momentous historical developments, notably the transitions from traditional to modern literacy and from marginal to expressive literacy, in her case both attained through nontraditional channels.

Rahel Gollup grew up in a small village in northwestern Russia, the oldest of five children in an extended family.[24] Her narrative re-creates an Old World tradition of reading and storytelling centered on religion and folk tales. At home she had access only to "a few volumes in Hebrew and

Yiddish pertaining to religion." In addition to the Old Testament, these included "'Rules for Proper Conduct,' a volume of the Psalms of David, a few prayer-books, and two or three volumes of narratives in Yiddish"—probably a fairly typical collection in shtetl households. As Cohen recalled, "Nothing was ever read to children for the purpose of entertaining, but many were the stories told us by our elders."[25]

That tradition was distinctly female. Her blind grandmother did most of the storytelling while knitting stockings or plucking feathers with Cohen's mother; her frighteningly vivid ghost stories alternated with tales from the Bible. Cohen reciprocated by reading aloud. By her own account, she was a pious child who pored over religious books whose "narratives of saints who became sinners, of sinners who became saints," and stories about the dead frightened her. She found consolation in the Psalms, whose rhythm she loved, and read them aloud in a sing-song voice in imitation of her father and grandfather, even though she understood only an occasional word of the Hebrew. Writing from the perspective of one who had shed her religion, Cohen subtly underscores the differential literacies of men and women: a girl could reproduce Hebrew sounds without comprehending their meaning.[26]

The Old World literacy recalled by Cohen resembled the pattern of traditional reading in colonial New England, where a few texts, virtually all of them religious, were read over and over again.[27] It was a world of piety, superstition, and fear in which oral tradition played an important part. Modernity entered when Rose was eleven and her father hired a tutor to teach the children "literary Russian," which Cohen considered a mark of cultivation, like learning music. Retrospectively, she claimed that by providing a respite from gloomy religious texts, the lessons lifted "the mantle of both religion and fear" a little. She may have been romancing, for she had "barely learned to read a few words" when the lessons ended with her father's departure for America. As the oldest child, Cohen followed soon after—she was twelve. Her mother and younger siblings came a year later.[28]

Cohen's literacy status when she arrived in New York in 1892 is uncertain. Unlike her parents, who could read but not write Yiddish, Rose could also write, although evidently not with ease. Her acquisition of literacy in the New World follows a common pattern among adult learners, described by one scholar as "a kind of patchwork whose configuration is closely linked to specific settings characterized by specific opportunities and constraints."[29] The chief constraint in this case was economic. Cohen went to work immediately, following her father into the garment industry. It was a harsh life of long hours, low pay, and frequent layoffs and one that foreclosed the possibility of further education.

But the move also brought opportunities. No longer bound by traditional religious structures and strictures, Cohen gained access to a new type of literature.[30] The new era began when she happened on "Yiddish books, stories!" in a neighbor's kitchen. She had almost forgotten how to read and had "to spell out the words." As they fell into place she lost herself in the book until it became too dark to read. Astonished that the volume was not about religion but "just a story," she became a regular customer at a soda-water stand, borrowing books at five cents a volume, plus a fifteen-cent deposit.[31]

The discovery not only enhanced the quality of her life but also enabled her to become more competent in Yiddish. Insecure in her knowledge of her native language, at first she read only books in which diacritical marks under the Hebrew letters indicated the vowels.[32] When she exhausted the supply, she pressed on and before long was able to read without the vowels: "And now reading material was not so limited. A flying newspaper in the street, a crumpled advertisement sheet, I would smooth out tenderly and carry off home, happy in the expectation of what was awaiting me." She read even if she did not understand, "For just to read became a necessity and a joy. There were so few joys" (191).

Borrowing one 250-page volume a week, Cohen "got all I could out of it." She and another sister spent "many happy evenings" reading to their mother and the younger children. The reading matter (secular rather than religious) and setting were new, but the practice of intergenerational reading and storytelling was familiar. Adding a creative touch of her own, Cohen memorized songs or poems from the books and then found an "appropriate" melody from her stock of Russian peasant songs which she sang for visitors on the Sabbath (188–89).

On her own, Cohen reread each story and "lived it when I was not reading." A self-described dreamy child who had had several imaginary playmates, Cohen threw herself into the world of make-believe. She read passionately and at first indiscriminately. With titles like "The Executioner from Berlin," the stories were "depicted in the most extravagant language, with unnatural characters and impossible plots."[33] Mainly romances translated from European literatures, they transported her into realms far removed from the daily grind of work and poverty: "And I lived now in a wonderful world. One time I was a beautiful countess living in a palace, another time I was a beggar's daughter singing in the street" (189). Her confession that she read "in a feverish state, my face hot, my nerves tingling, reading breathlessly" echoes numerous erotically charged descriptions of early adolescent reading.[34]

Then Cohen encountered *David Copperfield*. Dickens was one of the most popular writers on the Lower East Side—in Yiddish translation as well as in English—as he was among young Americans generally.[35] Starting with the title of the first chapter—"I Am Born"—the book electrified her. Never before had she read a first-person narrative, and its intimate tone filled her "with a strange feeling of happiness. . . . Someone was talking to me—I could almost hear the voice!" The experience launched a new phase in which Cohen sought greater connection between her reading and her life: "I used to love to know that things I read were real." Her experiences in the labor force and the family's extreme poverty left no doubt that Dickens's tale of hardship and hunger was real. Later she discovered "'a whole shelf of books by Dickens' and I read them all," this time in English, but *David Copperfield* remained her favorite: "In some of the other volumes there were often pages that I wanted to skip. But a man who has once been hungry cannot bear to waste a crumb."[36] The hero's dramatic change of fortune from abused and famished orphan to successful writer must have held out hope for a happier future.

Twice the size of the earlier volumes, the story entranced the family for two full weeks: "We lived little David's life over with him." Her mother cried at David's separation from his nurse, Peggotty, "and then she laughed, at her tears, remembering that it was 'only a story.'" The novel inhabited Cohen's mental life: she rehearsed the previous evening's episode as she felled sleeve lining and looked forward joyfully to the evening when she would resume reading to the others. For all of them, reading *David Copperfield* was an intensely emotional experience, something to be recapitulated and savored before resuming life as usual. When they reached the end, "we felt as if we had parted from a dear friend. We could not bear to read anything else for a whole week" (190–91).

This scene of happy, participatory family reading contrasted with a painful episode that occurred during Cohen's brief engagement to a young grocer. At sixteen, she was unenthusiastic about the prospective marriage, which was arranged by a matchmaker, but acquiesced to her family's wishes. During the awkward moments of the couple's first time alone, she hoped that two dusty books she found in the store would help them form a bond. One, a mix of letters and diary translated from Russian into Yiddish, captivated her. As with *David Copperfield*, "the intimate tone of the first person in which it was written made me feel as if that some one were actually talking to me." Her fiancé's rejection of her offer to read the book aloud—"What is the use?"—exposed a chasm that could not be bridged (220). She broke off the engagement soon after.[37]

The incident precipitated her first hesitant efforts at authorship (if we except the poems to which she assigned melodies). Observing her younger siblings writing out their lessons, she recalled the diary and took up paper and pencil herself. Her initial efforts at writing were halting, and she rubbed out most of the words. One clear sentence remained: "I feel new joy in life and in freedom." Determined to keep a diary, she copied over the first night's writing—in Yiddish of course—into a small penny notebook she bought for the purpose. Her first entry was bold and disturbing: "I hate the shop, I feel sick, I feel tired, I cannot see any meaning in life" (229–30).

By this time Cohen's reading went well beyond the stage of vicarious adventure. Books had become an instrument of self-expression and emotional connection (or a sign of its absence in the case of the fiancé). Reading the diary had triggered a desire to express herself in personal writing; it may also have authorized her to bring into the open painful truths she might otherwise have been unable to acknowledge, let alone express.[38] Diary keeping and self-awareness were mutually reinforcing. The diary encouraged introspection, but the desire to keep one and the rejection of marriage to an incompatible man signaled an already heightened self-consciousness.

Following her brief engagement, Cohen began to study English. It was her first venture outside her neighborhood after five years in the United States. The initial stop was night school, as it was for many Jewish women, who constituted an estimated 40 percent of New York women attending them.[39] Cohen enrolled after leaving her job due to ill health, as did her sister, who, in classic pattern, had been forced to quit day school in order to make up the lost wages.[40] The experience was excruciating. Barely able to follow when "the girls" read aloud, Cohen lost her place if she lifted her finger from the page. When her turn came, she "would hear a queer sound like of someone sick"; by persisting, she "learned painfully a word or two at a time" (198).[41] Her misery underscores Jane Addams's wisdom in insisting on sociability as an essential ingredient of evening classes at Hull-House.

Cohen's encounters with three other American institutions—settlement house, library, and hospital—proved more rewarding. Settlements and libraries were traditional intermediaries between immigrants and American culture, but in Cohen's case it was an uptown hospital that occasioned her first glimpse of life beyond Cherry Street and her initial progress in English.

Through the intercession of Lillian Wald of the Nurses' (later Henry Street) Settlement, Cohen entered Presbyterian Hospital when she was seventeen.[42] During a three-month stay, she had her first encounters with English-language books and with Gentiles, cultivated Americans whose kindness to an impoverished Jewish immigrant amazed her. Forced to speak English in a foreign environment, she learned in an atmosphere of unaccustomed sociability with people whose language was utterly unlike the "Yiddish English" of the Lower East Side. Among them was the daughter of a millionaire who read *Under the Red Robe* (1894), a swashbuckling novel set in the age of Cardinal Richelieu that moved both women to tears.

More problematic for one raised in an Orthodox household was the first text she tried to read on her own: a New Testament.[43] Although troubled by the efforts of a female missionary to convert her, she decided it could not be a sin to read the Bible of people who had been so good to her. But first she had to demystify the volume, which she had not dared to touch, by naturalizing it: "It had a musty smell like any other book that was old and little used; here and there the pages stuck together with a bit of food" (244). She struggled to read it, spelling out the words to a nearby patient, who explained their pronunciation and meaning. Learning English in these circumstances pointed to the possibility of betrayal. Sensing the drift of things, Mary Brewster, cofounder of the Nurses' Settlement, refused Cohen's request for a New Testament, presenting her instead with a love story—her first English book—in its own way a symbol of the new order.[44]

Progress was slow and uneven. Like other immigrants, Cohen found the disparity between her intellectual development and her limited skill in an unfamiliar tongue painful. Elated when she finished reading the love story, she was soon cast down by her inability to decipher a handwritten letter: "And then like any poor illiterate old woman I had to run to a drug store and ask a clerk to read my letter to me" (250). Cohen dates the beginning of her education "if it can be so called" to her inability to understand more than an occasional word of a talk on Shakespeare at the Nurses' Settlement. For help, she looked to the Aguilar Free Library, a circulating library founded by Jews. Although awed by "the shelves and shelves of books and the stream of people hastening in and out with books under their arms," she asked for "the best thing that Shakespeare wrote" and was surprised at the "pretty Jewish-American" librarian's uncertainty on the point. After struggling with *Julius Caesar* for two weeks, Cohen nerved herself to ask the librarian for an English book "'like for a child.' She brought me 'Little Women'" (252–53).

Delighted by the availability of free books, Cohen read a great deal, good books when she could get them, anything when she could not. Longfellow's "The Day Is Done" had special appeal as "a beautiful song." It may also have spoken to the budding writer, for she found "very wonderful" the poet's wish to hear from

> . . . some humbler poet.
> Whose songs gushed from his heart . . .
> Who, through long days of labor,
> And nights devoid of ease,
> Still heard in his soul the music.

Understanding remained elusive. She "had to dig and dig to get the meaning" of *Dreams* (1890) by the feminist South African writer Olive Schreiner. A series of allegories—many in the form of dreams—the book raises questions about life's ultimate meanings, about freedom and love, heaven and hell, seeking and suffering. Cohen loved it because of its difficulty "and because of the short simple sentences, the short words. I studied this little book."[45] Simplicity of language is an apt description of Cohen's later essays and stories about Jewish and peasant life in Russia; perhaps she was absorbing Schreiner's style even as she struggled with the meaning.

As her reading transported her to new worlds, she became increasingly alienated from her old life. Recalling this period, she observed, "A child that came to this country and began to go to school had taken the first step into the New World. But the child that was put into the shop remained in the old environment with the old people, held back by the old traditions, held back by illiteracy. . . . Now that I had had a glimpse of the New World, a revolution took place in my whole being. I was filled with a desire to get away from the whole old order of things" (246).

The inevitable family conflict ensued: "Father did not take kindly to my reading. How could he! He saw that I took less and less interest in the home, that I was more dreamy, that I kept more to myself." Fearing what would come of associating with non-Jews and reading "Gentile books," he went so far as to fling one of her library books out the window when his son told him it contained the word Christ. Cohen was furious when she saw the torn cover and scattered pages: "I wept aloud that I had a right to know, to learn, to understand. I wept bitterly that I was horribly ignorant, that I had been put into the world but had been denied a chance to learn" (254).

For support in her new pursuits, as well as for practical assistance, Cohen looked to sympathetic American reformers. After an unpleasant experience in which male coworkers oppressed her with coarse jokes, Lillian Wald found her a place in a cooperative dressmaking workshop at the Nurses' Settlement. The instructor, Leonora O'Reilly, a charismatic woman of working-class Irish parentage, was an inspiration to associates of all classes in the labor and social reform movements in which she was active. The venture reminded Cohen of the cooperative sewing shop in Nikolay Chernyshevsky's *What Is to Be Done?*, an influential Russian utopian novel, both feminist and socialist, that she was reading at the time: "The little shop turned out to be more and more like a shop in a dream. . . . In this book there was an ideal sewing shop and I felt as if our little shop too was out of a story" (279). Evidently too dreamlike to survive the cutthroat conditions of the garment industry, the New York cooperative soon went under.[46]

Overcoming her shyness, Cohen found intellectual stimulation and companionship in a community of young working-class women who formed around O'Reilly. As they pursued common cultural interests, she credits the teacher and a young woman in the class who "read greedily" with unlocking her intellectual curiosity. O'Reilly later asked Cohen to assist her in setting up the Manhattan Trade School for Girls and remained an important person in her life, the recipient of confidences about personal matters and about her literary efforts. In what must have been an act of enormous gravity, Cohen dedicated *Out of the Shadow* to her.[47]

Cohen now read not only to remedy her intellectual deficits or improve her English, but also to gain perspective on her own life and to know that she was not alone. Reading not to escape her situation, but to comprehend it, she turned to George Eliot's *Silas Marner*, which a friend recommended when there was trouble at home: "It was so that I loved best to read—when I could see a connection between life and literature. Literature, to me, was as real as life. Literature was life. Many an amusement that was within my reach I gave up, to read." Literature that was "as real as life" offered the solace that made her own situation easier to bear, elicited a sensibility that helped her understand it, and provided her with a language into which she could translate her experience. But what did she mean when she declared that "Literature was life"? That she lived in books rather than in her impoverished and conflicted surroundings? That literature made life bearable? That she could not live without it? Perhaps something of all of these.[48]

Cohen's narrative leaves off somewhere between the end of adolescence and the beginning of womanhood. It ends on an ambiguous note, with Cohen still struggling to learn English, this time to read and write script, at first in order to correspond with a man whose letters she "almost lived for."[49] Nothing came of the relationship, and she drew close to the man's unnamed friend who was well-read in both Russian and English. Their common interest in books was central to their growing intimacy, which, Cohen hints, might lead to marriage, as it did.[50]

Little is known about Joseph Cohen, except that in later years he had "a newspaper-cigarette stand" in an office building. The couple's only child, Evelyn, was born in 1905.[51] After her marriage, Cohen began taking writing courses, a practice she continued at several institutions over the years. *Out of the Shadow* originated as an exercise in an advanced English course at the Socialist Rand School taught by Joseph Gollomb, himself an immigrant writer who encouraged her to write about her own experience. After struggling to begin the composition that became the first chapter of her book, she hit on the first lines: "I was born in a small Russian village"—perhaps an echo of the opening of *David Copperfield* that had captured her imagination years before.[52] Gollomb challenged her to keep on writing, and he read each chapter aloud to the class.

Bent on making literature out of her life, Cohen continued on her own. To try out her work on an audience, she read chapters aloud to her husband and young daughter. Writing was at once a torment and a necessity, an act of will by a woman who never overcame her intellectual insecurity. "I cannot write even a short letter without hardship and shame," she wrote, "I am hopelessly ignorant." But as the years passed, she kept on with her life story, almost as a fate. She was so overwhelmed when the publisher's acceptance notice came that her daughter had to read it to her.[53]

Out of the Shadow appeared in 1918 to favorable reviews that praised it as an authentic story of immigrant life. Accenting the hardships the author endured, the reviewer for *Life and Labor*, the journal of the Women's Trade Union League, heard in Cohen's autobiography, as in *Uncle Tom's Cabin* and *Oliver Twist*, "the voice of the story of multitudes."[54] The realistic scenes of tenement life and sweatshops convinced readers of the book's essential truth, prompting the reviewer in the Socialist *New York Call* to agree with the publisher that it was "the fruit of unconscious art." For its part, the *Outlook* considered it "An autobiography that reads like a novel. How a Russian emigrant girl could write such a story as this is one of the mysteries of the thing we call genius."[55] In fact, Cohen's writing had been shaped by years of immersing herself in stories, both in books and in the oral culture of her family. And by her painstaking efforts to perfect her craft.

Out of the Shadow was translated into French, Danish, and Russian. In the next few years, Cohen published almost a dozen short works, including autobiographical essays, sensitive articles on Easter and Thanksgiving that examined similarities and differences between Old World and New, and short stories of Russian village life.[56] One of them, "Natalka's Portion," was selected for inclusion in a volume of the best stories of 1922 (one of six reprintings). It is a well-wrought and moving tale of a mother's anguished efforts to persuade her miserly husband to provide a marriage portion for their daughter; she succeeds at the last moment, but only by chance. Despite its Russian subject, the editor believed that "Natalka's Portion," like the other stories in the collection, by "uniting genuine substance and artistic form in a closely woven pattern with such sincerity . . . may fairly claim a position in American literature."[57] Describing the emotionally intense process of the story's creation, Cohen observed that when the "pictures" came to her, she fell to weeping with the peasant mother: "I was no longer building a story. I was living the life of my childhood over again."[58]

The writer who had struggled so hard for self-expression went on to receive prestigious fellowships at the MacDowell Colony in Peterborough, New Hampshire, where she spent the summers of 1923 and 1924. She died the following year at the age of forty-five, an event that can be traced only by a date appended to her record at MacDowell. Cohen's last years are shrouded in mystery. From her letters to Leonora O'Reilly we know that she separated from her husband in the early 1920s and that she was economically hard-pressed and still struggling with her writing. Otherwise the historical record trails off. Cohen's surviving siblings evidently talked little about her, but a niece recalls her mother telling her that Cohen committed suicide.[59]

Although best known for her sensitive portrayal of a Jewish woman's struggles to overcome the hardships of immigrant life, Cohen did not want to be restricted in subject. Moving away from the first-person in her fiction, she wrote stories of Russian peasant life, of love and work. "My aim is to write, telling of the life among the Jews on Cherry Street from which I come, among the Russian peasants from whom I come, and among the Americans among whom I am."[60] This ambitious project may have exceeded her emotional as well as creative resources. Integrating these multiple selves seems to have eluded her during the difficult last years. But even if Rose Cohen could not sustain her literary success, her moment in the sun represents a triumph of spirit and will by one who traveled an enormous cultural and intellectual distance in a short lifetime.

.   .   .   .

Where Rose Cohen's autobiography is a story of hesitant progress out of the shadow of illiteracy, Mary Antin's *The Promised Land* is a paean to the

Portrait of Mary Antin, ca. 1915.
Courtesy of the Boston Public
Library, Print Department.
Photograph by Falk Studio.

power of her adoptive country to refashion a humble Jewish immigrant girl
into an American citizen. It is a story of Americanization and class mobility
made possible by circumstances quite different from those experienced by
Cohen. Better educated on arrival, Antin went to American schools, had
paternal support and easy access to books, and from her earliest years in
the United States found intermediaries who supported her in her burning
desire to become a writer. The opening lines capture the theme and tone:
"I was born, I have lived, and I have been made over. Is it not time to write
my life's story? . . . I can analyze my subject, I can reveal everything; for *she*,
and not *I*, is my real heroine. My life I have still to live; her life ended where
mine began."[61]

Published in 1912, when Antin was thirty-one, *The Promised Land* was
wildly successful, no doubt because its story of America was so celebratory.
Widely and on the whole favorably reviewed, it became a best seller and went
through thirty-four editions by the time of the author's death in 1949.[62] It also
launched a vogue for ethnic autobiography, of which *Out of the Shadow* is a
prime example.[63] Unremitting in its praise of the author's adoptive country,

The Promised Land became *the* story of the Jewish American experience—male or female—and remains so to this day. Together with Abraham Cahan, the influential editor of the *Jewish Daily Forward*, Antin has been credited with "inventing the Jew" in American Jewish autobiography.[64] Such preeminence was unthinkable for a Jewish woman in the Old World.

Like *Out of the Shadow*, *The Promised Land* is a tale of emancipation from the benighted customs, language, and religion of the Old World. Antin did not dwell on tenements and sweatshops (she had no experience of the latter) but on the triumph over her non-American origins by an ambitious girl whose childhood was consumed with books, school, and libraries. She arrived in Boston in 1894 at about the same time and age as Cohen; at thirteen, she was young enough to master English and had the opportunity to do so. Unlike Cohen, birth order was in her favor: her older sister Frieda was the one who went to work, while Mary attended school. Antin also had unwavering support from her father, who took pride in her every achievement and, despite the family's precarious economic circumstances, allowed her to attend high school at a time when few children, immigrants or natives, did so.[65] Steeped in Jewish learning in Russia, Joseph Antin left off observance in the United States, as did his daughter. He became an American at the first opportunity, an act that conferred citizenship on his children as well. For Mary Antin, learning English and acquiring American citizenship were the essential portals of entry into the new life she celebrated so extravagantly.

For Antin, the principal sites of deliverance were public school and library. A "green" pupil in September who did not know the days of the week in English, by February she had written an extravagant homage to George Washington, a patriotic verse of many stanzas, which she recited "with a foreign accent, indeed, but with plenty of enthusiasm" (206). She gave it her all, for "I must tell them what George Washington had done for their country—for *our* country—for me" (230). Antin's involvement with the father of her adoptive country was far from casual. Her voice shook and her hands trembled when it came her turn to read her poem aloud, and she "gazed with adoration" at the portraits of the first president and his wife. But—and this was the point—however heroic, he was not beyond the reach of a schoolgirl: "this George Washington . . . was like a king in greatness, and he and I were Fellow Citizens." Thrilled that she now understood the meaning of "my country," she concluded that Washington himself "could not mean more than I when [he] said 'my country,' after I had once felt it. For the Country was for all the Citizens, and *I was a Citizen*" (224–25). Her poem contrasted this welcome with life in Europe, where Jews were a people without a country doomed to permanent exile and where the emblems of Russian nationhood under the Romanoffs—flag, country, and war heroes—symbolized only terror.[66]

Among the privileges of citizenship, none was greater than the public library, which Antin referred to as a "palace" and as "paradise." Discovering the local branch one summer, she spent hours in the reading room, where she welcomed the unaccustomed quiet and the opportunity to learn at her own pace, "without being obliged to stop for stupid little girls and inattentive little boys to catch up with the lesson" (256). Lining up before the library opened, she borrowed and read a book a day—the maximum allowed. In this way she became familiar with the literature of American childhood, the works of Louisa May Alcott, Horatio Alger, and Jacob Abbott in particular.

But it was the Boston Public Library that elicited her greatest flight of fancy. As a high school student, she loved to linger at the entrance to read the carved inscriptions: *"Public Library—Built by the People—Free to All.* Did I not say it was my palace? Mine, because I was a citizen; mine, though I was born an alien; mine, though I lived on Dover Street. My palace—*mine!"* In her "right to be there," and to say *"This is mine"* and *"This is ours,"* she felt at home with "all these eager children, all these fine-browed women, all these scholars going home to write learned books." Best of all was the vast reading room: "Everything I read in school, in Latin or Greek, everything in my history books, was real to me here, in this courtyard set about with stately columns." Antin's definition of what is real diverges sharply from Cohen's, to whom Dickens rang true. Perhaps only by locating herself amid stately columns in a grand space could Antin mediate the distance between the Greeks and the ghetto she was so eager to escape: "Dover Street was never really my residence" (340–42).

In the reading room she made a point of recalling her birthplace, "the better to bring out the wonder of my life." Born in "the prison of the Pale," it was a miracle that she roamed at will in the land of freedom: "That I who had been brought up to my teens almost without a book should be set down in the midst of all the books that ever were written was a miracle as great as any on record. That an outcast should become a privileged citizen, that a beggar should dwell in a palace—this was a romance more thrilling than poet ever sung. Surely I was rocked in an enchanted cradle" (341–43). In this telling, Antin becomes the heroine of her own romance, princess in her own fairy tale. In contrast to the usual romance, however, hers is a story—and a reversal of fortune—centered on books and learning rather than on marriage to the prince. It is a striking departure from the Orthodox belief that a woman could not enter heaven without a man: in America, a woman did not need a prince to enter paradise.

Antin does not explicitly invoke gender in her discussion of becoming a citizen (or comment on its limited application to women, who could not vote in most parts of the United States). She simply notes her acquisition of citizenship by virtue of her father's naturalization. But elsewhere her resentment at the limitations placed on girls, in particular their exclusion from learning in the Old World, blazes forth. When her younger brother entered heder, like his male peers, he became "the hero of the family," while "a girl's real schoolroom was her mother's kitchen" (32, 34). "A girl was 'finished' when she could read her prayers in Hebrew, following the meaning by the aid of the Yiddish translation especially prepared for women. If she could sign her name in Russian, do a little figuring, and write a letter in Yiddish . . . she was called . . . well educated" (111). For Antin, American citizenship, with its access to public schools and libraries, signified the possibilities open to her not just as a Jew but as a woman.

Antin came to the United States at a time when a girl raised in a shtetl could find institutional support for her desire to make something of herself. Female immigrants in particular often found themselves the objects of intervention by sympathetic (although often patronizing) natives eager to promote their adaptation to American life. The New York City Board of Education signaled such an interest when it added Edith Horton's *A Group of Famous Women* to its booklist in 1914. The author observed that although women then voted in ten states and therefore needed to be educated for citizenship, material about the important role women had played and would continue to play in American life was difficult to come by in schools. All girls needed this knowledge, but "many foreign born girls in our schools have practically no means of acquiring any adequate idea of the ideal standard of American womanhood—a standard radically different from that in their own native lands." Although Horton's introduction closes with a formulaic reminder that "the home and the family are the bulwarks of the country," the biographical sketches offer sympathetic portrayals of nonconformists like Margaret Fuller, Susan B. Anthony, and Lucy Stone, as well as Louisa May Alcott and Harriet Beecher Stowe. Ostensibly chosen "because of their direct influence upon events of world-wide significance," these subjects often challenged the gender norms of their day by virtue of their feminism, their rejection of marriage, or both.[67]

Antin's precocious experience as a writer would in any event have suggested the possibilities open to women in the United States—even "a little

Jewish girl from Polotzk." *Primary Education* published her composition on "Snow," which a favorite teacher—the first of many American patrons—sent as an example of what a young Russian Jewish child could do after studying English for "only four months" (211). On her own, Antin took her poem on Washington to several newspapers, including the *Boston Herald*, which published it. Fascinated by seeing her name in print, Antin wondered, "Was this really I?" (213). It was a reasonable question, not least because "Mary Antin" was a name she acquired in the New World, where "Mary" replaced "Mashke." As if to consolidate her literary precocity, letters she had written to an uncle about the voyage to America appeared in English translation in book form as *From Plotzk to Boston* (1899) while she was still in her teens.[68] The girl who had scoured the dictionary for words fitting to praise Washington later scrutinized encyclopedia entries of famous people, beginning with her hero, but most often her favorite authors. She experienced "an enormous ambition that devoured all my other ambitions . . . that I should live to know that after my death my name would surely be printed in the encyclopaedia." This secret longing took concrete form when she saw that "Antin, Mary" would come not far from "Alcott, Louisa M." (258–59). By juxtaposing her name with that of the preeminent American writer for girls, Antin linked herself to a native female literary tradition. It was a move that depended on approximating an American girlhood—as much as a non-native could.

. . . .

Mary Antin was not alone in her infatuation with libraries or her belief that they embodied America's democratic best. Writing of the library from a radical perspective, labor organizer Elizabeth Hasanovitz observed: "I was not accustomed to being served so readily and receiving every book for which I asked. . . . It was there that I found my coveted *America*; it was there I found *freedom* and *equality!*" Hesitant at first to patronize institutions named for capitalists, she concluded: "Never mind Astor, never mind Lenox—'t is ours, ours—everybody's!"[69]

Voting with their feet, Jewish children, those born in the United States and those who arrived at young ages, flocked to the libraries that sprang up on the Lower East Side at the turn of the twentieth century. A librarian's account of a crowd that turned out on an early March day in 1901, not for a nickel movie, but for the opening of a new branch of the Aguilar Free Library, on 7th Street and Avenue C, captures the spirit: "The children commenced to flock to the library at precisely three o'clock and it required the services of the policeman, janitor and seven monitors to keep them in order—the line extending round the corner as far as Avenue D." She reported with pride that "fully two thousand readers came to draw books"; in all, 1,479 books, 927 of them juveniles, circulated. New applicants for library cards were asked to return the following day.[70] Uncommon excitement was to be expected at the launching of a new branch of a free circulating library in New York's overcrowded tenement district. Even on ordinary days at the Aguilar's East Broadway branch, the line extended down the stairs, as impatient children jostled one another while waiting for books in the after-school hours. Here, too, a policeman was on hand to help prevent accidents.[71] Librarians at nearby branches of the New York Public Library, like the Aguilar patronized primarily by eastern European Jews, also reported long lines, overcrowding, and a perennial shortage of books: on one occasion, only eighty-four volumes remained on the shelves of the Children's Room of the Seward Park Branch.[72]

Many observers, even those who otherwise considered Russian Jews uncouth, commented on their apparent "book hunger." With some frequency, articles appeared in the press with titles like "Jew Babes at the Library" and claims that the "*Bible* goes out like the last new novel."[73] Librarians who worked on New York's Lower East Side exulted that a smaller proportion of fiction circulated at their branches than elsewhere—and that "of the very best." Believing that foreign children were older "in experience & taste" than Americans of the same age, they approved youthful predilections for history and science and even "adult" fiction.[74] One children's librarian proclaimed with delight that "Shakespeare ought to rise up and make a bow."[75] Even the city's police commissioner declared with astonishment: "Think of it! Herbert Spencer preferred to a fairy story by boys and girls."[76] The belief that Jews were superior in intellect and, in consequence, also in character derived from long-standing racial preconceptions embraced by many Jews as well as Gentiles at the turn of the century.[77] In fact, fairy tales were the most popular children's books in Jewish neighborhoods as they were elsewhere.

Contemporaries and historians alike have tended to equate this passion for reading with intellectual seriousness and a specifically Jewish desire for education. It is true that Jews made excellent use of the opportunities available in New York City. Free public education, including secondary schools after 1898, and colleges for both men and women (City College and the Normal College—later Hunter College—respectively), conferred benefits unknown in eastern Europe and, as far as college goes, not yet widely available in the United States.[78] But the purely instrumental reasons for reading are easily overstated, important though they were for a group that had been denied access to public education and professional advancement in eastern Europe. As the crush of children at the Avenue C library suggests, enthusiasm for reading preceded any specifically vocational ambition.

Puzzled by children's eagerness to read and their willingness to undergo almost any inconvenience to secure a desired book, a librarian at the Seward Park Branch mused:

> I do not quite comprehend the phsycology [*sic*] of it all in the case of the children.
>
> To be eager to come day after day to a place so thronged, to wait as they sometimes do literally for hours at a time in the hope of securing some special book,—and then do it all over again at the very earliest opportunity—is proof conclusive that something more is effected than any tangible benefit.[79]

There were, of course, tangible as well as intangible benefits for readers of all ages, especially for children. Gaining entrance could be daunting; in addition to the long lines, librarians refused to admit anyone with dirty hands, and some confiscated the cards of repeat offenders. Once inside, however, libraries were welcoming places that offered refuge from overcrowded and noisy tenements—and from parental oversight. To Philip Roth, who grew up in the 1940s, the library signified not only "the idea of communal ownership, property held in common for the common good" ("books . . . weren't mine alone, they were everybody's") but the opportunity "to sit in a strange place, beyond the reach of parent and school and read whatever one chose, in anonymity and peace."[80] This desire for self-direction, evident as well in Antin's pleasure at reading at her own pace, was nowhere more apparent than in children's joy at having their own library cards and freedom in their choice of books—policies instituted early in the twentieth century by the child-friendly librarian in charge of children's work for the New York Public Library. Some librarians no doubt fell short of her instructions to treat every child with respect, but many strove to do so, some it seems successfully.[81] In a study of twenty-six immigrant men and women educated in New York City public schools, "*Every* informant spoke lovingly of books and the library, and several recounted strategies they employed to up the two-book-per-visit quota."[82]

In addition to encouraging individual enthusiasms, libraries offered sociability. Very young Jewish children listened with rapt attention at story hours, another innovation of the period, an enthusiasm some librarians attributed to the absence of storytelling and bedtime reading at home.[83] Following the practice of settlements, some branches instituted or encouraged the formation of young people's clubs, generally along sex-segregated lines, while the Seward Park Branch organized a mothers' club and reached out to women who did not know English.[84] Library reading rooms enabled individuals to pursue their own reading interests in a public rather than an isolated setting.

Librarians also assisted with homework. Frequently requested subjects at the Rivington Branch in February 1909 encompassed literature (Browning's poems, the lives of Longfellow and Victor Hugo); history (the Creek Indian War, "the number of presidents we have had"); biography (from Newton to Helen Keller); deportment ("Poems on politeness and obedience"); patriotism ("Uncle Sam how he looks, what he wears & how he serves his country"); contemporary relevance (woman suffrage); and subjects with an apparently ethnic focus (St. Patrick and "What nationality was Marconi").[85] Girls were often the main questioners, even on subjects of presumed interest to boys like General Grant.[86]

Girls were also enthusiastic borrowers, judging from the titles of the most widely circulated books. Of the ten titles most often mentioned by children's librarians in 1910 as "never in," eight were written by women, with the majority falling into the category of girls' books. Except for fairy tales—always in short supply—these included the *Brownie* series (Palmer Cox), *Rebecca of Sunny Brook Farm* (Kate Douglas Wiggin), *The Lamplighter* (Maria Cummins), *Little Women*, Frances Hodgson Burnett's *Little Princess*, and Margaret Sidney's *Five Little Pepper* series.[87] Books that appealed to children's imaginations, as these did, were not readily available elsewhere. Few immigrants— or working-class natives, for that matter—could afford to buy books of any kind. Newspapers were more plentiful and carried serial stories, but none written specifically for children: despite a rich storytelling tradition in eastern Europe, a juvenile Yiddish literature did not evolve until after 1910.[88]

For bookish girls without family resources, libraries were places of amusement, as entertaining to some as Coney Island but more affordable. Like other sites of reading, they helped to cement the bonds of female friendship. Bella (Cohen) Spewack's *Streets: A Memoir of the Lower East Side* captures with some immediacy the joys of trolling the neighborhood for books.[89] Born in Transylvania, Spewack came to the United States at the age of three shortly after the turn of the twentieth century. When she was eleven or twelve, she had a flourishing friendship with "another bookworm" that "consisted simply of going to the library together, to school together, and sometimes doing our lessons together." They scoured the libraries that blanketed

Children at charge desk covering their books with wrapping paper. Hamilton Fish
Branch Library, ca. 1910. Photograph by Lewis Hine. The New York Public Library Archives,
The New York Public Library, Astor, Lenox and Tilden Foundations.

the Lower East Side almost as personal preserves: "Seward Park Branch,
Tompkins Park Branch, Bond Street Branch, Rivington Street Branch, and
the Second Avenue Branch saw us both, eyes alight." At each, they sought
favorite books—the Gypsy Breynton series at one, the Hildegarde and Patty
books at others. Sometimes they spent hours at a circulation desk waiting
for the return of a volume they longed to read, pouncing on it with glee if it
turned up (54–55).

What they read had little to do with their lives. In Spewack's case that
was the point. At twelve, she was acutely conscious of the "sordidness" of
life around her; to escape, she hid behind her books and built up a life of her
own in public school, settlement, and library (66). Jews did not appear in
these stories, nor did the ravages of tenement life. Reading books like *Little
Women* and even fairy stories, Spewack inferred that the characters were "all
Krishts. No Jews were mentioned, therefore where it was not stated, I assumed that they were all Krishts." After she observed a woman with a Jewish

name who "acted like a Krisht—'refined'—and wore gloves," she concluded that wearing gloves, speaking perfect English, and not arguing about paying children's trolley fares constituted the essential characteristics of "Krishts" and informed her mother that she wanted to be one (29–30).

For Spewack, Jews and "Krishts" could be distinguished by attributes, like dress and deportment, that we associate with class. Reading American books permitted children of the ghetto, struggling with poverty and premature responsibility, to enter into the lives of middle-class children and to dream of a future in which they could partake of such niceties. Spewack's early dreams, like Antin's, included a literary career, but she had different models and decorated her windowless bedroom with pin-ups of James Whitcomb Riley, Robert Louis Stevenson, and Rudyard Kipling, popular writers at the time (137). After a brief stint as a reporter, she became a successful playwright, working with her husband Samuel Spewack. The high point of their careers was *Kiss Me, Kate*, a collaboration with Cole Porter, for which they wrote the book and libretto.

As with Rose Cohen, books—and Spewack's absorption in them—became a source of family conflict. Spewack does not mention her mother's reactions to her interest in American ways or the desire she expressed to become a "Krisht." But reading—and its counterpart, writing—offered Spewack the fastest way out of the ghetto, a prospect that alarmed her mother, who accused Bella of "throwing your mother away for books" and threatened to "burn them all." Despite such outbursts and the family's extreme poverty—they were receiving charity—her mother allowed her to remain in high school (138).

Spewack's account, though more lighthearted than Cohen's and less hortatory than Antin's, like theirs points to books as a principal source of knowledge about American life and the possibilities it held out to Jews. Access to American culture was not without its hazards. Each of the three accounts underscores the author's estrangement—from family, religion, or both. For Cohen and Spewack, reading was a source of open family conflict. Beyond this, Cohen and Antin expressed their discontent with traditional Jewish culture and religion; both also displayed at least a passing interest in Christianity. Antin married a Christian and was interested in such alternative spiritual paths as mysticism and anthroposophy.[90]

Of course reading American books did not by itself alienate immigrant women from Jewish tradition. For those who sought them out, these books may have helped them to analyze, and perhaps even act on, feelings of which they may previously have been only dimly aware. Beyond specifically religious or ethnic issues, reading allowed Jewish girls and young women, as it did their non-Jewish counterparts, to test emerging values and contemplate the future, including the kind of women they wished to become. Given reading's power to transform emotions, it offered women like Cohen, Antin, and Spewack not only occasions to reimagine themselves but also the pragmatic skills with which to reinvent themselves in the world.

Their stories of reading were those of a minority of Jewish immigrants. Most never completed the transition to the New World, which, as in the instances discussed here, often marked a transition to middle-class American life as well. Those who came as adults, even if they made the effort, often found it difficult to read and write English, especially works that demanded sophisticated vocabulary or syntax.[91] But there were Yiddish books and a Yiddish press that remained strong until about 1940.[92] Newspapers published short stories and serial fiction, much in the form of romances (known as *schund*) deplored by high-minded editors, but popular with women readers. Like their English-speaking sisters, many Yiddish readers had a distinctly secular outlook, in the case of women writers, often militantly so.[93]

Attainment of expressive literacy in English brought access to a culture that promised some Jewish women immigrants greater freedom and gender equality, including citizenship and integration into a more welcoming society than they had known, attainments that often put them at odds with the dictates of their religion and the values of their Old World parents. The contrast with the reading practices of African American women is striking. Unlike immigrant women seeking to escape from what they came to view as an oppressive patriarchal religious tradition, African American women's literary traditions promoted the communal ties needed for survival in a hostile environment. Formerly enslaved Americans and their children learned to read and write at missionary schools. Daughters often helped their mothers with the alphabet, binding the generations together in a once forbidden activity whose potency they well understood. If for many Jews America seemed like the land of opportunity, African Americans, with their long experience in the United States, knew very well that they would not be entering the promised land any time soon.

. . . .

CHAPTER NINE

With Pen and Voice

Ida B. Wells, Race, Literature, and Politics

Ida B. Wells possessed a faith in the fruits of literacy shared by many women of the Progressive generation, black as well as white. Proficiency with words was central to her development as a child and her identity as an adult. It became the source of her livelihood as well, first as a teacher, then as a journalist. By hard work and determination she demonstrated that a woman born into slavery could transcend her origins and leave her mark on history. Her masterful use of pen and voice in her campaign against lynching carried her to the front ranks of African American leaders in the 1890s.

Wells came of age at a rare moment of opportunity for African American women. Given the conspicuous needs of a newly freed people, they had a central role to play in blacks' entry into civil society.[1] Like their white counterparts, black women clustered in teaching. By the 1880s, with the proliferation of race-based newspapers, talented women could also look to careers in journalism and to more formal literary achievement as well: a growing number of African American women turned to writing fiction in the 1890s, as white women had done in the 1850s.[2] Wells would try her hand at all of them.

With the early death of both parents, she had to make her own way in the world while supporting younger siblings. She was better educated than most African Americans of her generation, but to attain full command of her speaking and writing voice, she supplemented her years of schooling with education of an informal kind. In pursuit of expressive literacy, she was more fortunate than Rose Cohen, for she had full support from the African American community, for whom literacy was a collective enterprise.

A seeker after culture throughout her life, Wells displayed the passion for self-improvement common to many Americans of humble origin. As a young woman, she honed her literary and performance skills at a literary society in Memphis where she took part in diverse pursuits, oral and written, public and private. In the African American oratorical tradition in which a reader was not so much a person who pours silently over the pages of a book as one who excels in recitation, she became a noted "elocutionist." Her oral and literary skills blended when she became editor of the group's newsletter, which she wrote and then read aloud.[3] These avocational efforts served her well in her career as a journalist and in her antilynching crusade, in which reading, writing, and speaking coalesced.[4]

Wells's faith in literature as a means of self-improvement had a racial as well as an individual dynamic. Like many of her peers, she hoped that a "race literature" that portrayed African Americans more accurately would offset the debilitating stereotypes then circulating in serious literature as well as in popular culture. Those who wrote a people's history and literature were those who had, if not necessarily the last word, at least a significant voice in the struggle for truthful representation. In this context, Wells merits a place as a producer as well as a consumer of literature.

· ·

Ida B. Wells was born in July 1862 in Holly Springs, Mississippi, in the waning days of slavery. In her posthumously published autobiography, *Crusade for Justice*, she locates her family at the apex of both the slave and free black hierarchies. Her mother, Elizabeth Warrenton Wells, was "a famous cook" of part Indian descent, her father a man of high standing in the community. Apprenticed at eighteen by his white father-owner to his future wife's master, James Wells became a skilled carpenter who later supported himself and his growing family by his trade. He was a political activist who could not be intimidated, a trait he passed on to his daughter. When his employer locked him out of the shop because he refused to vote the Democratic ticket, Jim Wells "bought a new set of tools, and went across the street and rented another house." His attendance at political meetings kept his wife pacing the floor for fear of Ku Klux Klan reprisals. He was also a "master Mason" and a trustee of Shaw University, where his children went to school.[5]

As the most immediate symbol of their newly acquired freedom, literacy took on an almost sacred meaning to the Wells family and others emerging from slavery: its attainment became an essential precondition for U.S. civic identity. Despite laws that prohibited teaching slaves to read or write, an estimated 5–10 percent of enslaved African Americans had attained some degree of literacy, often at considerable risk.[6] During and after the war, men and women flocked to schools established by missionary societies of several denominations and by the United States Freedmen's Bureau; later they attended public schools set up by state governments. Accounts by white and black teachers who went south to participate in the great experiment emphasized the eagerness of the new students, with the middle-aged taking their places alongside their children in the hope of learning the fundamentals, often in order to read the Bible. As a result of hard work under difficult circumstances, African American illiteracy declined to an estimated 70 percent by 1880, 45 percent by 1900, and 30 percent ten years later.[7] A considerable racial gap remained, but given the community's history, this was by any standards an impressive achievement. By 1910 African American women's literacy surpassed that of their male counterparts. Among the causes of this gender imbalance—the reverse of that for Jews—was the exceptionally high concentration of black women in teaching, the chief alternative to domestic service.[8]

As an African American growing up in the turbulent years following emancipation, Ida B. Wells had a different relationship to literacy from that of native-born whites. Like others in similar circumstances, she did not start with a reserve of parental book learning. Her mother and probably to a degree her father depended on Ida, their oldest child, in this regard: according to the census of 1870 Jim Wells could read but not write.[9] This reversal of the usual order of things heightened the salience of literary endeavor for Wells and other African Americans emerging from slavery.

In her autobiography, Wells places literacy at the core of her identity. It is the subject of her revealing first words about herself: "I do not remember when or where I started school. My earliest recollections are of reading the newspaper to my father and an admiring group of his friends. He was interested in politics and I heard the words Ku Klux Klan long before I knew what they meant."[10] Here Wells represents herself as rendering a useful and appreciated community service by performing literacy for adult men, most of them probably illiterate or at best marginally literate. The scene illustrates the continuity between oral and print cultures in the African American community and the political nature of both. Wells seems to be suggesting that these sessions, at which the men undoubtedly discussed the news they heard, constituted her initiation into racial politics. The association between literacy and racial politics is striking: Wells's retrospective account intimates both an early affinity for the literary form—the newspaper—and the coupling of newspapers and racial politics that marked her career.

Wells's inability to remember when or where she started school—presumably where she learned to read—seems to imply that she always knew how.[11] Despite the omission, she makes it clear that school was central to the Wells children and their parents. "Our job was to go to school and learn all we could," she declared, adding that her "mother went along to school with us until she learned to read the Bible" and subsequently visited "to see how we were getting along."[12] Literacy for Wells was thus associated with her mother and religion as well as with her father and politics.

Her schooling reinforced her home religious training. Shaw (later Rust) University was established in Holly Springs by the Freedmen's Aid Society of the Methodist Episcopal Church after the war. Like most of the missionary institutions founded for southern blacks prior to 1880, it was less a university than a primary and secondary school—of necessity, since students lacked basic skills. African American residents supported the enterprise wholeheartedly and subscribed $2,000 toward the erection of its first building. For their part, local whites excoriated the white president for treating blacks as social equals and supporting their right to vote. True to its religious mission, Shaw required all pupils to study the Bible and to attend daily chapel, weekly prayer meetings, and Sunday school; in later years, at least, there were frequent revival meetings.[13]

Along with family, school, and religion, Wells included fiction among the formative influences of childhood. She went so far as to claim that she "knew nothing of life except what I had read." A self-described "voracious reader" who "read all the fiction in the Sunday school library and in Rust College," she professed, "I had formed my ideals on the best of Dickens's stories, Louisa May Alcott's, Mrs. A. D. T. Whitney's, and Charlotte Brontë's books, and Oliver Optic's stories for boys. I had read the Bible and Shakespeare through, but I had never read a Negro book or anything about Negroes."[14] These authors might have been claimed by any middle-class female reader. Three of them wrote for the burgeoning market in adolescent fiction. Brontë was a favorite of adolescent girls, while Dickens was the most popular author with readers of all ages. Shakespeare and the Bible were considered universal, and Wells's locution suggests that familiarity with them was expected.

In the absence of evidence, it is difficult to know how Wells read herself into these texts in childhood and early adolescence. The rather casual mention of the Bible in her list of formative reading is curious. Given the religious emphasis at school and at home, where the Bible was the only acceptable Sunday reading, one might expect greater stress on its role in shaping her core ethical values. The diary she kept as a young woman is full of religious striving, and she remained a churchgoer all her life, sometimes attending three or four services on Sundays. But the religious note in her autobiography is restrained.[15] Frequently at odds with African American clergymen, whom she censured for their moral and political shortcomings, including their failure to support her antilynching campaign, she may have been disinclined to link her work to a patriarchal religious tradition, a politically quiescent one at that.[16] The seriousness she attached to religion may also have prompted her to separate the spiritual from the temporal. When as a young woman she decided to teach a Sunday school class for youth, she observed, "the bible & its truths are dealt with too flippantly to suit me."[17]

Wells's striking assertion that she "had never read a Negro book or anything about Negroes" presumably meant no fiction, since she had grown up with newspapers. Despite this gap, she seems to have had no difficulty reading herself into texts by white authors. Indeed, she depicts the important early influences outside her family as mainly white. Of Shaw University, she writes: "All my teachers had been the consecrated white men and women from the North who came into the South to teach immediately after the end of the war. It was they who brought us the light of knowledge and their splendid example of Christian courage."[18] In her campaign against lynching, she emulated their example.

The prevalence of these early influences in no way diminished Wells's commitment to advancing the legal and political status of African Americans. In her campaign against lynching and her legal challenges to segregated railroad cars, this engaged and uncompromising woman held up Anglo-American political and moral traditions as universal standards for judgment. Claiming white as well as black abolitionists as forebears, the Declaration of Independence and the Constitution, she ended an antilynching speech to a white audience by quoting the ringing hymn to freedom, "My country! 'tis of thee."[19] In this context, her later attention to African American literature was not a negation of her earlier interests but an enlargement of them. She saw no contradiction between the particular and the universal. By joining Dickens and Shakespeare in pursuing fundamental human truths, African Americans would bring blacks within the circle of humanity.

．　．　．　．　．　．　．　．　．　．　．　．　．　．　．　．　．　．　．　．

Wells's education, like her childhood, ended abruptly in 1878 with the deaths of both parents and a younger sibling in a yellow fever epidemic. The oldest of six surviving children, sixteen-year-old Ida assumed responsibility for her siblings by becoming a teacher, an occupation that neither pleased nor interested her. Taking up her duty in "country schools," she left Shaw without receiving a high school degree.[20] She later expressed anger and regret at her failure to graduate and the resulting deficits in her knowledge. During this lonely period of her life, three and a half long years, she turned to books for solace: "In the country schools . . . my only diversion was reading and I could forget my troubles in no other way."[21]

Wells's move to Memphis in the early 1880s gave her a much larger stage on which to act out her ambitions. Supporting herself and two sisters as a teacher, first in a country school, then in Memphis, she joined a thriving community of middle-class African Americans who were struggling to maintain their rights in the deteriorating racial climate that followed the end of Reconstruction. She was an eager participant in the cultural life of this community and took advantage of the opportunities for self-improvement it afforded. Wells also established her credentials as a race activist by protesting her exclusion from first-class railroad cars. Her career as a journalist evolved from this mix of avocational interests and racial politics.

A diary Wells kept between December 29, 1885, and September 18, 1887, offers fascinating insights into the life and thought of a spirited young woman who was at once seeking to establish herself professionally, set herself right as a Christian, and navigate Victorian gender norms in her relations with prospective suitors. It documents the early stages of her entry into journalism, demonstrating the ways in which amateur endeavors, many of them literary, provided the skills, experience, and contacts needed to launch her career as a writer, editor, and speaker. The diary reveals as well the fundamental continuity between reading, speaking, and writing in the African American community.

Wells cultivated these skills as a member of a lyceum composed mainly of teachers. These forums for self-improvement flourished among African Americans in the Gilded Age, fostering a tradition of public oratory that endured into the late twentieth century, especially in the South.[22] Like its counterparts elsewhere, the Memphis lyceum was a mixed-media affair which featured "recitations, essays, and debates interspersed with music." It was "a breath of life to me," Wells recalled, "for this program was like the Friday afternoon oratoricals in school." An enthusiastic participant, she gave recitations and delivered at least one talk, intriguingly titled "What Lack We Yet?" Like other African American cultural groups, this one had a political as well as a social and intellectual agenda. When P. B. S. Pinchback, an African American and former governor of Louisiana, spoke there at Wells's invitation, the organizers evidently used the occasion to make a political announcement to the large crowd that turned out.[23]

Whether out of sensitivity about her educational deficits and small-town beginnings—some of her new associates had college degrees—or because she wanted to excel at whatever she did, Wells made the most of the opportunities for self-improvement Memphis offered. She took elocution lessons from Mrs. Fannie J. Thompson, a fellow teacher with whom she labored over Lady Macbeth's letter-reading and sleepwalking scenes. The results were mixed, she thought, when she recited both scenes at a concert organized by a friend in early July 1886. She received loud applause for her rendition of the former but judged her performance in the sleepwalking scene, in which she wore a loose, flowing gown known as a mother hubbard, "not so effective as I would have wished."[24]

Shakespeare was the pinnacle of high culture in the Memphis African American community, as he was elsewhere at the time. So it is not surprising that Wells recited soliloquies from his plays or worked hard to get them right. More striking is the choice of role, especially in view of her later reputation as a dominating woman and charges that she usurped male authority. Lady Macbeth is Shakespeare's fiercest portrait of a woman, one who steels her husband's nerve to murder the king to advance his career but goes mad under the strain: she is the dark opposite of everything a Victorian woman was supposed to be, an object lesson of what comes of violating gender norms.[25]

Two decades later, the *Conservator*, a paper owned by her husband, issued a fierce challenge to African American men: "God grant the race a few more Lady Macbeths like Ida [Wells-]Barnett to pump self respect into our loud-mouthed Negro leaders."[26] Given the contemporary rhetorical emphasis on reclaiming black manhood, this was provocation of a high order.

The Memphis African American community was not all high culture. The group enjoyed less rarified moments, including humorous and dramatic, not to say melodramatic, recitations. Wells delivered a dialect poem, "The Widder Budd," written in the voice of a rural widow wary of the mercenary motives of prospective suitors. She also gave a dramatic recitation of "Le Marriage de Conveniance [sic]," of which she claimed: "every one admired it. Indeed Judge Latham paid me a very high compliment when he said it was the most artistic piece of elocution he had ever heard."[27]

The refinement of Wells's oratorical skills went hand in hand with a growing taste for the theater. She saw the celebrated Shakespearean actor Edwin Booth perform in *Hamlet* and, as Iago, in *Othello* (she preferred the former) and also attended *The Count of Monte Cristo* and *The Mikado* as well as vaudeville. Whether high culture or low, theater was still suspect among the godly, and the son of the pastor of a church she attended reprimanded her for setting a bad example for her students. Wells, who had "not so keenly" seen the wrong, prayed that she would receive strength to do her duty. But she did not change her ways.[28]

Wells's interest in the theater was far from casual. An exacting critic, she declared a reading of *Macbeth* at the lyceum "exceedingly dull & tiresome & some of the pronunciation . . . execrable in the extreme."[29] During the Memphis years she fashioned herself into a skilled performer who garnered accolades for her toasts and "entertainments" at social events. In a scene from the *Rival Queens* judged to be "the crowning literary effort" of one lyceum meeting, she took the part of Mary Stuart, with a fellow teacher playing Elizabeth; both wore costumes.[30] Wells may or may not have been contemplating a career as an actress, as a Washington, D.C., newspaper intimated, but a New York editor went so far as to invite her "to read up Emilia in 'Othello,' as 'he may need me' in that part."[31] In addition to organizing a dramatic club, she asked a friend to buy a copy of *Aesthetic Physical Culture* by Oskar Guttmann, manager of the Stadt Theatre in Hamburg. If she received and read the volume, which was intended for "all cultured circles" as well as for "oratorical and dramatic artists," she would have found instruction on the principles of bodily, gestural, and facial movement, or what the author called "aesthetic gymnastics." There were tips on the use of the hands, the position of the head, how to lift a dress while walking, and a host of exercises to attain proficiency in aesthetic movement—all with the goal of having the body "so in one's power that the moods of the soul may be easily and gracefully rendered." With gymnastics encompassing decorum and manners, the author claimed that a reader could learn about proper posture and behavior (drinking tea, the use of the handkerchief).[32] In tandem with elocution lessons, the book might well have helped an upwardly mobile reader like Wells eliminate lingering marks of her country origins. It would also have fostered the physical presence, confidence, and self-control that later characterized her talks on lynching.

By successfully performing at the lyceum and other Memphis venues, Wells augmented skills that proved useful for her burgeoning career in journalism. Members acknowledged her proficiency in October 1886 by electing her "editress" of the *Evening Star*, the "spicy journal prepared and read by the editor" at the close of each meeting. She had sole responsibility for assembling the "news, literary notes, criticisms of previous offerings on the program, a 'They Say' column of pleasant personalities—and always some choice poetry." Already known for her articles in the African American press, with the *Evening Star* Wells became a one-woman literary show—as writer, editor, and reader.[33]

Enjoyable though group activities and public performances were, at twenty-three Wells felt she was "drifting along with no visible improvement. Yet it is not altogether procrastination, I don't know what books to read that will do the most good & know not where I am to obtain the knowledge."[34] To remedy this lack, and perhaps also to prepare herself for a position higher than elementary school teaching, in the spring of 1886 she took lessons from Theodore W. Lott, a well-regarded teacher at her school. The scope of the lessons is not clear, but on one occasion she asked Lott to buy her "a philosophy" and on another asked him to read an article she was writing. Of her progress she variously observed, "Have taken 3 lessons with Mr. L & find it hard to rouse my sluggish nature to study" and "Am getting along nicely in my studies. Hope I'll have perseverance to continue."[35] Taking stock on her twenty-fifth birthday, Wells lamented "the wasted opportunities" in picking up "the crumbs of knowledge" within her reach: "Consequently I find myself at this age as deficient in a comprehensive knowledge as the veriest schoolgirl just entering the higher course."[36]

While still taking lessons from Lott, in November 1886 Wells joined the Chautauqua Literary and Scientific Circle (CLSC) and subscribed to the *Chautauquan*, its monthly magazine. The cost was $2.00, with another $7.00 for books she ordered by mail.[37] Coming on top of payments for lessons with her elocution teacher and with Lott, this was a hefty outlay for a woman who was financially responsible for siblings, had a weakness for fine clothes, and always had trouble making ends meet on a teacher's salary.[38] It is possible that in this endeavor, as in her lessons with Lott, Wells was hoping for professional advancement. About the time she joined the CLSC, the white superintendent of the Memphis public schools advised her "to study up &

get a principal's certificate & he would give me a school. I believe it's worth the trial."[39]

After receiving the books and the December issue of the *Chautauquan*, she goaded herself on: "Am not keeping up as I could wish but will resume after Christmas."[40] Since this is the last entry on the subject, we don't know whether she continued. If she did, she would have found in the December issue required readings on geology, women's clerical work, the shift from craft to industrial production, an evolutionary perspective on housing, and optional selections by well-known writers. Subsequent numbers included a piece on journalism by Ida Tarbell, a series on "Practical Suggestions on English Composition," several articles on women's work, and one on Sojourner Truth, all of which might have been of greater interest. But Wells would have found most of the readings tangential to her deepening preoccupation with racial issues. By this time, too, she was advancing in journalism, a career that offered an ambitious young woman considerably more scope than teaching.

Fiction was far more engaging. Her reading during the period of the diary included *She* (1886), H. Rider Haggard's best-selling adventure novel about matriarchal rule in Africa, Scott's *Ivanhoe* (she found "a peculiar charm" in the author's "simple language yet strong portraiture of the characters"), and *Bricks without Straw* (1880) by white progressive Albion Tourgée, a novel which, although set in "the Reconstruction era of Negro freedom," she liked only "somewhat."[41] In extended comments on *Vashti; or, "Until Death Us Do Part"* (1869) by Augusta Jane Evans, she noted the author's "pedantic" style and penchant for certain character types that had "almost grown monotonous." Despite these reservations, Wells, who had read the novel before, went on to enthuse: "Her references, quotations, and general language and especially her dialogue—are all elegant, the language chaste and the thought pure & elevating, the dialogue cutting, witty masterpieces," all qualities that made Wells long to know the author.[42]

Wells's most revealing remarks were reserved for heroines and their romances. *Vashti* disappointed because of its failed romance: the hero spurns the admirable woman who loves him, making him "more of a god than a natural human being with heart & soul," while "the idea of her never marrying because of her hopeless love seems unnatural." Wells disparaged Evans's female characters, who had such "an exorbitant ambition that they feed, & trample every thing & every body under their feet to accomplish." But of Victor Hugo's *Les Misérables* she declared: "I do not like his heroine—she is sweet, lovely and all that, but utterly without depth, or penetration—fit only for love, sunshine & flowers."[43] These comments cast light on Wells's own efforts to achieve something in the world without sacrificing romance. They also suggest the complexity of doing so while avoiding exorbitant ambition on the one hand, and shallowness and excessive sweetness on the other. Wells, who had several suitors during her Memphis years but was by February 1887 the only unmarried female teacher at her school, seemed to be searching for fictional heroines who combined drive and femininity.[44] Was there no role model of a forceful woman this side of Lady Macbeth—one who acted on her own rather than through a husband?

For a time Wells was exhilarated by the prospect of writing a novel of her own: "The stupendous idea of writing a work of fiction causes me to smile in derision of myself at daring to dream of such a thing."[45] The subject occupied a central place in her extended correspondence with Charles Morris, a young Louisville journalist and prospective suitor. How seriously she took the project is difficult to say, but fiction was gaining cachet at the time, and it is not surprising that an ambitious and passionate reader like Wells wanted to try her hand at it.[46] If completed, the novel would have placed her in the vanguard of African American fiction writers.[47]

Morris encouraged Wells to make the novel "classical, representative and standard and I shall make myself loved, honored & respected." Responding to his suggestion that they write "in partnership," she mailed him "the plot(?) of our novel." She judged the outline he returned to her "too much on the style of other novels—rather sensational."[48] Wells had other ideas. Outraged at the escalating hostility to African Americans, she recorded episodes of racial offense in her diary—to make sure she would remember them when she wrote her own novel. One involved the sentencing of a black girl to a workhouse for nearly a year for fighting back when a white girl tried to push her off a narrow wooded path. After registering this incident, Wells noted two preposterous episodes resulting from the ban on interracial marriage.[49] By bringing the news into her novel, she would have combined fact with fiction, journalism with literature. Whether or not she hoped to write for the ages as Morris suggested ("classical, representative and standard"), she clearly aspired to write a "Negro book." Perhaps one with the power of *Uncle Tom's Cabin*, in Wells's view a novel in which a "woman's influence . . . was indirectly one of the causes of the abolition of slavery."[50]

Wells got as far as starting a short story in September 1886: "Today witnessed my first essay in story-writing; I have made a beginning. I know not where or when the ending will be. I can see and portray in my mind all the elements of a good story but when I attempt to put it on paper my thoughts dissolve into nothingness."[51] Story writing was not her line, as evidenced by "Two Christmas Days: A Holiday Story," published eight years later in the *AME Zion Church Quarterly*. A classic temperance tale, it is the story of a man rescued from his vice by the love of a good woman, a resolution in line with the idealized roles envisioned by and for middle-class women of African as well as European ancestry. The story conforms to standard gender conventions rather than breaking the kind of literary ground represented by her projected inclusion of controversial racial incidents in a novel.[52]

In view of the hardening of racial lines and the growing violence against African Americans by the mid-1880s, it is understandable that Wells might find it difficult to translate racial realities into fiction: the facts were dramatic enough. With journalism she was on surer ground. The direct and pungent writing style she cultivated, though ill suited to the genteel standards and circumlocutions of contemporary fiction, was well adapted to newspaper reporting and commentary.

Wells's career in journalism evolved from her protests against racial discrimination in railroad travel. She resisted conductors' efforts to remove her from the first-class cars reserved for "ladies"—only white women qualified—and relegate her to the "smoking car," which was not only inferior but coded male. Given the gender and class conventions of the day, this arrangement left no space where black women could travel in comfort and with pride and status intact. In 1883 Wells was put off the train, but not before she bit the conductor. She sued the railroad and initially won an award of $500 that elicited the headline "A Darky Damsel Obtains a Verdict for Damages against the Chesapeake and Ohio Railroad" in a white newspaper. But she lost the case when the railroad successfully appealed. A second case went the same way.[53]

In her early twenties, Ida B. Wells was herself news. So it is not surprising that she was invited to write about the case in the *Living Way*, a local religious paper, probably in late 1883 or early 1884. Soon she was writing regular weekly "letters" in which, she later claimed, she hoped to deal with the problems of people with little or no education "in a simple, helpful way." She signed them "Iola."[54] She made no secret of her authorship and occasionally blurred the line between her public and private identities, as did others.[55]

Her articles attracted attention from the outset. African American newspapers in other cities reprinted or commented on them, and editors asked for original copy. By the middle of 1886, she was writing for several papers, including the *New York Freeman* (later the *New York Age*), the *Gate City Press* (Kansas City, Missouri), the *Watchman* (Memphis), and the *Detroit Plain-*

dealer, as well as for the *AME Church Review,* the premier African American journal. Of her many patrons, she credits Rev. William J. Simmons, editor of the *American Baptist* and *Our Women and Children,* for his encouragement and for being the first to pay for her work. Soon she was writing regular columns for his papers.[56] Wells also covered a white woman suffrage speaker and a Knights of Labor meeting and wrote occasionally for the white-owned *Memphis Scimitar,* a newspaper that excoriated her after her antilynching articles appeared.

Many of Wells's early pieces addressed "women's subjects." For the most part they were conventional renderings that endorsed Victorian morality, women's nurturing qualities, and the virtues of motherhood.[57] For a middle-class black woman, these hard-won virtues were not to be dismissed lightly, and Wells was quick to applaud a white Memphis newspaper that defended African American women against charges of immorality. Despite her celebrations of traditional womanhood, like Carey Thomas, Wells insisted that a true woman was not "a fashion plate, a frivolous inanity, a soulless doll, a heartless coquette—but a strong, bright presense [*sic*], thoroughly imbued with a sense of her mission on earth and a desire to fill it."[58] And although she felt a bit tongue-tied when asked to respond to a talk on "Woman in Journalism" at the National Colored Press Association, she hoped she would have another opportunity to "urge the young women to study & think with a view to taking places in the world of thought & action."[59]

She succeeded in making such a place for herself. Where most women journalists, white and black, covered the women's and children's beat, Wells made her name writing about racial politics. She expressed herself forcefully on such subjects as party affiliation (she favored choice, even if it meant breaking ranks with the Republican Party) and self-segregation (she criticized African Americans who promoted segregated schools).[60] Urging racial unity as a means of advancing blacks' dual position as Negroes and as Americans, Wells exhorted her colleagues to follow the examples of Jewish, Irish, and Italian Americans, groups she believed were establishing themselves as full citizens in Memphis. Only through self-help could African Americans develop "more race love" and "a proper self-respect."[61]

In June 1889 Wells became editor and one-third owner of the *Free Speech and Headlight* of Memphis, a position that enhanced her freedom to express her often controversial views. Two years later, in an editorial condemning the inferior conditions in local African American schools, she raised the specter of interracial sex by suggesting that white members of the school board hired unqualified black women teachers with whom they had illicit affairs.

Although she did not sign the article, retribution was swift: the school board did not renew her contract. Wells subsequently devoted herself full-time to promoting the *Free Speech*. By traveling through Mississippi, Arkansas, and Tennessee on the Delta spur of the Illinois Central Railroad and by adopting a distinctive format (pink paper, which she later learned was mistaken for the racy *Police Gazette*), she increased circulation and soon earned almost as much as she had as a teacher. Wells thus completed the transition from amateur to professional journalist.[62] An excellent businesswoman, even early in her career she insisted on being paid for her labor, a circumstance evidently unusual enough to invite (unfavorable) press comment.[63]

Wells was an established figure in African American journalism well before the Memphis lynchings, the event that carried her to national and international celebrity. Influential in her profession as well as successful at her craft, she was elected first assistant secretary of the National Colored Press Association in August 1887 and two years later became general secretary, beating out a prominent male competitor for the position. She delivered addresses to the group on "How I Would Edit a Paper" in 1887 and, five years later, on "The Requirements of Southern Journalism." She was active as well in the short-lived Southern Press Association.[64]

Wells later claimed that she had "no literary gifts and graces," but others hailed her as "brilliant" and "a genius" and even compared her to Frederick Douglass in being "prompted by the highest motives to be a benefactress to her race."[65] One woman journalist noted that she had made the name Iola "a power," while another claimed: "No writer, the male fraternity not excepted, has been more extensively quoted; none struck harder blows at the wrongs and weaknesses of the race."[66] Dubbed the "Princess of the Press," Wells made news in addition to commenting on it: articles reported on her ambition, her plans, and her standing as a Memphis belle too busy to pay attention to her many suitors. Gendered comments were not unusual. Male journalists seemed disconcerted by the contrast between her femininity (she was under five feet tall, well turned out, and personally engaging) and the power of her pen; no doubt they resented her sometimes caustic remarks and her star quality as well. Their comments were often condescending, sexist, or just plain mean.[67] Even sympathetic journalists, like T. Thomas Fortune, himself the "Prince of Journalists" and later her patron at the *New York Age*, declared: "She handles her subjects more as a man than as a woman."[68] In an age of extremely polarized gender norms, Wells's forthrightness brought her to the edge—and sometimes to the other side—of boundaries many thought a woman should not cross.

Wells smarted at the criticism, but flourished in her new life. With journalism, she later observed, she "had at last found my real vocation," work that expressed "the real 'me.'"[69] It was a self she had carefully constructed. As with her oratorical performances, she had cultivated her literary skills: the diary and the growing correspondence with journalists over which she took great pains helped her hone her craft. But, even after seeing herself praised in print as "one of the foremost among the female thinkers of the race today," she still harbored doubts:

> I think sometimes I can write a readable article and then again I wonder how I could have been so mistaken in myself. A glance at all my "brilliant?" productions pall[s] on my understanding, they all savor of dreary sameness, however varied the subject, and the style is monotonous. I find a paucity of ideas that makes it a labor to write freely and yet—what is it that keeps urging me to write notwithstanding all?[70]

Wells did not answer her question at the time, at least not in her diary. No doubt the urge to write had multiple sources, including her desire to excel in a realm proscribed to her ancestors. In addition, the passion that prompted her to challenge the second-class status and dangers daily experienced by blacks drove her on. Anger fueled her pen.

With lynching, Wells discovered an apparently inexhaustible subject. The practice was on the rise, peaking in the early 1890s just as Wells began her campaign. Not all the victims were black, but the vast majority were.[71] As early as 1886, Wells reacted bluntly to the brutal murder of a black woman accused of poisoning a white woman: "Wrote a dynamitic article . . . almost advising murder! . . . O my God! can such things be and no justice for it?"[72] Under such circumstances, it is not surprising that she considered the Negro's Mutual Protective Association, a Memphis organization to defend African Americans' civil rights, "the best thing out."[73] Responding to a lynching in Kentucky a few years later, an unsigned editorial in the *Free Speech* urged self-defense: "Of one thing we may be assured, so long as we permit ourselves to be trampled upon, so long we will have to endure it. Not until the Negro rises in his might and takes a hand resenting such cold-blooded murders, if he has to burn up whole towns, will a halt be called in wholesale lynching."[74] Strong words, they anticipated those that later led to Wells's exile and brought her to the world's attention.

Wells had lived in Memphis for about a decade when three black men were lynched in the city on March 9, 1892. All three were associated with the People's Grocery Company, a joint-stock store. Their "offense": defending themselves when a white competitor tried to destroy the store following a racial incident. They were dragged from jail and shot; as in most such episodes, the perpetrators were never tried. Taking place on Wells's home turf, the event was all the more shocking because she was a friend of one of the victims and godmother to his daughter, and it led her to question accepted truths about lynching.[75] In blunt editorials she challenged the racial order in Memphis—and elsewhere in the South. Concluding that economic motives were often at the root of lynchings, she encouraged African Americans to boycott Memphis streetcars and to head west. To the distress of the city's businessmen, many heeded her advice and joined an exodus then gaining force nationally. Even more boldly, she urged self-defense in the face of white violence and bought a gun. "A Winchester rifle should have a place of honor in every black home," she observed a short time later.[76]

Her greatest assault on white southern sensibilities came when she challenged the myth that most lynchings occurred because of sexual aggression by African American men against white women. She took up the point in an editorial published on May 21, 1892: "Nobody in this section of the country believes the old thread bare lie that Negro men rape white women. If Southern white men are not careful they will over-reach themselves and . . . a conclusion will then be reached which will be very damaging to the moral reputation of their women."[77] These were inflammatory words in Memphis in 1892. The subsequent destruction of the *Free Speech* office and the threat against Wells's life spelled the end of her career in the South.

Reviewing the federal government's refusal to take action, in an address to the National Colored Press Association on "The Requirements of Southern Journalism" Wells called for a "fearlessly edited press" that would answer every false claim made by whites, especially those that justified lynching as a punishment for the rape of white women. By publishing the facts and exposing the injustice and hypocrisy surrounding lynching, journalists could educate African Americans to their true standing in the United States—and to their rights—in this way raising race consciousness and paving the way for united action. To this end, Wells urged her colleagues to "cultivate race reading," a process that entailed increasing circulation as well as publishing thought-provoking material. Recognizing the difficulties of doing this in the South, she advocated a mobile press that, when threatened in one place, would take root in another.[78]

Deprived of her home and livelihood, Wells took her campaign north. Extending her critique of lynching, she published her findings in a long editorial in the *New York Age* on June 25, 1892. It was widely circulated—10,000 copies were printed—and, along with subsequent writings and lectures, mobilized African Americans, women especially. Both as individuals and in groups, women raised funds, arranged meetings, and in other ways supported Wells's cause. Victoria Earle Matthews, a New York writer and journalist, and Maritcha Lyons, a respected public school teacher from Brooklyn, organized a testimonial at New York City's Lyric Hall on October 5, 1892. A committee of 250 women helped to publicize the event, which drew a large audience, including prominent African American women from Boston and Philadelphia.

After preliminary speeches, resolutions, and music, Wells rose to tell her story. Behind her, electric lights spelled out "Iola." Years later she recalled her fright on learning she must speak: "I had some little reputation as an essayist from schoolgirl days, and had recited many times in public recitations which I had committed to memory. In canvassing for my paper I had made talks asking for subscriptions. But this was the first time I had ever been called on to deliver an honest-to-goodness address." Even though the lynching was "imprinted" on her memory, she committed the talk to paper. When she started to read, she felt homesick for the friends and days that were gone. She panicked when the tears came, but "kept on reading the story which they had come to hear." Although she was mortified at this exhibition of weakness, her performance was a great success. The sponsors gave her a gold brooch in the shape of a pen, "an emblem of my chosen profession," and $500. She wore the brooch, she claimed, "on all occasions" for the next twenty years and used the money to publish *Southern Horrors: Lynch Law in All Its Phases* (1892), which she dedicated "to the Afro-American women of New York and Brooklyn . . . [who] made possible its publication."[79] The pamphlet, with a testimonial from Frederick Douglass, was a reissue of her June article in the *Age*.

Already a seasoned journalist, at Lyric Hall and after, Wells came into her own as a speaker. For the next few years she occupied center stage. As has so often been the case for African Americans, triumphal tours of England, in 1893 and again in 1894, enhanced her reputation at home as the preeminent campaigner against lynching. During the second trip, a series of letters she wrote for the *Inter-Ocean*, a white-owned Chicago paper that "persistently denounced lynching," kept her in the public eye.[80]

Some likened Wells's impact to that of *Uncle Tom's Cabin*, a comparison she did not disclaim. The association is not surprising given the power of her rhetoric and her frequent invocation of abolitionist heroes, white as well as black.[81] Her talks combined gruesome details of brutal murders with carefully assembled statistical data on the number of lynchings (which she took from white newspapers so she could not be accused of exaggeration) and on the alleged crimes of the victims (fewer than one-third were even charged with rape). Imbued with the reformist faith of the Progressive generation that only ignorance of the facts prevented remedial action against injustice, she informed anyone who would listen.

To this effort, she brought all her resources to bear. To largely white audiences she invoked the moral standards of a Christian and civilized society, but especially the American democratic values systematically violated where blacks were concerned. Linking the lawlessness of lynching to that of slavery, Wells juxtaposed the failure to guarantee legal protection to blacks (of life as well as citizenship) with the promise of freedom heralded by the Constitution and the nation's secular hymns. Her second pamphlet, *A Red Record* (1895), a sociological survey of lynching victims in the early 1890s, was "Respectfully submitted to the Nineteenth Century civilization in 'the Land of the Free and the Home of the Brave.'"[82] Wells used her skills as an investigative journalist to challenge the lynching-for-rape myth invoked to justify mob murder. Drawing on Shakespeare as well, she claimed that intimate relationships between black men and white women were often consensual, "the story of Desdemona and Othello, minus the marriage tie."[83] Her carefully researched talks and pamphlets incorporated formative influences from her past, the Christian and abolitionist principles of her white teachers (leavened by the occasional literary reference) and the protest tradition of her father, into a political program that called for full rights for blacks.

Wells proved a master of rhetorical style as well as substance. Even before the Memphis lynchings, the *New York Age* called her "eloquent, logical, and dead in earnest. . . . She should use the gift of speech God has given her to arouse the women of the race to a full sense of their duty."[84] African American women did become her strongest allies, but Wells used her gifts in cosmopolitan fashion, addressing whites as well as blacks, men as well as women, Europeans as well as Americans. With her head and heart full, she could speak on the subject of lynching for two hours without a note, in a voice, according to one listener, that "resembled the low strains of pathetic music which steals in upon the soul and touches the heart."[85] The *Manchester Guardian* stressed her "reliance on the simple eloquence of facts," while another British observer commented that by "this marvelous self-restraint . . . she moves us all the more profoundly." Wells's self-possession and control over her material and herself contrasted not only with the drama of her gruesome story but with negative preconceptions about African American

Ida B. Wells, ca. 1893–94.
Courtesy of Special Collections
Research Center, University of
Chicago Library.

women.[86] Having found her subject, she employed the principles of elocution she had once mastered as an exercise in the service of a mighty cause.
With her refined delivery of a powerful message, she reached members of
the British upper classes who endorsed her campaign by forming an Anti-
Lynching League. Thus challenged, the formerly silent white American
press took up the subject of lynching; for the most part, northern as well as
southern newspapers questioned Wells's methods and condemned her for
maligning white womanhood.[87]

If Wells's public career began as a "reader" of newspapers to her father's
friends, it culminated in the mid-1890s, when she traveled widely to spread
her own news: that lynching was an instrument of terror designed to control
African Americans and to keep them from prospering and from exercising
rights they had gained during Reconstruction. Lynching was increasing not
because of the degradation of blacks but because they were coming up in
the world.

In delivering this message, Wells viewed herself not as an orator in the
Frederick Douglass mold, but as a "mouthpiece through which to tell the
story of lynching and I have told it so often that I know it by heart. I do
not have to embellish; it makes its own way."[88] Like many black and white

women before her, in claiming a public role Wells made herself out to be a plain speaker of truth whose words mirrored the stark reality, the medium who transmitted a transparent message. (The stance was familiar, but unlike many of her African American predecessors, she did not invoke the deity.) She may have been bowing to the gender conventions that prohibited women from claiming public space on their own. But by so doing, she understated her own agency, discounting her careful research, the originality of her argument, and the art of her rhetoric. This message came to a woman who had prepared herself to receive and deliver it.

Wells's campaign activated African American women, galvanizing a trend toward organizing already under way. With the rise of a small but articulate middle class, urban black women came together in the 1890s for cultural and social purposes, much as their white counterparts had done earlier. Local and regional women's groups coalesced to form the National Association of Colored Women (NACW) in 1896. An inflammatory charge by a Missouri journalist that African American women lacked virtue and character, an attack many thought to be directed at Wells, provided an external impetus. Sensitive to such allegations because of the legacy of slavery and because they accepted the sexual norms of middle-class Victorian America, black club women rallied in defense of their name. But even before this catalyst, they were working together to overcome the virulent prejudice of the era and to improve the lives of less-favored members of the race.[89]

By the mid-1890s Wells had become a "race heroine" to many African Americans.[90] With confidence in her cause and scant patience with more timid souls, she may have cast herself in this role as well: she viewed her antilynching work as a crusade, something she did for "my people." For their part, Wells's contemporaries often cast her in larger-than-life roles, many of them religious. She was Queen Esther, who saved the Jewish people from destruction and, more often, Joan of Arc, who donned male dress to fight for the French king and was martyred at the hands of the Inquisition.[91] In a sermon delivered to the Ida B. Wells Club in Chicago, AME minister Reverdy Ransom likened her to Deborah and Jael. Like these female prophets of the Old Testament, he maintained, at the time of the Memphis lynching Wells had "the courage to speak out, the courage to speak the courageous word when the men and the manhood of the race ought to have rushed to the defense."[92] These are powerful associations: Deborah roused the troops to battle when male leaders lacked courage, while Jael drove a stake through the head of the leader of the opposing army after luring him to her tent. They are Lady Macbeth with a vengeance, though acting in honorable causes and on their own rather than through men. These images stand in stark contrast with Wells's view of herself as a medium or transmitter of the truth, a divergence that may have presaged her later estrangement from former allies.[93]

Wells's antilynching career peaked in the mid-1890s when she was much in the news, especially during and right after her second British tour. She became less central to the national reform scene after 1895. Her marriage that year to attorney and publisher Ferdinand L. Barnett of Chicago, followed by the birth of four children between 1896 and 1904, brought new duties. But family obligations by themselves did not sideline her. With her firstborn son and a nurse in tow, she attended the 1896 inaugural meeting of the NACW, where she read the body's forthright resolutions condemning racism.[94] And although she gave up her work on the *Conservator* (the newspaper she had purchased from her husband) after the birth of her second son the following year, she had sufficient help with childcare to remain active in many causes.[95]

With the death of Frederick Douglass in 1895, Ida Wells-Barnett lost an influential patron who had not only helped launch her career and supported her during difficult moments, but shared her radical protest agenda. Predictably, she was soon at odds with his conservative successor, Booker T. Washington, on whom whites thrust the mantle of race leadership after Douglass's death. Still eager to continue her work, she headed the Anti-Lynching Bureau of the Afro-American Council, in which capacity she wrote *Mob Rule in New Orleans* (1900). But the group was short-lived, and Wells was bypassed by leaders of new national organizations that challenged the racial status quo, first the abortive all-black Niagara Movement, then the interracial NAACP. Her militancy threatened black male leaders, the images of Joan of Arc and Deborah too close for comfort. In addition, the NAACP made antilynching work its priority and adopted organizational and legal approaches that departed from Wells's inspirational rhetorical mode.[96] Wells remained active in antilynching work for the rest of her life, primarily at the local and regional level where she was sometimes called in to investigate murders or irregular judicial procedures. But the center of action had moved on.

· · · · · · · · · · · · · · · · · · ·

In September 1892, at the start of her antilynching campaign, Wells delivered a lecture on "The Afro-American in Literature" to the Concord Literary Circle of Brooklyn. Appearing on the program with a male and a female singer and a woman who read an essay on patriotism, she "completely captivated" her audience.[97] Three months later she wrote up an exhibition of

African American artists shown in the home of a member of the Woman's Loyal Union of New York and Brooklyn, a group that organized around her campaign under the leadership of Victoria Earle Matthews. The show, which had been mounted to "stimulate race pride," was so successful that it became an annual affair.[98]

These modest ventures signaled Wells's connection to an emerging movement to encourage African American cultural production. Unfortunately, no copy of her talk has survived. She may have censured the literary depictions of blacks by whites or examined African Americans' portrayals of themselves. In either case, she would have addressed subjects of growing concern to intellectuals eager on the one hand to refute negative racial images and on the other to produce a literature of their own. By undermining recurrent racist representations and creating a high-culture tradition, such a literature would, proponents believed, demonstrate African Americans' worth in the eyes of whites. Many assumed that it would also promote a more positive identity among blacks.[99] As Wells observed several years earlier, "When pride of race is the theme, one must be able to point with pride to resources developed, victories won, conquests recorded or the achievements of the race in question, in letters, arts and sciences."[100] On literature, then, there rested a heavy burden. It must expose acts of racial aggression (whether of commission or omission) and, by documenting all aspects of the past, song and story as well as history, create both a faithful record of that past and a vital cultural present. If promoting art and literature seemed less imperative than taking action against lynching, in this reading, culture too was a political vehicle for advancing racial interests.

For some, fiction held a special place in this campaign. Mary Church Terrell, first president of the NACW, observed that if she could relive her life, she "would somehow force myself into the ranks of successful story writers. I believe the deplorable conditions under which many of us live can be pictured more vividly and can be improved more quickly and more surely through the medium of the short story than in any other way."[101] Terrell's faith in fiction had its roots in the impact of *Uncle Tom's Cabin*, and she longed to write a work of comparable power. She settled instead for an article about Stowe, who remained an important writer in this African American community long after her reputation among white critics declined.[102]

Fiction was not the only genre for advancing the African American cause. Wells contributed to the movement as a journalist. Her conviction that blacks must counter white prejudice by setting forth the facts was central to her journalistic practice—and not only about lynching. *The Reason Why the Col-*

ored American Is Not in the World's Columbian Exposition (1893), the protest pamphlet she orchestrated, included, in addition to a history of blacks' exclusion written by Ferdinand L. Barnett and her own work on lynching, an article by I. Garland Penn titled "The Progress of the Afro-American since Emancipation." The pamphlet's subtitle, *The Afro-American's Contribution to Columbian Literature*, hints at its larger purpose, as does Penn's documentation of the achievements of a recently enslaved people in the arts, religion, and economic life. When juxtaposed with the atrocities recounted by Wells, they amounted to an impressive record.[103] Several years later, Daniel Murray, a bibliographer at the Library of Congress who collected 1,400 works by African American authors, observed, "this showing must undoubtedly raise the Negro to a plane previously denied him, but which, in spite of every drawback he has honestly won."[104]

Though not included in Murray's list, Wells's writings counted as race literature under the generous definition advanced by Victoria Earle Matthews, a central figure in African American women's organizations during the 1890s and a respected fiction writer and journalist who wrote for white as well as African American publications. In her 1895 address before the First Congress of Colored Women of the United States (the precursor of the NACW), Matthews offered a critique of racist portrayals of African Americans and elaborated on what a genuine race literature would look like. Citing Czech composer Antonin Dvořák's claim that the future music of America would be founded on "the original Negro melodies of the South," she asserted that an African American literature must build on the distinctive individuality that derived from the unique history of the race.[105] Her own best-known work of fiction, *Aunt Lindy* (1893), was an early dialect story about the aftermath of slavery, set in her hometown in Georgia.[106]

Even as she pioneered an emerging genre, Matthews defined race literature broadly as "all the writings emanating from a distinct class—not necessarily race matter; but a general collection of what has been written by the men and women of that Race: History, Biographies, Scientific Treatises, Sermons, Addresses, Novels, Poems, Books of Travel, miscellaneous essays and the contributions to magazines and newspapers." Since literature was "a collective body of literary productions, embracing the entire results of knowledge and fancy, preserved in writing," one could speak of the literature of race as one did of the literature of chemistry. Matthews viewed Wells and other journalists as unsung heroes and heroines of this literature; by serving as "counter-irritants" against falsehoods, they "have made a nobler fight than the brilliant Parnel [*sic*] in his championship of Ireland's cause." Hers was a still-generous definition of literature as encompassing all humane learning and not simply the high arts of fiction and belles lettres, an approach that was becoming dominant by the 1890s.[107]

Matthews spoke to a receptive audience. Women were in the forefront of those exploring race literature—as consumers, promoters, and producers. The African American women's club movement was in full flower in the 1890s. In addition to reading black authors, members contributed to the *Woman's Era*, the Boston-based journal of the NACW. Local clubs also generated a plethora of print documenting their activities—constitutions, yearbooks, and histories.[108] African American clubs practiced many of the rituals common to white women's groups and read many of the same authors, but they also incorporated African American subject matter into their programs. The Chautauqua Circle, for example, an elite group of fifteen women, many of them connected with Atlanta University, combined an interest in Tennyson, Robert Burns, and Ella Wheeler Wilcox with African American subjects. They heard papers on "The Negro in Literature and Art," "Negro Musicians of Note," and "The Influence of Slavery upon Literature" as well as on "The Beginnings of English Literature." African American writer Benjamin G. Brawley spoke on "Race History" and read a chapter from W. E. B. Du Bois's *The Souls of Black Folk*; the opening quotations on that occasion were from Brawley's own work. At other times, members recited quotations from Paul Laurence Dunbar and James Weldon Johnson and sometimes sang Johnson's "Negro National Hymn."[109] The blending of African American and European American traditions by many literary clubs suggests the possibility of multiple cultural identifications, bearing out critic Frances Foster's claim that "the tradition and models of Shakespeare or Whittier, Pope and Stowe were as much the heritage of African Americans as were the laws and political structures within which they asserted their case for full participation."[110] In the late nineteenth and early twentieth centuries, interest in race literature represented a bid for inclusiveness rather than exclusiveness.

In addition to studying texts from diverse literary traditions, most African American women's clubs with literary interests combined cultural work with socially useful projects. These ranged from raising funds for settlements to lobbying for better schools. Committed to what Elizabeth McHenry calls "public literacy" from the start, in addition to publishing records of their own history, clubs established reading rooms and in other ways extended both literature and literacy to a wider public.[111] White women's organizations also made books available to others, but given the inheritance of slavery, inferior public education, and blacks' exclusion from public libraries, the importance of African American women's voluntary associations in making books accessible to members of their race cannot be overstated. The Sojourner Truth Club of Montgomery, Alabama, which met "for personal improvement and for social service" and devoted one of its two monthly meetings to literary subjects, established a Free Reading Room and Library when African Americans were refused admission to the local Carnegie Library. It raised funds from churches and citizens and kept the room open six hours a day. By 1909 the Reading Room had some 500 volumes of "good literature" and had become a lending library as well. The club also offered a prize to the high school junior or senior who wrote the best paper on a subject connected with the history of the race.[112] At an even more basic level, the Woman's League of Kansas City, which conducted sewing classes and gave women a place to sell their goods, also engaged in literacy outreach by offering classes in reading and writing to formerly enslaved women.[113]

Where white women's clubs usually began as purely cultural groups, African Americans' were political from the start.[114] One of the principal goals of the Woman's Loyal Union of New York and Brooklyn (WLU) was "the diffusion of . . . information" about the civil and social status of African Americans in order to promote "intelligent assertion of their rights" and united action. To this end, the group sent circular letters throughout the South and West requesting information about the conditions of African American families. Club president Victoria Matthews followed up by visiting the Black Belt. Members gathered signatures for a petition supporting a resolution introduced by Congressman Henry Blair of New Hampshire to fund a federal investigation of lynching (10,000 people eventually signed, but the bill was defeated). The WLU also raised a purse so that elocutionist Hallie Quinn Brown could visit England to solicit funds for a library at Wilberforce College to be named for Frederick Douglass.[115]

By the fall of 1895, the WLU focused on establishing a library and reading room that would initially contain mainly "works written by colored authors, or those that discuss the race question," but that would expand in time to include "all works of standard value in literature."[116] Two years later when Matthews established the White Rose Mission, a nonsectarian Christian settlement to assist black girls and women migrating to New York from the South, she began to fulfill this goal by building up a literary collection. The library included the works of such well-known contemporary writers as Charles Chesnutt, Paul Laurence Dunbar, and Booker T. Washington, a second edition of poems by Phillis Wheatley, and a bound volume of *Anglo-African Magazine* (1859) which included an account of John Brown's raid on

Harpers Ferry. In accord with Matthews's broad definition of race literature, it was a library about, as well as by, African Americans and included writings by white abolitionists. Matthews taught a course on race history that focused on the lives and works "of all the great abolitionists," surely one of the first of its kind.[117] Although the promotion of race literature and history was central to Matthews's conception of her work, mention of the collection disappears from the organization's records after her death in 1907: without the founder's driving interest, literature gave way to the demanding task of finding jobs for young female migrants.[118]

.   .   .   .

When Ida Wells-Barnett founded her own settlement in 1910, like Matthews she tried to blend reading and race literature with practical assistance. The Negro Fellowship League (NFL) had its origin two years earlier when members of her men's Bible class at Grace Presbyterian Church began meeting to counteract the apathetic response to the lynching of three African Americans in Springfield, Illinois. The NFL's most visible face was its Reading Room and Social Center, located on State Street in the heart of Chicago's Black Belt. Having heard from prisoners, many of them recent migrants from the South, that they had first gone wrong there, Wells-Barnett considered it "our duty to try to see that some sort of a lighthouse was established on State Street." Viewing the saloon as the only local institution that currently welcomed blacks, she thought its influence (and that of gambling houses and poolrooms) might be counteracted "if we could have a modern, up-to-date reading room set down there in the midst of all those temptations, and a consecrated young man in charge."[119] For all her political radicalism, like other middle-class women, Wells-Barnett viewed reading as a means of racial uplift. But the NFL was unusual among female-initiated social welfare ventures, African American or white, in catering principally to men and boys.[120]

When the NFL Reading Room and Social Center opened in May 1910, the *Chicago Defender* noted its "well selected library of history, biography, fiction and race literature especially," including newspapers and magazines; six weeks later the *Defender* proclaimed it "one of the finest reading rooms in the city, especially for men and boys."[121] Staffed by a paid aide and by young male volunteers, it was open from 9:00 A.M. to 10:00 P.M. Whether or not the reading room kept "penniless boys, girls, and men" from becoming public charges, as a 1916 report claimed, for those with time on their hands it offered a place to read, write, and play checkers. A newspaper report that over 300 people visited the reading room during a week of inclement weather in February raises the question of how much interest there was in reading and how much in keeping warm.[122] Either way, the reading room was fulfilling its founder's goals.

The NFL offered considerably more than a place to read and write. With initial funding from a white philanthropist, at its peak the organization provided a men's lodging house (above the reading room), food for the hungry (chits to a nearby restaurant), and, through its employment bureau, jobs for those seeking work. In addition to serving as a meeting place for many black women's organizations, the reading room held a Sunday lecture series that featured celebrities such as Jane Addams, the distinguished black physiologist Ernest Just, and William Monroe Trotter, a journalist and radical activist, as well as a Pullman conductor who lost his job for trying to organize his coworkers. There were also sessions on ward politics, white slavery (the kidnapping of women for purposes of prostitution), and the U.S. invasion of Mexico in 1916. Above all, the organization was a launching pad for Wells-Barnett's many causes, including her antilynching work and efforts to secure legal justice for African Americans, especially prisoners. The NFL joined other groups in successfully opposing an Illinois law to segregate public transportation (according to the *Defender* Wells-Barnett was "on the firing line all the time"), the social segregation of black students at Wendell Phillips High School, and a congressional bill to prohibit interracial marriage in Washington, D.C.[123]

The NFL and its leader also worked both sides of the cultural front. On the one hand, they promoted African American culture and history, and on the other, they protested endeavors denigrating to blacks. In the former category, Wells-Barnett and her husband organized a well-received exhibit of work by African American painter William A. Harper at Chicago's prestigious Art Institute in 1910.[124] On a broader scale, the NFL sponsored an orchestra and the Emancipation (or Fellowship) Chorus of 100 voices that sang Negro folk songs as well as "music by the great masters."[125] Wells-Barnett was especially proud of the chorus, which performed at annual Lincoln and Douglass Day celebrations. And each year on the first of January, the NFL celebrated Emancipation, joining forces in 1913 with other groups for an impressive fiftieth anniversary commemoration of this historic milestone.

Beyond promoting African American culture, through the NFL Wells-Barnett also mobilized protests against racist depictions of blacks. In 1911 she led a delegation that tried, without success, to block the opening of *The Sins of the Father*, a play by Rev. Thomas Dixon Jr., author of *The Clansman*, an incendiary novel that depicted blacks during Reconstruction as little better than animals and the entire period as a blot on the nation's history. Three years later, concerned Chicagoans tried, again unsuccessfully, to secure a ban on the screening of D. W. Griffith's blockbuster film, *The Birth of a Nation* (based on *The Clansman*).[126] Dissatisfied, the NFL held a meeting to discuss "What Can the Negro Do about 'The Birth of a Nation'?"[127]

Wells-Barnett expressed her views on the negative consequences of racial stereotypes most pointedly in a 1910 article on northern African American women. While not as disadvantaged by caste as their southern sisters, she thought they suffered by their exclusion from "uplifting and refining" influences such as the theater and concert halls and that the brave woman who accepted public invitations in mixed groups "schools herself to be deaf, dumb and blind to gibe, insult or hostility." Wells-Barnett blamed much of the negative view of black women on white writers' representations of them as lacking in love for their families; she excepted Stowe, whose portrait of mother love in the figure of Eliza crossing the ice to save her child from slavery Wells-Barnett considered both positive and realistic. But for the most part she believed that to set the record straight African Americans must write their own history and literature for the reason given by the lion in Aesop's fable and by "the red Indian" when asked why his people were always worsted by the white man: "It was because the white man wrote the stories."[128]

Wells-Barnett's interest in having blacks tell their own stories—and in encouraging young people to engage their own history—is apparent in her support of an annual essay contest on an African American theme. Details of the first contest appear in a rare surviving copy of the *Fellowship Herald*, a paper Wells-Barnett published and edited for the NFL for several years beginning in May 1911. A front-page clipping from the December 21, 1911, issue features the literary contest on "Negro Authors" sponsored by the Bethel AME Church, with participants from the NFL and other local organizations. Irene McCoy, representing the University Club, delivered the winning talk on "Negro Authors of Africa and Europe." The *Herald* looked forward to publishing it, pronouncing McCoy "a new literary Star" and the talk notable both as a literary production and for its delivery.[129]

The *Fellowship Herald* was Wells-Barnett's last publishing venture. The *Chicago Broad Ax* greeted its appearance favorably, calling the editor a "keen, logical, and forcible writer." And in 1914 a Dane who had lived in the United States for some years went so far as to call it "the best paper the Negro has here in Chicago" and Wells-Barnett "the Jane Addams among the

Negroes."[130] But the fortunes of the parent organization were declining, and Wells-Barnett closed its doors in 1920, several years after the paper ceased publication. Still concerned about negative stereotypes, even after her formal career as a journalist came to an end, she wrote letters to editors to protest the use of racial slurs, which she considered a spur to racial violence.[131]

Wells-Barnett remained an avid consumer and promoter of African American culture to the end of her life. A pocket diary for 1930 reveals continuity with the patterns of a lifetime. When distressed by a crisis involving one of her sons, she "read to keep from thinking." While running for state senator, she found time to speak to young people at St. Thomas's Church on "Negro books & plays," observing: "Few out but very interested." She also attended a meeting of a "local Negro History club" that discussed a book by Carter G. Woodson, a prominent African American historian and founder of the Association for the Study of Negro Life and History, who had once lectured at the NFL. It was a book, she tartly observed, "in which is no mention of my anti-lynching contribution."[132]

Wells-Barnett died in 1931 at the age of sixty-eight. In her eulogy, Irene McCoy Gaines, now a community leader in her own right, spoke movingly of Wells-Barnett's distress that so few African Americans knew of black people's contributions to world history and culture: "She knew how white publicists & statesmen had denied Negro's courage & valor & how white historians have sustained the denial by leaving from their histories the N[egro]'s contributions to civilization." One of Wells-Barnett's last official acts, Gaines noted, was to ask women's clubs to participate in a book shower she organized to benefit the YMCA by sending "books *by* N[egro]. authors."[133]

As Wells-Barnett's acid comment about Woodson's omission of her antilynching work demonstrates, even black authors could not be relied on to tell the whole story. (She did not explore, as we might, the gendered dimension of the oversight.) Perhaps anticipating such neglect, she began work on her autobiography in 1928 after a young black woman compared her to Joan of Arc, but could not say why. Wells-Barnett wanted to set the record straight about how the agitation against lynching began, "for the young people who have so little of our race's history recorded. . . . I am all the more constrained to do this because there is such a lack of authentic race history of Reconstruction times written by the Negro himself."[134] Here she positions herself as an authentic witness of a long-past era by virtue of having lived it. It was a daunting task, for at the time she wrote, the historiography of Reconstruction was mired in the white supremacist distortions of the dominant prosouthern school of historians whose views were barely distinguishable from those of *Birth of a Nation*. To portray the years of her childhood and young adulthood more accurately, as a time when blacks first gained and then lost rights that should have been theirs all along—and to secure the historical place she deserved—Wells-Barnett, like "the red Indian," knew she would have to tell her own story.

She did not live to complete it. Forty years went by before *Crusade for Justice* appeared in print, brought to light through the editorial efforts and persistence of her youngest child, Alfreda Duster. Following on the heels of important civil rights victories at the national and local levels, the book's publication in 1970 came at a time of emerging interest in the historical achievements of blacks and women. Wells-Barnett quickly became a heroine to a new generation—to blacks of both sexes and to women of both races, indeed to anyone supporting African Americans' unfinished struggle for full citizenship.

Crusade for Justice is a passionate book centered on Wells-Barnett's antilynching and other race work.[135] Like other autobiographies by women of her generation, it focuses almost exclusively on her public life. Its protagonist is a visionary but embattled woman often frustrated by the refusal of other blacks to follow her lead in the struggle to claim their rights. But if her sense of grievance is painfully manifest, so is her righteous anger at racial injustice. The book is the heroic story of a fearless woman who in her twenties exposed a growing evil and continued to fight for racial justice throughout her life. Intended to keep alive the author's vision of the past, to let the lion tell her own story, *Crusade for Justice* is, finally, "the Negro book" its author never read in her youth.

. . . .

From Then to Now

The Gilded Age literary culture did not disappear overnight. Girls and young women continued to read voraciously and to lose—and find—themselves in books. They still do, and for many of the same reasons: to remove themselves from their everyday lives, encounter novel situations, learn more about life, perhaps reinvent themselves or discover who they really are. But for the most part by 1920 or so reading lost the cultural cachet it once possessed.[1]

The question is not what happened to the Gilded Age culture of reading but what happened to American society that undermined reading as an institution. There is no easy answer to this question, but there are signposts that point to crucial cultural shifts in the past century. Of these the most basic concern the transformations in middle-class women's lives.

The Gilded Age culture of reading was closely linked to middle-class family life and to women's new role as purveyors of culture within and outside the home. As both a sanctified activity and an approved entertainment— arguably *the* major form of entertainment for men and women of the comfortable classes and those who aspired to join them—this reading culture had unusual power and piquancy for the women who grew up in it. Young women's collective reading culture, which combined serious engagement with literature, opportunities for learning and dreaming, and emotional intimacy with other women, provided imaginative space in which to invent new lives and develop the necessary skills and self-confidence to act on them. The ability to fulfill such dreams depended on circumstances as varied as new educational and professional opportunities and late-Victorian restraints on social interaction between the sexes.

By the early twentieth century an evolving middle-class youth culture began to challenge the family as the principal shaper of values, particularly during adolescence. As high school attendance became the norm, young people came increasingly under the sway of peers whose values often ran counter to those of parents. Unlike the homosocial culture of the nineteenth century, the new peer culture was assertively heterosocial. Liberating in many ways from the most repressive aspects of Victorian morality, the new "heterosexual imperative" emphasized popularity with members of the opposite sex and dating as a training ground for marriage.[2]

New forms of entertainment also challenged the primacy of the family-based literary culture. None more so than movies, which, beginning in the 1890s, became popular first with working-class and then middle-class audiences. This powerful visual medium, with its fashionable and seductive stars, projected new models of femininity, as did a burgeoning advertising industry that fostered insecurities about popularity and appearance. Other popular entertainments followed, many to be enjoyed with members of the opposite sex, not only radio and television, but also sports, dancing, and music. As sports and entertainment stars like Gertrude Ederle and Mary Pickford replaced writers like Louisa May Alcott as role models, adolescents who had once expressed interest in literary careers became preoccupied with subjects like dress, dieting, and dating.[3]

As reading became one among many activities competing for leisure time, reading practices changed significantly. In *Middletown*, their 1929 landmark study of Muncie, Indiana, Robert and Helen Merrell Lynd found that women were the main book borrowers from public libraries and that men were "almost never heard discussing books." But although women were still more interested in literature than men, their participation in formal or semiformal literary programs declined, among them Chautauqua and young women's reading circles, along with literary evenings in churches. The trend was especially marked among younger women, who belonged to clubs where they were more apt to play bridge than to read.[4]

The literary clubs patronized by older women continued to meet in Muncie and elsewhere. But membership declined from a peak in the early twentieth century, as the clubs' political orientation and clout diminished with the waning of Progressive politics after World War I. As adult education became the province of academic institutions and women attended college in greater numbers, the educational role of women's clubs also declined.

With the upgrading of professional standards in many fields, the informal educational efforts of clubs and lyceums came to seem amateurish. By the 1920s it became fashionable to ridicule women's clubs as promoting mindless consumption of literature and ostentatious display of at best superficial knowledge.[5]

If changing gender and sexual norms and new forms of entertainment undermined the Gilded Age culture of reading, so did the success of women of the Progressive generation in overturning some of the barriers that had traditionally shut them out of public life. Their very achievements helped to undercut the perceived need for women's collective endeavors.

In *The Second Twenty Years at Hull-House* (1930), Jane Addams expressed puzzlement at the "contrasts in a post-war generation," including younger women's lack of interest in the social ideals that animated her contemporaries and the new emphasis on sex as the most important avenue for fulfillment.[6] While it is true that young women no longer had the same sense of gender consciousness—in its dual connotation of privilege and obligation—that motivated many women of Addams's generation, they did not simply opt for exclusively private lives. But most were unwilling to make the choice between career and marriage that their predecessors took for granted. Fortified by the vote, and not much interested in female bonding, successive generations of women learned firsthand what the Progressive generation had assumed: that without institutional supports, career and motherhood were difficult to combine.

For the most part, women of Addams's cohort worked in single-sex institutions or in sex-typed fields for which women were often thought to have special talents. Professional niches of this sort became less common in the twentieth century: women's medical schools and hospitals closed as training requirements increased, and women's colleges employed more male professors as concern about students' heterosexual adjustment and the fear of lesbianism—a newly invented label—made women's friendships suspect. The post–World War II ideology that Betty Friedan called "the feminine mystique," with its renewed premium on marriage and motherhood, dampened enthusiasm for living public lives. Then came the women's movement in the late 1960s and in its wake professional attainments and public lives that even a dreamer like Carey Thomas might have found difficult to imagine.

IN OUR OWN TIME, women have again become collectively visible in the world of letters, as readers, writers, and cultural arbiters. Noting that there were more female than male authors under the age of forty, a journalist concluded in 1989 that literature is "a woman's world now."[7] At a time when alarmist reports about the decline of literary reading are routine, this assessment may offer cold comfort. But it points to the continued attraction of literary pursuits for women.

Women have been the mainstay of the book clubs that are so conspicuous a feature of the contemporary cultural landscape. Although there are all-male and mixed-sex book clubs, reading groups appeal mainly to women, as they did in the nineteenth century. The current movement has roots in the 1980s and took off in earnest in the 1990s when just about everyone seemed to be joining a group. A book club professional estimated that there were half a million book clubs in 1999 (double the number just five years earlier), with a membership of five to ten million.[8] It is impossible to keep track of a grass-roots phenomenon that typically begins when a handful of people decide to read books and talk about them together. But reading groups have remained a force in women's lives in the early years of the twenty-first century, among women of color as well as white women.

Women have been the main followers of Oprah's Book Club, launched in September 1996 "'to get America reading' again." An estimated thirteen million viewers watched the book club segment of the *Oprah Winfrey Show*, and it was claimed that at least half a million had read or at least dipped into the book by airtime, when a few readers were invited to join Winfrey and the author on the show.[9] (In the process, Winfrey became the nation's most important gatekeeper for contemporary fiction. Her selections catapulted to best-seller lists, selling anywhere from 700,000 to 1.5 million copies.) Unlike reading groups, which generally appeal to women who describe themselves as "great readers," Oprah's Book Club included women who claimed they had not read a book in years. Some professed that the book club changed their lives, as Winfrey claimed reading changed hers.[10]

The popularity of reading groups and Oprah's Book Club underscores the renewed importance of reading in women's lives, accompanied by a desire to talk about books with others. Clubs, both past and present, have blended the intellectual, social, and personal, a powerful combination for women. A comparison between such seemingly dissimilar individuals as Oprah Winfrey and her fellow Chicagoan, Jane Addams, yields significant similarities as well as differences. Reading was an important vehicle for personal development in each case. In Winfrey's account, "Books opened windows to the world for me. If I can help open them for someone else, I'm happy."[11] Both women made their reading skills and preferences available to others less favored, Addams through reading parties and classes at Hull-House,

Oprah much more widely through her book club, with its on-air and on-line components.

Despite their common faith in reading, the approaches of Addams and Winfrey diverge, in part no doubt because they came to books in dissimilar ways and because of differences in their mediums and objectives. Where Addams grew up in privilege, Winfrey came from a background of poverty, neglect, and abuse and found in books "an open door to dwell in possibility." She echoes the stories of Jewish immigrants a century earlier when she observes, "Getting my library card was like citizenship, it was like American citizenship."[12] Given the distance she has traveled, Winfrey's emphasis on the personal impact of reading is not surprising: "The reason I love books . . . is because they teach us something about ourselves." As she told one author, "We all look for the parts of ourselves that are in your story."[13] Since many of her selections feature heroines who overcome dysfunctional families, abusive relationships, or mental illness, what they teach is self-awareness and determination. The message: you are responsible for your own life—take charge of it.[14] Addams, too, believed in the transformative possibilities of reading. But where Winfrey emphasizes transformation of the self, Addams articulated the civic uses of literacy and the responsibilities of the privileged to use the insights gained from literature to promote a more equitable society: "The real question is not what we read, but what social use do we make of the mental and physical life we have thus acquired."[15] Believing that literature could foster imaginative engagement with individuals from every background, she viewed reading as a means by which men and women of privilege could transcend the limitations of their class.

Considering Addams and Winfrey as preeminent cultural leaders of their times, their outlooks tell us a great deal about changes in American life in the past century, and not only about the loss of self-assurance of Addams's generation and the culture of disclosure of Winfrey's. Perhaps most striking is the changed professional and political situation of American women. Today, when roughly half of law and medical students are female, girls grow up with expectations about their lives that those of us who grew up in the first two-thirds of the twentieth century—let alone the nineteenth—did not. At the same time, new opportunities brought about in part by two women's movements result in less leisure for middle-class women, who experience continued gender disparities both on the job and at home, where they still bear the brunt of family responsibilities.

Where voluntary organizations like the literary clubs provided a launching pad for public activities of various kinds a century or so ago, today's clubs seem more like places of refuge. Then, when women were assumed to be limited to domestic life, they fashioned an ostensibly private activity into an effective public instrument. In so doing, they used an activity that began at home to claim first semi-public and then overtly public space.

And today? What accounts for the popularity of an activity that has been hailed as obsolete and lacks the tangible goals associated with so many self-directed endeavors? What still makes reading so compelling for women?

A freelance male writer provides an oblique answer in assessing why men rarely join book groups. He tells us that it is for the same reason they do not read Amy Tan or go to see the film version of *Little Women* or cry if they do: because doing so would violate "the 'Guy Code.'" Men view book clubs as "one more form of 'women's work' to be avoided at all costs," think that too much fiction and too many books by women authors are read, and prefer more "'objective' impersonal groups."[16]

What men find objectionable is precisely what attracts women to book groups. Aficionadas speak of self-discovery and intimacy, "verification" and self-esteem, connection and community. Some join "because they want 'to do something for me,'" some because they "want to have someone besides an uninterested husband, roommate, or baby to share their book-related thoughts with." Others talk about the expanded horizons that follow serious encounters with books, especially those they would not read on their own. But when members speak of groups as "life support" and "safe places," it is clear that the appeal of groups is "more than talking about books."[17] Whatever the initial motivation, a women's book group is also about female bonding. It is the personal dimension of the interchanges—the emotional satisfaction that comes from shared moments of intimacy over book talk— that is often most compelling. As one book club leader put it: "The books and the groups serve as a starting point for connection. Women want to explore issues in depth and search for meaning. Books and the structure of book groups allow that."[18]

Where women's literary groups in the late nineteenth century were often about the process of becoming, today's offer a respite from busy professional and personal lives, whether lived mainly at home, in the paid work force, or both. In earlier times, groups appealed to women of all ages, many of them seeking support for their aspirations as well as knowledge; today's attract those who have already begun to live out their dreams. Yet, as Elizabeth Long observes so compellingly, today's book club members are still eager to explore their own lives and to measure themselves against the lives of others, whether these others be female characters or their fellow bookies. In that sense, reading groups are still about women's identity.[19]

If today's book clubs seem drained of their activist edge, their popularity indicates that reading once again plays an important role in women's lives, one that is collective rather than purely private. Despite the tremendous changes in their lives, the need to touch base with other women persists, particularly at a time when gender-segregated activities in daily life are fewer than they once were. The resurgence of reading groups also suggests that each generation of women must find anew ways to promote female agency and that this is often best done in spaces inhabited by women—both real and imagined.

NOTES

INTRODUCTION

1 The Progressive era derives its name from the diverse and sometimes contradictory reform movements that flourished in the United States from the 1890s through 1917. Except where otherwise indicated, I have used the designation in a generational rather than in a political sense.

2 See the synthesis of recent work by J. A. Appleyard, *Becoming a Reader: The Experience of Fiction from Childhood to Adulthood* (Cambridge: Cambridge University Press, 1990).

3 See, for example, Lewis M. Terman and Margaret Lima, *Children's Reading: A Guide for Parents and Teachers*, 2nd ed. (New York: D. Appleton & Co., 1931), who find that "at every age girls read more than boys" and read more fiction (68); and National Endowment for the Arts, *Reading at Risk: A Survey of Literary Reading in America*, Research Division Report #46 (Washington, D.C.: National Endowment for the Arts, 2004), 23–24.

4 As Jerome Bruner observes, "It is through our own narratives that we principally construct a version of ourselves in the world, and it is through its narrative that a culture provides models of identity and agency to its members"; *The Culture of Education* (Cambridge, Mass.: Harvard University Press, 1996), xiv.

5 Anna Quindlen suggests that "Perhaps only a truly discontented child can become as seduced by books as I was"; *How Reading Changed My Life* (New York: Ballantine Publishing Group, 1998), 4.

6 Roger Chartier, *The Order of Books: Readers, Authors, and Libraries in Europe between the Fourteenth and Eighteenth Centuries*, trans. Lydia G. Cochrane (Stanford: Stanford University Press, 1994), 3. This book is a thoughtful summing up of Chartier's influential work on reading. Among historians, he has forcefully articulated the importance of reading practices in the construction of meaning; elaborated on the concept of appropriation, that is, the reader's ability to wrest personal meaning from a text; and questioned the equation of "cultural cleavages . . . organized according to pre-existent social divisions" (7).

7 Janice A. Radway, introduction to *Reading the Romance: Women, Patriarchy, and Popular Literature* (1984; reprint, Chapel Hill: University of North Carolina Press, 1991), 7. In this pioneering ethnographic study of romance readers, Radway underscores the importance of the act of reading itself. She suggests that by taking time out from other tasks, housewives who reiteratively read romances were engaging in a mild form of self-assertion and even protest against the exclusively domestic existence to which they otherwise subscribed.

8 Clifford Geertz, *The Interpretation of Cultures: Selected Essays* (New York: Basic Books, 1973), esp. 5–6, 14, 443–53.

9 I have defined "reading community" somewhat loosely, to include a family and a feminist literary circle as well as larger social groupings. I prefer the term to "interpretive community," the designation employed by Stanley Fish, *Is There a Text in This Class?: The Authority of Interpretive Communities* (Cambridge, Mass.: Harvard University Press, 1980). The latter term derives from the reading practices of academic communities for whom interpretation is the primary thing one does with texts and is based on fixed theoretical approaches rather than on reading practices.

10 The history of the book (or reading), a burgeoning field of inquiry for the past two decades, has been a critically important influence on my work. For surveys of the field as practiced by Americanists, see David D. Hall, "Readers and Reading in America: Historical and Critical Perspectives," in *Cultures of Print: Essays in the History of the Book* (Amherst: University of Massachusetts Press, 1996), 169–87; Janice Radway, "Beyond Mary Bailey and Old Maid Librarians: Reimagining Readers and Rethinking Reading," *Journal of Education for Library and Information Science* 35 (Fall 1994): 1–21; and Joan Shelley Rubin, *Songs of Ourselves: The Uses of Poetry in America* (Cambridge, Mass.: Harvard University Press, 2007), 1–10. See also the classic early statement by a historian of France, Robert Darnton, "What Is the History of Books?," *Daedalus* 3 (Summer 1982): 65–83.

11 Keith Oatley, "Emotions and the Story Worlds of Fiction," in *Narrative Impact: Social and Cognitive Foundations*, ed. Melanie C. Green, Jeffrey J. Strange, and Timothy C. Brock (Mahwah, N.J.: Lawrence Erlbaum, 2002), 39–69; quotations 39, 65. Oatley maintains that reading biography and narrative history can also be transformative.

12 The phrase is Oatley's, in ibid., 41.

CHAPTER ONE

1 Zelda, "Just between Ourselves, Girls," English Department, *Jewish Daily News* (*Yiddishes Tageblatt*, New York), July 12, 1903. Measured against this advice, there is no little irony in Pastor's own story: a few years later she entered a storybook marriage to a wealthy Gentile of the sort featured in the "cheap" romances she condemned; later still, she joined first the socialist, then the communist left. For her story, see *"I Belong to the Working Class": The Unfinished Autobiography of Rose Pastor Stokes*, ed. Herbert Shapiro and David L. Sterling (Athens: University of Georgia Press, 1992); Arthur Zipser and Pearl Zipser, *Fire and Grace: The Life of Rose Pastor Stokes* (Athens: University of Georgia Press, 1989); and Harriet M.

Sigerman, "Daughters of the Book: A Study of Gender and Ethnicity in the Lives of Three American Jewish Women" (Ph.D. diss., University of Massachusetts, 1992).

2 "'Zelda' on Books," *Jewish Daily News*, Aug. 4, 1903. After Alcott, Pastor recommended Dickens, George Eliot, and—her audience squarely in mind—Grace Aguilar, a respected nineteenth-century Anglo-Jewish writer, as well as Jewish and general history.

3 Although *Little Women* was not published as a single volume until 1880, I will refer to it in the singular except when one volume is specifically intended. For additional references on Alcott and *Little Women* and more on the novel's publishing history, see Barbara Sicherman, "Reading *Little Women*: The Many Lives of a Text," in *U.S. History as Women's History: New Feminist Essays*, ed. Linda K. Kerber et al., 245–66 (Chapel Hill: University of North Carolina Press, 1995). Nearly 598,000 copies of *Little Women* had been printed by Roberts Brothers by 1909 (excluding foreign sales); Joel Myerson and Daniel Shealy, "The Sales of Louisa May Alcott's Books," *Harvard Library Bulletin*, n.s., 1 (Spring 1990): esp. 69–71, 86. See also Roberts Brothers Cost Book D [I], Little, Brown & Co. Papers, *87M-113, the Houghton Library, Harvard University.

Sales of course are only part of the story. Library use was high at the outset and remained so. Thomas Niles to Alcott, fragment [1870?], Louisa May Alcott Papers, bMS Am 1130.8 (18), the Houghton Library, Harvard University. See also "Popularity of 'Little Women,'" Dec. 22, 1912, "Press . . .[illegible] Albany," Alcott Papers, bMS Am 800.23, the Houghton Library, Harvard University.

4 For a fascinating analysis of this shift, see Richard H. Brodhead, "Starting Out in the 1860s: Alcott, Authorship, and the Postbellum Literary Field," ch. 3 in *Cultures of Letters: Scenes of Reading and Writing in Nineteenth-Century America*, 69–106 (Chicago: University of Chicago Press, 1993).

5 Dorothea Lawrence Mann, "When the Alcott Books Were New," *Publishers Weekly* 116 (Sept. 28, 1929): 1619.

6 "'Little Women' Leads Poll," *New York Times*, Mar. 22, 1927, 7, reprinted in Madeleine B. Stern, ed., *Critical Essays on Louisa May Alcott* (Boston: G. K. Hall, 1984), 84.

7 For a wide-ranging account see Gloria T. Delamar, *Louisa May Alcott and "Little Women": Biography, Critique, Publications, Poems, Songs and Contemporary Relevance* (Jefferson, N.C.: McFarland, 1990).

8 Janice M. Alberghene and Beverly Lyon Clark, eds., *Little Women and the Feminist Imagination: Criticism, Controversy, Personal Essays* (New York: Garland, 1999), xviii–xix. The introduction provides a thoughtful appraisal of the novel's popular and critical reception.

9 The 1994 movie may have prompted renewed interest in the book: *Books in Print, 1999–2000* listed sixty-nine editions, up from twenty seven years earlier.

10 Frank Luther Mott, *Golden Multitudes: The Story of Best Sellers in the United States* (New York: Macmillan, 1947), 102.

11 For an analysis of well-loved texts that takes *Little Women* as a point of departure, see Catharine R. Stimpson, "Reading for Love: Canons, Paracanons, and Whistling Jo March," *New Literary History* 21 (Autumn 1990): 957–76.

12   Cynthia Ozick, "Spells, Wishes, Goldfish, Old School Hurts," *New York Times Book Review*, Jan. 31, 1982, 24.

13   Victor Nell, *Lost in a Book: The Psychology of Reading for Pleasure* (New Haven: Yale University Press, 1988), 2.

14   For a critique of the essentialist position that readers must occupy a subject-position based on predetermined, mutually exclusive categories, for example, "male" or "working-class," see Diana Fuss, *Essentially Speaking: Feminism, Nature and Difference* (New York: Routledge, 1989), 32–35.

15   Emily Dickinson, Poem No. 1286, in *The Poems of Emily Dickinson: Reading Edition*, ed. R. W. Franklin (Cambridge, Mass.: Harvard University Press, 1999), 501.

16   Hans Robert Jauss, "Literary History as a Challenge to Literary Theory," in *New Directions in Literary History*, ed. Ralph Cohen (Baltimore: Johns Hopkins University Press, 1974), 38, 37. A member of the German reception-aesthetics school, Jauss developed the "horizon of expectations" concept as an aspect of literary criticism, but ordinary readers too judge books in a comparative context, based on their everyday lives as well as their prior reading experiences.

17   "Literature," *Putnam's Magazine* 2 (Dec. 1868): 760.

18   *One Hundred Influential American Books Printed before 1900: Catalogue and Addresses; Exhibition at the Grolier Club* (New York: Grolier Club, 1947), 106.

19   Richard L. Darling, *The Rise of Children's Book Reviewing in America, 1865–1881* (New York: R. R. Bowker, 1968). An excellent starting point for considering the new children's literature is Anne H. Lundin, "Victorian Horizons: The Reception of Children's Books in England and America, 1880–1900," *Library Quarterly* 64 (1994): 30–59.

20   On age, see an ad for a series of "Books for Girls" whose intended audience was those "between eight and eighteen. . . . for growing-up girls, the mothers of the next generation," in *American Literary Gazette and Publishers' Circular* 17 (June 1, 1871): 88. One critic characterized the genre as "something above mere baby tales" but not "novels of a sort which should be read only by persons capable of forming a discreet judgment"; Edward G. Salmon, "What Girls Read," *Nineteenth Century* 20 (Oct. 1886): 522.

21   Hellmut Lehmann-Haupt et al., *The Book in America: A History of the Making and Selling of Books in the United States* (New York: Bowker, 1951), 160–61. On *Little Women*'s readership, see, for example, Frank Preston Stearns, *Sketches from Concord and Appledore* (New York: G. P. Putnam's Sons, 1895), 81–82. Many reviews indicated its crossover appeal.

22   On the gendering of juvenile literature, see Elizabeth Segel, "'As the Twig Is Bent . . .': Gender and Childhood Reading," in *Gender and Reading: Essays on Readers, Texts, and Contexts*, ed. Elizabeth A. Flynn and Patrocinio P. Schweickart, 165–86 (Baltimore: Johns Hopkins University Press, 1986), a useful, brief analysis; Kimberley Reynolds, *Girls Only?: Gender and Popular Children's Fiction in Britain, 1880–1910* (Philadelphia: Temple University Press, 1990), esp. 50–90; and Martin Green, *Dreams of Adventure, Deeds of Empire* (New York: Basic Books, 1979), esp. 203–34. See also Daniel T. Rodgers, *The Work Ethic in Industrial America, 1850–1920* (Chicago: University of Chicago Press, 1978), 125–52; and R. Gordon Kelly, ed., *Children's Periodicals of the United States* (Westport, Conn.: Greenwood Press, 1984).

23 "What Our Boys Are Reading," *Scribner's Monthly* 15 (Mar. 1878): 681.

24 Entry for May 1868, *The Journals of Louisa May Alcott*, ed. Joel Myerson, Daniel Shealy, and Madeleine B. Stern (Boston: Little, Brown, 1989), 165–66 (hereafter cited as *Journals*). On rereading this entry years later, Alcott quipped, "Good joke." Niles evidently asked her to write a girls' story after observing the hefty sales of boys' adventure stories at a nearby publishing house.

25 Angela M. Estes and Kathleen Margaret Lant, "Dismembering the Text: The Horror of Louisa May Alcott's *Little Women*," *Children's Literature* 17 (1989): 98–123. See also Judith Fetterley, "*Little Women*: Alcott's Civil War," *Feminist Studies* 5 (Summer 1979): 369–83; and Linda K. Kerber, "Can a Woman Be an Individual?: The Limits of Puritan Tradition in the Early Republic," *Texas Studies in Literature and Language* 25 (Spring 1983): 165–78.

26 Henry James, review of *Eight Cousins*, *Nation* 21 (Oct. 14, 1875): 250–51, reprinted in Madeleine Stern, *Critical Essays*, 165–66. See also Janet S. Zehr, "The Response of Nineteenth-Century Audiences to Louisa May Alcott's Fiction," *American Transcendental Quarterly*, n.s., 1 (Dec. 1987): 323–42.

27 A sign of the changing times was the banning of the Elsie books by some libraries on the grounds that they were commonplace and not true to life; Esther Jane Carrier, *Fiction in Public Libraries, 1876–1900* (New York: Scarecrow Press, 1965), 356–60.

28 For comparisons of the two authors, see review of *An Old-Fashioned Girl*, *Nation* 11 (July 14, 1870): 30; and Niles to Alcott, Jan. 13, 1871, Alcott Papers, bMS Am 1130.8 (20). Niles reported that Harriet Beecher Stowe wanted to know why Alcott's books were "so much more popular" than Mrs. Whitney's, which she considered "equally as good." By permission of the Houghton Library, Harvard University.

29 David E. Smith, *John Bunyan in America* (Bloomington: Indiana University Press, 1966), discusses *Little Women* and the changed standing of *Pilgrim's Progress* in postwar America, 93–102.

30 Review of *Little Women* by Louisa May Alcott, in *Ladies' Repository* 28 (Dec. 1868): 472.

31 Critics who find this less overt method of discipline more coercive than physical punishment include Steven Mailloux, "The Rhetorical Use and Abuse of Fiction: Eating Books in Late Nineteenth-Century America," *boundary 2* 17 (Spring 1990): 133–57. See also Brodhead, *Cultures of Letters*, ch. 3.

32 Alcott's depiction of home theatricals evidently drew the wrath of evangelicals. Niles to Alcott, Oct. 26, 1868, Alcott Papers, bMS Am 1130.8 (3). The *Christian Union*, edited by Henry Ward Beecher, evidently did not include her books on its Sunday School list, to Niles's great irritation; Lawrence F. Abbott to Roberts Brothers, June 6, 1882, with appended note by Niles to Alcott, Alcott Papers, bMS Am 1130.8 (128), the Houghton Library, Harvard University.

33 See Sharon O'Brien, "Tomboyism and Adolescent Conflict: Three Nineteenth-Century Case Studies," in *Woman's Being, Woman's Place: Female Identity and Vocation in American History*, ed. Mary Kelley (Boston: G. K. Hall, 1979), 351–72, which includes a section on Alcott; Alfred Habegger, "Funny Tomboys," in *Gender, Fantasy, and Realism in American Literature* (New York: Columbia University Press, 1982), 172–83; and Michelle Ann Abate, *Tomboys: A Literary and Cultural*

History (Philadelphia: Temple University Press, 2008), esp. 24–49. An ad for *Little Men* noted that "when a girl, [Jo] was half a boy herself." *American Literary Gazette and Publishers' Circular* 17 (May 15, 1871): 49.

34 The first book in the long-lived series was *What Katy Did* (1872). "Susan Coolidge" was the pen name of Sarah Chauncey Woolsey.

35 Niles to Alcott, July 25, 1868, Alcott Papers, bMS Am 1130.8 (2). By permission of the Houghton Library, Harvard University.

36 *Little Women*, ed. Madelon Bedell (New York: Modern Library, 1983), 290. All quotations are taken from this volume, which "utilizes two of the earliest editions published by Roberts Brothers" (l).

37 Nov. 1 [1868], *Journals*, 167; Alcott to Elizabeth Powell, Mar. 20, [1869], in *The Selected Letters of Louisa May Alcott*, ed. Joel Myerson, Daniel Shealy, and Madeleine B. Stern (Boston: Little, Brown, 1987), 125. Erin Graham, "Books That Girls Have Loved," *Lippincott's Monthly Magazine* 60 (Sept. 1897): 428–32, makes much of Bhaer's foreignness and ungainliness.

38 For girls in early adolescence and/or for lesbian readers, the young Jo may have been the primary romantic interest.

39 A conversation with Dolores Kreisman contributed to this analysis.

40 Alcott, *Little Women*, 601.

41 See Rachel Blau DuPlessis, *Writing beyond the Ending: Narrative Strategies of Twentieth-Century Women Writers* (Bloomington: Indiana University Press, 1985).

42 Review of *Little Women, Part II*, by Louisa May Alcott, *Harper's New Monthly Magazine* 39 (Aug. 1869): 455–56, reprinted in Madeleine Stern, *Critical Essays*, 83.

43 Stearns, *Sketches from Concord and Appledore*, 82.

44 Niles to Alcott, Apr. 14, 1869, Alcott Papers, bMS Am 1130.8 (4). By permission of the Houghton Library, Harvard University.

45 Sales fell off in the late 1870s but picked up again in the 1880s with the repackaging of *Little Women* as a single volume and publication of eight titles in a "'Little Women' Series." See Roberts Brothers Cost Books, including summary in Cost Book D [I], Little, Brown & Co. Papers, *87M-113, the Houghton Library, Harvard University; and Myerson and Shealy, "The Sales of Louisa May Alcott's Books" (see note 3). The repackaged text was newly illustrated and purged of some of its slang; Elaine Showalter, "*Little Women*: The American Female Myth," in *Sister's Choice: Tradition and Change in Women's Writing* (Oxford: Clarendon Press, 1991), 55–56.

46 Letter in *St. Nicholas* 5 (Feb. 1878): 300.

47 "Little Things," at first handwritten, then typeset on a small press, was part of a national phenomenon. See Paula Petrik, "The Youngest Fourth Estate: The Novelty Toy Printing Press and Adolescence, 1870–1886," in *Small Worlds: Children and Adolescents in America, 1850–1950*, ed. Elliott West and Paula Petrik (Lawrence: University Press of Kansas, 1992), 125–42. The Alcott sisters had their own Pickwick Club in 1849. Alcott's correspondence with the Lukens sisters, which extended over fourteen years, is reprinted in Myerson, Shealy, and Stern, *Selected Letters*; it was published earlier in the *Ladies' Home Journal* 13 (Apr. 1896): 1–2.

48 *Boston Evening Transcript*, Sept. 30, 1868, 3. Newspaper coverage sustained this view. An undated source, for example, claimed, "It was known to friends and acknowledged by Miss Alcott herself that 'Little Women' is the transcript, more or

less literal, of her own and her sisters['] girlhood"; torn clipping, probably an obituary, bMS Am 800.23, Louisa May Alcott Papers. By permission of the Houghton Library, Harvard University. See also [Franklin B. Sanborn], "The Author of 'Little Women,'" *Hearth and Home* 2 (July 16, 1870).

49 Niles to Alcott, Aug. 30, 1870, and Aug. 14, 1871, bMS Am 1130.8 (16, 29). By permission of the Houghton Library, Harvard University. Unfortunately, only a few letters from Alcott's fans survive.

50 The equation of author and character continued after Alcott's death. When her sister Anna Pratt supervised publication of *Comic Tragedies* (1893), a volume of childhood plays, she wrote the foreword as "Meg," and the title page read "Written By 'Jo' And 'Meg' And Acted By The 'Little Women.'"

51 Letter from "Nelly," dated Mar. 12, 1870, reproduced in Delamar, *Louisa May Alcott*, 146.

52 Entry for April [1869], *Journals*, 171.

53 Louisa May Alcott to Amos Bronson Alcott, [Oct. 18, 1875], in Myerson, Shealy, and Stern, *Selected Letters*, 198. See also entries for September and October 1875, *Journals*, 196–97.

54 See, for example, Louise Chandler Moulton, "Louisa May Alcott," in *Our Famous Women* (Hartford: A. D. Worthington, 1884), 29–52, which was prepared with Alcott's assistance. Reports of Alcott's financial success appeared frequently in the press. An obituary estimated her earnings for *Little Women* alone at $200,000; "Death of Miss Alcott," *Ladies' Home Journal* 5 (May 1888): 3. The figure is high, but it attests to the belief in her success.

55 "American Literature," [1878–79], in *The Jane Addams Papers*, ed. Mary Lynn McCree Bryan (Ann Arbor: University Microfilms International, 1984), reel 27, frames 0239–95.

56 Undated review of *Little Men* ("Capital" penciled in), bMS Am 800.23, Louisa May Alcott Papers. By permission of the Houghton Library, Harvard University.

57 Stearns, *Sketches from Concord and Appledore*, 84. See also Franklin B. Sanborn, *Recollections of Seventy Years* (Boston: Richard G. Badger, 1909), 2:342, 338.

58 Theodore Roosevelt, *An Autobiography* (1913; reprint, New York: De Capo Press, 1985), 17.

59 Addams to Vallie Beck, Mar. 16, 1876, in *The Jane Addams Papers*, reel 1.

60 Nina Baym, *Woman's Fiction: A Guide to Novels by and about Women in America, 1820–1870* (Ithaca, N.Y.: Cornell University Press, 1978).

61 Charlotte Perkins Gilman, *The Living of Charlotte Perkins Gilman* (1935; reprint, New York: Harper & Row, 1975), 35.

62 S. Josephine Baker, *Fighting for Life* (New York: Macmillan, 1939), 17, 9.

63 M. Carey Thomas Journal, June 20, 1870, in *The Papers of M. Carey Thomas in the Bryn Mawr College Archives*, ed. Lucy Fisher West (Woodbridge, Conn.: Research Publications, 1982), reel 1. See chapter 5 for more on Thomas's reading.

64 Alcott, *Little Women*, 51.

65 Ibid., 172–82, quotation on 178.

66 Ibid., 328–29.

67 See Nina Auerbach, *Communities of Women: An Idea in Fiction* (Cambridge, Mass.: Harvard University Press, 1978), 55–73.

68 See Lee Virginia Chambers-Schiller, *Liberty, a Better Husband: Single Women in America; The Generations of 1780–1840* (New Haven: Yale University Press, 1984).

69 Simone de Beauvoir, *Memoirs of a Dutiful Daughter*, trans. James Kirkup (Cleveland: World, 1959), 94–95. Despite differences in culture and religion, de Beauvoir found many parallels between the March family and her own, in particular the belief "that a cultivated mind and moral righteousness were better than money" (94). According to her biographer, de Beauvoir had read *Little Women* by the time she was ten; Deirdre Bair, *Simone de Beauvoir: A Biography* (New York: Summit Books, 1990), 68–71.

70 Bair, *Simone de Beauvoir*, 69; de Beauvoir, *Memoirs*, 111.

71 Showalter, "*Little Women*," 42.

72 These conclusions emerge from my reading and from discussions and correspondence with approximately three dozen women. They were highly educated for the most part and mainly over fifty, but some women under thirty also felt passionately about *Little Women*. Most of my informants were white, but not all. A black high school student in Jamaica rewrote the story to fit the locale. When she learned of my project, a young African American academic interjected, as if continuing an ongoing conversation, that it was unfair of Aunt March to take Amy rather than Jo to Europe. And an Asian American high school student chose the novel as the subject of her college entrance essay.

   Passionate statements may also be found in Alberghene and Clark, *Little Women and the Feminist Imagination*, esp. xv–xvii and 173–83; Shirley Abbott, *The Bookmaker's Daughter: A Memory Unbound* (New York: Ticknor and Fields, 1991), 133–35; and Lynne Sharon Schwartz, *Ruined by Reading: A Life in Books* (Boston: Beacon Press, 1996), 66–67.

73 Mary Church Terrell, *A Colored Woman in a White World* (Washington, D.C.: Ransdell, 1940), 26; Alfreda M. Duster, ed., *Crusade for Justice: The Autobiography of Ida B. Wells* (Chicago: University of Chicago Press, 1970), 7, 21–22.

74 *Middletown Press*, June 1, 1994, B1; and Ann Petry to author, letter postmarked July 23, 1994. Thanks to Farah Jasmine Griffin for this reference and to James A. Miller for insight into the interaction of race and class in African American women's reading practices.

75 Edith Wharton, *A Backward Glance* (New York: D. Appleton-Century Co., 1934), 51; italics in the original. Annie Nathan Meyer, a member of New York's German Jewish elite who extols the authors in the family library as "impeccable," claims that Alcott was the only writer of children's books she could "endure"; *It's Been Fun: An Autobiography* (New York: Henry Schuman, 1951), 32–33.

76 Dorothy Richardson, *The Long Day: The Story of a New York Working Girl* (1905; reprint, New York: Quadrangle Books, 1972), 84–85. For a thoughtful analysis of fiction read by working-class women that includes a discussion of an episode reported by Richardson, see Nan Enstad, *Ladies of Labor, Girls of Adventure: Working Women, Popular Culture, and Labor Politics at the Turn of the Twentieth Century* (New York: Columbia University Press, 1999), 31–60, esp. 56–58.

77 The others were Mrs. A. D. T. Whitney and Edgar Allan Poe. United Workers and Woman's Exchange in Hartford, *Annual Report* (Hartford, 1888), 1:8.

78 Richardson, *The Long Day*, 75–86; quotation 86. *The Long Day* must be used with

caution. Published anonymously, it purports to be a firsthand account by a "working girl." The author, a journalist, calls it "absolutely a transcript from real life," but the editor of a recent edition considers it both "the product of good investigative reporting" and "fictionalized autobiography." Cindy Sondik Aron, introduction to *The Long Day* (Charlottesville: University Press of Virginia, 1990), ix–xi.

79 For an analysis of Libbey's work, including *Little Rosebud's Lovers* as a "Cinderella tale," see Michael Denning, *Mechanic Accents: Dime Novels and Working-Class Culture in America* (London: Verso, 1987), 188–200, esp. 197–200. Joyce Shaw Peterson, "Working Girls and Millionaires: The Melodramatic Romances of Laura Jean Libbey," *American Studies* 24 (Spring 1983): 19–35, considers Libbey's romance formula a "success myth for women" in which working girls emerge as ladies. In Europe, at least, working-class traditions were less likely to foster an individualistic outlook; see Regenia Gagnier, "Social Atoms: Working-Class Autobiography, Subjectivity, and Gender," *Victorian Studies* 30 (Spring 1987): 335–63; and Mary Jo Maynes, "Gender and Narrative Form in French and German Working-Class Autobiographies," in *Interpreting Women's Lives: Feminist Theory and Personal Narratives*, ed. The Personal Narratives Group (Bloomington: Indiana University Press, 1989), 103–17.

80 Elizabeth G. Stern, *My Mother and I* (New York: Macmillan, 1917), 69–71. For an assessment of Stern and her work, see Ellen M. Umansky, "Representations of Jewish Women in the Works and Life of Elizabeth Stern," *Modern Judaism* 13 (1993): 165–76. See also Sicherman, "Reading *Little Women*," 423.

81 Stern, *My Mother and I*, 71–72. A male writer raised as an Orthodox Jew also read *Little Women* as a vehicle for assimilation into American middle-class life; Leo Lerman, "Little Women: Who's in Love with Miss Louisa May Alcott? I Am," *Mademoiselle*, Dec. 1973, reprinted in Madeleine Stern, *Critical Essays*, 113.

82 See, for example, *The Louisa Alcott Reader: A Supplementary Reader for the Fourth Year of School* (1885; reprint, Boston: Little, Brown, 1910); and Fanny E. Coe, ed., *The Louisa Alcott Story Book* (Boston: Little, Brown, 1910). The former included fairy tales, the latter, more realistic stories, with the moral printed beneath the title in the table of contents, e.g., "Kindness to horses" and "Wilfulness is punished."

83 Mary Antin, *The Promised Land* (Boston: Houghton Mifflin, 1912), 257, 258–59.

84 On cultural work, see Jane Tompkins, *Sensational Designs: The Cultural Work of American Fiction, 1790–1860* (New York: Oxford University Press, 1985).

85 For nineteenth- and early twentieth-century reviews, mainly in newspapers, see bMS Am 800.23, Louisa May Alcott Papers, the Houghton Library, Harvard University; and Zehr, "The Response of Nineteenth-Century Audiences," 323–42 (see note 26), which draws on this mostly undated collection.

86 On continuities and changes in female adolescence, see Joan Jacobs Brumberg, *The Body Project: An Intimate History of American Girls* (New York: Random House, 1997).

87 Carolyn G. Heilbrun emphasizes the lack of female models in literature and the exceptional nature of Jo; *Reinventing Womanhood* (New York: W. W. Norton, 1979), 190–91, 212. See also Heilbrun, *Writing a Woman's Life* (New York: W. W. Norton, 1988). Half the female graduate student respondents in one survey named *Little Women* as one of ten books read in childhood that they could recall most easily;

their other selections clustered around a few works. Men's choices were far more varied; Lewis M. Terman and Margaret Lima, *Children's Reading: A Guide for Parents and Teachers*, 2nd ed. (New York: D. Appleton & Co., 1931), 69.

88 These scenes are identified in Jesse S. Crisler, "Alcott's Reading in *Little Women*: Shaping the Autobiographical Self," *Resources for American Literary Study* 20 (1994): 27–36.

CHAPTER TWO

1 See the 1960 Census monograph, John K. Folger and Charles B. Nam, *Education of the American Population* (Washington, D.C.: Government Printing Office, 1967), 113–15. Other useful guides to the complex subject of literacy are Lee Soltow and Edward Stevens, *The Rise of Literacy and the Common School in the United States: A Socioeconomic Analysis to 1870* (Chicago: University of Chicago Press, 1981); Carl F. Kaestle, "Studying the History of Literacy," in Kaestle et al., *Literacy in the United States: Readers and Reading since 1880* (New Haven: Yale University Press, 1991), 3–32; and Harvey J. Graff, *The Literacy Myth: Literacy and Social Structure in the Nineteenth-Century City* (New York: Academic Press, 1979). Aggregate literacy rates conceal inequalities in distribution. In 1850 white illiteracy was considerably higher in the South and other sparsely populated regions (an estimated one out of seven people in North Carolina could neither read nor write). By 1870 regional disparities had declined and the literacy rates of the native and foreign-born converged, with some variation among ethnic groups. On African Americans' literacy, see chapter 9.

On the gender gap in literacy at the end of the eighteenth century, see Ross W. Beales and E. Jennifer Monaghan, "Practices of Reading, Part One: Literacy and Schoolbooks," in *The Colonial Book in the Atlantic World*, ed. Hugh Amory and David D. Hall, A History of the Book in America, vol. 1 (New York: Cambridge University Press, 2000), 380–81. See also E. Jennifer Monaghan, "Literacy Instruction and Gender in Colonial New England," *Reading in America: Literature and Social History*, ed. Cathy N. Davidson, 53–80 (Baltimore: Johns Hopkins University Press, 1989); and E. Jennifer Monaghan, *Learning to Read and Write in Colonial America* (Amherst: University of Massachusetts Press, 2005).

2 Martyn Lyons, "New Readers in the Nineteenth Century: Women, Children, Workers," in *A History of Reading in the West*, ed. Guglielmo Cavallo and Roger Chartier; trans. Lydia G. Cochrane (Amherst: University of Massachusetts Press, 1999), 313. Ronald J. Zboray, *A Fictive People: Antebellum Economic Development and the American Reading Public* (New York: Oxford University Press, 1993), 83–84, 196–201, gives a combined 60 percent literacy rate for British men and women; while Kaestle, "Studying the History of Literacy," 18–19, cites a 33⅓ percent rate for British women in 1850.

3 The classic statement is Linda K. Kerber, *Women of the Republic: Intellect and Ideology in Revolutionary America* (Chapel Hill: University of North Carolina Press, 1980).

4 Mary Kelley has documented advances in women's education at all-female academies and seminaries in the antebellum period and argues that they were on a par with male colleges; *Learning to Stand and Speak: Women, Education, and*

Public Life in America's Republic (Chapel Hill: University of North Carolina Press, 2006), esp. 66–111. The book provides a rich guide to the vast literature bearing on the subject. See also Kerber, *Women of the Republic*; Anne Firor Scott, "The Ever-Widening Circle: The Diffusion of Feminist Values from the Troy Female Seminary, 1822–1872," in *Making the Invisible Woman Visible* (Urbana: University of Illinois Press, 1984), 64-88; and Sally Schwager, "Educating Women in America," *Signs* 12 (Winter 1987): 333–72.

5 Daniel Scott Smith, "Family Limitation, Sexual Control, and Domestic Feminism in Victorian America," in *Clio's Consciousness Raised: New Perspectives on the History of Women*, ed. Mary S. Hartman and Lois Banner (New York: Harper & Row, 1974), 122–23.

6 Although they cannot fully explain the trend, demographers agree that declining fertility is positively correlated with female education.

7 David B. Tyack, *The One Best System: A History of American Urban Education* (Cambridge, Mass.: Harvard University Press, 1974), 61. The demand for women teachers helps account for the greater number of female than male students attending high school—some 53 percent of the total in 1872, 57 percent in 1900; John L. Rury, *Education and Women's Work: Female Schooling and the Division of Labor in Urban America, 1870–1930* (Albany: State University of New York Press, 1991), 17–18. See also Joel Perlmann and Robert A. Margo, *Women's Work?: American Schoolteachers, 1650–1920* (Chicago: University of Chicago Press, 2001).

8 See Patricia Okker, *Our Sister Editors: Sarah J. Hale and the Tradition of Nineteenth-Century American Women Editors* (Athens: University of Georgia Press, 1995); and Nina Baym, *American Women Writers and the Work of History, 1790–1860* (New Brunswick, N.J.: Rutgers University Press, 1995).

9 Susan Coultrap-McQuin, *Doing Literary Business: American Women Writers in the Nineteenth Century* (Chapel Hill: University of North Carolina Press, 1990), 2, 86. On women's literary activities, see also Nina Baym, *Woman's Fiction: A Guide to Novels by and about Women in America, 1820–1870* (Ithaca, N.Y.: Cornell University Press, 1978); Mary Kelley, *Private Woman, Public Stage: Literary Domesticity in Nineteenth-Century America* (New York: Oxford University Press, 1984); Joan D. Hedrick, *Harriet Beecher Stowe: A Life* (New York: Oxford University Press, 1994); Mary P. Ryan, *The Empire of the Mother: American Writing about Domesticity, 1830–1860* (New York: Institute for Research in History/Haworth Press, 1982); and Okker, *Our Sister Editors*.

10 This estimate of women students in higher education includes those studying at normal schools; Colin B. Burke, *American Collegiate Populations: A Test of the Traditional View* (New York: New York University Press, 1982), 217. On women's higher education and the career trajectories of college women, see also Barbara Miller Solomon, *In the Company of Educated Women: A History of Women and Higher Education in America* (New Haven: Yale University Press, 1985); John Mack Faragher and Florence Howe, eds., *Women and Higher Education in American History* (New York: W. W. Norton, 1988), esp. Barbara Sicherman, "College and Careers: Historical Perspectives on the Lives and Work Patterns of Women College Graduates," 130–64; and Patricia Ann Palmieri, *In Adamless Eden: The Community of Women Faculty at Wellesley* (New Haven: Yale University Press, 1995).

11 See, for example, Margaret W. Rossiter, *Women Scientists in America: Struggles and Strategies to 1940* (Baltimore: Johns Hopkins University Press, 1982); and Regina Markell Morantz-Sanchez, *Sympathy and Science: Women Physicians in American Medicine* (New York: Oxford University Press, 1985).

12 Kathleen D. McCarthy questions the degree of women's authority as culture builders, before or after the Civil War; *Women's Culture: American Philanthropy and Art, 1830–1930* (Chicago: University of Chicago Press, 1991).

13 Burton J. Bledstein, *The Culture of Professionalism: The Middle Class and the Development of Higher Education in America* (New York: W. W. Norton, 1976), emphasizes the status-seeking aspects of education and professional training in setting the middle class apart from the working class.

14 Unless otherwise indicated, generalizations refer to the broad middle class. Defining class in the United States remains a vexed and vexing intellectual problem. In an important synthesis, Stuart M. Blumin analyzes five major indicators of middle-class status: work, family organization and strategy, consumption, residential location, and formal and informal voluntary associations; *The Emergence of the Middle Class: Social Experience in the American City, 1760–1900* (Cambridge: Cambridge University Press, 1989), esp. 11. See also *The Middling Sorts: Explorations in the History of the American Middle Class*, ed. Burton J. Bledstein and Robert D. Johnston (New York: Routledge, 2001). Historians who study the relationship between consumption and class emphasize the higher disposable income of middle-class families as one key to their greater expenditure on consumer items. In addition, Blumin finds that middle-class families spent more for home furnishings and cultural artifacts like pianos than did artisans of similar means, a finding he relates to the more precarious economic position of the latter as well as to divergent views on the "proper character . . . of the physical home"; *The Emergence of the Middle Class*, ch. 5, quotation on 163. On the evolution of middle-class vacations, see Cindy S. Aron, *Working at Play: A History of Vacations in the United States* (New York: Oxford University Press, 1999).

15 The phrase is Pierre Bourdieu's in *Distinction: A Social Critique of the Judgement of Taste*, trans. Richard Nice (Cambridge, Mass.: Harvard University Press, 1984), 2. Bourdieu's influential analysis of the close relationship of cultural preferences to class and educational status should be balanced by Roger Chartier's caution against assuming hard and fast cultural cleavages based on class; "Intellectual History or Sociocultural History?: The French Trajectories," in *Modern European Intellectual History: Reappraisals and New Perspectives*, ed. Dominick LaCapra and Steven L. Kaplan, 13–46 (Ithaca, N.Y.: Cornell University Press, 1982).

16 Noah Porter, *Books and Reading; or, What Books Shall I Read and How Shall I Read Them?* (1870; reprint, New York: Charles Scribner's Sons, 1883), 1–5.

17 Louise L. Stevenson, *The Victorian Homefront: American Thought and Culture, 1860–1880* (New York: Twayne, 1991), quotation on 2. See also Mary Lynn Stevens Heininger, *At Home with a Book: Reading in America, 1840–1940* (Rochester, N.Y.: Strong Museum, 1986); Richard L. Bushman, *The Refinement of America: Persons, Houses, Cities* (New York: Vintage Books, 1993); Peter C. Marzio, *The Democratic Art: Chromolithography, 1840–1900; Pictures for a 19th-Century America* (Boston: David R. Godine, 1979); and Shirley Wajda, "A Room with a Viewer: The Parlor

Stereoscope, Comic Stereographs, and the Psychic Role of Play in Victorian America," in *Hard at Play: Leisure in America, 1840–1940*, ed. Kathryn Grover, 112–38 (Amherst: University of Massachusetts Press, 1992).

18 Mary Austin, *Earth Horizon: Autobiography* (Boston: Houghton Mifflin, 1932), 100, 102, 86.

19 Joan Shelley Rubin, in *The Making of Middlebrow Culture* (Chapel Hill: University of North Carolina Press, 1992), analyzes the development of an ideology of culture that pitted genuine culture against the marketplace. For a more gendered take on the subject, see Kirsten Swinth, *Painting Professionals: Women Artists and the Development of Modern American Art, 1870–1930* (Chapel Hill: University of North Carolina Press, 2001).

20 Austin, *Earth Horizon*, 100–102. Austin may well have been familiar with the analysis of Thorstein Veblen, *The Theory of the Leisure Class: An Economic Study of Institutions* (1899; reprint, New York: Modern Library, 1934).

21 Horace Mann, "Report for 1848," in *Life and Works of Horace Mann* (Boston: Lee and Shepard, 1891), 4:277.

22 William E. Channing, "Address on Self-Culture," in *The Works of William E. Channing, D.D.*, 20th ed. (Boston: American Unitarian Association, 1871), 1:354, 378.

23 Raymond Williams traces these and other definitions of "culture" in *Keywords: A Vocabulary of Culture and Society*, rev. ed. (New York: Oxford University Press, 1983), 87–93, quotation on 90.

24 Austin, *Earth Horizon*, 100. On religious trends see Paul A. Carter, *The Spiritual Crisis of the Gilded Age* (DeKalb: Northern Illinois University Press, 1971).

25 Matthew Arnold, *Culture and Anarchy: An Essay in Political and Social Criticism* (London: Smith, Elder, 1869), viii.

26 Arthur John, *The Best Years of the Century: Richard Watson Gilder,* Scribner's Monthly, *and the* Century Magazine, *1870–1909* (Urbana: University of Illinois Press, 1981).

27 By "sacralization of culture" I mean the spiritual, even quasi-religious, veneration of culture from any quarter. This usage differs from that of Lawrence W. Levine, *Highbrow/Lowbrow: The Emergence of Cultural Hierarchy in America* (Cambridge, Mass.: Harvard University Press, 1988), who popularized the term and applied it to efforts by urban elites to refine cultural practices in ways that excluded working-class audiences. Joan Shelley Rubin uses "desacralization" to refer to the diffusion of culture by a burgeoning publishing industry; *The Making of Middlebrow Culture*, 15–19.

28 Hedrick, *Harriet Beecher Stowe*; and William G. McLoughlin, *The Meaning of Henry Ward Beecher: An Essay on the Shifting Values of Mid-Victorian America, 1840–1870* (New York: Alfred A. Knopf, 1970), 83. See also Debby Applegate, *The Most Famous Man in America: The Biography of Henry Ward Beecher* (New York: Doubleday, 2006). Beecher's shift notwithstanding, to proponents of a still strong evangelical culture, secular fiction and art often remained suspect; Candy Gunther Brown, *The Word in the World: Evangelical Writing, Publishing, and Reading in America, 1789–1880* (Chapel Hill: University of North Carolina Press, 2004). See also David Paul Nord, *Faith in Reading: Religious Publishing and the Birth of Mass Media in America* (New York: Oxford University Press, 2004).

29 The classic analysis of the shift from traditional to modern literacy is David D. Hall, "The Uses of Literacy in New England, 1600–1850," in *Printing and Society in Early America*, ed. William L. Joyce, David D. Hall, Richard D. Brown, and John Hench, 1–47 (Worcester, Mass.: American Antiquarian Society, 1983).

30 The pirating of books by foreign authors prior to the signing of an international copyright agreement in 1891 contributed to the expansion of the fiction and belles lettres categories at reduced prices. See Raymond Howard Shove, *Cheap Book Production in the United States, 1870 to 1891* (Urbana: University of Illinois Library, 1937); and on working-class expenditures on reading, David Paul Nord, "Working-Class Readers: Family, Community, and Reading in Late-Nineteenth-Century America," *Communication Research* 13 (April 1986): 156–81.

31 Ronald J. Zboray and Mary Saracino Zboray, "Political News and Female Readership in Antebellum Boston and Its Region," *Journalism History* 22 (Spring 1966): 2–14, challenges the standard view.

32 John, *The Best Years of the Century*, 13, 233; Frank Luther Mott, *A History of American Magazines* (Cambridge, Mass.: Harvard University Press, 1938), 3:6.

33 Many aspects of the production, distribution, and consumption of books before and during the Gilded Age are treated in *The Industrial Book, 1840–1880*, ed. Scott E. Casper, Jeffrey D. Groves, Stephen W. Nissenbaum, and Michael Winship, A History of the Book in America, vol. 3 (Chapel Hill: University of North Carolina Press, 2007); and *Print in Motion: The Expansion of Publishing and Reading in the United States, 1880–1940*, ed. Carl F. Kaestle and Janice A. Radway, A History of the Book in America, vol. 4 (Chapel Hill: University of North Carolina Press, 2009). See also Donald H. Sheehan, *This Was Publishing: A Chronicle of the Book Trade in the Gilded Age* (Bloomington: Indiana University Press, 1952); John Tebbel, *A History of Book Publishing in the United States*, vols. 1 and 2 (New York: R. R. Bowker, 1972, 1975); Michael Winship, *American Literary Publishing in the Mid-Nineteenth Century: The Business of Ticknor and Fields* (Cambridge: Cambridge University Press, 1995); Frank Luther Mott, *A History of American Magazines*, vols. 1–3 (Cambridge, Mass.: Harvard University Press, 1938); John Tebbel and Mary Ellen Zuckerman, *The Magazine in America, 1741–1990* (New York: Oxford University Press, 1991); Richard Ohmann, *Selling Culture: Magazines, Markets, and Class at the Turn of the Century* (London: Verso, 1996); and Ellen Gruber Garvey, *The Adman in the Parlor: Magazines and the Gendering of Consumer Culture, 1880s to 1910s* (New York: Oxford University Press, 1996).

34 Porter, *Books and Reading*, 15, 232, 76, 9. See also M. F. Sweetser, "What the People Read," *Hints for Home Reading: A Series of Papers on Books and Their Use*, ed. Lyman Abbott, 5–14 (New York: G. P. Putnam's Sons, 1880). For analysis of the advice literature, see Stevenson, *The Victorian Homefront*, 30–47. On the growing acceptance of fiction in an earlier period, see Nina Baym, *Novels, Readers, and Reviewers: Responses to Fiction in Antebellum America* (Ithaca, N.Y.: Cornell University Press, 1984). See also Scott E. Casper, "Biographical Mania: The Transformation of Biographical Theory in Nineteenth-Century America," *Nineteenth-Century Prose* 22 (Fall 1995): 39–62, on the transformation of biography from a mode of instruction to a literary art.

35 See, for example, *The Best Hundred Books: By the Best Judges* (*Pall Mall Gazette*

"Extra," No. 24 [1886]), a compendium of articles published earlier in the *Pall Mall Gazette*; and *List of Books for Girls and Women and Their Clubs*, ed. Augusta H. Leypoldt and George Iles (Boston: Library Bureau, 1895).

36 Pictorial and verbal representations of women readers are analyzed by Okker, *Our Sister Editors*; Linda J. Docherty, "Women as Readers: Visual Interpretations," *Proceedings of the American Antiquarian Society* 107, part 2 (1997): 335–88; and Catherine J. Golden, *Images of the Woman Reader in Victorian British and American Fiction* (Gainesville: University Press of Florida, 2003). For Great Britain, see Kate Flint, *The Woman Reader, 1837–1914* (New York: Oxford University Press, 1993).

37 On book ownership, see Soltow and Stevens, *The Rise of Literacy*, 77–85. Home libraries were principally the preserve of the upper and upper-middle classes. By the end of the century, decorating manuals considered them essential in every cultured home; Martha Crabill McClaugherty, "Household Art: Creating the Artistic Home, 1868–1893," *Winterthur Portfolio* 18 (Spring 1983): 17–18.

38 William Allen White, *The Autobiography of William Allen White* (New York: Macmillan, 1946), 34.

39 Meta Lilienthal, *Dear Remembered World: Childhood Memories of an Old New Yorker* (New York: Richard R. Smith, 1947), 13. See also Vida Dutton Scudder, *On Journey* (New York: E. P. Dutton, 1937).

40 Information about the Abbotts comes from Edith Abbott, "X. Books in the Prairie Days," typescript, Sept. 17, 1945, Edith and Grace Abbott Papers, Series 4, Special Collections Research Center, University of Chicago Library. See also Othman A. Abbott, "Recollections of a Pioneer Lawyer," part 3, *Nebraska History Magazine* 11 (July–Sept. 1928): esp. 151 and photograph facing 155; Elizabeth Abbott is one of the dignitaries observing President Theodore Roosevelt break ground for the new library building in 1905.

41 Edith Abbott, "Books in the Prairie Days," 9, 13, 8. For a thoughtful discussion of children's books, see Anne H. Lundin, "Victorian Horizons: The Reception of Children's Books in England and America, 1880–1900," *Library Quarterly* 64 (January 1994): 30–59.

42 William Allen White, for one, highlighted his mother's passion for books, her role in founding the public library in Eldorado, Kansas, and the joy he had in listening to her read aloud. His father objected to the practice, evidently believing that it would keep his son from reading on his own; *Autobiography*, 44, 60–61, 84. This volume is full of recollections about family reading practices during childhood and youth.

43 Edward A. Ross, *Seventy Years of It: An Autobiography* (New York: D. Appleton-Century, 1936), 7–9.

44 Hamlin Garland, *A Son of the Middle Border* (1917; reprint, New York: Macmillan, 1956), 35.

45 For an excellent examination of reading venues in a small town, see Christine Jane Pawley, *Reading on the Middle Border: The Culture of Print in Late-Nineteenth Century Osage, Iowa, 1870–1900* (Amherst: University of Massachusetts Press, 2001).

46 Lela B. Costin, *Two Sisters for Social Justice: A Biography of Grace and Edith Abbott* (Urbana: University of Illinois Press, 1983), 17.

47 William Allen White, *Autobiography*, 61.

48 See, for example, Edith Abbott, "Books in the Prairie Days," 4. For the changing meaning of *Pilgrim's Progress*, see David E. Smith, *John Bunyan in America*
(Bloomington: Indiana University Press, 1966), 93–102.

49 William Allen White, *Autobiography*, 60–61.

50 Christine Pawley, "What to Read and How to Read: The Social Infrastructure of
Young People's Reading, Osage, Iowa, 1870–1900," *Library Quarterly* 68 (July 1998):
287–92. A similar point about the overlap between men's and women's book-
charging patterns for an earlier period is made by Zboray, *A Fictive People*, 162–73;
a similar caveat applies.

51 Edward G. Salmon, "What Girls Read," *Nineteenth Century* 20 (October 1886):
515–29, and *Juvenile Literature as It Is* (London: Henry J. Drane, 1888), esp. 11–32.
"Favorite books" followed gender expectations to a greater degree than did "favorite authors": Kingsley's *Westward Ho!* was the girls' reported favorite, with Susan
Warner's *The Wide, Wide World* and the Bible in second and third places; *David
Copperfield* was sixth, just ahead of *Little Women*. *Robinson Crusoe* was the boy's
favorite, followed by *Swiss Family Robinson* and *The Pickwick Papers*. For further
analysis of Salmon's study, see Jonathan Rose, "How Historians Study Reader Response; or, What Did Jo Think of *Bleak House?*," in *Literature in the Marketplace:
Nineteenth-Century British Publishing and Reading Practices*, ed. John O. Jordan
and Robert L. Patten (Cambridge: Cambridge University Press, 1995), 196–202.

52 Elaborating on this point are Lundin, "Victorian Horizons," esp. 40–42; Pawley,
"What and How to Read," 290–91; and Anne Scott MacLeod, *American Childhood:
Essays on Children's Literature of the Nineteenth and Twentieth Centuries* (Athens:
University of Georgia Press, 1994), 114–26.

53 See Robert Morss Lovett, "A Boy's Reading Fifty Years Ago," *New Republic* 48 (November 17, 1926): 334–36.

54 *Children's Periodicals of the United States*, ed. R. Gordon Kelly (Westport, Conn.:
Greenwood Press, 1984), xxv–xxvi.

55 Austin, *Earth Horizon*, 67. For another example, see Jane Addams, *Twenty Years at
Hull-House* (New York: Macmillan, 1910), 47.

56 In *Songs of Ourselves: The Uses of Poetry in America* (Cambridge, Mass.: Harvard
University Press, 2007), Joan Shelley Rubin analyzes the many uses of poetry and
the continuity of its claims on individuals. Of particular relevance here are her discussions of memorization and the long-lasting impact of school poetry recitations.
Rubin focuses on the years 1890 to 1935, but recitations were the norm much earlier. On oral reading instruction and elocution, see Nila Banton Smith, *American
Reading Instruction* (Newark, Del.: International Reading Association, 1986), esp.
38–42, 71, and 91.

57 Abbott, "Books," 2, 4, 12.

58 Edith Abbott, "Books in the Prairie Days," 10–13.

59 For an admirably thorough and wide-ranging study of literary practices in everyday life that draws on a vast array of archival sources for an earlier period, see
Ronald J. Zboray and Mary Saracino Zboray, *Everyday Ideas: Socioliterary Experience among Antebellum New Englanders* (Knoxville: University of Tennessee Press,
2006).

60 On diaries, see Jane H. Hunter, "Inscribing the Self in the Heart of the Family:

Diaries and Girlhood in Late-Victorian America," *American Quarterly* 44 (March 1992): 51–81. Diaries are usually considered Protestant undertakings, but Melissa R. Klapper has uncovered numerous diaries kept by middle-class Jewish girls during the period; *Jewish Girls Coming of Age in America, 1860–1920* (New York: New York University Press, 2005). For a later period, see Joan Jacobs Brumberg, "The 'Me' of Me: Voices of Jewish Girls in Adolescent Diaries of the 1920s and 1950s," in *Talking Back: Images of Jewish Women in American Popular Culture*, ed. Joyce Antler (Hanover, N.H.: Brandeis University Press, 1998), 53–67.

61 In a study that highlights women's letter writing in maintaining family ties, Marilyn Ferris Motz observes that letters were widely viewed as "a characteristically feminine occupation." Not only did magazines promote the view that "a good letter . . . is eminently woman's forte and function," but men's reluctance to write them seems to have been accepted by the women in her sample; *True Sisterhood: Michigan Women and Their Kin, 1820–1920* (Albany: State University of New York Press, 1983), 5–6, 8–9, 52–81, quotations on 53, 62. For a stimulating analysis of women's emotional work in the late twentieth century, see Micaela di Leonardo, "The Female World of Cards and Holidays: Women, Family, and the Work of Kinship," *Signs* 12 (Spring 1987): 440–53.

62 See Barbara Sicherman, *Alice Hamilton: A Life in Letters* (Cambridge, Mass.: Harvard University Press, 1984), esp. 211–17.

63 Joan D. Hedrick, in "Parlor Literature: Harriet Beecher Stowe and the Question of 'Great Women Artists,'" *Signs* 17 (Winter 1992): 275–303, elaborates on a tradition of domestically based literary production she calls "parlor literature." Her focus is on the antebellum period, but the tradition continued into the Gilded Age, even as the conditions of authorship and publishing were becoming more professionalized.

64 Porter, *Books and Reading*, 248.

65 The phrase is Charlotte Perkins Gilman's, *The Living of Charlotte Perkins Gilman: An Autobiography* (1935; reprint, New York: Harper & Row, 1975), 28.

66 Mary Church Terrell, *A Colored Woman in a White World* (Washington, D.C.: Ransdell, 1940), 26; Edith Abbott, "Books in the Prairie Days," 12; Gilman, *Living*, 28; Austin, *Earth Horizon*, 92–93.

67 Terrell, *Colored Woman*, 26; Austin, *Earth Horizon*, 70.

68 Austin, *Earth Horizon*, 150; entries for May 20 and Oct. 16, 1872, Alice Stone Blackwell diary, Blackwell Family Papers, Library of Congress (microfilm edition). Two of Blackwell's published poems are reprinted in *Growing Up in Boston's Gilded Age: The Journal of Alice Stone Blackwell, 1872–1874*, ed. Marlene Deahl Merrill (New Haven: Yale University Press, 1990), 254–55.

69 For a brief but suggestive discussion comparing three generations of American autobiographies, see Robert F. Sayre, "The Proper Study—Autobiographies in American Studies," *American Quarterly* 29 (1977): 241–62. On women's autobiographies, see *Interpreting Women's Lives: Feminist Theory and Personal Narratives*, ed. The Personal Narratives Group (Bloomington: Indiana University Press, 1989), and *Women's Autobiography: Essays in Criticism*, ed. Estelle C. Jelinek (Bloomington: Indiana University Press, 1980).

70 On the intersection of gender and class in Jane Addams's life and writing, see Dorothy Ross, "Gendered Social Knowledge: Domestic Discourse, Jane Addams,

and the Possibilities of Social Science," in *Gender and American Social Science: The Formative Years*, ed. Helene Silverberg (Princeton: Princeton University Press, 1998), 235–64.

CHAPTER THREE

1 The material about Kelley in this and the next two paragraphs comes from Florence Kelley, "My Philadelphia," *Survey Graphic* 57 (Oct. 1, 1926): 51–52. "My Philadelphia" and three other published articles that constitute Kelley's autobiography have been collected, with an introduction and notes, as *Notes of Sixty Years: The Autobiography of Florence Kelley*, ed. Kathryn Kish Sklar (Chicago: Charles H. Kerr, 1986). See also Sklar, *Florence Kelley and the Nation's Work: The Rise of Women's Political Culture, 1830–1900* (New Haven: Yale University Press, 1995).

2 Kelley, "My Philadelphia," 9, and Kelley, "When Co-Education Was Young," *Survey Graphic* 57 (Feb. 1, 1927): 557.

3 Jane Addams, *Twenty Years at Hull-House* (New York: Macmillan, 1910), 13.

4 Quotations are from the Alice Stone Blackwell diary in the Blackwell Family Papers, Library of Congress, microfilm edition (hereafter cited as Diary). The diary has been published with commentary as *Growing Up in Boston's Gilded Age: The Journal of Alice Stone Blackwell, 1872–1874*, ed. Marlene Deahl Merrill (New Haven: Yale University Press, 1990). I am relying on Merrill's count of what Blackwell read, 2–3.

5 Diary, March 16, May 1, 1872.

6 Diary, Feb. 11, Feb. 15, 1872. The full title is *Westward Ho! or, The Voyages and Adventures of Sir Amyas Leigh, Knight, of Burrough in the County of Devon, in the Reign of Her Most Glorious Majesty Queen Elizabeth* (1855).

7 Diary, April 27, 1873. *Tom Brown at Oxford* (1861) was a sequel. "T.B. at Rugby" refers to the earlier volume, *Tom Brown's School Days* (1857). Blackwell often commented on heroes, not always favorably: she considered both leading men in *Jane Eyre* "detestable" and was "furious" at the romantic pairing at the end of Thackeray's *Pendennis*. Diary, April 14, Dec. 18, and Dec. 22, 1872.

8 Diary, July 11, 1873.

9 Diary, Feb. 7, 1872. Charles Kingsley was among those who came in for her strictures. After reading his Christian Socialist novel *Yeast* (1851), she observed that Kingsley "doesn't believe in woman's rights, so I don't altogether believe in him, though he says some splendid good things" (Diary, May 26, 1873).

10 Diary, Jan. 28, 1873.

11 Robert Morss Lovett, "A Boy's Reading Fifty Years Ago," *New Republic* 48 (Nov. 17, 1926): 335.

12 Hamlin Garland, *A Son of the Middle Border* (1917; reprint, New York: Macmillan, 1956), 186–87.

13 M. Carey Thomas to Mary Garrett, July 7, 1878, *The Papers of M. Carey Thomas in the Bryn Mawr College Archives*, ed. Lucy Fisher West (Woodbridge, Conn.: Research Publications, 1982), reel 15.

14 Annie Nathan Meyer, *It's Been Fun: An Autobiography* (New York: Henry Schuman, 1951), 37.

15 Diary, Oct. 23, Sept. 4, and May 1, 1872. The entry "*no Ledger*" is underlined three times. See also Diary, May 9, 1872.

16 "Mark Heber's Luck; or, Life on the Plains," by Leon Lewis, appeared in forty installments between February 24 and July 6, 1872. Quotation from the first installment: *New York Ledger* 28, no. 1 (Feb. 24, 1872): 1.

17 See, for example, Diary, Oct. 5 and Dec. 22, 1872.

18 Diary, Feb. 18, 1872. The book was probably *The Physical Geography of the Sea* by Matthew Fontaine Maury.

19 Diary, March 28, 1874. The dedicated revolutionary's name was Enjolras.

20 Diary, Feb. 18, 1872. See also Diary, Feb. 11, 1872. During the period of the diary, Blackwell read at least nine novels by Henry Kingsley, Charles Kingsley's younger and less successful brother—the most by a single author. *Ravenshoe* (1861), which takes place during the Crimean War and is generally considered his best, is a convoluted story that centers on problematic identities and contested inheritances.

21 Diary, Feb. 27, 1872. Plutarch had a prominent place in many homes, including that of James Weldon Johnson, a distinguished African American author, songwriter, civil rights activist, and diplomat who grew up in Florida; *Along This Way: The Autobiography of James Weldon Johnson* (New York: Viking Press, 1933), 17.

22 See chapter 6 for John Huy Addams's efforts to persuade his daughter Jane to read "instructive literature."

23 Diary, Feb. 6, 1872, Nov. 5, 1872, and March 26, 1873. Blackwell's dream occurred the night before a history test.

24 Jeannette Porter Meehan, *The Lady of the Limberlost: The Life and Letters of Gene Stratton-Porter* (Garden City, N.Y.: Doubleday, Doran, 1928), 58.

25 Diary, March 7, 1873.

26 M. M. Bakhtin, *The Dialogic Imagination: Four Essays*, ed. Michael Holquist, trans. Caryl Emerson and Michael Holquist (Austin: University of Texas Press, 1981), 39, 32, 37–38; see also 247.

27 Nancy Armstrong develops the somewhat parallel argument that "written representations of the self allowed the modern individual to become an economic and psychological reality" and argues that "a modern gendered form of subjectivity developed first as a feminine discourse in certain literature for women." *Desire and Domestic Fiction: A Political History of the Novel* (New York: Oxford University Press, 1987), quotations on 8, 14. Armstrong's main interest is discourse, while my focus is on the behavioral (including emotional) consequences that result from a certain kind of reading formation, one in which the domestic literature she analyzes played a minor role and in which reading activities often took women out of their homes.

28 Erik H. Erikson, *Identity: Youth and Crisis* (New York: W. W. Norton, 1968), 53, 87. Erikson tends to ignore the ways in which social location can restrict imagination, but I find his emphasis both on the possibilities of identification with fictional characters and on choosing among models useful. For a thoughtful developmental study of reading, see J. A. Appleyard, *Becoming a Reader: The Experience of Fiction from Childhood to Adulthood* (Cambridge: Cambridge University Press, 1990).

29 On changing historical definitions and patterns of adolescence, see Joseph F. Kett, *Rites of Passage: Adolescence in America, 1790 to the Present* (New York: Basic Books, 1977); and Joan Jacobs Brumberg, *The Body Project: An Intimate History of American Girls* (New York: Random House, 1997).

30 The heaviest users of the Osage Public Library were between twelve and thirty, with females accounting for 58 percent of the users in that age category; Christine Pawley, "What to Read and How to Read: The Social Infrastructure of Young People's Reading, Osage, Iowa, 1870 to 1900," *Library Quarterly* 68 (July 1998): 276–97. In *Becoming a Reader*, Appleyard suggests that in more recent times voluntary reading seems to peak at ages twelve and thirteen (80).

31 Mary Austin, *Earth Horizon, Autobiography* (Boston: Houghton Mifflin, 1932), 104. Joan Shelley Rubin wisely cautions that highlighting childhood reading was an autobiographical convention of the time; "What Is the History of the History of Books?," *Journal of American History* 90 (Sept. 2003): 574–75. Conventions of this kind may distort an author's claims about earlier reading experiences, but starting with the often idiosyncratic choice of signature books like Mary Austin's, many have a ring of authenticity and some are supported by contemporary evidence from diaries and letters.

32 On men's reading, see Thomas Augst, *The Clerk's Tale: Young Men and Moral Life in Nineteenth-Century America* (Chicago: University of Chicago Press, 2003); and Joseph F. Kett, *The Pursuit of Knowledge under Difficulties: From Self-Improvement to Adult Education in America, 1750–1990* (Stanford: Stanford University Press, 1994).

33 William Allen White, *The Autobiography of William Allen White* (New York: Macmillan, 1946), is a rich source of information about men's reading.

34 In more recent times, too, women learn best and achieve most in settings in which collaborative learning that is noncompetitive and nonhierarchical prevails. See, for example, Mary Field Belenky et al., *Women's Ways of Knowing: The Development of Self, Voice, and Mind* (New York: Basic Books, 1986).

35 Charlotte Perkins Gilman, *The Living of Charlotte Perkins Gilman: An Autobiography* (1935; reprint, New York: Harper & Row, 1975), 100.

36 Ibid., 36–37. See also Ann J. Lane, *To Herland and Beyond: The Life and Work of Charlotte Perkins Gilman* (New York: Pantheon, 1990), 34; Mary A. Hill, *Charlotte Perkins Gilman: The Making of a Radical Feminist, 1860–1896* (Philadelphia: Temple University Press, 1980); and Denise D. Knight, ed., *The Diaries of Charlotte Perkins Gilman*, vol. 1, *1879–1887*, and vol. 2, *1890–1935* (Charlottesville: University Press of Virginia, 1994) (hereafter cited as *Diaries of CPG*). On the Society to Encourage Studies at Home, see Jean Strouse, *Alice James: A Biography* (New York: Bantam Books, 1982), 185–93.

37 Todd Steven Gernes has written persuasively about the group's literary culture in "Houp La!: Charlotte Perkins Gilman, Martha Luther Lane, and Young Women's Literary Culture in Nineteenth-Century Providence," ch. 5 in "Recasting the Culture of Ephemera: Young Women's Literary Culture in Nineteenth-Century America" (Ph.D. diss., Brown University, 1992), 221–79. See, too, the references in the preceding note, especially *Diaries of CPG*, vol. 1.

38 *Diaries of CPG*, vol. 1: Feb. 22, 1879 (9), Jan. 25, 1879 (7), April 12, 1880 (20); Hill, *Charlotte Perkins Gilman*, 83.

39 Gernes, "Recasting the Culture of Ephemera," esp. 248–61.

40 Gilman, *Living*, 79–80.

41 *Diaries of CPG*, vol. 1: July 22, 1881 (70–71), May 12, 1880 (20).

42 Martha A. L. Lane and Mabel Hill, comps., *American History in Literature* (Boston: Ginn & Co., 1905), iii.

43 On the CLSC, see Herbert B. Adams, "Chautauqua: A Social and Educational Study," U.S. Commissioner of Education, *Report for 1894–95* (Washington, D.C.: Government Printing Office, 1896), 1:977–1077; Theodore Morrison, *Chautauqua: A Center for Education, Religion, and the Arts in America* (Chicago: University of Chicago Press, 1974), 53–70; Joseph F. Kett, *The Pursuit of Knowledge*, 160–66, 174–75, 182–86; and especially Andrew C. Rieser, *The Chautauqua Moment: Protestants, Progressives, and the Culture of Modern Liberalism* (New York: Columbia University Press, 2003), 161–206.

44 A useful contemporary source on circle procedures and on Jewish and Catholic branches is Adams, "Chautauqua," 1011–14 and 1065–77. See also Thomas F. O'Connor, "American Catholic Reading Circles, 1886–1909," *Libraries and Culture* 26 (Spring 1991): 334–47; and Rieser, *The Chautauqua Moment*, 104–8.

45 The extensive literature on women's study clubs includes Karen J. Blair, *The Clubwoman as Feminist: True Womanhood Redefined, 1868–1914* (New York: Holmes and Meier, 1980), 57–71; Theodora Penny Martin, *The Sound of Our Own Voices: Women's Study Clubs, 1860–1910* (Boston: Beacon Press, 1987); and Anne Ruggles Gere, *Intimate Practices: Literacy and Cultural Work in U.S. Women's Clubs, 1880–1920* (Urbana: University of Illinois Press, 1997), which offers comparative class, race, and ethnic data, as does Anne Ruggles Gere and Sarah R. Robbins, "Gendered Literacy in Black and White: Turn-of-the-Century African-American and European-American Club Women's Printed Texts," *Signs* 21 (Spring 1996): 643–78; and Elizabeth McHenry, *Forgotten Readers: Recovering the Lost History of African American Literary Societies* (Durham, N.C.: Duke University Press, 2002). Elizabeth Long, *Book Clubs: Women and the Uses of Reading in Everyday Life* (Chicago: University of Chicago Press, 2003), is a thoughtful analysis of the clubs from their origins to the present.

46 Long, *Book Clubs*, 45.

47 Ibid., ch. 2. See also Christine Pawley, "'Not Wholly Self Culture': The Shakespearean Women's Club, Osage, Iowa, 1892–1920," *Annals of Iowa* 56 (Winter/Spring 1997): 12–45; and references in note 45 above.

48 The term "semi-public" is Long's in *Book Clubs*, 49. Gere and Robbins, "Gendered Literacy," analyzes clubs' public productions.

49 McHenry, *Forgotten Readers*, esp. 241.

50 Anne Firor Scott, "Women and Libraries," *Journal of Library History* 21 (Spring 1986): 400–405, and *Natural Allies: Women's Associations in American History* (Urbana: University of Illinois Press, 1991); Paula D. Watson, "Founding Mothers: The Contributions of Women's Organizations to Public Library Development in the United States," *Library Quarterly* 64 (July 1994): 233–69; Gere, *Intimate Practices*,

122–23, 307; Daniel F. Ring, "Outpost of New England Culture: The Ladies' Library Association of Kalamazoo, Michigan," *Libraries and Culture* 32 (Winter 1997): 38–56. See also Joanne E. Passet, "Reaching the Rural Reader: Traveling Libraries in America, 1892–1920," *Libraries and Culture* 26 (Winter 1991): 101–18.

51 On women's literary presence at the Exposition, see Jeanne M. Weimann, "Mob of Scribbling Women," in *The Fair Women* (Chicago: Academy Chicago, 1981), 353–92; and Sarah Wadsworth and Wayne A. Wiegand, "'Right Here I See My Own Books': A Cultural History of the Woman's Library of the World's Columbian Exposition, Chicago, 1893," unpublished paper in the author's possession.

52 Quoted in Gere, *Intimate Practices*, 211.

53 On 1890s rhetoric, see John Higham, "The Reorientation of American Culture in the 1890s," in *Writing American History: Essays on Modern Scholarship* (Bloomington: Indiana University Press, 1970), 73–102; on masculinity, see also E. Anthony Rotundo, *American Manhood: Transformations in Masculinity from the Revolution to the Modern Era* (New York: Basic Books, 1993).

54 Kirsten Swinth, *Painting Professionals: Women Artists and the Development of Modern American Art, 1870–1930* (Chapel Hill: University of North Carolina Press, 2001). On the deteriorating situation for American women writers, see Joan D. Hedrick, *Harriet Beecher Stowe: A Life* (New York: Oxford University Press, 1994); on Great Britain, see Gaye Tuchman, with Nina E. Fortin, *Edging Women Out: Victorian Novelists, Publishers, and Social Change* (New Haven: Yale University Press, 1989).

55 *Diaries of CPG*, vol. 2: Feb. 10, 1893 (517), March 3, 1893 (519).

56 Frances E. W. Harper, "Woman's Political Future," *The World's Congress of Representative Women*, ed. May Wright Sewall (Chicago: Rand, McNally, 1894), 433–34.

CHAPTER FOUR

1 Edith Hamilton to "Dearest Jeddie" [Jessie Hamilton], [postmarked Aug. 3, 1892], Hamilton Family Papers, Schlesinger Library, Radcliffe Institute for Advanced Study, Harvard University. All citations from archival sources not otherwise identified are from this collection.

2 Agnes Hamilton Diary, Jan. 26 [1890] (hereafter cited as Diary).

3 See, for example, Jerome Bruner, *The Culture of Education* (Cambridge, Mass.: Harvard University Press, 1996), xiv, 39.

4 Edith to Jessie Hamilton, Oct. 3 [1883], folder 591, and to Jeddie, Friday [n.d.], folder 590; Doris Fielding Reid, *Edith Hamilton: An Intimate Portrait* (New York: W. W. Norton, 1967), 30.

5 Jessie to Agnes Hamilton, May 1, 1887.

6 See Allyn C. Wetmore, "Allen Hamilton: The Evolution of a Frontier Capitalist" (Ph.D. diss., Ball State University, 1974).

7 Edith and Alice's only brother, Arthur, was thirteen years younger than Norah; the younger brothers in the cousins' family were considered "children" and do not figure in this story, nor do the much younger Wagenhals cousins. On the family, see Alice Hamilton, *Exploring the Dangerous Trades* (Boston: Little, Brown, 1943) (hereafter cited as *EDT*); and Barbara Sicherman, *Alice Hamilton: A Life in Letters* (Cambridge, Mass.: Harvard University Press, 1984), esp. 11–22 and genealogy (xvi).

8 Israel George Blake, *The Holmans of Veraestau* (Oxford, Ohio: The Mississippi Valley Press, 1943), and "Jesse Lynch Holman: Pioneer Hoosier," *Indiana Magazine of History* 39 (March 1943): 25–51.

9 *The Prisoners of Niagara; or, Errors of Education; A New Novel; Founded in Fact* (Frankfort, Ky.: William Gerard, 1810). Jesse Holman later bought up copies and tried to suppress the work because he considered its morals unsound; Blake, "Jesse Lynch Holman," 27.

10 Diary, Aug. 18 [1889]. See also obituaries, *Fort Wayne News, Fort Wayne Journal-Gazette*, and *Fort Wayne Sentinel*, August 1889, and "Last Will and Testament of Emerine J. Hamilton," Allen County Court, Fort Wayne, Ind.

11 *EDT*, 23–24; Diary, Nov. 1 [1890].

12 Robert S. Robertson, *History of the Maumee River Basin: Allen County, Indiana* (Indianapolis: Bowen and Slocum, 1905), 2:350–58. Hamiltons possessed half the private libraries deemed worthy of mention in this volume, among them Ellen Wagenhals, Allen and Emerine's middle daughter. She and her husband, Samuel Wagenhals, a Lutheran clergyman, owned more than 4,000 volumes, many on theology. See also Charles Elihu Slocum, *History of the Maumee River Basin: From the Earliest Account to Its Organization into Counties* (Defiance, Ohio: published by the author, 1905), 633.

13 Robertson, *Maumee River Basin*, 2:354–58. Holman Hamilton's "Books of Childhood: A Senior Speech," and book orders from the 1870s to 1895, the year he died, are in the A. Holman Hamilton Papers, Indiana State Library, Indianapolis. I am grateful to Marybelle Burch, who generously researched and provided materials from this collection.

14 Montgomery Hamilton to A. Holman Hamilton, Jan. 25, 1854, June 24, 1854, and Oct. 6, 1856; see also letters of Dec. 21, 1858, and Nov. 11, 1859.

15 Montgomery Hamilton to A. Holman Hamilton, June 4, 1864.

16 Robertson, *Maumee River Basin*, 2:353–54.

17 Ibid., 337–40, quotation on 337; and library file in the Indiana Collection, Vertical File, Allen County Public Library, Fort Wayne.

18 Robertson, *Maumee River Basin*, 2:351–53. Some of the books had most likely belonged to her mother. Margaret's brother-in-law, Samuel Wagenhals, was also involved in founding and overseeing the public library, and her niece Katherine later took her place on the Library Committee. Information from "Minutes of the Public Library Committee" and other materials from the Allen County Public Library.

19 On the art school, see Albert F. Diserens, "The Fort Wayne Art School and Museum," *Old Fort News* 15 (March, June 1952). On Margaret Vance Hamilton as an art patron, see Edith Hamilton to Jessica, Wed. evening [May 5, 1886]. Losing her purpose after the deaths of her mother and aunt, Margaret Vance Hamilton escaped to Europe in the mid-1890s, where she studied bookbinding and Italian and tried her hand at translating "Afternoon," a story by Ouida (Marie Louise de la Ramée), an English writer, many of whose novels were considered sensational. As the family's economic situation deteriorated, she contemplated earning money from bookbinding. Margaret Vance Hamilton to Jessie Hamilton, Feb. 24, 1895, to Phoebe Taber Hamilton (sister-in-law), Dec. 8, 1895, and letters to her nieces between December 1894 and January 1896.

20 *EDT*, 18–19. Portraying Edith as the older and more precocious sister, Alice claims that she "slipped back to the 'Katy' books," but also that she learned Keats's "The Eve of St. Agnes" by hearing Edith recite it. In the cousins' family too, older siblings fostered the reading habit, first as renowned storytellers, later as tutors who listened to younger children's recitations and made sure they got them right.

21 *EDT*, 19. Sophie May was the pen name of Rebecca Clarke, Susan Coolidge that of Sarah Chauncy Woolsey. In her catalogue of childhood reading, Alice also recalled the "Schönberg-Cotta books" (actually one book) and Yonge's *The Daisy Chain*, a novel about the May family. The books all feature large families.

   The scholarship on children's literature is vast. Most relevant to the works cited here is Shirley Foster and Judy Simons, *What Katy Read: Feminist Re-Readings of "Classic" Stories for Girls* (Iowa City: University of Iowa Press, 1995). On children's reading in the United States, see Anne H. Lundin, "Victorian Horizons: The Reception of Children's Books in England and America, 1880–1900," *Library Quarterly* 64 (January 1994): 30–59; R. Gordon Kelly, *Mother Was a Lady: Self and Society in Selected American Children's Periodicals, 1865–1890* (Westport, Conn.: Greenwood Press, 1974); and Anne Scott MacLeod, *American Childhood: Essays on Children's Literature of the Nineteenth and Twentieth Centuries* (Athens: University of Georgia Press, 1994). See also Elizabeth Segel, "'As the Twig Is Bent . . .': Gender and Childhood Reading," in *Gender and Reading: Essays on Readers, Texts, and Contexts*, ed. Elizabeth A. Flynn and Patrocinio P. Schweickart (Baltimore: Johns Hopkins University Press, 1986), 165–86.

22 [Montgomery Hamilton], "Heroines," *Nassau Literary Magazine* 22 (March 1862): 271–77; Diary, Thursday [Dec. 27, 1883]. According to Alice, her father stressed the Scottish side of his ancestry, while the younger generation was fascinated by the Irish connection; *EDT*, 22–23.

23 On Scott's popularity in the United States, see Andrew Hook, "Scott and America," in *From Goosecreek to Gandercleugh: Studies in Scottish-American Literary and Cultural History* (Edinburgh: Tuckwell Press, 1999), 94–115; Emily Bishop Todd, "The Transatlantic Context: Walter Scott and Nineteenth-Century American Literary History" (Ph.D. diss., University of Minnesota, 1999); and James D. Hart, *The Popular Book: A History of America's Literary Taste* (Berkeley and Los Angeles: University of California Press, n.d.), 68–69, 73–78. See also John Henry Raleigh, "What Scott Meant to the Victorians," in *Time, Place, and Idea: Essays on the Novel* (Carbondale: Southern Illinois University Press, 1968), 96–125.

24 Margaret Vance Hamilton to Jessie Hamilton, July 15, 1879. The trip included a visit to Hamilton, near Glasgow, which Margaret called "the cradle of the Hamilton family." Margaret was especially close to her oldest niece, Katherine, whom she often addressed as "Kitrine." On American tourists in Scotland, see Todd, "The Transatlantic Context," 172–212, and Hook, *From Goosecreek to Gandercleugh*, 77–93.

25 Agnes Hamilton's diary is the most comprehensive source of information about the Hamiltons' reading and includes lists of books she read between 1885 and 1897.

26 Agnes to Jessie Hamilton, July 14, 1894.

27 Agnes Hamilton to Edith Trowbridge, Aug. 19, 1895, folder 405.

28 Jessie to Phoebe Taber Hamilton, June 17, 1883.

29 See Robert Lee Wolff, *Gains and Losses: Novels of Faith and Doubt in Victorian England* (New York: Garland, 1977), for a discussion of religious novels, many of them read by the Hamiltons. On religious publishing in the United States, see Candy Gunther Brown, *The Word in the World: Evangelical Writing, Publishing, and Reading in America, 1789–1880* (Chapel Hill: University of North Carolina Press, 2004).

30 *EDT*, 30. Alice's description of her parents' reading is gender-marked; of her mother, she wrote: "She was no lover of Scott or Macaulay. For her I learned Gray's *Elegy* by heart and with her we read aloud *The Mill on the Floss* and *Adam Bede*." *EDT*, 32.

31 On the political milieu of the Holman (and Hamilton) families, see Jean H. Baker, *Affairs of Party: The Political Culture of Northern Democrats in the Mid-Nineteenth Century* (Ithaca, N.Y.: Cornell University Press, 1983), esp. 33–37.

32 Jessie to Agnes Hamilton, March 30, 1887. See also Edith to "Dearest Jeddie," [June 4, 1893].

33 Agnes called a book trashy because it was "written by a person sufficiently clever to entice but not enough so to give any good." Agnes to Jessie Hamilton, Sept. 8, 1889.

34 Edith to Jessie Hamilton, July 14 [1889], folder 607. The book was *The Silence of Dean Maitland* by Maxwell Gray (pseudonym for Mary Gleed Tuttiett); Edith later wished she could have heard the title character preach on the day's text; Edith to Jessie Hamilton, Sept. 14 [1889], folder 589.

35 *EDT*, 18–19. Forbidden books turn up often in autobiographies of the period. The term French novel was virtually generic for racy; in addition to Sue, George Sand was often mentioned. See Nina Baym, *Novels, Readers, and Reviewers: Responses to Fiction in Antebellum America* (Ithaca, N.Y.: Cornell University Press, 1984), 178–80, 184–86, 213. A. Holman Hamilton's library included some pornography, the most costly books for which prices are available; Montgomery Hamilton ordered at least one pornographic book. A. Holman Hamilton Papers, Indiana State Library.

36 Diary, Oct. 21 [1888], folder 332; Agnes to Alice Hamilton, Aug. 10, 1881. Katherine declared reading forbidden novels as "that greatest of all pleasures." Katherine to Agnes Hamilton, [1887?], folder 145.

E. Marlitt (the pen name of Eugenie John) was considered trashy by the Hamiltons, but not by everyone. For an analysis of the author's popularity in the United States, see Lynne Tatlock, "Domesticated Romance and Capitalist Enterprise: Annis Lee Wister's Americanization of German Fiction," in *German Culture in Nineteenth-Century America: Reception, Adaptation, Transformation*, ed. Lynne Tatlock and Matt Erlin, 153–82 (Rochester, N.Y.: Camden House, 2005).

37 On the educational practices discussed in this and the following paragraphs, see *EDT*, 27–31. According to Reid, *Edith Hamilton*, Edith considered her father "the world's worst teacher" (23). The cousins attended public schools at times, but much of their education was also self-directed. In the months before departing for boarding school, for example, Agnes studied Latin, German, and Greek and read four volumes of Charles Knight's history of England. Diary, Aug. 2 [1885], March 31, and July 29 [1886].

38 *EDT*, 31, 29, 27. Katherine and Jessie kept tabs on the progress of their younger brothers in memorizing *The Lady of the Lake*; each was under ten at the time of the

inquiry. Katherine to Taber Hamilton, [1882–83], folder 150; Jessie to Phoebe Taber Hamilton, May 28, 1881.

39 See, for example, Edith to Jessica, Tuesday evening [Jan.? 1882], folder 590; and Edith to "My dear little girl" [Jessie Hamilton], Sunday, Feb. 21 [1886].

40 Edith to Jessie Hamilton, Thursday, Mar. 13 [1884]. For a subtle analysis of Scott and history writing and of the gendered nature of the literary field, see Ina Ferriss, *The Achievement of Literary Authority: Gender, History, and the Waverley Novels* (Ithaca, N.Y.: Cornell University Press, 1991), 195–236.

41 Edith to Jessica, Tuesday evening [Jan.? 1882], folder 590.

42 Edith to Jeddie, Saturday, [early 1882], folder 591. On the construction of femininity in the *Spectator* and its predecessor, the *Tatler*, see Kathryn Shevelow, *Women and Print Culture: The Construction of Femininity in the Early Periodical* (London: Routledge, 1989).

43 Edith Hamilton to "dearest Jeddie," [postmarked Aug. 3, 1892]. In a similar vein, several years after the *Spectator* assignment Edith urged Jessie to destroy her "weekly effusions" for the sake of her "future reputation"; "My dear, dear child," Sunday evening [late Feb. 1886], folder 590. See also Edith to "Dearest Jeddie," Thursday, July 24 [1884], and to "My dear little girl" [Jessie Hamilton], Sunday, Feb. 21 [1886].

44 *EDT*, 35–37; Louise L. Stevenson, "Sarah Porter Educates Useful Ladies, 1847–1900," *Winterthur Portfolio* 18 (Spring 1983): 39–59, and *Miss Porter's School: A History in Documents, 1847–1948*, vol. 1, ed. Louise L. Stevenson (New York: Garland, 1987). See also Amy K. Johnson, "Miss Sarah Porter and Her School: Bastions of Conservatism or Precursors of Feminism?," Independent Study Project, Trinity College, 1983, in the author's possession.

45 Erik H. Erikson, *Identity: Youth and Crisis* (New York: W. W. Norton, 1968), 155–56.

46 For a pathbreaking analysis of the social nature of reading, see Elizabeth Long, "Textual Interpretation as Collective Action," in *The Ethnography of Reading*, ed. Jonathan Boyarin, 180–211 (Berkeley and Los Angeles: University of California Press, 1992).

47 Matei Calinescu, *Rereading* (New Haven: Yale University Press, 1993), quotation on xi. Calinescu's focus is on literary texts, but he questions the sharp division others have made between reflective and pleasure reading (165), a central point of this chapter.

48 Janice A. Radway, *A Feeling for Books: The Book-of-the-Month Club, Literary Taste, and Middle-Class Desire* (Chapel Hill: University of North Carolina Press, 1997), 280–94, and 391–94, quotation on 290.

49 See Nancy J. Chodorow, *The Power of Feelings: Personal Meaning in Psychoanalysis, Gender, and Culture* (New Haven: Yale University Press, 1999), esp. 4.

50 Agnes is quoting Jessie, Diary, March 29 [1886].

51 Jessie to Agnes Hamilton, Feb. 4, 1887. *The Mice at Play* (1860) was by Charlotte Yonge, *Johnnykin and the Goblins* (1876) by Charles Godfrey Leland.

52 Agnes Hamilton to Edith Trowbridge, Aug. 19, 1895. Agnes continued to revisit her favorites by reading them aloud to her younger siblings and her Sunday school students.

53 Allen Hamilton Williams to "My dear Bag" [Agnes Hamilton], Aug. 11, 1890.

54 Louisa M. Gray, *The Children of Abbotsmuir Manse* (London: T. Nelson & Sons, 1887), quotations on 9, 16, 93–94, 73, 215, 245; "A Tale for the Young" appears on the cover. The Hamiltons read several of Gray's novels; some tended toward the heavy moral, this one less so. On Motley, see *EDT*, 24.

55 Elizabeth Rundle Charles, *Chronicles of the Schönberg-Cotta Family* (New York: Tibbals & Whiting, 1865).

56 Diary, Nov. 29 [1896].

57 Agnes to Katherine Hamilton, Feb. 1–4, 1882; and undated fragment in folder 408, which completes the letter. In a later letter, Agnes offered to write "another series of the 'Hamilton's Lady Book'" [signed fragment, n.d.], folder 407.

58 Agnes to Jessie Hamilton, Mar. 18, 1888; and undated fragment, folder 407. *Memorials of a Quiet Life* (1872) is a two-volume work by Maria Leycester Hare's adopted son, Augustus J. C. Hare.

59 For her part, Jessie hoped to write a biography of Edith but feared she could not do her "very splendid" cousin justice. Jessie to Agnes Hamilton, Mar. 13, 1887.

60 Allen Williams to Agnes Hamilton, Aug. 6, 1895; Williams to "Dear James" [Jessie], Jan. 4, 1896 [1897], folder 723; and Williams to "Dear Bag" [Agnes], Dec. 2, 1896.

61 Jessie to Agnes Hamilton, Jan. 27, 1887. Laura Goshorn, the librarian, had a poem accepted by *Connoisseur* magazine, which was published in 1888. See also Agnes to Allen Hamilton, April 17, 1891.

62 Diary, April 25 [1885]. See also entries for July 31 and Sept. 5 [1886].

63 Jessie to Agnes Hamilton, Jan. 9, 1887. See also Jessie to Agnes Hamilton, Jan. 19, and Jan. 23, 1887; and Allen Hamilton Williams to Agnes Hamilton, June 1, 1887.

64 Jessie to Agnes Hamilton, Jan. 23, 1887.

65 Jessie to Agnes Hamilton, Jan. 23, 1887. See also Jessie to Agnes Hamilton, Feb. 11, 1887.

66 Jessie to Agnes Hamilton, March 11, 1888; see also Jessie to Agnes Hamilton, Feb. 13, 1887.

67 Diary, Feb. 17 [1889].

68 To Jessie Hamilton, [early 1882], folder 385. The books, by Susan Coolidge, Elizabeth Stuart Phelps (Ward), and Joanna Hooe Mathews, respectively, were published in the late 1860s and early 1870s. On school stories, see Sally Mitchell, *The New Girl: Girls' Culture in England, 1880–1915* (New York: Columbia University Press, 1995), 74–102.

69 Alice to Agnes Hamilton, [June? 1896].

70 Edith to Jessie Hamilton, [fall 1896]; and Edith to Jessie Hamilton, [Dec. 18? 1896].

71 Diary, Dec. 6 [1883]. Elsè is a central character in Elizabeth Rundle Charles's *Chronicles of the Schönberg-Cotta Family*, Olive Drayton a diarist in the same author's *The Draytons and the Davenants: A Story of the Civil Wars* (1866). Kate is the heroine of Elizabeth Payson Prentiss's *Stepping Heavenward* (1869), which is discussed below. All three novels have a religious focus. See also Alice to Agnes Hamilton, Aug. 6, 1893, for a similar range of choices, not all of them fictional.

72 Benjamin Franklin quoted in Cathy N. Davidson, *Revolution and the Word: The Rise of the Novel in America* (New York: Oxford University Press, 1986), 52.

73 Allen Hamilton Williams to "Dear Bag" [Agnes Hamilton], Aug. 11, 1890. Polly and Reginald were young cousins in Mrs. Ewing's *A Flatiron for a Farthing* (1872);

Polly is a tomboy who takes the lead in their early play. For more on Ellen Daly and Nora Nixon, see below.

74 Margaret Vance Hamilton to Agnes Hamilton, May 6, 1895.

75 Alice to Agnes Hamilton, [postmarked Nov. 9, 1896].

76 Edith to "My dear child" [Jessie Hamilton], Sunday afternoon, Jan. 31 [1886], folder 587.

77 Diary, Sept. 21 [1896]. For his part, Allen viewed his cousins' vacation letters from Mackinac Island as "a little like a story-book" because they lived such different lives than they did in Fort Wayne. Allen Williams to "My dear Bag," Aug. 11, 1890.

78 Allen Hamilton Williams to "Dear Bag," July 30, 1896; Williams to "My dear girl" [Alice Hamilton], Aug. 15[?], 1896.

79 Alice to Agnes Hamilton, Sept. 12 [1896]. The full text is reprinted in Sicherman, *Alice Hamilton*, 101–4.

80 Allen Hamilton Williams to "Dear child" [Alice Hamilton], Sept. 17, 1896.

81 Alice to Margaret Hamilton, Sunday [July 7,] 1918, Alice Hamilton Papers, Schlesinger Library, Radcliffe Institute, Harvard University. The book was *The First Violin* (1877) by Jessie Fothergill, which Agnes at nineteen had characterized as "a very trashy book but great fun." Diary, July 29 [1888].

82 Interview with Hildegarde Wagenhals Bowen, Dec. 30, 1976. It is possible that the type of romantic hero admired by Alice reinforced the women's penchant for singlehood, since of course no real-life hero "could be so noble." There were more pragmatic reasons, including the fact that the marriages in their parents' generation were mainly unhappy, and fathers and uncles "difficult" at best. Then too, sisters and cousins discouraged one another from leaving the family and, since they stuck together, it was a brave young man who attempted to breach the ranks.

83 [Montgomery Hamilton], "Heroines" (see note 22); Montgomery Hamilton to A. Holman Hamilton, July 30, 1864, and June 4, 1864. The Bulwer-Lytton novel was *Alice; or, The Mysteries* (1838).

84 There is no direct evidence that Nora and Ellen were as important models of female heroism to the women as they were to Allen, but their letters contain numerous references to *Quits* and *Castle Daly*. See, for example, Edith Hamilton to Jessica, Tuesday evening [Jan.? 1882], folder 590; and Edith to Jeddie, Sunday, [winter 1892?], folder 607. Their aunt Margaret's Farmington cottage was named the "Happy-Go-Lucky Lodge," the home of the beloved Irish aunt in *Castle Daly*, Anne O'Flaherty. She was single, independent, and had a strong sense of responsibility for her Irish tenants. Some Hamilton women may have been named for fictional heroines, among them Norah (occasionally referred to as Leonorah, Nora Nixon's given name).

85 Martha Vicinus, "What Makes a Heroine?: Nineteenth-Century Girls' Biographies," *Genre* 20 (Summer 1987): 171–88.

86 Agnes to Jessie Hamilton, Mar. 18, 1888. For Agnes's personal and vocational trajectory, see Mina J. Carson, "Agnes Hamilton of Fort Wayne: The Education of a Christian Settlement Worker," *Indiana Magazine of History* 80 (Mar. 1984): 1–34. Jane H. Hunter discusses Agnes Hamilton in a study of adolescent females that draws extensively on diaries, *How Young Ladies Became Girls: The Victorian Origins of American Girlhood* (New Haven: Yale University Press, 2002), 50–51, 65–66, 182–84.

87 Agnes Hamilton to Edith Trowbridge, Aug. 19, 1895; Diary, July 31 [1887].

88 Diary, April 8, [1890]; Agnes Hamilton to Edith Trowbridge, Aug. 19, 1895. Agnes's descriptions of her reading experiences mark her as an exemplary pleasure reader. Victor Nell, *Lost in a Book: The Psychology of Reading for Pleasure* (New Haven: Yale University Press, 1988), treats the subject, but draws too hard and fast a line around what constitutes pleasurable reading.

89 Diary, Jan. 26 [1890]. For a sophisticated analysis of reading that is often dismissed as escapist, see Janice A. Radway, *Reading the Romance: Women, Patriarchy, and Popular Literature* (Chapel Hill: University of North Carolina Press, 1984), esp. chs. 2 and 3.

90 Diary, May 7 [1890].

91 Agnes Hamilton to Edith Trowbridge, Aug. 19, 1895. The book was *The Old Mam'selle's Secret* (1868), by E. Marlitt, which Agnes described as "utter stuff."

92 Diary, May 7 [1890].

93 Elizabeth Payson Prentiss, *Stepping Heavenward* (New York: Anson D. F. Randolph & Co., 1869). The novel sold over 100,000 copies in the nineteenth century. I am following the interpretation of *Stepping Heavenward's* theology by Candy Gunther Brown, *The Word in the World*, 99–105. The message was underscored for Agnes by Professor Henry Drummond's *Natural Law in the Spiritual World* (1883), which she was also reading at the time.

94 Agnes to Jessie Hamilton, Dec. 31, 1886. The book that prompted the comment was Charles Kingsley's *Hypatia*, which Agnes liked "almost as well as any book I ever read."

95 Agnes to Jessie Hamilton, Wed., April 12 [1887?], folder 370; and Agnes Hamilton to Edith Trowbridge, Aug. 19, 1895.

96 Agnes to Phoebe Taber Hamilton, May 28, 1903; Diary, Jan. 26 and Dec. 10 [1890], and Aug. 18 [1889].

97 Diary, Dec. 10 [1890].

98 Diary, Jan. 26 and Dec. 10 [1890]; Agnes to Jessie Hamilton, Wed., Apr. 12 [1887?], folder 370. Quotation from Augustus J. C. Hare, *Memorials of a Quiet Life*, American edition, reprinted from the 9th English edition (New York: George Routledge & Sons / Anson D. F. Randolph, 1872), vi.

99 Diary, Dec. 13 [1896].

100 See, for example, Rachel M. Brownstein, *Becoming a Heroine: Reading about Women in Novels* (New York: Penguin, 1984).

101 Norman Holland suggests that the reader identifies not so much with a particular character as with the total interaction of characters, some satisfying the need for pleasure, others the need to avoid anxiety. Holland's concept of "identity themes," characteristic modes of response that influence reading as well as other behaviors, is useful for historians since it provides a key to individual reading preferences that can be applied to the past; *The Dynamics of Literary Response* (New York: W. W. Norton, 1975), esp. 262–80.

102 *EDT*, 26. Alice Hamilton also attributes the growing awareness of social problems she and Agnes shared to reading Kingsley and Maurice. Claiming "we knew nothing about American social evils," she ignores their work at the sabbath mission school in Nebraska. Since Alice was interested in "slumming" by age eighteen,

which was probably before she or Agnes read the English social theorists, this seems to have been another case of literature seeming more real than life. *EDT*, 26–27.

103 This conflict is the focus of Barbara Sicherman, "Working It Out: Gender, Profession, and Reform in the Career of Alice Hamilton," in *Gender, Class, Race, and Reform in the Progressive Era*, ed. Noralee Frankel and Nancy Schrom Dye, 127–47 (Lexington: University Press of Kentucky, 1991), and an important theme in Sicherman, *Alice Hamilton*.

104 Edith to Jeddie, Sept. 14 [1889], folder 589, and Wed. evening, March 20 [1889], folder 607.

105 On Edith Hamilton, see Helen H. Bacon, "Edith Hamilton," in *Notable American Women: The Modern Period*, ed. Barbara Sicherman and Carol Hurd Green (Cambridge, Mass.: Harvard University Press, 1980), 306–8; and Judith P. Hallett, "Edith Hamilton (1867–1963)," *Classical World* 90 (Nov./Dec. 1996–Jan./Feb. 1997): 107–47. I am grateful to Hallett for sharing information on Edith Hamilton.

106 Edith to Jessie Hamilton, July 24 [1884].

107 Diary, Sept. 5 [1893]. The Hamiltons' disdain for rich pleasure seekers was likely influenced by a religious tradition that discouraged display as well as by their intellectual culture.

108 Edith to "My dear" [Jessie Hamilton], [May 1895], folder 595.

109 Alice considered her mother "more original and independent in her approach to life" than her father; *EDT*, 31. The exact nature of the conflict is shrouded in the family's secretiveness. The elder Hamiltons seem to have disapproved what they perceived as the sisters' lack of filial duty to their father and the use of scarce resources for education.

110 Diary, Sept. 22 [1895]. The discussion ended with the women laughing at their "fixed opinions on subjects that never will touch us in any way."

111 See, for example, J. A. Appleyard, *Becoming a Reader: The Experience of Fiction from Childhood to Adulthood* (Cambridge: Cambridge University Press, 1990), esp. 55–56. In this context, the connection between reading and play is especially important, as is the affective nature of reading's impact.

112 Edith to "My dearest Jeddie," Thursday [late summer, late 1890s], folder 604.

CHAPTER FIVE

1 M. Carey Thomas Journal, Nov. 10, Feb. 26 [1871], *The Papers of M. Carey Thomas in the Bryn Mawr College Archives*, ed. Lucy Fisher West (Woodbridge, Conn.: Research Publications, 1982), microfilm edition, reel 1. All citations from archival sources not otherwise identified are from this edition. Thomas's journal will be cited as Journal; youthful misspellings have been retained. Thomas's name is abbreviated hereafter as MCT.

2 On "the place of elsewhere," see Keith Oatley, "Emotions and the Story Worlds of Fiction," in *Narrative Impact: Social and Cognitive Foundations*, ed. Melanie C. Green et al. (Mahwah, N.J.: Lawrence Erlbaum, 2002), 41.

3 As Thomas explained her desire for a vocation at fourteen: "I can[']t stand being dependent on any body even Mother & Father & I want to do something else besides eating reading & dressing." Journal, June 20 [1871], reel 1.

4 Journal, Sept. 23, 1877, reel 1; see also Journal, Jan. 1, 1872, reel 1.

5 Journal, Mar. 18 [1878], reel 2.

6 For biographical information on Thomas and her family, see Helen Lefkowitz Horowitz, *The Power and Passion of M. Carey Thomas* (New York: Alfred A. Knopf, 1994); Helen Thomas Flexner, *A Quaker Childhood* (New Haven: Yale University Press, 1940); Edith Finch, *Carey Thomas of Bryn Mawr* (New York: Harper, 1947); James Thomas Flexner, *An American Saga: The Story of Helen Thomas and Simon Flexner* (Boston: Little, Brown, 1984); Logan Pearsall Smith, *Unforgotten Years* (Boston: Little, Brown, 1939); and Marjorie Housepian Dobkin, ed., *The Making of a Feminist: Early Journals and Letters of M. Carey Thomas* (Kent, Ohio: Kent State University Press, 1979), which includes selections from Thomas's journals and letters.

7 "Autobiographical Materials," reel 74, frame 0860; Flexner, *A Quaker Childhood*, 11. According to Helen Thomas Flexner, Thomas's much younger sister, relatives with "grave, terrifying personalities" sometimes stayed for weeks; *A Quaker Childhood*, v–vi.

8 Certainly Thomas thought so; see "Autobiographical Materials," reel 74, frame 0874. See also MCT, "Burn 1864–1866," a section of her "Autobiography" in the Simon Flexner Papers, Series 2, American Philosophical Society, Philadelphia (hereafter cited as APS). The sections constitute partial drafts, often with several takes on a subject, rather than a finished manuscript. There is overlap with "Autobiographical Materials," reel 74.

9 On *The Arabian Nights* and other stories and poems read and recited to her during her illness, see MCT, "IV. Burn, 1864–1866 Section V," 15–17, "Autobiography," APS.

10 "Autobiographical Materials," reel 74, frames 0857–58. "A Romantic Victorian" has been substituted for "a very different child" and "probably" for "much." Thomas sometimes played on this identity, claiming, for example, that she would "read & weep & weep & read in true Victorian fashion," thereby ruining the finish on the dining room table; reel 74, frame 0861; see also frames 0862–63.

11 MCT, "III. Childhood, Second Section after Burn," 8–14, 25–27, "Autobiography," APS.

12 Thomas's activities may be followed in her journal. On the secret society, see her correspondence with her cousin Franklin Whitall Smith, reels 29 and 58; and [Hannah Whitall Smith], *The Record of a Happy Life: Being Memorials of Franklin Whitall Smith, a Student of Princeton College; By His Mother* (Philadelphia: privately printed, 1873). See also sections on "Childhood," in "Autobiography," APS.

13 "Autobiographical Materials," reel 74, frame 0497. Thomas incorrectly gave the age at which she left for boarding school as thirteen; reel 74, frame 0455.

14 On the submissions to *Harper's*, see Journal, Jan. 2, 1872, reel 1; the poem "The Lovers" appears in "My Poetical Effusions," reel 1, frames 0351–52. The year before, Thomas noted that another poem, "Snowflakes," appeared in *Leisure Moments* (probably *Our Leisure Moments*, a juvenile magazine published in Buffalo); Journal, Feb. 8, 1871, reel 1. Thanks to Christopher Densmore for tracking down *Our Leisure Moments*. See also "Selections from Prose Masters" (the copybook), reel 1, frames 0417–36.

15 Thomas claimed she could read by the age of three, having been taught by her

mother, who pricked out letters on a pin cushion: "Apart from this memory of the pincushion I cannot remember a time when I did not read, and at every available moment ever since sick or well at home or abroad I have been reading. . . . It has been the greatest resource and happiness of my life." "Autobiographical Materials," reel 74, frames 0420, 0422.

16 The entry on her mother continues: "It was one of the few occasions on which she hurt my feelings & afterwards I carefully hid my emotion" (ibid., frames 0551–52). Of her father's transgression, she observed: "I was so angry that for a long time I never spoke to him about my reading. I missed a great deal as he could have helped me" (ibid., frame 0868).

17 Journal, Feb. 23, 1872, reel 1; "Autobiographical Materials," reel 74, frame 0858.

18 Journal, Nov. 19, Nov. 12, June 20, 1870, reel 1. Thomas's reading can be followed in her journal and in the lists she kept between 1873 and 1882, reel 1, frames 0541–72. In the early years, her categories were books she wanted to buy, those she "got some new thoughts from!," those that were "utterly worthless!," and those she liked. Despite her formulaic remonstrances about reading trash, Thomas seems to have been little troubled by the secular nature of her reading, a matter of great concern to her cousin Frank Smith, to whom she was exceptionally close. See [Hannah Whitall Smith], *The Record of a Happy Life*, esp. 182–99.

19 "The History of a Pin," reel 74, frames 1084–87.

20 Journal, Oct. 1, 1871, reel 1; see also MCT to Anna Shipley, Oct. 31, 1877, reel 29.

21 Thomas and Smith (who was two and a half years her senior) spoke of the time they spent reading and planning together as "armor-making." Finding it difficult to reenter the humdrum world after spending time in the land of the "opium-eaters" with his cousin, Smith wondered whether it was best for him "to have [his] mind filled with an indescribable, romantic, day-dreamish sort of desire to do, and to be, something great" ([Hannah Whitall Smith], *The Record of a Happy Life*, 205, 179).

22 Friedrich de la Motte Fouqué, *Sintram and His Companions: A Northern Tale* (New York: Wiley and Putnam, 1845).

23 Journal, November 16, 1874, reel 1, frames 0513, 0515–16; this entry is out of chronological sequence and appears both before and after the entry for August 3, 1874.

24 Flexner, *A Quaker Childhood*, 2–4.

25 Journal, Nov. 16, 1874.

26 Oatley, "Emotions and the Story Worlds of Fiction," quotation on 65; see also 40. Oatley notes that "in fiction we are more subject to tears than in ordinary life" (63). See also D. W. Harding, "Psychological Processes in the Reading of Fiction," in *The Cool Web: The Pattern of Children's Reading*, ed. Margaret Meek et al., 58–72 (London: Bodley Head, 1977).

27 Journal, June 20, [1870], reel 1; there is an earlier, fragmentary journal. As a model for diary keeping, Jo was a transitional figure; by 1872 Thomas kept the journal in her own name.

28 Franklin Whitall Smith to MCT, Feb. 20, 1870, reel 58.

29 *Little Women*, ed. Madelon Bedell (New York: Modern Library, 1983), 178.

30 Elizabeth King Ellicott to MCT, Nov. 23 [1879], reel 39.

31 Journal, Mar. 12 [1871], reel 1. The prose selections include Mahomet, Dante, and Luther from *On Heroes*, one from *Sartor Resartus*, and an entry about Carlyle,

"Selections from Prose Writers, 1871–1872," reel 1, frames 0417–36; Elizabeth King Ellicott to MCT, May 14 [1882], reel 39.

32 A taste for Carlyle seems to have marked a stage for men as well as women of the era. Sociologist Edward A. Ross claimed that he was "a thrall of Carlyle" at twenty but outgrew hero worship and "Carlylese" two years later; *Seventy Years of It: An Autobiography* (New York: D. Appleton-Century, 1936), 21, 30. On Jane Addams and Carlyle, see chapter 6.

33 Thomas Carlyle, *On Heroes, Hero-Worship, and the Heroic in History: Six Lectures; Reported, with Emendations and Additions* (New York: D. Appleton, 1841), 1, 178; MCT to Mary E. Garrett, June 10 [1881], reel 15.

34 Journal, Feb. 26 [1871], reel 1.

35 "Selections from Prose Writers," reel 1, frame 0435.

36 These seem to me to be the implications of works as diverse as Rachel M. Brownstein, *Becoming a Heroine: Reading about Women in Novels* (New York: Penguin, 1984); Jonathan Culler, *On Deconstruction: Theory and Criticism after Structuralism* (Ithaca, N.Y.: Cornell University Press, 1982), 43–64; Judith Fetterley, *The Resisting Reader: A Feminist Approach to American Fiction* (Bloomington: Indiana University Press, 1978); and Patrocinio P. Schweickart, "Reading Ourselves: Toward a Feminist Theory of Reading," in *Gender and Reading: Essays on Readers, Texts, and Contexts*, ed. Elizabeth A. Flynn and Patrocinio P. Schweickart, 31–62 (Baltimore: Johns Hopkins University Press, 1986).

37 Cora Kaplan, "*The Thorn Birds*: Fiction, Fantasy, Femininity," in *Sea Changes: Feminism and Culture* (London: Verso, 1986), 117–46. Defining fantasy "as 'daydream', as a conscious, written narrative construction, or as an historical account of the gendered imagination," Kaplan suggests that some romances invite "the female reader to identify across sexual difference and to engage with narrative fantasy from a variety of subject positions and at various levels." "A very free movement between masculine and feminine positions" may occur in consequence that permits women to read themselves as subjects rather than "see themselves narcissistically through the eyes of men" as objects (125, 120, 134, 123).

38 "Selections from Prose Writers," reel 1, frame 0435. Twenty-first century girls, too, frequently identify with male heroes. On their greater willingness to do so than for boys to identify with female protagonists, see Oatley, "Emotions and the Story Worlds of Fiction," 61–63.

39 Vallie Beck to Jane Addams, Aug. 10, 1877, *The Jane Addams Papers*, ed. Mary Lynn McCree Bryan (Ann Arbor: University Microfilms International, 1984), reel 1 (hereafter cited as *JAP*).

40 Klee, "The American Heroine," *Evening Transcript*, July 21, 1879, clipping in Katharine Lee Bates Papers, Scrapbook of Writings (1876–85), Wellesley College Archives. Thanks to Patricia Palmieri for calling this reference to my attention and to Wilma Slaight for providing a copy.

41 I am grateful to Joan Hedrick for suggesting this connection.

42 "Some of the Representative Men of the Present Time" [1875], in "Autobiographical Materials," reel 74, frames 1091–96; Thomas's representative "men" were all writers. See also Charles Kingsley, "Heroism," in *Sanitary and Social Lectures and Essays* (1874; reprint, London: Macmillan, 1889), 225–54.

43 Journal, Mar. 14, 1872, reel 1. See also MCT to Franklin Whitall Smith, "I put no date," reel 29, frame 0483; and [May 4, 1872], frames 0430–44, which includes a poem, "Rex & Rush," written on the occasion of this fantasy. Smith interpreted the description of the carpet and fire as "a ridiculous hit at we male creatures"; Smith to MCT, Mar. 7, 1872, reel 58.

Before entering Cornell, Thomas exchanged her childhood nickname, Minnie, for the more grown-up—and gender-ambiguous—Carey. In her early twenties, she continued to assert the essential similarity of the sexes. Favoring an androgynous ideal that allowed for tenderness in men and strength in women, she sought to remove gendered labels from these traits and to redefine them as human. See, for example, MCT to Richard Cadbury, [1880–81], reel 13, frames 0260–61; and MCT to Mary Whitall Thomas, Feb. 27 [1881], reel 31.

44 Carolyn G. Heilbrun, *Writing a Woman's Life* (New York: W. W. Norton, 1988), 11. Heilbrun assumes that this writing occurs "unconsciously, and without [the woman's] recognizing or naming the process," but Thomas and many of her contemporaries consciously wrote their lives in advance. On Thomas and Bryn Mawr, see Helen Lefkowitz Horowitz, *Alma Mater: Design and Experience in the Women's Colleges from Their Nineteenth-Century Beginnings to the 1930s* (New York: Knopf, 1984), 105–33, and *The Power and the Passion*.

45 MCT to Mary Whitall Thomas, Nov. 25, 1882, reel 32. Thomas's mother and aunt, Hannah Whitall Smith, a religious writer, encouraged her ambitions.

46 Jane Addams, "Woman's Special Training for Peacemaking," *Proceedings of the Second National Peace Congress, Chicago, May 2–5, 1909* (1909): 252; Vida Scudder quoted in Arthur Mann, *Yankee Reformers in the Urban Age: Social Reform in Boston, 1880–1900* (Chicago: University of Chicago Press, 1954), 201.

47 Oatley, "Emotions and the Story Worlds of Fiction," 43, emphasizes the creative and transformative power of emotions produced during reading.

48 Addams to Ellen Gates Starr, Aug. 11, 1879, reel 1, *JAP*; Mercedes M. Randall, *Improper Bostonian: Emily Greene Balch* (New York: Twayne, 1964), 45. *Undine* (1811) by the German romantic Friedrich de La Motte Fouqué, author of *Sintram*, was popular with American girls; both stories are mentioned in *Little Women*.

49 For literary trends that may have stimulated such readings, see Martha Vicinus, "What Makes a Heroine?: Nineteenth-Century Girls' Biographies," *Genre* 20 (Summer 1987): 171–88, which notes the downplaying of sexuality and the marriage plots in girls' biographies; and Rachel Blau DuPlessis, *Writing beyond the Ending: Narrative Strategies of Twentieth-Century Women Writers* (Bloomington: Indiana University Press, 1985), which suggests that in nineteenth-century fiction, quest (Bildung) and romance "could not coexist and be integrated for the heroine at the resolution" (3).

50 Mary White Ovington, *The Walls Came Tumbling Down* (1947; reprint, New York: Arno Press, 1969), 3–4. Ovington links these literary associations to the family culture, noting that the stories she heard from her abolitionist grandmother also fueled her imagination: "I did not get all the material for my dreams from books" (4).

51 Jerome L. Singer, *Daydreaming: An Introduction to the Experimental Study of Inner Experience* (New York: Random House, 1966), 211, 173. Singer analyzes several of his own recurrent adolescent fantasies—some stimulated by books—which

revolved around heroic figures bound for great success (15–28). Among his research subjects, daydreaming peaked between ages fourteen and seventeen (172).
Late-twentieth-century children's interest in heroes and heroines seems to have
peaked earlier (ages seven to twelve); J. A. Appleyard, *Becoming a Reader: The Experience of Fiction from Childhood to Adulthood* (Cambridge: Cambridge University Press, 1990), 57–93.

52 James Britton, *Language and Learning* (London: Allen Lane/Penguin Press, 1970),
109–10. Britton is building on the analysis of D. H. Harding.

53 MCT to Mary E. Garrett, Wednesday evening, [July 31, 1884], reel 15.

54 On Thomas's two years in Baltimore following her graduation from Cornell see
Horowitz, *The Power and the Passion*, 74–107. On the many ways in which formal
and informal institutions were stacked against women at this time, see Margaret W.
Rossiter, *Women Scientists in America: Struggles and Strategies to 1940* (Baltimore:
Johns Hopkins University Press, 1982), especially the sections on Christine Ladd-
Franklin, 38–50 passim. A distinguished psychologist, Ladd-Franklin was, like
Thomas, a special student at Hopkins. She completed all requirements for the
Ph.D. in 1882, but Hopkins did not award her the degree until 1926.

55 Journal, Aug. 27, 1878, reel 2. King withdrew from art school after she contracted
tuberculosis.

56 In addition to Horowitz, *The Power and Passion*, the Friday Night is discussed in
Dobkin, *The Making of a Feminist*; and Barbara Landis Chase, "M. Carey Thomas
and the 'Friday Night': A Case Study in Female Social Networks and Personal
Growth" (M.A. thesis, Johns Hopkins University, 1990). I am grateful to Barbara
Chase for sending a copy of her thesis. There are articles on Elizabeth King El-
licott, Mary Elizabeth Garrett, and Julia Rebecca Rogers in *Notable Maryland
Women*, ed. Winifred G. Helmes (Cambridge, Md.: Tidewater, 1977). See also
Hugh Hawkins, "Mary Elizabeth Garrett," in *Notable American Women, 1607–1950*,
ed. Edward T. James, Janet Wilson James, and Paul S. Boyer (Cambridge, Mass.:
Harvard University Press, 1971), 2:21–22; "Autobiographical Materials" (on Garrett), reel 75, frames 551–672; and "In Memoriam Mary Gwinn Hodder," *Bryn
Mawr Alumnae Bulletin* (Jan. 1941), 19. Biographical data on group members was
also obtained from Bryn Mawr College, the Enoch Pratt Free Library, the Maryland Historical Society, and Goucher College.

57 Mary E. Garrett Diary, Tuesday [June 14, 1870], Mary E. Garrett Papers, Bryn
Mawr College Archives. Garrett also rejected Ruskin's strictures against a woman's
studying theology. On Ruskin, see *Sesame and Lilies: Three Lectures* (1865; reprint,
New York: John Wiley & Sons, 1890). At about the same time, Garrett, Rogers, and
King participated in an informal reading group. Thomas was invited to join, but it
is unclear whether she did. Garrett Diary, Sat. [June 11, 1870] and Friday [June 17,
1870], Garrett Papers.

58 Journal, Feb. 2 [1878], reel 2. Gwinn later recalled that the initiative for the group
came from Garrett, Rogers, and King, who "had been projecting a small club of
the like-minded, to convene at one another's houses fortnightly and read to one
another bookish papers." Mary Mackall Gwinn Hodder to Logan Pearsall Smith,
Feb. 17, 1938, Mary Mackall Gwinn Faculty File, Bryn Mawr College Archives.

59 In Germany, Thomas and Gwinn made a practice of reading novels during their

periods, the time physicians deemed women most liable to injure themselves by studying. Indulging in a pleasure they sometimes denied themselves, they turned a negative image of women reading to their own purposes—while also hedging their bets. MCT to Mary E. Garrett, Nov. 30 [1880], reel 15.

60 Journal, June 1 and Feb. 2, 1878, reel 2.

61 Garrett to MCT, July 15, 1879, reel 42.

62 Elizabeth King Ellicott to MCT, [May 1880], reel 39; MCT to Mary Whitall Thomas, [July 12, 1880], reel 31. Thomas defined "*nous autres*" as "the Gautier, Rossetti school"; in the context of the letter (a reply to one from her mother, June 22, 1880, reel 61) she seems to be referring principally to the group's commitment to literary excellence. Helen Lefkowitz Horowitz in "'Nous Autres': Reading, Passion, and the Creation of M. Carey Thomas," *Journal of American History* 79 (June 1992): 68–95, and *The Power and Passion*, emphasizes the importance of Thomas's reading in creating an identity based on acknowledged passion for women. She views this identity, which she links especially to Thomas's reading of Swinburne and Théophile Gautier's *Mademoiselle de Maupin*, as falling in time and nature between the sentimental friendships of "the female world of love and ritual" described by Carroll Smith-Rosenberg and a full-fledged lesbian identity. Horowitz and I both stress the importance of reading in shaping Thomas's identity, but I emphasize the quest rather than the (female) romance plot and the younger age at which reading influences identity formation.

63 Journal, Thanksgiving 1874, reel 1, frame 0516. Most likely she read Shelley's *Queen Mab* and the accompanying prose notes, an all-out attack on religion and on repressive institutions like monarchy.

64 Thomas read the *Vindication*, as well as Godwin's *Memoirs of Mary Wollstonecraft*, but curiously did not comment on Wollstonecraft's views: perhaps her brand of feminism was too tame, her life too shocking.

The Godwin-Shelley circle inspired the women's collective novel (reel 2, frames 0916–78). Set in the aftermath of the French Revolution, the novel begins with the story of a humanitarian philosopher and the woman he loves and lives with chastely. After his death, she tries to raise his son according to the father's values, but the son, a poet named Percy, sows his wild oats before following in his father's footsteps. Thomas's segments contain echoes of Tom Paine—another member of the circle—in such phrases as "royalist editors and hireling reviewers" (0977). For a critical assessment, see Horowitz, *The Power and the Passion*, 77–78. Thomas claimed she was shocked to discover social injustice on reading Godwin, but the impact seems to have been temporary.

65 MCT to Richard Cadbury, Apr. 4, 1880, reel 13.

66 MCT to Garrett, [Nov. 11, 1880], reel 15, frame 0224; Thomas to Anna Shipley, Nov. 21 [1875] and Jan. 30 [1876], reel 29.

67 For Thomas's defense of Swinburne, see MCT to Anna Shipley, Nov. 21 [1875], reel 29. On French novels, see Garrett to MCT, Nov. 30, 1879, reel 42; and MCT to Mary Whitall Thomas, incorrectly dated "first day 8th mo. 25th" [July 25, 1880], reel 31. On Shelley and Swinburne's politics, see Stephanie Kuduk Weiner, *Republican Politics and English Poetry, 1789–1874* (New York: Palgrave Macmillan, 2005); for the latter's challenge to religion and conventional sexual norms, see Thaïs E.

Morgan, "Swinburne's Dramatic Monologues: Sex and Ideology," *Victorian Poetry* 22 (1984): 175–95.

68 MCT to Mary E. Garrett, [postmarked July 24, 1879], reel 15.

69 Journal, Feb. 2 [1878], reel 2. Cf. Gwinn Hodder to Logan Pearsall Smith, Feb. 17, 1938, Bryn Mawr College Archives. Gwinn also proclaimed herself a follower of Thomas Malthus and declared that she did not want children.

70 Journal, Apr. 6, 1878, reel 2. See also MCT to Mary Whitall Thomas, [July 25, 1880], reel 31; Nancy F. Cott, "Passionlessness: An Interpretation of Victorian Sexual Ideology, 1790–1850," *Signs* 4 (Winter 1978): 219–36.

71 Elizabeth King Ellicott to MCT, Saturday [1884], reel 39; MCT to Margaret Hicks Volkmann, [Aug. 30, 1880], reel 32; see also Journal, Mar. 24 [1878], reel 2. Thomas's abortive romance is treated extensively in her journal for 1878 (reel 2) and is analyzed by Horowitz, *The Power and Passion*, 78–82, 100–102.

Gwinn wrote an essay on seven intellectual women who attained sufficient success in art, philosophy, mathematics, and languages from the fourteenth century through the eighteenth to warrant portraits at the University of Bologna. Some had been honored with university chairs as well as portraits. Intrigued by these role models, Gwinn hunted down the meager available facts about their lives. These hinted at the difficulties under which even women of exceptional talent and privilege labored: in some cases, their accomplishments seemed to end with marriage, while others, though single, retreated into private life. Mary Mackall Gwinn Hodder, "The Friday Night, 1878–1879," reel 71, frames 0005–14.

72 MCT to Mary Whitall Thomas, Nov. 13, 1880, reel 31. The ins and outs of these relationships are analyzed by Horowitz, *The Power and Passion* and "'Nous Autres.'" On Thomas's sexual identity also see note 62; Lillian Faderman, *Odd Girls and Twilight Lovers: A History of Lesbian Life in Twentieth-Century America* (New York: Columbia University Press, 1991), 28–31, 37; Carroll Smith-Rosenberg, "The New Woman as Androgyne: Social Disorder and Gender Crisis, 1870–1936," in *Disorderly Conduct: Visions of Gender in Victorian America* (New York: Alfred A. Knopf, 1985), esp. 273–74; and Dobkin, *The Making of a Feminist*, esp. 77–87.

73 MCT to Mary E. Garrett, New Year's Eve [1880], reel 15; Journal, Mar. 24 [1878], reel 2; and MCT to Richard Cadbury, June 26 [1880], reel 13.

74 MCT to Mary Whitall Thomas, Feb. 7, 1880, reel 31.

75 Journal, June 26, 1878, reel 2. On the consecration of the classics as high culture in the Gilded Age, see Caroline Winterer, *The Culture of Classicism: Ancient Greece and Rome in American Intellectual Life, 1780–1910* (Baltimore: Johns Hopkins University Press, 2002), 99–151.

76 Journal, Oct. 4, 1877, reel 1; Apr. 21, 1878, reel 2.

77 Journal, Feb. 2, 1885, reel 2.

78 Journal, June 1 and July 6, 1878, reel 2. The book's full title is *Literature and Dogma: An Essay towards a Better Apprehension of the Bible.*

79 Journal, May 2 [1878], reel 2; MCT to Mary E. Garrett, Sunday afternoon, July 7, 1878, reel 15; Journal, July 6 [1878], reel 2. The first volume of *The Principles of Sociology* was published in 1876.

80 Journal, Aug. 25, 1878, reel 2, frame 0894.

81 Ibid., frames 0894–95; this entry precedes the one for Aug. 23.

82 MCT to Mary E. Garrett, Aug. 27/Sept. 22 [1878], reel 15; this account of the episode is nearly identical to the one in her journal.

83 Andrew H. Walsh, e-mail to author, Oct. 20, 2006. I am grateful to Prof. Walsh for insight into the meaning of "dying daily" in Christian, especially Protestant, thought.

84 MCT to Mary E. Garrett, July 7, 1878, reel 15. See also Journal, June 26 [1878], reel 2. At times, Thomas also regarded her intense friendships as deterrents to her ambition.

85 Journal, Mar. 24 and July 6 [1878], reel 2. See also MCT to Mary E. Garrett, July 7, 1878.

86 Journal, July 6 [1878], reel 2. *Pascarel: Only a Story* (1873) was by Ouida, a sensation writer Thomas "particularly object[ed] to"; MCT to Mary E. Garrett, July 7, 1878. The other novels she read at the time also fell into the light or objectionable categories.

87 MCT to Mary E. Garrett, Nov. 2 [1880] and Oct. 15 [1881], reel 15. Cf. Julia Rogers, who, noting that she could hardly make herself put *Bleak House* down, thought it was "rather late in life . . . to be absorbed in this way by such books"; Rogers to Garrett, [Sept. 10, 1880], reel 71. And at twenty, Mamie Gwinn resented "an author's endeavor to make [her] feel"; Gwinn to Mary E. Garrett, Sept. 9, 1880, reel 71, frame 0124.

In the twentieth century, at least, book and magazine reading tended to decrease with age. Carl F. Kaestle et al., *Literacy in the United States: Readers and Reading since 1880* (New Haven: Yale University Press, 1991), 190, 201.

88 This story is told in part by Horowitz, *The Power and Passion*, 233–38; Alan M. Chesney, *The Johns Hopkins Hospital and the Johns Hopkins University School of Medicine: A Chronicle*, vol. 1 (Baltimore: Johns Hopkins University Press, 1943); and Hugh Hawkins, *Pioneer: A History of the Johns Hopkins University, 1874–1889* (Ithaca, N.Y.: Cornell University Press, 1960). On the Bryn Mawr School, see Rosamond Randall Beirne, *Let's Pick the Daisies: The History of the Bryn Mawr School, 1885–1967* (Baltimore: Bryn Mawr School, 1970).

89 For an excellent analysis of Thomas's graduate career, see Horowitz, *The Power and Passion*, 108–81.

90 MCT to Mary E. Garrett, Oct. 13, 1880, reel 15; and MCT to Richard Cadbury, Nov. 23, 1880, reel 13.

91 MCT to Mary E. Garrett, Dec. 12, 1880, and Nov. 19, 1880, reel 15, frame 0228; MCT to Richard Cadbury, Nov. 23, 1880, reel 13.

92 MCT to Richard Cadbury, Nov. 23, 1880, reel 13.

93 Mary Whitall Thomas to MCT, June 28, 1880, reel 61. An article by Thomas on recent excavations of statues at Pergamus was published in the "Notes" section of the *Nation*, no. 765 (Feb. 26, 1880): 156. Earlier, she contributed short pieces on education to the *Quaker Alumnus* 1 (1879): 36–37, 57–58, 64; for a time Thomas's and King's names appeared on the masthead.

94 MCT to Mary E. Garrett, [Mar. 20, 1884], and Apr. 26, 1884, reel 15.

95 MCT to Mary E. Garrett, [Oct. 9, 1884], reel 15.

96 Thomas's educational philosophy is best approached through her speeches, several of which are reprinted in *The Educated Woman in America: Selected Writings of*

Catharine Beecher, Margaret Fuller, and M. Carey Thomas, ed. Barbara M. Cross (New York: Teachers College Press, 1965), 139–75, esp. 169. On Thomas's racism and anti-Semitism, see Horowitz, *The Power and Passion*.

97 MCT, "Autobiographical Materials," reel 74, frame 0497.

98 The manuscript "Autobiography" in the American Philosophical Society consists of drafts and notes on "Youth" and "Girlhood" that take Thomas up to her departure for boarding school, when she was fifteen and a half.

99 MCT to Mary E. Garrett, May 28, 1884, reel 15.

100 Thomas claimed that her autobiography would be frank, but it is possible that she was reluctant to analyze her relationships with Gwinn and Garrett for public consumption. In the nineteenth century emotionally close relationships of this kind had been viewed as romantic but not sexual. By the time Thomas was writing, however, they were labeled lesbian, a subject she read up on for the project. Thomas's biographer suggests that her sister, Helen Thomas Flexner, destroyed the sections after childhood, presumably because of their frankness. Horowitz, *The Power and Passion*, 448–51.

101 Journal, Aug. 23 [1878], reel 2, frame 0896.

102 MCT to Mary E. Garrett, Wednesday evening [July 31, 1884], reel 15.

CHAPTER SIX

1 The most insightful overview of Addams's ideas on culture, though brief and unfootnoted, is James Dougherty, "Jane Addams: Culture and Imagination," *Yale Review* 71 (Spring 1982): 363–79. See also Harriet Averbuch Katz, "Cathedral of Humanity: A Study of Jane Addams's Ideas on Art and Culture" (D.S.W. diss., Yeshiva University, 1975).

2 For an overview of the female-based social reform movement in which Addams played a central part, see Robyn Muncy, *Creating a Female Dominion in American Reform, 1890–1935* (New York: Oxford University Press, 1991).

3 The starting point for any study of Addams is *Twenty Years at Hull-House* (New York: Macmillan, 1910). The literature on her is vast. Two recent biographies build on the heroic labors of Mary Lynn McCree Bryan and her colleagues who collected the Jane Addams Papers and published them in microfilm and hardcover editions (see note 8): Victoria Bissell Brown, *The Education of Jane Addams* (Philadelphia: University of Pennsylvania Press, 2004); and Louise W. Knight, *Citizen: Jane Addams and the Struggle for Democracy* (Chicago: University of Chicago Press, 2005), which includes an extensive bibliography. Brown takes Addams through 1894; Knight, through 1899. Both volumes serve their subject well while wrestling with the question of how Jane Addams became Jane Addams and should be consulted for details and interpretations. Both confirm rather than alter the conclusions of this chapter, which was drafted before their publication. Earlier influential interpretations include the biography by her nephew, James Weber Linn, *Jane Addams: A Biography* (New York: D. Appleton-Century, 1935); John C. Farrell, *Beloved Lady: A History of Jane Addams' Ideas on Reform and Peace* (Baltimore: Johns Hopkins University Press, 1967); Allen F. Davis, *American Heroine: The Life and Legend of Jane Addams* (New York: Oxford University Press, 1973);

and Christopher Lasch, *The New Radicalism in America, 1889–1963: The Intellectual as a Social Type* (New York: Alfred A. Knopf, 1965).

4 This quotation and others describing Addams's London encounter and the meditation that followed are from Addams, *Twenty Years*, 67–71. Addams's name is abbreviated hereafter as JA.

5 Thomas De Quincey, "The English Mail-Coach. Section the Second.—The Vision of Sudden Death" [1849], in *Confessions of an English Opium-Eater, and Kindred Papers*, 41st ed. (Boston: Houghton Mifflin, 1851), 566, 554.

6 On Arnold as a more complex critic than he is often given credit for being, see Raymond Williams, *Culture and Society, 1780–1950* (New York: Columbia University Press, 1983), esp. 110–29. See also Joseph Carroll, *The Cultural Theory of Matthew Arnold* (Berkeley and Los Angeles: University of California Press, 1982).

7 For an analysis of "political autobiography" that distinguishes between "fact" and "truth," see Margo V. Perkins, *Autobiography as Activism: Three Black Women of the Sixties* (Jackson: University Press of Mississippi, 2000), esp. 88–89.

8 JA to John Weber Linn, Oct. 29, 1883, *The Jane Addams Papers*, ed. Mary Lynn Mc-Cree Bryan (Ann Arbor: University Microfilms International, 1984), reel 1. All archival sources not otherwise identified come from this edition. Some of Addams's writings have been reprinted in *The Selected Papers of Jane Addams*, vol. 1, *Preparing to Lead, 1860–81*, ed. Mary Lynn McCree Bryan, Barbara Bair, and Maree De Angury (Urbana: University of Illinois Press, 2003).

9 "The Notion of Conscience," [1880s], reel 46, frames 0100–101. See also "Fear as a Conservative Element," Jan. 7, 1880, reel 46, frames 0143–44. According to one of Addams's textbooks, De Quincey was considered a master of English prose; see *A Complete Manual of English Literature*, by Thomas B. Shaw, M.A., edited, with notes and illustrations, by William Smith, LL.D.; with a sketch of American literature, by Henry T. Tuckerman (New York: Sheldon & Co., 1871), 470, 472. In *Twenty Years*, Addams claimed that, in a "restless attempt" to gain experience, she and several classmates tried opium "to understand De Quincey's marvelous 'Dreams' more sympathetically" (46).

10 Addams alludes to her mental paralysis in JA to Ellen Gates Starr, Feb. 7, 1886; and JA to Alice Addams Haldeman, Feb. 17, 1886, both reel 2.

11 See JA to Ellen Gates Starr, Feb. 21, 1885, reel 2. In view of Addams's religious concerns during these years, it seems significant that the reference invoked here is to the "doubt and inaction" of Ben Hur, eponymous hero of the novel by Lew Wallace, at the "supreme moment" of the Passion. A passage in her college notebook also links De Quincey's views on "the treachery of nature" to the "'indifference'" of Christ's disciples in the garden; notebook [March 1880], reel 27, frame 0375. See also JA, "Three Days on the Mediterranean Subjectively Related," *Rockford Seminary Magazine* 14 (Jan. 1886): 14, reel 46, frames 0442–46; and poem on Thomas De Quincey, n.d. [1898?], reel 46, frame 0842.

12 Addams suggests that the emphasis on her father was partly a rhetorical strategy: because he "was so distinctly the dominant influence . . . it has seemed simpler to string these first memories on that single cord" (*Twenty Years*, 1).

13 Curiously, Addams does not mention the loss of her mother as a reason for her childhood nighttime terrors. Of a recurrent nightmare in which she was the only

person left in the world but failed to carry out an assigned responsibility, she said that it was "doubtless compounded in equal parts of a childish version of Robinson Crusoe and of the end-of-the-world predictions of the Second Adventists" (ibid., 5–6). Like the De Quincey episode, this passage suggests the power Addams accorded books as well as the disturbances they could produce.

14 Ibid., 12–13. In her mid-twenties Addams noted that she had driven "past this little public library Pa read through." JA to Alice Addams Haldeman, Mar. 31, 1886, reel 2.

15 The Library Company was a social library open to anyone who could pay the initial sum of two dollars and a yearly membership fee of fifty cents. John Huy Addams, one of the founders, was the library's first treasurer and librarian. *Rules and By-Laws of the Cedar Creek Union Library Company* (Freeport: E. D. Carpenter, Printer, 1847), reel 28, frames 0852–56, includes a catalogue of the library; a typed list entitled "Addams Family Library," which contains additional titles, follows, frames 0857–69.

16 JA, *Twenty Years*, 13.

17 Ibid., 47. Washington Irving's *Life of George Washington* appeared in five volumes between 1855 and 1859.

18 See Meyer Reinhold, *Classica Americana: The Greek and Roman Heritage in the United States* (Detroit: Wayne State University Press, 1984), esp. 250–64, and Carl J. Richard, *The Founders and the Classics: Greece, Rome and the American Enlightenment* (Cambridge, Mass.: Harvard University Press, 1994). Emerson was one of those who praised Plutarch's heroes; see "Heroism" and "Self-Reliance"in Ralph Waldo Emerson, *Essays and Lectures*, ed. Joel Porte (New York: Library of America, 1983), 373, 280.

19 On the importance of biography, see Scott E. Casper, "Biographical Mania: The Transformation of Biographical Theory in Nineteenth-Century America," *Nineteenth-Century Prose* 22 (Fall 1995): 39–62, and *Constructing American Lives: Biography and Culture in Nineteenth-Century America* (Chapel Hill: University of North Carolina Press, 1999). In this tradition, Addams distributed biographies in her early Hull-House years; *Twenty Years*, 36.

20 JA, *Twenty Years*, 23, 34.

21 Ibid., 21–22.

22 See, for example, JA, "The Subjective Necessity for Social Settlements," *Philanthropy and Social Progress* (New York: Thomas Y. Crowell, 1893), 1–26; "The Settlement as a Factor in the Labor Movement," *Hull-House Maps and Papers* (New York: Thomas Y. Crowell, 1895), 183–204; "Claim on the College Woman," *Rockford Collegian* 23 (June 1895): 59–63; and "A Modern Lear," *Survey* 29 (Nov. 2, 1912): 131–37.

23 JA, *Twenty Years*, 22. The original reads: "He wrapt *his little daughter* in his large/Man's doublet, careless did it fit or no" (emphasis added). The substitution of "me" for the third person suggests Addams's investment in the passage. Elizabeth Barrett Browning, *Aurora Leigh*, in *Aurora Leigh and Other Poems* (London: Women's Press, 1978), 60.

24 JA to Alice Addams Haldeman, Mar. 12, 1871; see also John Weber Addams to JA, May 8, 1868; JA to Alice Addams Haldeman, Jan. 28, 1870; and John Greenleaf Whittier to JA, Feb. 15, 1873, reel 1.

25 Linn, *Jane Addams*, 29–30. Altogether, extant documents point to a less morbid girlhood than does *Twenty Years*. In the reconstituted family circle, Jane played piano duets (with George Haldeman) and games (with George and her step-mother), among them chess, bamboozle, Authors, and "Sam Slick's Trip to Paris." According to a lone surviving diary, Addams also rode horseback, told stories to her nephew, and indulged in snowball fights and April Fool's Day pranks. She was a critical attender of sermons as well. JA Diary, 1875, reel 28.

26 JA Diary, esp. Jan. 29, June 2, Jan. 13, Jan. 25, all 1875. In Addams's Dickens phase, the family renamed their dog "Buzfuz" (a character from *The Pickwick Papers*), which she called "a noted name from Dickens, which the other was not." JA Diary, June 11, 1875.

27 JA, *Twenty Years*, 32–33.

28 Ibid., 47; JA to Vallie Beck, Mar. 30/Apr. 2, 1876, reel 1.

29 JA to Vallie Beck, May 3, 1877, reel 1. By "instructive," she most likely meant historical.

30 See JA, "Boarding-School Ideals," in *Twenty Years*, 43–64, and, for an analysis, Sarah Robbins, "Rereading the History of Nineteenth-Century Women's Higher Education: A Reexamination of Jane Addams' Rockford College Learning as Preparation for her *Twenty Years at Hull-House* Teaching," *Journal of the Midwest History of Education Society* 21 (1994): 27–45. Some of Addams's criticisms of Rockford, including its religious emphasis, could be made of contemporary male colleges. See, for example, Thomas Le Duc, *Piety and Intellect at Amherst College, 1865–1912* (New York: Columbia University Press, 1946). Like Rockford, Amherst was Congregational.

31 Transcript, reel 27, frame 0462. Addams received the degree because she took many more courses than other students. On Rockford and its curriculum, see Lucy Forsyth Townsend, "Anna Peck Sill and the Rise of Women's Collegiate Curriculum" (Ph.D. diss., Loyola University of Chicago, 1985).

32 On the history of moral philosophy in collegiate education and its decline in the late nineteenth century, see D. H. Meyer, *The Instructed Conscience: The Shaping of the American National Ethic* (Philadelphia: University of Pennsylvania Press, 1972).

33 JA, *Twenty Years*, 62.

34 On the vogue of liberal culture, see James Turner, "Secularization and Sacralization: Speculations on Some Religious Origins of the Secular Humanities Curriculum, 1850–1900," in George Marsden and Bradley J. Longfield, eds., *The Secularization of the Academy*, 74–106 (New York: Oxford University Press, 1992).

35 JA, "Resolved, The Civilization of the 19th cent. tends to fetter intellectual life and expression. Aff." Feb. 18, 1880, reel 46, frames 0181–82.

36 Turner, "Secularization and Sacralization," 86.

37 On the changing role of the classics in American intellectual, including collegiate, life, see Caroline Winterer, *The Culture of Classicism: Ancient Greece and Rome in American Intellectual Life, 1780–1910* (Baltimore: Johns Hopkins University Press, 2002), and on their meaning to women, *The Mirror of Antiquity: American Women and the Classical Tradition, 1750–1900* (Ithaca, N.Y.: Cornell University Press, 2007).

38 The first, "Bellerophon" [1880–81], was the "Greek Address" at the Junior

Exhibition, in which Addams recommended poetry as the best means of conquering modern delusions just as the winged horse Bellerophon conquered the monster Chimera; reel 46, frames 0091–94. The title is written in Greek, but Louise Knight thinks it unlikely that Addams delivered the address in Greek; *Citizen*, 440. The second address, "Cassandra," is discussed below.

39 JA, *Twenty Years*, 38.

40 JA to Anna Haldeman Addams, Jan. 14, 1880, and JA to Alice Addams Haldeman, Jan. 23, 1880; see also JA to Ellen Gates Starr, Jan. 29, 1880, reel 1.

41 JA to Alice Addams Haldeman, Jan. 19, 1881, reel 1.

42 When Addams visited Greece several years after graduation, she wrote, "I found to my mortification that I knew enough Greek to read streets & signs and an occasional inscription—but not much else" (JA to Ellen Gates Starr, June 8, 1884, reel 1).

43 Ellen Gates Starr to JA, Apr. 28, 1885, reel 2; JA, "The Macbeth of Shakespeare," *Rockford Seminary Magazine* 8 (Jan. 1880): 13–16, reel 46, frames 0138–40. Commenting on Addams's early writing, Starr observed that she "reluctantly decided to burn" some early letters because she considered them inferior in spelling and construction; Ellen Gates Starr to JA, Dec. 3, 1885, reel 2.

44 Comment on "Cicero and Caesar," Nov. 10, 1879, reel 46, frame 0071. (The four men included Napoleon and Erasmus.) The subjects of some essays coincided with Addams's courses in rhetoric, critical reading, and English literature.

45 "The Gipsies of Romance[,] Meg Merrilies thier [*sic*] queen," Oct. 15, 1879, reel 46, frame 0051.

46 Making many of the stops I do here, Victoria Bissell Brown traces the evolution of Addams's ideas in her early essays and letters away from a Carlylean emphasis on heroic individualism to a more democratic and "feminine" model of leadership; *Education*, esp. 83–84, 166. See also Louise Knight, *Citizen*, 80–108, which traces many of Addams's quotations to their sources.

47 JA to Eva Campbell, July 25/29, 1879, reel 1. The Carlyle passage Addams liked urged readers to select only those books that appealed to them at the time, advice at odds with those who advised systematic reading. See also JA to Ellen Gates Starr, Aug. 11, 1879, reel 1.

48 See Thomas Carlyle, *On Heroes, Hero-Worship, and the Heroic in History* (New York: D. Appleton & Co., 1841), esp. 1. For Addams's later view, see *Twenty Years*, 36.

49 JA to Ellen Gates Starr, May 15, 1880, reel 1. The biography was by Herman Friedrich Grimm.

50 JA, undated and untitled essay on Goethe, reel 45, frame 1611, and "One Office of Nature," *Rockford Seminary Magazine* 7 (June 1879): 156, reel 46, frame 0022. See also "An Allogory [*sic*]," [1877–81], reel 45, frame 1606. Emerson viewed Goethe as a man "coming into an over-civilized time and country, when original talent was oppressed under the load of books and mechanical auxiliaries"; *Representative Men: Seven Lectures*, in Emerson, *Essays and Lectures*, 760.

51 JA, "Savonarola," [1877–81], reel 45, frames 1654–55; "Darkness *versus* Nebulae," June 14, 1880, reel 46, frame 0213; and "George Eliot's view of Savonarola," reel 45, frame 1623.

52 JA to Ellen Gates Starr, Mar. 9, 1884; see also JA to Alice Addams Haldeman, Mar. 6, 1884, both in reel 1.

53 JA, "'Follow Thou Thy Star,'" *Rockford Seminary Magazine* 7 (July 1879): 183–84, reel 46, frames 0031–32. The title is from a quotation of Dante by way of Carlyle.

54 "The Gipsies of Romance[,] Meg Merrilies thier [*sic*] queen," Oct. 15, 1879, reel 46, frame 0051. A second version of the essay follows, frames 0041–48. On the impact of Romanticism on Addams, see Dorothy Ross, "Gendered Social Knowledge: Domestic Discourse, Jane Addams, and the Possibilities of Social Science," in *Gender and American Social Science: The Formative Years*, ed. Helene Silverberg, 235–64 (Princeton, N.J.: Princeton University Press, 1998).

55 JA, "The Gipsies of Romance," reel 46, quotation at frame 0050. In this essay, Addams noted how difficult it was to "thoroughly be ourselves, to follow steadily our own individuality & to keep ourselves from falling into a sort of indifference & imitation." A list of questions on *Guy Mannering*, presumably from the teacher, highlights historical subjects; reel 27, frames 0236–38.

Addams, who had a long-standing fascination with the female primitive, also wrote about the "primordial" Egyptian goddess, "the great brooding mother to whom time & knowledge were as nothing." See "Darkness *versus* Nebulae," June 14, 1880, reel 46, quotation at frame 0209; and "The Nebular Hypothesis," Jan. 28, 1880, reel 46, frames 0156–62.

56 JA, "Affirmative. Resolved; that the French women have had more influence through literature than polotics [*sic*]. Rep. women—George Sand and Md'e De Staël." [1878, ca. Nov. 13], reel 45, frames 1796–1807, quotation at 1800. There are two other versions with the same title and date: frames 1809–18 and 1820–23.

57 JA, Opening Address at the Junior Exhibition, *Rockford Seminary Magazine* 8 (Apr. 1880): 110–11, reel 46, frames 0196–97, reprinted in Bryan et al., *Selected Papers*, 1:350–54. "Bread givers" was the class motto. Phrases from this talk reappear in "Our debts: and how shall we pay them," [Oct. 8, 1887], reel 46, frames 0105–12.

58 JA, "Cassandra," *Rockford Seminary, Thirtieth Commencement, Essays of Graduating Class, Wednesday, June 22, 1881* (DeKalb, Ill.: News Stream Press, 1881), 36–39, reel 27, frames 0458–61. In this published version, *auethoritas* is a misprint for *auctoritas*, a term of respect for Roman civic leaders; Knight, *Citizen*, 107. "Cassandra" is reprinted in Bryan et al., *Selected Papers*, 1:428–32. Addams had recently published an article about Heinrich Schliemann's archeological expeditions to uncover the ancient city of Troy; "Self Tradition," *Rockford Seminary Magazine* 9 (Apr. 1881): 97–100, reel 46, frames 0314–16.

59 Earlier, Addams wrote of the poet Aurora Leigh, eponymous heroine of Elizabeth Barrett Browning's long narrative poem: "and while she cannot comprehend a million sick [she] weeps with pity over a pale factory child," in "The Passion of revenge and mercy as a producing element in Literature" [1880–81?], reel 46, frame 0116.

60 JA, "Tramps," Apr. 10, 1878, reel 45, frame 1758. For another American subject, see "The Present Policy of Congress," Dec. 5, 1877, reel 45, frames 1686–89, which argues that the post–Civil War South "should be treated with justice and not mercy."

61 While preparing her Cassandra address, Addams asked her stepbrother for a "little

dissertation" on "the impact of the Scientific method of education on habits of mind" (JA to George Haldeman, May 29, 1881, reel 1).

62 JA, "Resolved. The Civilization of the 19th cent. tends to fetter intellectual life and expression. Aff.," Feb. 18, 1880, reel 46, frames 0181–84. See Thomas Henry Huxley, "A Liberal Education, and Where to Find It," in *Lay Sermons, Addresses, and Reviews* (New York: D. Appleton & Co., 1870), 27–53.

There is a marked similarity between Addams's views on scientific training and those of John Stuart Blackie, professor of Greek at the University of Edinburgh, whom she read while working on the Cassandra address. He urged young men to commence their studies "by direct OBSERVATION of FACTS, and not by the mere inculcation of statements from books." To this end, he recommended the natural sciences; *On Self-Culture: Intellectual, Physical, and Moral; A Vade Mecum for Young Men and Students*, 4th ed. (Edinburgh: Edmonston and Douglas, 1874), 2.

63 When she spoke in her senior year of "a settled passion" for studying medicine in Edinburgh as the "next thing to old Athens itself," Addams contrasted the medical culture there with Germany, which "is very fine but still it is mostly learning" (JA to Ellen Gates Starr, Feb. 13, 1881, reel 1).

64 Ibid.

65 JA to Ellen Gates Starr, Aug. 11, 1879, reel 1. See also JA to Ellen Gates Starr, Nov. 22, 1879, reel 1.

66 JA, "Compilers," [1881], reel 46, frames 0273–78.

67 "Editorial," *Rockford Seminary Magazine* 9 (May 1881): 153, reel 46, frame 0352.

68 JA, "Resolved, The Civilization of the 19th cent.," reel 46, frames 0181–84.

69 JA, *Twenty Years*, 49.

70 JA to Ellen Gates Starr, May 15, 1880, reel 1; "Editorial," *Rockford Seminary Magazine* 9 (March 1881): 88–89, reel 46, frame 0308; JA to Alice Addams Haldeman, Jan. 3, 1886, reel 2.

71 Addams was also impressed by the missionary's emphasis on the intellectual side of this work, including the knowledge of languages; JA to Eva Campbell, July 25/29, 1879, reel 1, reprinted, with commentary, in Bryan et al., *Selected Papers*, 1:268–78. In an earlier essay on "Dress," Addams considered Africans and South Sea Islanders "barbarians" because they never had to exert themselves even enough to clothe themselves; Mar. 15, 1878, reel 45, frames 1730–35.

72 She copied one of the missionary's points into her commonplace book: "Self culture impales a man on his personal pronouns" ("Notebook," 1878–?), reel 27, frame 0168.

73 JA, "The *Magnificence* of Character," Oct. 5, 1880, reel 46, 0220–24.

74 Helen Harrington to JA, Apr. 15, 1882, reel 1. Harrington, who had read *King Lear* with Addams, thought that Lear's daughter, Cordelia, expressed her friend's "old idea."

75 In "The Snare of Preparation," ch. 4 of *Twenty Years*, Addams claimed that the phrase, which she sometimes gave as "the snare of self-preparation," came from Tolstoy (88).

76 Addams's fullest statement on this subject is *Democracy and Social Ethics* (1902; reprint, Cambridge, Mass.: Harvard University Press, 1964).

77 JA, *Twenty Years*, 73.

78 Ibid., 65. The recent discussions of Addams's medical condition in Louise Knight, *Citizen*, 119–25, and Victoria Bissell Brown, *Education*, 117–18, 124–25, modify earlier, more melodramatic and reductively psychoanalytic accounts.

79 JA to Ellen Gates Starr, Aug. 12, 1883, reel 1. In *Twenty Years*, Addams characteristically blamed herself for taking the easy route, claiming that after her recovery from surgery, she began Carlyle's *Frederick the Great* with "a lively sense of gratitude that it was not Gray's 'Anatomy,' having found, like many another, that general culture is a much easier undertaking than professional study" (65). Starr, however, viewed her friend's choice of this six-volume work as convalescent reading as a sign of her "thoroughly superior mind." Ellen Gates Starr to JA, Jan. 12 [1883], reel 1.

80 JA to Alice Addams Haldeman, Mar. 6, 1884, reel 1.

81 JA, *Twenty Years*, 73–75; JA to Alice Addams Haldeman, Jan. 17 [1884], reel 1; JA Diary, Jan. 15, 1884, reel 29.

82 JA to Mary Addams Linn, Mar. 31, 1884, reel 1.

83 JA to Sarah F. Blaisdell, Mar. 15/Apr. 26, 1884; see also JA to George Haldeman, Mar. 21, 1884, both on reel 1.

84 On the principles of positivism and its British varieties, see T. R. Wright, *The Religion of Humanity: The Impact of Comtean Positivism on Victorian Britain* (Cambridge: Cambridge University Press, 1986).

85 JA, *Twenty Years*, 82. See also Linn, *Jane Addams*, 77.

86 On George Eliot, see Wright, *The Religion of Humanity*, 173–201, quotation on 179.

87 J. B. Bullen, "George Eliot's *Romola* as a Positivist Allegory," *Review of English Studies*, n.s., 26 (1975): 425–35.

88 Addams explicitly linked George Eliot to Positivism in an important talk to the Chicago Woman's Club soon after founding Hull-House: "Positivism insists that the very religious fervor of man can be turned into love for his race, and his desire for a future life into content to live in the echo of his deeds. This is what George Eliot passionately voices." JA, "Outgrowths of Toynbee Hall" [Dec. 1890], 8, reel 46, frame 0488.

89 JA to Ellen Gates Starr, Mar. 9, 1884, reel 1.

90 On family relations, see the recollections of Addams's niece, Marcet Haldeman-Julius, "Jane Addams as I Knew Her," *Reviewer's Library* 7 (Girard, Kans.: Haldeman-Julius, 1936).

91 JA to Alice Addams Haldeman, Oct. 23, 1885, reel 2. For a *Romola* class at Hull-House, see chapter 7.

92 JA to George Haldeman, Mar. 8 1884, reel 1.

93 JA to Alice Addams Haldeman, Jan. 3, Feb. 28, Feb. 17, and Jan. 25, 1886, and JA to Ellen Gates Starr, Feb. 7, 1886, reel 2. Except for the course on United Italy, information about Addams's activities in this and the following paragraph comes from letters written in the winters of 1885–86 and 1886–87.

94 JA to Laura S. Addams, Dec. 1, 1886; JA to Alice Addams Haldeman, Dec. 8 and Dec. 15, 1886, and January [1887], reel 2.

95 JA, *Twenty Years*, 77.

96 Ibid.

97 JA to Ellen Gates Starr, Feb. 7, 1886, reel 2. Addams suggested that ill health may have been at the root of the trouble and thought she was on the road to recovery. But ten days later, she observed, "My faculties has [*sic*] been apparently paralyzed since I have been here, and I haven't studied 'worth a cent.' I hope to improve." JA to Alice Addams Haldeman, Feb. 17, 1886, reel 2.

98 JA to Laura S. Addams, Dec. 28, 1886; see also JA to Alice Addams Haldeman, Dec. 28, 1886, reel 2.

99 JA, "Our debts; and how shall we pay them," [Oct. 8, 1887], reel 46, frames 0105–12.

100 JA to George Haldeman, June 9, 1888; and JA to Alice Addams Haldeman, June 5, 1888, both on reel 2.

101 JA to Flora B. Guiteau, Jan. 7, 1888, reel 2.

102 JA, *Twenty Years*, 82–83.

103 JA to Flora B. Guiteau, Jan. 7, 1888.

104 JA, *Twenty Years*, 83. Addams claimed that she had "imagined from what the art books said that the cathedral horded [*sic*] a medieval statement of the Positivists' final synthesis, prefiguring their conception of a 'Supreme Humanity.'" Contemporary evidence on the point is lacking. Addams kept pocket diaries during these years, but the one for 1888, which may have been the "smug notebook" to which she refers, is missing.

It is curious that she did not mention Ruskin as an inspiration for her study of Gothic cathedrals in *Twenty Years* or in the Ulm letter. His vision of Gothic as a symbol of unity and religious renewal had great currency in the United States. Not only was Ruskin a great favorite of Starr's, but Addams was familiar with his work on painting and read his *Bible of Amiens* when she visited the cathedral there later on this trip.

105 JA, "A Visit to Tolstoy," *McClure's Magazine* 36 (Jan. 1911): 296. Addams claimed in *Twenty Years* (261) that she read *My Religion* "immediately after I left college," but the book was not translated into English until 1885. Her personal library included *What I Believe* (*My Religion* under a different title) in an 1885 English translation; "Books from Jane Addams's Personal Library," reel 28. It is likely that one of these versions was one of "the two Tolstois" she read in November 1886; JA to Alice Addams Haldeman, Nov. 24, 1886, reel 2.

106 JA, "A Book That Changed My Life," *Christian Century* 44 (Oct. 13, 1927): 1196–98. Addams dated her reading of *What to Do?* (later translated as *What to Do Then*) to "the late eighties." The work appeared in English translation under the title *What to Do?: Thoughts Evoked by the Census of Moscow* in 1887. A catalog card for an English translation of *What to Do?* in Addams's personal library at Hull-House is dated "[1888?]"; "Books from Jane Addams's Personal Library," reel 28.

107 JA to Ellen Gates Starr, Feb. 7 and July 17, 1886, reel 2. In the second letter, Addams reports her decision to frame "Melancholia," Dürer's powerful and brooding female figure singled out by Ruskin, rather than Michelangelo's Sibyl.

108 John Ruskin, *Modern Painters* (London: J. M. Dent; New York: E. P. Dutton, 1860–62), 5:222–32.

109 Addams was sufficiently interested in the Catacombs to teach a course of six lectures on the subject at the Deaconess's Training School in Chicago, "upon

the simple ground that this early interpretation of Christianity is the one which should be presented to the poor, urging that the primitive church was composed of the poor and that it was they who took the wonderful news to the more prosperous Romans" (*Twenty Years*, 84). The statement reflects an interest in simpler and more egalitarian forms of Christianity that surfaces frequently in Addams's writings. In the Ulm letter, for example, she noted that she had recently met some "'Old Catholics'" who "reject the infallibility of the Pope and all the other errors which have crept into the Church, and go back to the primitive catholicity to *the* church" (JA to Flora B. Guiteau, Jan. 7, 1888).

CHAPTER SEVEN

1 On Toynbee Hall, see Standish Meacham, *Toynbee Hall and Social Reform, 1880– 1914: The Search for Community* (New Haven: Yale University Press, 1987); and [Henrietta Octavia Rowland Barnett], *Canon Barnett: Warden of the First University Settlement, Toynbee Hall, Whitechapel, London; His Life, Work, and Friends; By His Wife* (Boston: Houghton Mifflin, 1919), esp. vol. 1. An important early statement of Addams's objectives is "Outgrowths of Toynbee Hall," typescript [Dec. 1890], in *The Jane Addams Papers*, ed. Mary Lynn McCree Bryan (Ann Arbor: University Microfilms International, 1984), reel 46, frames 0480–96. All otherwise unidentified manuscript citations are from this edition. Two recent biographies have enhanced our understanding of Addams's early years at Hull-House: Louise W. Knight, *Citizen: Jane Addams and the Struggle for Democracy* (Chicago: University of Chicago Press, 2005); and Victoria Bissell Brown, *The Education of Jane Addams* (Philadelphia: University of Pennsylvania Press, 2004). See also Kathryn Kish Sklar, *Florence Kelley and the Nation's Work: The Rise of Women's Political Culture, 1830–1900* (New Haven: Yale University Press, 1995), 171–315. For overviews of the female-based social reform movement in which Addams played a major role, see Robyn Muncy, *Creating a Female Dominion in American Reform, 1890–1935* (New York: Oxford University Press, 1991); Allen F. Davis, *Spearheads for Reform: The Social Settlements and the Progressive Movement, 1890–1914* (New York: Oxford University Press, 1967); and Mina Carson, *Settlement Folk: Social Thought and the American Settlement Movement, 1885–1930* (Chicago: University of Chicago Press, 1990). For a critical view of Hull-House in relation to recent immigrants, see Rivka Shpak Lissak, *Pluralism and Progressives: Hull House and the New Immigrants, 1890–1919* (Chicago: University of Chicago Press, 1989).

2 Jane Addams, *Twenty Years at Hull-House* (New York: Macmillan, 1910), 94. Addams's name is abbreviated hereafter as JA.

3 A major exception is Shannon Jackson, who makes an imaginative and persuasive case for the integral relationship between Hull-House's reform program and the aesthetic views of its founders; *Lines of Activity: Performance, Historiography, Hull-House Domesticity* (Ann Arbor: University of Michigan Press, 2001), esp. 16–17.

4 The settlement's charter defined its mission: "To provide a center for a higher civic and social life; to institute and maintain educational and philanthropic enterprises; and to investigate and improve the conditions in the industrial districts of Chi-

cago." *Hull-House Bulletin* 1 (Jan. 1910): 1, reel 53. For Addams's views on women's responsibilities, see, for example, JA, "Outgrowths," 2.

5 I am extending Deborah Brandt's concept of "sponsors of literacy" to sponsorship of culture at large, literacy included; *Literacy in American Lives* (Cambridge: Cambridge University Press, 2001).

6 Addams's early views appear in "Outgrowths," esp. 9–10. For a thoughtful analysis of Addams's ideas on culture, their sources, and their application to Hull-House, see Harriet Averbuch Katz, "Cathedral of Humanity: A Study of Jane Addams' Ideas on Art and Culture," D.S.W. diss., Yeshiva University, 1975. See also Helen Lefkowitz Horowitz, *Culture and the City: Cultural Philanthropy in Chicago from the 1880s to 1917* (Lexington: University Press of Kentucky, 1976), 126–44.

7 JA, "The Subjective Necessity for Social Settlements," in *Philanthropy and Social Progress* (New York: Thomas Y. Crowell, 1893), 9–10, and "Outgrowths," 11.

8 JA, "Outgrowths," 11.

9 JA, "Subjective Necessity," 6, and "Hull House as a Type of College Settlements [*sic*]," Wisconsin State Conference of Charities and Correction, *Proceedings* (1894), 112. For men and women of "former education and opportunity" brought low by misfortune, Addams believed the settlement would provide the opportunity to reconnect with a happier past; "The Objective Value of a Social Settlement," *Philanthropy and Social Progress* (New York: Thomas Y. Crowell, 1893), 39.

10 Shannon Jackson has done pioneering work in reconstructing daily life at Hull-House. Drawing on the field of performance studies, in *Lines of Activity* she provides a stimulating guide to the ambiguities of Hull-House rhetoric and settlement practices, ending up on the positive side of the ledger.

11 JA to Alice Addams Haldeman, Oct. 8, 1889, reel 2. Information in this and the following paragraph is drawn mainly from the Jane Addams Diary, 1889–90, reel 29; letters of Addams and Starr, reel 2; and *Twenty Years*. For an overview, see Mary Lynn McCree, "The First Year of Hull-House, 1889–1890, in Letters by Jane Addams and Ellen Gates Starr," *Chicago History* 1 (1970): 101–14.

12 JA to Alice Addams Haldeman, Oct. 8, 1889; JA Diary, Oct. 18, 1889.

13 As with other services initiated by the settlement, like the public bath and the playground, the library was later taken over by the city.

14 "Hull-House: A Social Settlement," in *Hull-House Maps and Papers*, by Residents of Hull-House (New York: Thomas Y. Crowell, 1895), 208.

15 See, for example, John C. Farrell, *Beloved Lady: A History of Jane Addams' Ideas on Reform and Peace* (Baltimore: Johns Hopkins University Press, 1967), 59–60; and Allen F. Davis, *American Heroine: The Life and Legend of Jane Addams* (New York: Oxford University Press, 1973), 67.

16 JA Diary, esp. entries for Jan. 30, Feb. 24, and March 3, 1890, reel 29.

17 JA, *Twenty Years*, 101. The photographs, which Addams and Starr had collected in Europe, were among the prized possessions in their new home.

18 See Nancy Schrom Dye, *As Equals and as Sisters: Feminism, the Labor Movement, and the Women's Trade Union League of New York* (Columbia: University of Missouri Press, 1980); and Louise Levitas Henriksen, *Anzia Yezierska: A Writer's Life* (New Brunswick, N.J.: Rutgers University Press, 1988).

19 Hilda Satt Polacheck, *I Came a Stranger: The Story of a Hull-House Girl*, ed. Dena J. Polacheck Epstein (Urbana: University of Illinois Press, 1991), 74–75, 86. For other neighbors who reacted positively to Addams, see Jean Bethke Elshtain, *Jane Addams and the Dream of American Democracy: A Life* (New York: Basic Books, 2002), 8–14.

20 Abraham Bisno, *Abraham Bisno: Union Pioneer* (Madison: University of Wisconsin Press, 1967), 118, 119. On cross-class alliances, see Kathryn Kish Sklar, "Hull House in the 1890s: A Community of Women Reformers," *Signs* 10 (Summer 1985): 658–77.

21 JA, *Twenty Years*, 101.

22 JA Diary, Dec. 11, 1889, reel 29.

23 Joseph Wiesenfarth, "George Eliot (Mary Ann Evans)," *Dictionary of Literary Biography*, vol. 21, *Victorian Novelists before 1885*, ed. Ira B. Nadel and William E. Fredeman (Detroit: Gale Research Co., 1983), 162; and "George Eliot," *Nineteenth-Century Literature Criticism*, ed. Laurie Lanzen Harris and Sheila Fitzgerald (Detroit: Gale Research Co., 1983), 4:101.

24 Jane Reoch to Ellen Gates Starr, Aug. 31, 1909, Ellen Gates Starr Papers, Sophia Smith Collection, Smith College. See also Jennifer Lynne Bosch, "The Life of Ellen Gates Starr, 1859–1940" (Ph.D. diss., Miami University, 1990).

25 "Hull-House: A Social Settlement," in *Hull-House Maps and Papers*, 208–9. By "humanities" Addams and Starr meant nonvocational courses, not necessarily those in literature and art. By October 1896, the designation "advanced" replaced "college extension" classes in the *Hull-House Bulletin*. See Maureen A. Fay, "Origins and Early Development of the University of Chicago Extension Division, 1892–1911" (Ed.D. diss., University of Chicago, 1976).

26 [Jane Addams and Ellen Gates Starr], *Hull-House: A Social Settlement; An Outline Sketch* (privately printed, dated Feb. 1, 1894), 4, 6–10, reel 53, frames 1528–32. Similar in title to the appendix in *Hull-House Maps and Papers*, this pamphlet has many details about early classes. For earlier classes, see "Hull-House College Extension Classes . . . Beginning on Monday, September 28, 1891," reel 50, frames 0862–64.

27 On winter 1894 college extension classes, see Addams and Starr, *Hull-House: A Social Settlement*, 4–10; and JA, "Objective Value," 39–44.

28 Information on Addams's classes comes from Hull-House program announcements on reel 50. The titles are inconsistent. Her classes on *The Marble Faun* are listed in the programs beginning September 28, 1891, and April 18, 1892; *Les Misérables* in the programs beginning April 6 and September 6, 1891; *Felix Holt* in the programs beginning January 11 and March 1, 1892; and *Alton Locke* in the programs beginning October 17, 1892, and January 2, 1893. Addams also led reading parties at the Hull-House summer school held at Rockford College, one on *Les Misérables* in 1891, a second on George Eliot the following year.

29 JA to Starr, Dec. 28, 1879, reel 1; JA to Alice Addams Haldeman, Sept. 13, 1889, reel 2.

30 Starr, a founder and first president of the Chicago Public School Art Society, was the primary catalyst for the settlement's enthusiastic embrace of the visual arts. Its second building was an art gallery, and exhibits there figured in the founding of the Chicago Society of Arts and Crafts, as did Starr. Eileen Boris, *Art and Labor:*

Ruskin, Morris, and the Craftsman Ideal in America (Philadelphia: Temple University Press, 1986), 180–83, 46.

31 The reading party designation, which was adopted from Toynbee Hall, seems to have applied to groups in which the main activity was reading aloud; by 1900, at least, there was no charge for them.

32 Information on Starr's classes and other offerings is taken from Hull-House announcements of class schedules between 1890 and 1896. Starr taught during each session. Thereafter, course offerings are listed in the *Hull-House Bulletin* (1896–1906) and the *Hull-House Year Book* (1906–7).

33 *Hull-House Bulletin* 3, nos. 8 and 9 (Jan. and Feb. 1899): 6, and "The Mazzini Celebration," *Hull-House Bulletin* 7, no. 1 (1905–6): 23, both on reel 53.

34 The term is Shannon Jackson's, from *Lines of Activity*, 19.

35 Addams's nephew and biographer attributes his aunt's interest in "reading-clubs" to "the memory of . . . evenings of reading aloud" with her stepmother and stepbrother; James Weber Linn, *Jane Addams: A Biography* (New York: D. Appleton-Century, 1935), 30.

36 JA, "Subjective Necessity," 10.

37 See, for example, Madge C. Jenison, "A Hull House Play," *Atlantic Monthly* 98 (July 1906): 83–92.

38 JA, "Objective Value," 40.

39 Polacheck, *I Came a Stranger*, written in the author's early seventies, is dedicated to Addams and bears the imprint of the author's Hull-House mentors whose reform values Polacheck continued to embrace. Details of Polacheck's career may be followed in the excellent and detailed notes by her daughter, Dena J. Polacheck Epstein. Page references are henceforth incorporated in the text.

40 Polacheck also became a demonstrator of Navajo weaving techniques at the Labor Museum; *Hull-House Bulletin* 5, no. 2 (1902): 10.

41 See *Hull-House Year Book* (Sept. 1, 1906–Sept. 1, 1907), 8.

42 See "Ariadne Club," *Hull-House Bulletin* 5, no. 1 (1902): 10.

43 The story is told in Polacheck, *I Came a Stranger*, 111–26. In a characteristic gesture, Addams served kosher chicken at the wedding reception, unaware that the presence of dairy products subverted her intent (126). On "The Walking Delegate," see Laura Dainty Pelham, "The Story of the Hull-House Players," *Drama* (May 1916): 253–54. One reviewer called the play "uncanny in its realism"; quoted in Jackson, *Lines of Activity*, 242.

44 For Polacheck's publications, see *I Came a Stranger*, Appendix B, 189–93.

45 Information about the class composition comes from "Hull-House: A Social Settlement," in *Hull-House: Maps and Papers*, 208. For a male perspective, see Philip Davis, *And Crown Thy Good* (New York: Philosophical Library, 1952), 81–93.

46 Edward L. Burchard to Starr, Jan. 16, 1938, Starr Papers.

47 See Rosalind Rosenberg, *Beyond Separate Spheres: Intellectual Roots of Modern Feminism* (New Haven: Yale University Press, 1982), esp. 43–51. In the early 1900s, the University of Chicago segregated women undergraduates in a separate junior college and also created separate departments for professional specialties in which women were concentrated.

48 "Hull-House: A Social Settlement," *Hull-House Maps and Papers*, 208.

49 The fact that local high school teachers constituted the first Latin class suggests that even esoteric subjects could have vocational possibilities. On classics at Hull-House, see Judith P. Hallett, "The Lessons of 'Cassandra': Classical Learning and the Classical Legacy of Jane Addams and Hull House," unpublished paper in the author's possession.

50 "Syllabus of the *Tragedy of King Lear,* Hull-House College Extension" [1891–92], reel 50, frame 0871.

51 "Hull-House Shakespeare Club," *Hull-House Bulletin* 7, no. 1 (1905–6): 10; and *Hull-House Year Book* (Sept. 1, 1906–Sept. 1, 1907), 9.

52 Information from listings under the title "Hull-House Shakespeare Club." On *Othello,* see *Hull-House Bulletin* 6, no. 2 (Autumn 1904): 9–10. For membership estimate see *Hull-House Year Book* (Sept. 1, 1906–Sept. 1, 1907), 9.

53 "Hull-House Shakespeare Club," *Hull-House Bulletin* 7, no. 1 (1905–6): 10. On one occasion, Addams led a discussion of an essay on Shakespeare and religion by philosopher George Santayana.

54 "Hull-House Shakespeare Club," *Hull-House Year Book* (1910), 9.

55 The Shakespeare Club and class marked only one manifestation of interest in the bard, whose plays continued to be performed at Hull-House after the group's demise. Like reading, Shakespeare suffused settlement activities, including those of young people's groups, which often put on his plays.

56 Lawrence W. Levine has documented efforts by urban elites to redefine Shakespeare's plays as high culture and extrude the lower orders from legitimate theater, processes he associates with the "sacralization" of Shakespeare and culture more generally in the late nineteenth century; "William Shakespeare in America," *Highbrow/Lowbrow: The Emergence of Cultural Hierarchy in America* (Cambridge, Mass.: Harvard University Press, 1988), 14–81. The Hull-House example suggests that the bard still had broad appeal.

57 Jenison, "A Hull House Play," 85, 83.

58 Kate Clifford Larson, "The Saturday Evening Girls: A Progressive Era Literary Club and the Intellectual Life of Working Class and Immigrant Girls in Turn-of-the-Century Boston," *Library Quarterly* 71 (Apr. 2001): 195–230. Larson's study draws on the group's newsletter and later oral histories with members.

59 Quotations from JA, "Social Education of the Industrial Democracy: Settlement Problems in Educational Work with Adults, Labor Museum at Hull House," *Commons* 5 (June 30, 1900): 1, and *Democracy and Social Ethics* (1902; reprint, ed. Anne Firor Scott, Cambridge, Mass.: Harvard University Press, 1964), 199. See also ibid., 200; and JA, "Jane Addams's Own Story of Her Work: How the Work at Hull-House Has Grown," *Ladies' Home Journal* 32 (May 1906): 11–12, 48.

60 JA, "Social Education of the Industrial Democracy," 1.

61 JA, "Hull House as a Type of College Settlements," 113, and "Extracts from an Address on 'What the Theater at Hull House Has Done for the Neighborhood People,'" Third Monthly Conference, *Charities* 8 (Mar. 29, 1902): 285, reel 46, frame 1096. See also JA, "Objective Value," 34, and "Outgrowths of Toynbee Hall," 15.

62 Lissak, *Pluralism and Progressives,* 108–9.

63 The evolution of English classes may be followed in the *Hull-House Bulletin* and the *Hull-House Year Book,* under the rubric "Classes (Secondary)." Hull-House also

placed increased emphasis on sports after the completion of the gymnasium in 1893.

64 The culture classes did not disappear entirely. A "Class in Advanced Literature," organized as a "study class" with twelve members about 1908, had nearly forty members five years later and continued until 1932, under the direction of W. L. Richardson of the University of Chicago. The group read many types of literature at first, but then seemed to concentrate on drama (it purchased thirty volumes of English drama "for study and reference"). Likened by the *Hull-House Year Book* to "an old-fashioned literary society," the group listened to six or seven reports on the evening's work and members submitted to a "searching oral examination" at the end of the year. *Hull-House Year Book* (1913), 8; *Hull-House Year Book* (1916), 8; *Hull-House Year Book* (1934), 6.

65 JA, "Hull House and Its Neighbors," *Charities* 12 (May 7, 1904): 450. Addams explicitly linked the two activities in "Jane Addams's Own Story of Her Work," 12.

66 "Extracts from an Address," 284.

67 JA, "House of Dreams," in *The Spirit of Youth and the City Streets* (1909; reprint, Urbana: University of Illinois Press, 1972), 75–103.

68 "Extracts from an Address," 286. Despite Addams's well-known antagonism to cheap movies, Hull-House opened a nickel theater in 1907 that featured fairy tales, foreign scenes, and "dramatizations of great moral lessons" such as those contained in *Uncle Tom's Cabin*; JA, "To Whom It May Concern," *Show World* 1 (Aug. 3, 1907), reel 46, frame 1589.

69 On theater at Hull-House, see the settlement's publications; Jackson, *Lines of Activity*, 203–47; Stuart Joel Hecht, "Hull-House Theatre: An Analytical and Evaluative History" (Ph.D. diss., Northwestern University, 1983); Edith de Nancrede, "Dramatic Work at Hull House," *Neighborhood: A Settlement Quarterly* 1 (Jan. 1928): 23–28, an account by the dance teacher and director of the Marionette Club; and JA, "The Play Instinct and the Arts," *Religious Education* 25 (Nov. 1930): 808–19.

70 See Stuart J. Hecht, "Social and Artistic Integration: The Emergence of a Hull-House Theatre," *Theatre Journal* 34 (May 1982): 172–82; Pelham, "The Story of the Hull-House Players," 249–62; and Elsie F. Weil, "The Hull-House Players," *Theatre Magazine*, Sept. 1913, reprinted in *100 Years at Hull-House*, ed. Mary Lynn McCree Bryan and Allen F. Davis (Bloomington: Indiana University Press, 1989), 92–95.

71 JA, "Extracts from an Address," 285; Elizabeth C. Barrows, "The Greek Play at Hull House," *Commons* 9 (Jan. 1904): 6. Cf. Lissak, *Pluralism and Progressives*, 104–7.

72 The Hull-House Players, though ethnically unmarked because of the group's English-language and high culture productions, had Irish affiliations: nearly half the actors were of Irish parentage, and the group produced many Irish plays and maintained relationships with theater groups in Ireland. See Pelham, "The Story of the Hull-House Players," 249–62; de Nancrede, "Dramatic Work at Hull House," 23; and Jackson, *Lines of Activity*, 233.

73 *First Report of the Labor Museum at Hull House, 1901–1902* (Privately printed, 1902), reel 46; JA, "The Humanizing Tendency of Industrial Education," *The Chatauquan* 39 (May 1904): 266–72; "Social Education of the Industrial Democracy," 17–20; and "Immigrants and Their Children," ch. 11 of *Twenty Years*. The progress of the Labor Museum may be followed in the *Hull-House Bulletin* and *Hull-House*

Year Book; see esp. "The Labor Museum" and "Art and the Labor Museum," *Hull-House Bulletin* 4 (Autumn 1900): 8–9. For an imaginative recent analysis, see Jackson, *Lines of Activity*, 253–82; for a contemporary account, see Marion Foster Washburne, "A Labor Museum," *Craftsman* 6 (Sept. 1904): 570–79.

74 Starr, who had studied bookbinding for nearly two years with T. J. Cobden-Sanderson, a British master craftsman, had charge of the bookbinding room.

75 For a thoughtful evaluation of the ambiguities of the educational ideas and programs of Dewey and his colleagues at the University of Chicago, with special reference to their views on labor, see Andrew Feffer, *The Chicago Pragmatists and American Progressivism* (Ithaca, N.Y.: Cornell University Press, 1993), esp. 91–146. Like Dewey, Addams emphasized mediation and education as ways of preventing class conflict.

76 JA, "Immigrants and Their Children," in *Twenty Years*, esp. 243–45.

77 JA, "Jane Addams's Own Story of Her Work," 12.

78 For Addams's views on the Labor Museum and on education more generally, particularly in relation to Dewey's ideas, see Farrell, *Beloved Lady*, 80–103.

79 For the views of Dewey and other contemporaries, see Robert B. Westbrook, *John Dewey and American Democracy* (Ithaca, N.Y.: Cornell University Press, 1991), 173–82; and Feffer, *The Chicago Pragmatists and American Progressivism*, esp. 131–41.

80 JA, *Twenty Years*, 45. Addams attributes the quotation to a "portentous statement from Aristotle which we found quoted in Boswell's Johnson."

81 JA, "A Function of the Social Settlement," *Annals of the American Academy of Political and Social Science* 13 (May 1899): 36. Tolstoy's *What Is Art?* appeared in an English translation in 1898. By "infection," he meant that the receiver of a work experiences the emotions of the creator. He considered genuine art a connecting force between people. See also JA, "Tolstoy's Theory of Life," *Chautauqua Assembly Herald* 27 (July 14, 1902): 2–3.

82 JA, *Democracy and Social Ethics*, 8–9. Addams's choice of language echoes the title of Walter Besant's *All Sorts and Conditions of Men* (1882), one of several books proposing cultural remedies to social problems that electrified American and British readers in the late 1880s. Addams predicted that readers for whom immigrants or the unemployed had been individualized in this way would never again cast ugly words or thoughts in their direction; JA, "The Newer Ideals of Peace," *Chautauqua Assembly Herald* 27 (July 8, 1902): 5. If Addams's views on these subjects seem naive or utopian, they reveal her affinity with other progressives who believed that for people of goodwill, knowing something was virtually a guarantee for acting on it.

For an excellent, brief discussion of Addams's views on the relation between culture and imagination, see James Dougherty, "Jane Addams: Culture and Imagination," *Yale Review* 71 (Spring 1982): 363–79. Martha C. Nussbaum, *Poetic Justice: The Literary Imagination and Public Life* (Boston: Beacon Press, 1995), esp. xiii–xix and 1–12, and Lynn Hunt, *Inventing Human Rights: A History* (New York: W. W. Norton, 2007), have recently argued for fiction's capacity to promote empathy and compassion for groups otherwise viewed as alien and lacking in individuality.

83 JA, "The Hull House Woman's Club," *Club Worker* 3 (Nov. 1901): 1.

84 JA, "A Function of the Social Settlement," 37–38. *Children of the Ghetto: A Study of*

a Peculiar People was popular in England and the United States; published in 1892, it went through nine editions by 1938 and was widely praised for its realism.

85 JA, "The Newer Ideals of Peace," 5. Addams compared the novelist's efforts to understand all sorts of people "done in a spirit of reverent truth seeking" with those of the scientist; "The New Social Spirit," *Proceedings of the National Council of Jewish Women* (1902): 18.

86 For Addams, interpretation was a key concept. For an analysis of her views on social science and the way in which her literary imagination provided a basis for them, see Dorothy Ross, "Gendered Social Knowledge: Domestic Discourse, Jane Addams, and the Possibilities of Social Science," in *Gender and American Social Science: The Formative Years*, ed. Helene Silverberg, 235–64 (Princeton, N.J.: Princeton University Press, 1998).

87 For Addams's interpretation of the deficits of the traditional charity worker, see *Democracy and Social Ethics*, ch. 1. See Dorothy Ross, "Gendered Social Knowledge," for a thoughtful analysis of the message and structure of this book, in particular Addams's role as an intermediary in each chapter.

88 JA, *Twenty Years*, 249–50, 246–47, 162.

89 JA, "A Function of the Social Settlement," 36.

90 Although Addams was deeply influenced by Tolstoy and visited him in 1896, she did not accept his controversial aesthetic or other theories uncritically (he dismissed Shakespeare and other celebrated artists because they did not reach the masses). For an account that includes her rejection of Tolstoy's injunction that everyone should perform physical labor, see "Tolstoyism," ch. 12 of *Twenty Years*.

91 Addams was fond of quoting Dewey: "Knowledge is no longer its own justification; the interest in it has at last transferred itself from accumulation and verification to its application to life" ("A Function of the Social Settlement," 34). For the relationship between Addams and pragmatist philosophers, in particular Addams's influence on Dewey, see Charlene Haddock Seigfried, *Pragmatism and Feminism: Reweaving the Social Fabric* (Chicago: University of Chicago Press, 1996), esp. 58–59, 73–79, 135, 227–33; and Louis Menand, *The Metaphysical Club* (New York: Farrar, Straus and Giroux, 2001), esp. 306–16.

92 Quoted in Westbrook, *John Dewey and American Democracy*, 89.

93 "A Modern Lear" is also a feat of considerable literary imagination. Begun in the aftermath of the 1894 strike, it was considered so controversial, despite the fact that Addams did not mention Pullman by name, that several publishers rejected it, and it did not appear in print until 1912; "A Modern Lear," *Survey* 29 (Nov. 2, 1912): 131–37. For a recent analysis, see Louise W. Knight, "Biography's Window on Social Change: Benevolence and Justice in Jane Addams's 'A Modern Lear,'" *Journal of Women's History* 9 (Spring 1997): 111–38.

94 Philip Davis, *And Crown Thy Good*; Jackson, *Lines of Activity*, 203–47.

CHAPTER EIGHT

1 This chapter focuses on Jewish women from Russia (which then included much of Poland) about whom information is most plentiful. The situation was different elsewhere in eastern Europe, especially for those living in the Austro-Hungarian

Empire. Paula E. Hyman, *Gender and Assimilation in Modern Jewish History: The Roles and Representation of Women* (Seattle: University of Washington Press, 1995), provides an excellent introduction to the gendered nature of Jewish educational and religious practices in a comparative context.

For a comprehensive study of Jewish women's literacy, see Iris Parush, *Reading Jewish Women: Marginality and Modernization in Nineteenth-Century Eastern European Jewish Society* (Hanover, N.H.: University Press of New England, 2004); on education, see Shaul Stampfer, "Gender Differentiation and Education of the Jewish Woman in Nineteenth-Century Eastern Europe," *Polin: A Journal of Polish-Jewish Studies* 7 (1992): 63–87.

2 Shaul Stampfer highlights the role of *heders* in maintaining social hierarchy among men and concludes that there was a significant status gap between Jewish scholars and ordinary men, as there was between men and women; "*Heder* Study, Knowledge of Torah, and the Maintenance of Social Stratification in Traditional East European Jewish Society," *Studies in Jewish Education* 3 (Jerusalem: Magnes Press, Hebrew University, 1988), 271–89. See also Parush, *Reading Jewish Women*, 5, 63–65; and Chava Weissler, "'For Women and for Men Who Are like Women': The Construction of Gender in Yiddish Devotional Literature," *Journal of Feminist Studies in Religion* 5 (1989): 7–24.

3 Quoted in Parush, *Reading Jewish Women*, 62. *Tiflut* may be translated as "foolishness" as well as "promiscuity." Either way, learning Hebrew was considered undesirable for a woman.

4 Some women, known as *zogerkes* (speakers), were proficient in Hebrew and helped others read and understand the prayer book. See Ellen Kellman, "Women as Readers of Sacred and Secular [Yiddish] Literature: An Historical Overview," in *Conference Proceedings, Di froyen: Women and Yiddish: Tribute to the Past, Directions for the Future* (New York: National Council of Jewish Women's New York Section, Jewish Women's Resource Center, 1997), 18, and Parush, *Reading Jewish Women*, 134–36 and 207–40.

5 Chava Weissler, "Prayers in Yiddish and the Religious World of Ashkenazic Women," in *Jewish Women in Historical Perspective*, ed. Judith R. Baskin (Detroit: Wayne State University Press, 1991), 167; Israel Zinberg, *A History of Jewish Literature*, vol. 7, *Old Yiddish Literature from Its Origins to the Haskalah Period* (Cincinnati: Hebrew Union College Press, 1975), 129–33; and Stampfer, "Gender Differentiation," 70–72. Authorities differ on how often the *Tsenerene* was reprinted—one estimate is as high as 300—but agree on its popularity.

On devotional literature for women, see also Weissler, "'For Women and for Men Who Are Like Women,'" 7–24, "The Religion of Traditional Ashkenazic Women: Some Methodological Issues," *AJS Review: Journal of the Association for Jewish Studies* 12 (Spring 1987): 73–94, and "The Traditional Piety of Ashkenazic Women," in *Jewish Spirituality: From the Sixteenth-Century Revival to the Present*, ed. Arthur Green, 245–75 (New York: Crossroad, 1989).

6 See Parush, *Reading Jewish Women*, 62, 88–89, and Deborah R. Weissman, "Education of Jewish Women," *Encyclopaedia Judaica Year Book* (Jerusalem: Encyclopaedia Judaica, 1986–87), 29–36. Stampfer emphasizes more modern values among well-

to-do families and the later age of marriage as factors in their willingness to educate daughters; "Gender Differentiation," 76–78.

7 Stampfer, "Gender Differentiation," 66. See also Isaac M. Rubinow, *Economic Condition of the Jews in Russia* (U.S. Bureau of Labor Bulletin 15, 1907; reprint, New York: Arno Press, 1975), 580.

8 Stampfer, "Gender Differentiation," 78. In general, girls fared better in Austrian Galicia; an estimated 40 percent of school-age Jewish girls attended public schools in 1890, compared to 25 percent of the boys; a decade later the proportions were 60 and 45 percent, respectively; ibid., 79–80.

9 S. M. Dubnow, *History of the Jews in Russia and Poland: From the Earliest Times until the Present Day*, trans. I. Friedlaender (Philadelphia: Jewish Publication Society of America, 1918), 2:350. See also *Jewish Grandmothers*, ed. Sydelle Kramer and Jenny Masur (Boston: Beacon Press, 1976), 91, 127, 142.

10 According to the Russian census of 1897, 22.5 percent of Jewish women over ten could read Russian; the figure for men was 42.9 percent. Rubinow, *Economic Condition*, 579–81. Rubinow claims that tutoring was within the means of even poor Jewish families, but Stampfer considers it expensive; "Gender Differentiation," 65.

11 Rose Pesotta, *Days of Our Lives* (Boston: Excelsior Publishers, 1958), 118–30.

12 Parush, *Reading Jewish Women*, makes a particularly strong case for "the benefit of marginality," 57–70, 88–89, 172–206. See also Iris Parush, "Readers in Cameo: Women Readers in Jewish Society of Nineteenth-Century Eastern Europe," *Prooftexts* 14 (Jan. 1994): 1–23; Hyman, *Gender and Assimilation*, 50–92; and Kellman, "Women as Readers," 19–21.

13 Pesotta, *Days of Our Lives*, 126–30, 169–80. Clara Lemlich Shavelson also read revolutionary literature in Russian, a language she studied despite her parents' disapproval; Paula Scheier, "Clara Lemlich Shavelson: 50 Years in Labor's Front Line," *Jewish Life* 9 (November 1954): 7–11. On Jewish women leaders of the American labor movement, see Annelise Orleck, *Common Sense and a Little Fire: Women and Working-Class Politics in the United States, 1900–1965* (Chapel Hill: University of North Carolina Press, 1995), and Joyce Antler, *The Journey Home: Jewish Women and the American Century* (New York: Free Press, 1997), 73–97.

14 The title of the most popular knightly romance, the *Bovo-Bukh*, written in the sixteenth century, was corrupted first to *Bobo-Bukh* and then to *Bobo-Maisse*, a combination of the words for "grandmother" (*bobo*) and "story" (*maisse*): an old-wives' tale; Sol Liptzin, *A History of Yiddish Literature* (Middle Village, N.Y.: Jonathan David, 1972), 5–8.

15 David G. Roskies, "Yiddish Popular Literature and the Female Reader," *Journal of Popular Culture* 10 (Spring 1977): 852–58; Charles A. Madison, *Yiddish Literature: Its Scope and Major Writers* (New York: Frederick Ungar, 1968), 24. Kellman, "Women as Readers," and Parush, "Readers in Cameo," both emphasize that men too read Yiddish fiction; Parush also analyzes the practice of addressing a female audience, 13–16.

16 Rubinow, *Economic Condition*, 577; Samuel Joseph, *Jewish Immigration to the United States from 1881 to 1910* (New York: Columbia University/Longmans, Green & Co., 1914), 192–94. The discrepancy between the two studies reflects at least in

part the youth of immigrants to the United States since literacy was greatest among younger cohorts. In the Russian census of 1897, for example, 43.7 percent of Jewish women ages 10–19 and 45.6 percent of those 20–29 were able to read in some language, as compared to 14.9 percent of those 60 years or over; Simon Kuznets, "Immigration of Russian Jews to the United States: Background and Structure," *Perspectives in American History* 9 (1975): 79–82. Since illiteracy was defined in the survey of entering immigrants as the inability to read *and* write, the figure most likely included women and men who could read but not write.

17 Joseph, *Jewish Immigration*, 148, 192–94. Illiteracy rates among neighboring Lithuanian, Polish, Russian, and Ruthenian immigrants for the year 1908, though higher among women and overall, were less skewed by gender.

18 On Jewish immigrant women's desire for education, see Sydney Stahl Weinberg, *The World of Our Mothers: The Lives of Jewish Immigrant Women* (New York: Schocken Books, 1988), 167–83. On school attendance, see Ruth Jacknow Markowitz, *My Daughter, the Teacher: Jewish Teachers in the New York City Schools* (New Brunswick, N.J.: Rutgers University Press, 1993), 6; and on the second generation, Deborah Dash Moore, *At Home in America: Second Generation New York Jews* (New York: Columbia University Press, 1981).

19 Pesotta, *Days of Our Lives*, 103.

20 Corinne Azen Krause, *Grandmothers, Mothers, and Daughters: An Oral History Study . . .*, cited in Paula E. Hyman, "Gender and the Immigrant Jewish Experience in the United States," in Baskin, *Jewish Women in Historical Perspective*, 225. See also Orleck, *Common Sense and a Little Fire*, 1–11.

21 Works on American Jewish women's history that consider the shifting gender balance in the transition from Old World to New include Hyman, *Gender and Assimilation*; Weinberg, *The World of Our Mothers*; and Susan A. Glenn, *Daughters of the Shtetl: Life and Labor in the Immigrant Generation* (Ithaca, N.Y.: Cornell University Press, 1990).

22 I wish to thank Helen Lang for suggesting the term "expressive literacy."

23 Published in 1918 by George H. Doran, *Out of the Shadow* was reprinted in 1995 by Cornell University Press, in a volume edited by Thomas Dublin; hereafter cited as *OOTS*. Otherwise unidentified quotations from Cohen are from this source; page references are given in the text.

24 A sixth sibling was born in the United States. Cohen's given name was Rahel. In the United States she was called "Ruth" and sometimes "Rose" and wrote under the name "Rose Cohen." Although the autobiography ends before her marriage, I refer to her as Cohen throughout.

25 Rose Cohen, "The Books I Knew as a Child," *Bookman* 49 (Mar. 1919): 15. The unnamed narratives might have included *The Arabian Nights*, *Sinbad the Sailor*, and *Robinson Crusoe*, all popular among Russian Jews at the time.

26 Cohen, "Books," 15–16. Of the Hebrew Psalms, Cohen wrote: "here and there I understood a few words and I put my whole soul into them." See also Cohen, "My Childhood Days in Russia," *Bookman* 47 (Aug. 1918): 592. Mary Antin similarly recounts her rote and uncomprehending recitation of the Psalms—in her case before an open window for passersby to hear; she too preferred them to other home reading; *The Promised Land* (Boston: Houghton Mifflin, 1912), 113.

27 On "traditional literacy," see David D. Hall, "The Uses of Literacy in New England, 1600–1850," in *Printing and Society in Early America*, ed. William L. Joyce et al., 1–47 (Worcester, Mass.: American Antiquarian Society, 1983).

28 Cohen, "Books," 16. The fact that Cohen received Russian lessons, however briefly, is one indication that shtetl life was becoming less restrictive during the last decades of the century. Thanks to Kenneth Moss for pointing this out.

29 Susan L. Lytle, "Living Literacy: Rethinking Development in Adulthood," *Literacy: A Critical Sourcebook*, ed. Ellen Cushman et al. (Boston: Bedford/St. Martin's, 2001), 382.

30 Some young Jews, particularly in larger cities, encountered secular books and magazines in Russia. Mary Antin discovered secular literature, including sensational books and magazines, when she visited an uncle in Vitebsk; *The Promised Land*, 156–58.

31 The story of Cohen's Yiddish reading discussed in this and the next paragraphs is from *OOTS*, 187–91, and "Books," 16–17. Like Rose Cohen, the philosopher Morris Raphael Cohen (no relation) recounts reading numerous books in Yiddish before he learned English; these too were translations, many of popular French authors. See *A Dreamer's Journey: The Autobiography of Morris Raphael Cohen* (Boston: Beacon Press, 1949), 72–73.

Beginning in the early 1890s, Yiddish translations and/or adaptations of fiction by western European authors were published in Europe and New York, often by booksellers. The subject has been too little studied, but see Moses Rischin, *The Promised City: New York's Jews, 1870–1914* (New York: Corinth Books, 1962), 130–32; Leo Wiener, *The History of Yiddish Literature in the Nineteenth Century* (New York: Charles Scribner's Sons, 1899), 224–26; and Charles A. Madison, *Jewish Publishing in America: The Impact of Jewish Writing on American Culture* (New York: Sanhedrin Press, 1976), 79–81. I am indebted to the late Dina Abramowicz of YIVO for her expert help in tracking down and translating several sources on Yiddish translations of European literatures.

32 In Hebrew, vowels are marked under the letters, but they are generally omitted in Yiddish. Paula Hyman, *Gender and Assimilation*, 82, suggests that vowel marks were included in a journal for women because of its "presumably minimally educated female readership."

33 For working-class women's preference for books of this sort, see Nan Enstad, *Ladies of Labor, Girls of Adventure: Working Women, Popular Culture, and Labor Politics at the Turn of the Twentieth Century* (New York: Columbia University Press, 1999).

34 Cohen, "Books," 16–17. Antin considered her period of "wild reading" a "debauch," but claims she suffered no harm from it; *The Promised Land*, 157–58.

35 *David Copperfield* was translated in 1894 by B. Gorin, the pen name of Isaac Goido, a Yiddish writer who migrated to New York. Harry Golden calls the novel "the standard book" of the lending libraries; *Les Misérables* was another; preface to Hutchins Hapgood, *The Spirit of the Ghetto: Studies of the Jewish Quarter of New York* (1902; reprint, New York: Schocken Books, 1966), xii.

36 Cohen, "Books," 17–18.

37 The fiancé allowed that he read when he had nothing better to do. Matters weren't

helped when he upbraided Cohen for incorrectly adding up a bill, which he insisted she do in front of a customer, despite her reluctance because of her innumeracy.

38 As a newcomer, Morris Raphael Cohen began keeping a journal after reading Benjamin Franklin's autobiography; *A Dreamer's Journey*, 85–86.

39 Charlotte Baum, Paula Hyman, and Sonya Michel, *The Jewish Woman in America* (New York: New American Library, 1975), 129; see also Mary Van Kleeck, *Working Girls in Evening Schools: A Statistical Study* (New York: Survey Associates, 1914).

40 Weinberg emphasizes the connection between birth order and educational opportunity: younger immigrant children were apt to go to school longer; *World of Our Mothers*, 173–76.

41 Cohen was not alone in her disappointment with night school. Not only were students exhausted from long hours of often arduous work, but many described classes as boring, useless ("I needed 'cat' and 'rat,' but we got Shakespeare"), or both. Quoted in Weinberg, *World of Our Mothers*, 170. Rose Pesotta, who found night school teaching methods antiquated and the teacher colorless and antagonistic to her students, learned English by reading novels from the East Ninety-sixth Street Branch of the public library, first in Russian, then in English, and by scrutinizing the daily press; *Days of Our Lives*, 247.

42 A doctor diagnosed Cohen's long illness as anemia (184); she once referred to it as "illness or semi-illness" (194–95). She spent several summers recuperating at a country farm connected with the settlement, where she assisted with younger children.

43 Cohen later wrote that she "learned to read English from the Bible in a hospital," but did not state that it was a New Testament; *The Best Short Stories of 1922*, ed. Edward J. O'Brien (Boston: Small, Maynard & Co., 1923), 309. In *OOTS*, she focused on the guilt, not on the achievement.

44 Cohen, "Books," 17.

45 Ibid., 18.

46 The novel, which advocated new gender and economic relationships, radicalized many Russian women.

47 Curiously, unlike Lillian Wald and other American settlement workers who appear in *OOTS* under their own names, Leonora O'Reilly is called Ann O'There. For O'Reilly's take on Cohen, see "Rahel of 'Out of the Shadow,'" *Life and Labor* 9 (May 1919): 103–5. There are additional comments about Cohen, the circle of young women, and O'Reilly's own literary interests in O'Reilly's diary, in *Papers of the Women's Trade Union League and Its Principal Leaders* (microfilm), ed. Edward T. James (Woodbridge, Conn.: Research Publications, 1979), reel 1.

48 Cohen, "Books," 18–19. This essay, published a year after *OOTS*, also suggests that literature was at times also a substitute for life: Cohen turned down a young man's offer of an outing, preferring to get back to *Middlemarch* to learn whether Dorothea Brooke would accept Causabon's proposal of marriage.

49 *OOTS*, 292–97. Although Jewish by birth, the man was studying at a Christian seminary. After more than a year, Cohen's father commanded her to stop writing, which, reluctantly, she did.

50 Of Rose and Joseph Cohen, O'Reilly observed: "They read much and deeply. They

shared their reading with others"; "Rahel of 'Out of the Shadow,'" 103–5, quotation on 103.

51 I am indebted to Tom Dublin for sharing information about Rose Cohen, including her daughter's birth year and her husband's later occupation.

52 Material in this and the following paragraph comes from Rose Gollup Cohen, "To the Friends of 'Out of the Shadow,'" *Bookman* 55 (Mar. 1922): 36–40. Cohen also took classes at the Thomas Davidson School of the Educational Alliance, a Jewish settlement, and at Columbia University. Gollomb suggested Antin's recently published *The Promised Land* as a model for writing her own experiences, but Cohen claims she could not locate a copy. *The Promised Land* begins, "I was born, I have lived, and I have been made over."

53 Cohen, "To the Friends," 36–37.

54 Edith Franklin Wyatt, "'Out of the Shadow': An Appreciation," *Life and Labor*, Apr. 1919, 79.

55 "'The Fruit of Unconscious Art,'" *New York Call*, Feb. 8, 1919, 11; "Out of the Shadow," *Outlook*, Nov. 6, 1918, 382. O'Reilly too claimed that "life has taught her to write"; "Rahel of 'Out of the Shadow.'" The *Call* observed that *OOTS* "makes . . . [Antin's] position as the only intelligent recorder of New York's Ghetto life exceedingly precarious."

56 See Thomas Dublin's introduction and bibliography in the 1995 edition of *OOTS*. Publications by Cohen not noted there are "The Meaning of Easter," *Life and Labor*, Apr. 1920; "The Thanksgiving of an Immigrant," *Life and Labor*, Nov. 1920; "Gittle," *Jewish Exponent* 72 (Nov. 5, 1920); "The Voice of the Sod," *Pictorial Review*, Oct. 1922; and "Katinka," *Pictorial Review*, May 1923.

57 O'Brien, *The Best Short Stories of 1922*, xviii. The assessment refers to all stories in the editor's highest category rather than to Cohen's alone.

58 Quoted in Blanche Colton Williams, introduction to *Thrice Told Tales: Thirteen Re-Reprints of Stories* (New York: Dodd, Mead, 1924), 14. "Natalka's Portion," first published in *Pictorial Review*, originated in Williams's advanced story writing course at Columbia University; *Thrice Told Tales*, 6.

59 Dublin's introduction to *OOTS* and his "Critical Essay" on the website of the Jewish Women's Archive (http://jwa.org/discover/inthepast/readingseries/cohen/criticalessay.html) provide the fullest published discussions of Cohen's last years. I am grateful to him for sharing his research materials and sources in frequent e-mail exchanges. Dublin tends to endorse the suicide theory. The evidence from family members—both the rumors and the silences—is suggestive, but not conclusive. It is not known whether Rose Gollup Cohen is the Rose Cohen the *New York Times* reported as having made an unsuccessful suicide attempt in 1922 (Sept. 17, 1922), 5. Whatever the case, Cohen's last years were difficult. Her letters to Leonora O'Reilly are the most revealing source of personal information for this period; see letters from "Rahel" [Cohen] to O'Reilly, in James, *Papers of the Women's Trade Union League*, reel 107.

60 Cohen, "To the Friends," 40.

61 Antin, *The Promised Land*, xi. Page references are given in the text.

62 There is an extensive literature on Antin. See especially Werner Sollors's thoughtful

introduction to *The Promised Land* (New York: Penguin Books, 1997), which is based on extensive use of primary sources and has a useful bibliography. See also Antler, *The Journey Home*, 17–26.

63 Other Russian Jewish women whose autobiographies were published in the second decade of the century include Elizabeth Stern, Elizabeth Hasanovitz, and Marie Ganz. Rose Schneiderman, Emma Goldman, and Rose Pesotta wrote in later years. Autobiographies of women who immigrated to the United States between 1882 and 1924 are discussed by Sally Ann Drucker, "'It Doesn't Say So in Mother's Prayerbook': Autobiographies in English by Immigrant Jewish Women," *American Jewish History* 74 (Autumn 1989): 55–71.

The vogue for ethnic autobiography deserves further study. The desire to read about the "authentic" experiences of exotic others accompanied the trend toward more realistic literary writing in the late nineteenth and early twentieth centuries. Interest in specifically immigrant stories may also have been fueled by the heated debates surrounding immigration and the upheavals of World War I. American intermediaries who encouraged immigrants to move outside their ethnic communities sometimes contrasted the vitality of the Lower East Side with the sterility of the denatured Protestant culture they sought to escape. An influential contemporary interpretation is Hapgood, *The Spirit of the Ghetto*.

64 On Antin as autobiographer, see Alvin H. Rosenfeld, "Inventing the Jew: Notes on Jewish Autobiography," *Midstream* 21 (Apr. 1975): 54–67; Magdalena J. Zaborowska, *How We Found America: Reading Gender through East European Immigrant Narratives* (Chapel Hill: University of North Carolina Press, 1995), 39–75; and Antler, *The Journey Home*, 17–26. See also Mary V. Dearborn, *Pocahontas's Daughters: Gender and Ethnicity in American Culture* (New York: Oxford University Press, 1986).

65 School attendance was not yet compulsory and high schools were new. In New York City, only about one-third of the students completed eighth grade in 1913; there was no public high school there until 1898. See Stephan F. Brumberg, *Going to America, Going to School: The Jewish Immigrant Public School Encounter in Turn-of-the-Century New York City* (New York: Praeger, 1986), and "The Schooling of Immigrant Jewish Girls on New York's Lower East Side at the Turn of the Twentieth Century" (1992), unpublished paper in the author's possession, esp. 4, 5.

66 Italics in the original. For an illuminating analysis of Antin that focuses on reading and writing poetry, see Joan Shelley Rubin, *Songs of Ourselves: The Uses of Poetry in America* (Cambridge, Mass.: Harvard University Press, 2007), 209–14.

67 Edith Horton, *A Group of Famous Women: Stories of Their Lives* (Boston: D. C. Heath, 1914), quotations on viii. See also Brumberg, *Going to America*, 132.

68 Antin, *From Plotzk to Boston*, foreword by Israel Zangwill (Boston: W. B. Clarke, 1899). "Plotzk" is a printer's error for "Polotzk," the correct spelling of Antin's birthplace.

69 Elizabeth Hasanovitz, *One of Them: Chapters from A Passionate Autobiography* (Boston: Houghton Mifflin, 1918), 162–63; italics in original.

70 Pauline Leipziger to the Library Committee, Mar. 18, 1901, Aguilar Free Library Society Records (hereafter AFLS), Box 3, "Library and Building Committees, Reports,

1898–1902," RG 4, Free Circulating Libraries Records, New York Public Library Archives; hereafter cited as NYPL Archives. The Aguilar Free Library was a circulating library, founded in 1886 by German Jews to bring books to "downtown" Jewish immigrants from eastern Europe. Its four branches were incorporated into the New York Public Library in 1903.

71 Pauline Leipziger to Library Committee, Jan. 20, 1902, AFLS, Box 3. The librarian had received several complaints about the policeman's rough manner with readers and suggested that a porter be substituted.

72 "Seward Park Children's Room: Report for March 1910," NYPL Archives, RG 8, Superintendent of Work with Schools Records, Branch Library Reports, 1907–10, Box 2. This collection is not catalogued and has been referred to in various ways in the past decade. I also consulted the reports of the East Broadway, Rivington, Tompkins Park, and Ottendorfer branches, all on the Lower East Side. Robert Sink, "Something Interesting Will Come of It: Reading Choices of New York City Children in 1910," unpublished paper, makes excellent use of these reports. I am grateful to him for permission to read and cite his paper. See also Jenna Weissman Joselit, "Reading, Writing, and a Library Card: New York Jews and the New York Public Library," *Biblion: The Bulletin of the New York Public Library* 5 (Fall 1996): 97–117.
   The photographs of Lewis Hine document city children's enthusiasm for reading. They are analyzed by Robert Sink, "Children in the Library: Lewis Hine's Photographs for the Child Welfare Exhibit of 1911," and Judith Mara Gutman, "Lewis Hine's Photographs: A Critic's View," *Biblion: The Bulletin of the New York Public Library* 1 (Spring 1993): 12–24 and 25–32.

73 *Evening Post*, Oct. 3, 1903, reprinted in *Portal to America: The Lower East Side, 1870–1925*, ed. Allon Schoener (New York: Holt, Rinehart and Winston, 1967), 133–34. See also "Do Not Take to Fiction," *New York Times*, Nov. 3, 1903, 4.

74 Rivington Street Branch, "Monthly Report of Children's Room," Sept. 1908, NYPL Archives.

75 "Seward Park Children's Room," Report for Nov. 1909, NYPL Archives.

76 Police commissioner quoted in Rischin, *The Promised City*, 199.

77 For an analysis of the "smart Jews" stereotype and the ways in which "praise becomes blame," see Sander L. Gilman, *Smart Jews: The Construction of the Image of Jewish Superior Intelligence* (Lincoln: University of Nebraska Press, 1996), 30.

78 See Sherry Gorelick, *City College and the Jewish Poor: Education in New York, 1880–1924* (New Brunswick, N.J.: Rutgers University Press, 1981). In a widely cited revisionist article, Selma C. Berrol argues that education followed rather than preceded economic mobility for Jews; "Education and Economic Mobility: The Jewish Experience in New York City, 1880–1920," *American Jewish Historical Quarterly* 65 (Mar. 1976): 257–71.

79 Seward Park, "Report for Children's Room," Jan. 1910, NYPL Archives.

80 Philip Roth, "The Newark Public Library," in *Reading Myself and Others* (New York: Farrar, Straus and Giroux, 1975), 175–77; quotations on 176.

81 Sink, "Something Interesting."

82 Brumberg, *Going to America*, 141; italics in original. See also *Jewish Grandmothers*.

83 A librarian contrasted Jewish and German children in this regard; Seward Park, "Report for Children's Room," June–Oct. 1910, NYPL Archives.

84 Joselit, "Reading, Writing, and a Library Card," 102–3.

85 Topics are drawn mainly from a list of questions asked by at least ten children on a given day at the Rivington Branch of the New York Public Library. "Report of Children's Room for February 1909," NYPL Archives.

86 "Report of the Children's Room," Rivington Branch, April 1908, NYPL Archives.

87 Sink, "Something Interesting," 6. Other titles in short supply included *Uncle Tom's Cabin* and *Pinocchio*. Sink's list is drawn from children's librarians across the city, but many of the titles were sought after on the Lower East Side. The librarian at the Rivington Branch routinely noted a shortage of books for older girls. "Reports of the Children's Room," Rivington Branch, Dec. 1909, Jan. 1910, NYPL Archives. Librarians in Jewish neighborhoods also mentioned categories of books in short supply other than fiction, including history, biography, science, and poetry.

88 Dina Abramowicz, "Yiddish Juvenilia: Ethnic Survival in the New World," *Wilson Library Bulletin* 50 (Oct. 1975): 138–45. I am grateful to Zachary Baker for this reference.

89 Bella Spewack, *Streets: A Memoir of the Lower East Side* (New York: Feminist Press, 1995). Spewack wrote the memoir in 1922, when she was in her early twenties. Page references are included in the text.

90 On Antin's alienation from Judaism, see Antler, *The Journey Home*, 17–26.

91 A Women's Bureau study of immigrant women workers in Philadelphia and the Lehigh Valley in the late 1920s found that Jewish women who immigrated when they were over fourteen learned to speak and even read English more frequently than women of other ethnic groups. Even so, 47 percent were unable to read English; these figures do not take into account length of residence in the United States; Caroline Manning, *The Immigrant Woman and Her Job* (1930; reprint, New York: Arno Press, 1970), 29–30. A study of the Yiddish press in the same period found that many individuals read English-language in addition to Yiddish newspapers, though not necessarily fluently; Mordecai Soltes, *The Yiddish Press: An Americanizing Agency* (1925; reprint, New York: Arno Press/New York Times, 1969), 33–42.

92 On the Yiddish press, see Rischin, *The Promised City*, 117–30; Irving Howe, *World of Our Fathers* (New York: Harcourt Brace Jovanovich, 1976), 518–51; and Soltes, *The Yiddish Press*. On Yiddish newspaper fiction, see Ellen Kellman, "Entertaining New Americans: Serialized Fiction in the *Forverts* (1910–1930)," in *Jews and American Popular Culture*, ed. Paul Buhle (Westport: Praeger, 2007), 2:199–211, and "The Newspaper Novel in the *Jewish Daily Forward* (1900–1940): Fiction as Entertainment and Serious Literature" (Ph.D diss., Columbia University, 2000).

93 See Norma Fain Pratt, "Culture and Radical Politics: Yiddish Women Writers in America, 1890–1940," in *Decades of Discontent: The Women's Movement, 1920–1940*, ed. Lois Scharf and Joan M. Jensen, 131–52 (Boston: Northeastern University Press, 1987); and Hagit Cohen, "The Demands of Integration—The Challenges of Ethnicization: Jewish Women's Yiddish Reading Circles in North America between the Two World Wars," *NASHIM: A Journal of Jewish Women's Studies and Gender Issues* 16 (2008): 98–129.

CHAPTER NINE

1 On African American women's public role in the transition from slavery to free-
dom, see Elsa Barkley Brown, "Negotiating and Transforming the Public Sphere:
African American Political Life in the Transition from Slavery to Freedom," *Public
Culture* 7 (1994): 107–46. Their achievements were celebrated in three volumes
published in the mid-1890s: M. A. Majors, *Noted Negro Women: Their Triumphs
and Activities* (Jackson, Tenn.: M. V. Lynk Publishing House, 1893); L. A. Scruggs,
Women of Distinction: Remarkable in Works and Invincible in Character (Raleigh,
N.C.: L. A. Scruggs, 1893); and Mrs. N. F. Mossell, *The Work of the Afro-American
Woman* (1894; reprint, New York: Oxford University Press, 1988). See also Katherine
Davis Chapman Tillman, "Afro-American Women and Their Work" (1895), in *The
Works of Katherine Davis Chapman Tillman*, ed. Claudia Tate (New York: Oxford
University Press, 1991), 70–92.

2 On the African American fiction boom, see Hazel V. Carby, *Reconstructing Womanhood: The Emergence of the Afro-American Woman Novelist* (New York: Oxford
University Press, 1987).

3 Elizabeth McHenry and Shirley Brice Heath, in "The Literate and the Literary:
African Americans as Writers and Readers, 1830–1940," *Written Communication* 11
(Oct. 1994): 419–44, make a strong case for the intertwined relationship between
orality and literacy in the African American community. In their words: "speaking
encircled reading and . . . reading—especially of literature—surrounded writing"
(424).

4 On the role of literary and oral performance (in this case in a familial context) in
the evolving career of Pauline Hopkins, a notable Boston writer and editor, see
the exquisitely researched study by Lois Brown, *Pauline Elizabeth Hopkins: Black
Daughter of the Revolution* (Chapel Hill: University of North Carolina Press, 2008).

5 *Crusade for Justice: The Autobiography of Ida B. Wells*, ed. Alfreda M. Duster (Chicago: University of Chicago Press, 1970), 7, 8–9, 16; hereafter cited as *Crusade*. In
the absence of primary documents, the autobiography, although inaccurate in
places, is still the basic source for Wells's Mississippi years.

Several recent biographies have greatly expanded knowledge about Wells: Linda
O. McMurry, *To Keep the Waters Troubled: The Life of Ida B. Wells* (New York: Oxford University Press, 1998), concentrates on the early career; Patricia A. Schechter,
Ida B. Wells-Barnett and American Reform, 1880–1930 (Chapel Hill: University of
North Carolina Press, 2001), breaks new ground on Wells's later career in Chicago;
and Paula J. Giddings, *Ida: A Sword among Lions: Ida B. Wells and the Campaign
against Lynching* (New York: Amistad, 2008), is a generously researched, full-
scale biography. All of them may be usefully consulted on many points touched
on here. See also Thomas C. Holt, "The Lonely Warrior: Ida B. Wells-Barnett and
the Struggle for Black Leadership," in *Black Leaders in the Twentieth Century*, ed.
John Hope Franklin and August Meier, 39–61 (Urbana: University of Illinois Press,
1982); and James West Davidson, *"They Say": Ida B. Wells and the Reconstruction of
Race* (New York: Oxford University Press, 2007).

6 On literacy among slaves, see Janet Duitsman Cornelius, *"When I Can Read My
Title Clear": Literacy, Slavery, and Religion in the Antebellum South* (Columbia: University of South Carolina Press, 1991); and Heather Andrea Williams, *Self-Taught:*

African American Education in Slavery and Freedom (Chapel Hill: University of North Carolina Press, 2005), 7–29.

7 Literacy statistics are from a 1960 Census monograph, John K. Folger and Charles B. Nam, *Education of the American Population* (Washington, D.C.: Government Printing Office, 1967), 114; and James D. Anderson, *The Education of Blacks in the South, 1860–1935* (Chapel Hill: University of North Carolina Press, 1988), 31. The census did not count as literate those who could read but not write, thereby understating skills. On postwar education, see Heather Andrea Williams, *Self-Taught*; Robert C. Morris, *Reading, 'Riting, and Reconstruction: The Education of Freedmen in the South, 1861–1870* (Chicago: University of Chicago Press, 1981); Ronald E. Butchart, *Northern Schools, Southern Blacks, and Reconstruction: Freedmen's Education, 1862–1875* (Westport, Conn.: Greenwood Press, 1980); and Jacqueline Jones, *Soldiers of Light and Love: Northern Teachers and Georgia Blacks, 1865–1873* (Chapel Hill: University of North Carolina Press, 1980). For an interpretive survey of the period, see Eric Foner, *Reconstruction: America's Unfinished Revolution, 1863–1877* (New York: Harper and Row, 1988), esp. 95–102, 144–48, 364–68.

8 Because domestic service was viewed as a lingering badge of servitude as well as dangerous because of sexually predatory male employers, families often kept girls in school longer than their brothers. On the gender gap in African American literacy, see Jacqueline Jones, *Labor of Love, Labor of Sorrow: Black Women, Work, and the Family from Slavery to the Present* (New York: Basic Books, 1985), 91, 97. See also Michael Fultz, "African-American Teachers in the South, 1890–1940: Growth, Feminization, and Salary Discrimination," *Teachers College Record* 96 (Spring 1995): 544–68. Thanks to Jack Dougherty for this reference.

9 Population Schedules of the Ninth Census of the United States, 1870, Roll 740, *Mississippi*, vol. 11, Marshall County.

10 *Crusade*, 9.

11 According to the 1870 Census, Ida Wells could read and write. Her age is listed as six, but she was a month shy of her eighth birthday.

12 *Crusade*, 9.

13 For the involvement of northern churches in the education of former slaves, see James M. McPherson, *The Abolitionist Legacy: From Reconstruction to the NAACP* (Princeton, N.J.: Princeton University Press, 1975), esp. 143–60. The early history of Shaw University may be followed in Ishmell Hendrex Edwards, "History of Rust College, 1866–1967" (Ph.D. diss., University of Mississippi, 1993), esp. 41–76. See also *Reports of the Freedmen's Aid Society of the Methodist Episcopal Church*, esp. *Third Annual Report* (for 1869), 10. Shaw graduated its first two male students in 1878, Wells's last year there; Freedmen's Aid Society, *Twelfth Annual Report* (for 1879), 30. Wells's course of study is not known.

14 *Crusade*, 21–22.

15 I am indebted to Jerry G. Watts for insights on this point. Shirley Wilson Logan also contrasts the scarcity of religious allusions in Wells's rhetoric with the appeals to religious authority of many African American female predecessors and contemporaries; *"We Are Coming": The Persuasive Discourse of Nineteenth-Century Black Women* (Carbondale: Southern Illinois University Press, 1999), 82. Schechter, on the other hand, emphasizes the importance of religion in Wells's antilynching

campaign; *Ida B. Wells-Barnett*. On Wells's early religious striving, see Emilie M. Townes, *Womanist Justice, Womanist Hope* (Atlanta: Scholars Press, 1993), esp. 107–30.

16 AME minister Reverdy C. Ransom observed that Wells "met cold, or indifferent support in most of the Negro Churches in America"; quoted in Eric Gerard Pearman, "The Reality of Leadership: Ida B. Wells-Barnett's Crusade for Social Justice," in *Ruts: Gender Roles and Realities*, ed. Anne Rankin Mahoney (Denver: Red Mesa Publishing, 1996), 129. Thanks to David L. Beckley for sending a copy of this article.

17 Ida B. Wells Diary, Jan. 3, 1887, Ida B. Wells Papers, Special Collections Research Center, University of Chicago Library; hereafter cited as Diary. The diary has been published, with useful historical and biographical commentary, as *The Memphis Diary of Ida B. Wells*, ed. Miriam DeCosta-Willis (Boston: Beacon Press, 1995); the published version will be cited as *Memphis Diary*.

18 *Crusade*, 22. Wells also claimed she had never seen a black bishop until she encountered the AME Church in Memphis.

19 Ida B. Wells, "Lynch Law in All Its Phases" (1893), in Mildred I. Thompson, *Ida B. Wells-Barnett: An Exploratory Study of an American Black Woman, 1893–1930* (Brooklyn: Carlson, 1990), 187.

20 An entry in a collective biographical work published in 1893—for which Wells was a likely source—claims that she continued to attend Shaw "between the terms" of teaching; T. Thomas Fortune, "Ida B. Wells, A.M.," in Scruggs, *Women of Distinction*, 35.

21 *Crusade*, 21. Linking this period of intense reading to her disappointment at the failure of the African American community to support her protest activities, Wells seems to be referring to country schools in Tennessee, but it is likely that reading kept her going in Mississippi as well.

22 African American literary clubs are discussed by Anne Meis Knupfer, *Toward a Tenderer Humanity and a Nobler Womanhood: African American Women's Clubs in Turn-of-the-Century Chicago* (New York: New York University Press, 1996), esp. 108–13. Lyceums had been popular among white Americans in the antebellum era. The Gilded Age African American lyceums may have hewed more closely to the original tradition of self-improvement than did the eclectic lecture system into which the earlier lyceums evolved. On antebellum lyceums, see Carl Bode, *The American Lyceum: Town Meeting of the Mind* (New York: Oxford University Press, 1956). For an informative survey of venues for self-improvement, see Joseph F. Kett, *The Pursuit of Knowledge under Difficulties: From Self-Improvement to Adult Education in America, 1750–1990* (Stanford: Stanford University Press, 1994).

23 *Crusade*, 23; Diary, Jan. 18 and May 2, 1887.

24 Diary, July 4, 1886.

25 A male correspondent chided Wells for using an "objectionable" expression about "Lady M." Diary, Jan. 21, 1886. Lady Macbeth also intrigued Wells's white female contemporaries. Texas club members at the turn of the century discussed her more often than any other female character in Shakespeare; Elizabeth Long, *Book Clubs: Women and the Uses of Reading in Everyday Life* (Chicago: University of Chicago Press, 2003), 46.

26 *Chicago Conservator*, Apr. 21, 1906, quoted in Schechter, *Ida B. Wells-Barnett*, 132. A similar sentiment appears in "Bethel Literary and Historical Club Doing Great Work," *Chicago Defender*, Jan. 1, 1910: "If we only had a few men with the backbone of Mrs. Barnett lynching would soon come to a halt in America." Wells, who often drew on Shakespeare, referenced *Macbeth* in less provocative fashion, calling "the race problem or negro [*sic*] question . . . the Banquo's ghost of politics, religion, and sociology"; Wells, "Lynch Law in All Its Phases," 171–72. See also *Crusade*, 370.

27 Diary, May 3, 1887; see also Diary, May 6, 1886. Wells may have recited the tragic and sentimental poem "Un Mariage de Convenance" (in English despite the French title) written from the perspective of a man whose wife perpetually mourns a lost love, which appeared in *Tinsley's Magazine* 1 (Nov. 1867): [512] and the *New York Times*, Nov. 3, 1867, or "Marriage de Convenance," a humorous "romance verse monologue" in the voice of a "society girl" who was marrying for money; *Werner's Readings and Recitations* (New York: E. S. Werner, 1890–), 47:104–5. "The Widder Budd" by Eugene J. Hall appears in *Ninety-nine Choice Recitations and Readings* (New York: J. S. Ogilvie & Co., [1881–83]), 2:43–44. Wells had a third piece at her command at this time, "The Doom of Claudius and Cynthia," a melodramatic story of Roman times by Maurice Thompson, in *Scribner's Monthly*, Feb. 1879, 547–52.

28 Diary, Feb. 20, 1887.

29 Ibid., Jan. 24, 1886.

30 "Memphis, Tenn.," *Cleveland Gazette*, Apr. 4, 1885. The other performer, Virginia Broughton, became prominent in Baptist women's organizations; Evelyn Brooks Higginbotham, *Righteous Discontent: The Women's Movement in the Black Baptist Church, 1880–1920* (Cambridge, Mass.: Harvard University Press, 1993), 69–73.

31 *Washington Bee*, reprinted in *New York Freeman*, Dec. 11, 1885; Diary, Feb. 25, 1886.

32 Diary, Feb. 14, 1886. The book's subtitle is *A Self-Instructor for All Cultured Circles, and Especially for Oratorical and Dramatic Artists* (Albany, N.Y.: Edgar S. Werner, 1884); quotation on vii. On his way up the class ladder, African American writer Charles W. Chesnutt copied passages from *A Handbook for Home Improvement* on such subjects as "The Daily Bath," "Change of Linen," and "Spitting" into his diary. *The Journals of Charles W. Chesnutt*, ed. Richard H. Brodhead (Durham: Duke University Press, 1993), 40–41.

33 Diary, Oct. 31, 1886; *Crusade*, 23. Elizabeth McHenry emphasizes the importance of reading aloud for a semiliterate population and its place in antebellum African American literary societies; *Forgotten Readers: Recovering the Lost History of African American Literary Societies* (Durham: Duke University Press, 2002), esp. 35–37, 53. Wells errs in linking her first journalistic assignment to her editorship of the *Evening Star*; by the time she became editor in 1886, her articles had been appearing in papers around the country for at least two years. On May 24, 1884, under the title "Doings of the Race," the *New York Globe* took note of an article she had written for the *Living Way* (Memphis).

34 Diary, Jan. 28, 1886.

35 Ibid., Mar. 18 and Apr. 3, 1886.

36 Ibid., July 16, 1887.

37 Ibid., Nov. 7 and Nov. 15, 1886. Although the main CLSC vehicle was the reading circle, there is no evidence to suggest that Wells joined a group.

38 Miriam DeCosta-Willis estimates that the average annual salary of black Memphis schoolteachers in 1885 was $450; "Ida B. Wells's *Diary*: A Narrative of the Black Community of Memphis in the 1880s," *West Tennessee Historical Society Papers* 45 (Dec. 1991): 40, 42–43.

39 Diary, Nov. 7, 1886.

40 Ibid., Dec. 21, 1886.

41 Ibid., Mar. 11, 1886. Wells and the author later became friends. Tourgée, an attorney and judge who worked for African American causes, argued the antisegregation side of the landmark case *Plessy v. Ferguson* before the Supreme Court. He sent Wells a set of George Eliot's works as well as a set of his own as a wedding present. Draft of letter from Ida B. Wells to Mrs. Albion Tourgée, Aug. 26, 1895, Wells Papers, University of Chicago Library.

42 Diary, Dec. 29, 1885.

43 Ibid., Dec. 29, 1885, July 29, 1887.

44 Ibid., Feb. 1, 1887.

45 Ibid., Jan. 28, 1886.

46 The St. Paul *Western Appeal*, July 9, 1887, reported that Wells planned to spend the summer writing a novel in a town near Memphis where she had previously taught. Cited in McMurry, *To Keep the Waters Troubled*, 98, 354.

47 See Dickson D. Bruce Jr., *Black American Writing from the Nadir: The Evolution of a Literary Tradition, 1877–1915* (Baton Rouge: Louisiana State University Press, 1989), esp. ch. 1; and Carby, *Reconstructing Womanhood*.

48 Diary, Jan. 28, Mar. 11, Aug. 22, and Sept. 4, 1886.

49 Ibid., Feb. 18, 1886.

50 "Woman's Mission," *New York Freeman*, Dec. 26, 1885, reprinted in *Memphis Diary*, 181.

51 Diary, Sept. 1, 1886.

52 Reprinted in Thompson, *Ida B. Wells-Barnett*, 225–34.

53 Wells sued following separate incidents in 1883 and 1884 because the state's separate car law passed in 1881 required trains to have first-class cars for each race. The story can be followed in Giddings, *Ida*, 60–68, 136–39, quotation on 67; Schechter, *Wells-Barnett*, 43–44, 71–72, 264; and *Crusade*, 17–20. (Wells refused to change cars on other occasions, but conductors did not make an issue of it.) The reversal by the Tennessee Supreme Court in the second case left Wells extremely discouraged; Diary, Apr. 11, 1887. The racial and gender dimensions of restricted railroad travel before and after the Jim Crow era are analyzed by Barbara Young Welke, *Recasting American Liberty: Gender, Race, Law, and the Railroad Revolution, 1865–1920* (Cambridge: Cambridge University Press, 2001), 280–322. Educator Anna Julia Cooper was among the women objecting to segregated cars; *A Voice from the South: By A Black Woman of the South* (1892; reprint, New York: Oxford University Press, 1988).

54 *Crusade*, 23–24. It has been suggested that the heroine of *Iola Leroy*, Frances Ellen Watkins Harper's important 1892 novel, may have been named for Wells. Frances

Smith Foster, *Written by Herself: Literary Production by African American Women, 1746–1892* (Bloomington: Indiana University Press, 1993), 183; Claudia Tate, *Domestic Allegories of Political Desire: The Black Heroine's Text at the Turn of the Century* (New York: Oxford University Press, 1992), 145.

55 Diary, Aug. 9, 1886; "'Iola' Wells," *Cleveland Gazette*, July 6, 1889.

56 *Crusade*, 31–34. Black Baptist publications sponsored many women journalists; Higginbotham, *Righteous Discontent*, 76–78. Many African American newspapers, including all three published in Memphis, were church-related. On Wells's career as a journalist, see Rodger Streitmatter, *Voices of Revolution: The Dissident Press in America* (New York: Columbia University Press, 2001), 80–96.

57 See, for example, Wells, "Functions of Leadership" (originally published in *Living Way*, Sept. 12, 1885), and "Woman's Mission," both reprinted in *Memphis Diary*, 178–82.

58 Wells, "Woman's Mission," 180. See also Wells, "A Story of 1900," a piece about a teacher's heroic mission in raising the condition of black children (first published in *Fisk Herald*, Apr. 1886), reprinted in *Memphis Diary*, 182–84.

59 Diary, Aug. 12, 1887.

60 Iola, "Freedom of Political Action," *New York Freeman*, Nov. 7, 1885; and "'Iola' on Discrimination," *New York Freeman*, Jan. 15, 1887.

61 Iola, "Race Pride," St. Paul *Western Appeal*, Mar. 5, 1887, reprinted from *American Baptist*. See also Iola, "Functions of Leadership," 178–79.

62 *Crusade*, 35–45. Wells, who insisted on becoming a co-owner as well as editor of the *Free Speech*, claims she was the only woman editor of a black newspaper, *Crusade*, 59.

63 "'Iola', Newspapers and Magazines," *Washington Bee*, Jan. 23, 1886. The editor of the *Bee* ridiculed Wells's writing as well as her claim that she was always paid for it. I am indebted to Jacqueline Goldsby for her insights into Wells's business acumen.

64 "The National Colored Press Association," *Washington Bee*, Aug. 20, 1887.

65 *Crusade*, 23; "Miss Ida B. Wells (Iola)," in Majors, *Noted Negro Women*, 187.

66 Mrs. N. F. Mossell, *Indianapolis Freeman*, Jan. 5, 1889, quoted in McMurry, *To Keep the Waters Troubled*, 112; and Lucy W. Smith, quoted in I. Garland Penn, *The Afro-American Press and Its Editors* (1891; reprint, New York: Arno Press, 1969), 408; the latter quote is reprinted in *Crusade*, 33.

67 For example: "Iola makes the mistake of trying to be pretty as well as smart. She should remember that beauty and brains are not always companions. George Eliot, George Sand, Harriet Beecher Stowe and many other bright minds of that sex were not paragons by any means" (*Indianapolis Freeman*, July 30, 1889, quoted in McMurry, *To Keep the Waters Troubled*, 115).

68 Fortune, "Ida B. Wells, A.M.," in Scruggs, *Women of Distinction*, 39. Because few thought a woman could write such hard-hitting articles, her editorials were sometimes attributed to her male co-owners.

69 *Crusade*, 41, 31.

70 *Washington Bee*, reprinted in *New York Freeman* (Dec. 11, 1885); Diary, Aug. 26, 1886.

71 Estimates of the number of African Americans lynched vary widely, but scholars agree that the practice was at a peak in the 1890s. Recent works include Philip

Dray, *At the Hands of Persons Unknown: The Lynching of Black America* (New York: Random House, 2002); and Leon F. Litwack, *Trouble in Mind: Black Southerners in the Age of Jim Crow* (New York: Random House, 1998), 280–325.

72 Diary, Sept. 4, 1886.

73 Ibid., Apr. 18, 1887.

74 Quoted in *Memphis Weekly Avalanche*; and McMurry, *To Keep the Waters Troubled*, 128–29.

75 On the Memphis "lynching at the curve," see David M. Tucker, "Miss Ida B. Wells and Memphis Lynching," *Phylon* 32 (Summer 1971): 112–22; Schechter, *Wells-Barnett*, 75–79; McMurry, *To Keep the Waters Troubled*, 130–49; Giddings, *Ida*, 156–87; and *Crusade*, 47–52.

76 Wells, *Southern Horrors: Lynch Law in All Its Phases*, reprinted in *Southern Horrors and Other Writings: The Anti-Lynching Campaign of Ida B. Wells, 1892–1900*, ed. Jacqueline Jones Royster (Boston: Bedford Books, 1997), 70.

77 Quoted in ibid., 52. On lynching and rape, see Crystal N. Feimster, *Southern Horrors: Women and the Politics of Rape and Lynching* (Cambridge, Mass.: Harvard University Press, 2009).

78 Wells, "The Requirements of Southern Journalism," *AME Zion Quarterly Review* (Apr. 1892): 189–96.

79 Wells, *Southern Horrors*, 50. For Wells's account of the Lyric Hall testimonial, see *Crusade*, 77–82; quotations on 79–80. She was somewhat disingenuous about her lack of experience since she had delivered talks to journalists and at the lyceum; perhaps she did not count them in the "honest-to-goodness" category.

80 Wells describes the British tour in detail, with extended excerpts from the *Inter-Ocean* and the British press, in *Crusade*, 83–223; quotation on 125.

81 Wells noted the comparison in an interview; Schechter, *Wells-Barnett*, 278 (n. 111). For a sophisticated analysis of Wells's rhetoric in relation to contemporary journalistic conventions, see Jacqueline Goldsby, *A Spectacular Secret: Lynching in American Life and Literature* (Chicago: University of Chicago Press, 2006), 43–104.

82 Wells, *A Red Record: Tabulated Statistics and Alleged Causes of Lynchings in the United States, 1892–1893–1894*, reprinted in *Southern Horrors and Other Writings*, 73–157. See also Wells, "Lynch Law in All Its Phases," 171–87.

83 Quoted in Patricia Schechter, "'To Tell the Truth Freely': Ida B. Wells and the Politics of Race, Gender, and Reform in America, 1880–1913" (Ph.D. diss., Princeton University, 1993), 150. On the race-sex dynamic in lynching discourse and practice, see Martha Hodes, *White Women, Black Men: Illicit Sex in the Nineteenth-Century South* (New Haven: Yale University Press, 1997), 176–208. On the race-gender dynamic, see Gail Bederman, "'The White Man's Civilization on Trial': Ida B. Wells, Representations of Lynching, and Northern Middle-Class Manhood," in *Manliness and Civilization: A Cultural History of Gender and Race in the United States, 1880–1917* (Chicago: University of Chicago Press, 1995), 45–76.

84 "Personal and Pertinent," *New York Age*, July 25, 1891.

85 Quoted in McMurry, *To Keep the Waters Troubled*, 226. Maritcha Rémond Lyons, who claims she bested Wells in a debate at the Brooklyn Literary Union, takes credit for teaching Wells to speak extemporaneously; "Memories of Yesterdays: All of Which I Saw and Part of Which I Was: An Autobiography," typescript, Harry A.

Williamson Collection, Schomburg Center for Research in Black Culture, New York Public Library.

86 Quoted in *Crusade*, 147. Logan, *"We Are Coming,"* 70–97, analyzes Wells's rhetoric and speaking style, as well as the restrained mode of speech adopted by other black women, including Frances Harper (49). See also Jacqueline Jones Royster, "To Call a Thing by Its True Name: The Rhetoric of Ida B. Wells," in *Reclaiming Rhetorica: Women in the Rhetorical Tradition*, ed. Andrea A. Lunsford (Pittsburgh: University of Pittsburgh Press, 1995), 167–84, and *Traces of a Stream: Literacy and Social Change among African American Women* (Pittsburgh: University of Pittsburgh Press, 2000).

87 For press coverage of Wells's campaign, see articles in the *Literary Digest*, July 28, Aug. 11, and Sept. 8, 1894; all refer to it as a crusade.

88 *Crusade*, 231.

89 On the formation of the NACW, see Deborah Gray White, *Too Heavy a Load: Black Women in Defense of Themselves, 1894–1994* (New York: W. W. Norton, 1999), 21–55; Dorothy Salem, *To Better Our World: Black Women in Organized Reform, 1890–1920* (Brooklyn: Carlson, 1990); and Paula Giddings, *When and Where I Enter: The Impact of Black Women on Race and Sex in America* (New York: Bantam Books, 1984), 75–117. Stephanie J. Shaw, "Black Club Women and the Creation of the National Association of Colored Women," *Journal of Women's History* 3 (Fall 1991): 10–25, emphasizes internal factors rather than external pressure for black women's organizing efforts at this time.

90 See, for example, *Woman's Era* 1 (Feb. 1895): 11.

91 A poem by African American writer Katherine Davis Tillman compared Wells to Charlotte Corday as well as Joan of Arc. The allusion to Corday, the assassin of the French revolutionary journalist Jean-Paul Marat who was put to death for the deed, seems idiosyncratic and does not appear in a later version; "Lines to Ida B. Wells," *Philadelphia Christian Recorder*, July 5, 1894, quoted in Schechter, *Wells-Barnett*, 103–4. Years later, in an article on Wells-Barnett's insistence on joining the Illinois delegation to a suffrage parade after white suffragists tried to exclude her, the *Chicago Defender* headlined her as "The Modern Joan of Arc," Mar. 8, 1913.

92 Reverdy C. Ransom, *Deborah and Jael . . . Sermon to the I.B.W. Woman's Club* (Chicago, 1897), 5; copy provided by Archives and Special Collections, Rembert E. Stokes Learning Resources Center, Wilberforce University. The Deborah analogy appeared the same year in Norman B. Wood, *The White Side of a Black Subject* (Chicago: American Publishing House, 1897), 381–82; the latter passage is quoted by Alfreda M. Duster, Wells's daughter and the editor of her autobiography; *Crusade*, xiii.

93 Despite her early close connections with women's clubs, Wells-Barnett soon found herself at odds with leaders of the NACW. The politics of respectability to which they subscribed meant taking a secondary role to male leaders and adhering to the rules of true womanhood. Wells believed in two of the pillars of female respectability, piety and purity, but not in submissiveness. Her radical temperament and impatience with half measures made for a difficult fit with many potential allies. On respectability and the ideology of racial uplift, see Kevin K. Gaines, *Uplifting the Race: Black Leadership, Politics, and Culture in the Twentieth Century* (Chapel

Hill: University of North Carolina Press, 1996); and Higginbotham, *Righteous Discontent.*

94 Of this reading, the *Woman's Era* observed, "The pathos was emphasized by the reading of them by Mrs. Ida B. *Wells* Barnett, in the musical monotone peculiar to that polished reader." "Additional Convention Notes," *Woman's Era* 3 (Aug.–Sept. 1896): 13.

95 *Crusade*, 248–49.

96 Wells was critical of the NAACP's antilynching work. Schechter analyzes their differences and underscores the gendered nature of the organization; *Wells-Barnett*, 135–68. See also Dray, *At the Hands of Persons Unknown*, esp. 171–73, 215–51. On black women's antilynching activities, see Rosalyn Terborg-Penn, "African-American Women's Networks in the Anti-Lynching Crusade," in *Gender, Class, Race, and Reform in the Progressive Era*, ed. Noralee Frankel and Nancy S. Dye (Lexington: University Press of Kentucky, 1991), 148–61.

97 Clarence Taylor, *The Black Churches of Brooklyn* (New York: Columbia University Press, 1994), 29, and "Miss Ida B. Wells," *Washington Bee*, Oct. 22, 1892.

98 "Report of the Women's [*sic*] Loyal Union of New York and Brooklyn," *Woman's Era* 2 (Aug. 1895): 5. Branches or chapters of the WLU were established in Charleston, Memphis, and Philadelphia.

99 Bruce elaborates on views on race literature; *Black American Writing*, esp. ch. 1, "Foundations of a Black American Literary Tradition, 1877–1896." The goals of the American Negro Academy, an elite and all-male organization founded in 1897, included promoting literary and scholarly works, aiding "youths of genius," gathering the works of African American authors into an archive, and aiding "by publications, the vindication of the race from vicious assaults, in all the lines of learning and truth"; quoted in Alfred A. Moss Jr., *The American Negro Academy: Voice of the Talented Tenth* (Baton Rouge: Louisiana State University Press, 1981), 24.

100 Iola, "Race Pride," St. Paul *Western Appeal*, Mar. 5, 1887.

101 Mary Church Terrell, "Needed: Women Lawyers," reprinted in Beverly Washington Jones, *Quest for Equality: The Life and Writings of Mary Eliza Church Terrell* (Brooklyn: Carlson, 1990), 327; see also Terrell, *A Colored Woman in a White World* (Washington, D.C.: Ransdell, 1940), 234. On the role of fiction, see also the prospectus for *Contending Forces*, a novel by Pauline Hopkins, editor of *Colored American Magazine*; "Prospectus . . . ," *Colored American Magazine* 1 (Sept. 1900): [195]. On Hopkins and the magazine, see Lois Brown, *Pauline Elizabeth Hopkins.*

102 On Terrell and Stowe, see Dorothy Sterling, *Black Foremothers: Three Lives*, 2nd ed. (New York: Feminist Press, 1988), 136; Terrell, *A Colored Woman*, 233, and "Harriet Beecher Stowe," Mary Church Terrell Collection, Moorland-Spingarn Research Center, Howard University, Washington, D.C. African American women's tributes to Stowe in the 1890s may be followed in the *Woman's Era.* The Woman's Loyal Union honored Stowe on her eighty-fifth birthday, and, at the time of her death the following year, the NACW recommended that clubs celebrate her birthday annually. See *A History of the Club Movement among the Colored Women of the United States of America* (1902; reprint, Washington, D.C.: National Association of Colored Women's Clubs, 1978), 52.

103 *The Reason Why* is reprinted in full in *Selected Works of Ida B. Wells-Barnett*,

comp. Trudier Harris (New York: Oxford University Press, 1991), 46–137. For a detailed analysis of African American participation in the exposition, which was greater in the end than *The Reason Why* suggested, see Christopher Robert Reed, *"All the World Is Here!": The Black Presence at White City* (Bloomington: Indiana University Press, 2000).

104 Daniel H. Murray, "A Bibliography of Negro Literature," *AME Church Review* 17 (July 1900): 19–27, quotation on 26. See also *Preliminary List of Books and Pamphlets by Negro Authors for the Paris Exposition and the Library of Congress*, comp. Daniel Murray, for the American Negro Exhibit, Paris Exhibition of 1900 (Washington, D.C.: Library of Congress, 1900); thanks to Wayne Wiegand for providing a copy of this document. For another contemporary statement, see Mrs. N. F. Mossell, "Life and Literature," *AME Church Review* 14 (Jan. 1898): 322–23.

105 Victoria Earle Matthews, "The Value of Race Literature: An Address," *Massachusetts Review* 27 (Summer 1986): 170–85, quotation on 172. Matthews drew on "The Negro as Presented in American Literature," Anna Julia Cooper's incisive, early critique of racist literary portrayals that appeared three years earlier in *A Voice from the South*, 175–227. On Matthews, see Logan, *"We Are Coming,"* 127–51.

106 *Aunt Lindy* was published under the name Victoria Earle in the prestigious *AME Church Review*. On Matthews's fiction, especially *Aunt Lindy*, see Bruce, *Black American Writing*, 51–55.

107 Matthews, "The Value of Race Literature," 170, 177, 182. On changing definitions of literature, see Kenneth Cmiel, *Democratic Eloquence: The Fight over Popular Speech in Nineteenth-Century America* (Berkeley and Los Angeles: University of California Press, 1990), esp. 165, 179–80; and for African Americans, see Carla L. Peterson, *"Doers of the Word": African-American Women Speakers and Writers in the North (1830–1880)* (New York: Oxford University Press, 1995).

108 For an excellent analysis of black women's clubs, see McHenry, *Forgotten Readers*, 187–250. On literary practices, see also Anne Ruggles Gere, *Intimate Practices: Literacy and Cultural Work in U.S. Women's Clubs, 1880–1920* (Urbana: University of Illinois Press, 1997); and Anne Ruggles Gere and Sarah R. Robbins, "Gendered Literacy in Black and White: Turn-of-the-Century African-American and European-American Club Women's Printed Texts," *Signs* 21 (Spring 1996): 643–78.

109 Minute Book 1, 1913–22, Chautauqua Circle, the Chautauqua Circle Collection, Robert W. Woodruff Library, Atlanta University Center. Although the group used the Chautauqua name, it voted at its inaugural meeting in 1913 to pursue "miscellaneous study" rather than the CSLC's prescribed home reading course. Minute Book 1: Oct. 17, 1913. For other groups that studied race literature or history, see *Efforts for Social Betterment among Negro Americans*, ed. W. E. B. Du Bois, Atlanta University Publications, No. 14 (Atlanta: Atlanta University Press, 1909), 50, 104.

110 Foster, *Written by Herself*, 19.

111 McHenry, *Forgotten Readers*, 241.

112 Du Bois, *Efforts for Social Betterment*, 117–18; this volume contains a great deal of information about African American women's organizations. See also Salem, *To Better Our World; A History of the Club Movement*; and Knupfer, *Toward a Tenderer Humanity and a Nobler Womanhood*, ch. 6. For the history of a library established for African American men and women, see Beverly Washington Jones,

Stanford L. Warren Branch Library: 77 Years of Public Service; A Phoenix in the Durham Community (Durham, N.C.: Durham County Library, 1990).

113 Marilyn Dell Brady, "Kansas Federation of Colored Women's Clubs, 1900–1930," Kansas History 9 (Spring 1986): 21.

114 At its inaugural meeting in 1896, the NACW adopted some two dozen resolutions, including condemnations of laws segregating railroads, the recent *Plessy v. Ferguson* decision that legalized them, the convict lease system, and lynching; they were read by Wells; *A History of the Club Movement*, 47–53.

115 "Report of the Women's [sic] Loyal Union of New York and Brooklyn," *Woman's Era* 2 (Aug. 1895): 5.

116 Ibid.; "Report of the Woman's Loyal Union of New York and Brooklyn," in *A History of the Club Movement*, 65–67, quotation on 66.

117 "White Rose Mission Settlement," 1910 program for Matinee Musicale with statement reprinted from the *New York Evening Post*, White Rose Folder, Schomburg Center for Research in Black Culture, New York City. I am grateful to Gabrielle Foreman for alerting me to this collection.

118 White Rose Annual Reports. See also Salem, *To Better Our World*, 44–45, 90–91.

119 *Crusade*, 301–2, 303. The activities of the NFL may be followed in *Crusade*, as well as in the *Chicago Defender* and *Chicago Broad Ax*. Wells-Barnett's Chicago activities go well beyond those covered here and may be followed in the biographies by Schechter and Giddings, and in *Crusade*. The tradition of African American reading rooms dates to the antebellum period; see McHenry, *Forgotten Readers*.

120 The NFL's goals included "developing loyalty to and fellowship within the race" and working to elevate "the moral, civic and social standards of the race, and especially of the young men"; "Clubs and Societies," *Chicago Defender*, Sept. 20, 1913. On African American women's organizations in Illinois, including those in which Wells-Barnett was active, see Wanda A. Hendricks, *Gender, Race, and Politics in the Midwest: Black Club Women in Illinois* (Bloomington: Indiana University Press, 1998); and Knupfer, *Toward a Tenderer Humanity*.

121 *Chicago Defender*, April 30 and July 11, 1910. See also Knupfer, *Toward a Tenderer Humanity*, 103.

122 *Chicago Defender*, Jan. 15 and Feb. 19, 1916.

123 The activities of the NFL and its campaigns may be followed in the *Chicago Broad Ax* and the *Chicago Defender*. On the transportation bill, see "Appomattox Club Kills 'Jim Crow' Bills in the State of Lincoln," *Chicago Defender*, Apr. 19, 1913. On Chicago black women's political and other activities, see Knupfer, *Toward a Tenderer Humanity*, 46–64.

124 "William A. Harpers [sic] Paintings Exhibited," *Chicago Defender*, Aug. 6, 1910.

125 "Fellowship Club," *Chicago Defender*, Oct. 18, 1913. The orchestra and chorus were both mentioned in Wells-Barnett's obituary, *Chicago Defender*, Mar. 28, 1931.

126 *Crusade*, 342–44.

127 *Chicago Defender*, June 12, 1915.

128 Wells-Barnett, "The Northern Negro Woman's Social and Moral Condition," *Original Rights Magazine* 1 (Apr. 1910): 33–37.

129 "Bethel's Literarl [sic] Society's Contest," *Fellowship Herald*, Dec. 21, 1911, Irene McCoy Gaines Papers, Box 1, folder 5, Chicago Historical Society (courtesy of

Chicago Historical Society). The paper was also the organ of the State and City Federation of Colored Women's Clubs. See also *Broad Ax*, Dec. 20, 1913; that year the contest was held under the auspices of the NFL.

130 *Broad Ax*, May 20, 1911; George Olsen, "The Negro in Chicago," *Chicago Defender*, Apr. 18, 1914; and McMurry, *To Keep the Waters Troubled*, 296. Olsen estimated that the paper had 500 subscribers.

131 Wells-Barnett attributed the NFL's difficulties to lack of support from the black elite who, in her view, shunned direct engagement with the organization's socially desperate clientele and to white philanthropists who threw their support to the new Urban League, which focused on improving housing and employment for blacks. *Crusade*, 297–307, 371–73. On her letters to the editor, see "Ida B. Wells-Barnett Scores Tribune—Disregards Race," *Chicago Defender*, May 9, 1914; and McMurry, *To Keep the Waters Troubled*, 313–14.

132 "The 1930 Chicago Diary of Ida B. Wells-Barnett," reprinted in *Memphis Diary*, May 19, Jan. 19, and Jan. 13, 1930. Woodson's book may have been *Negro Makers of History* (1928).

133 Irene McCoy Gaines, untitled talk [Mar. 30, 1931], Irene McCoy Gaines Papers, Box 1, folder 10, Chicago Historical Society.

134 *Crusade*, 4.

135 For an analysis of *Crusade for Justice*, see Joanne M. Braxton, *Black Women Writing Autobiography: A Tradition within a Tradition* (Philadelphia: Temple University Press, 1989), 102–38.

EPILOGUE

1 The National Endowment for the Arts found in two recent studies that there has been a general decline in what it calls "literary reading," but that women still did more of it than men. See Sunil Iyengar and Don Ball, *To Read or Not to Read: A Question of National Conscience*, Research Report 47 (Washington: D.C.: NEA, 2007); and *Reading at Risk: A Survey of Literary Reading in America*, Research Report 46 (Washington, D.C.: NEA, 2004).

2 John Modell, "Dating Becomes the Way of American Youth," *Essays on the Family and Historical Change*, ed. Leslie Page Moch and Gary D. Stark, 91–126 (College Station: Texas A&M University Press, 1983); Mary P. Ryan, *Womanhood in America: From Colonial Times to the Present*, 3rd ed. (New York: Franklin Watts, 1983), 217–52; Joan Jacobs Brumberg, *The Body Project: An Intimate History of American Girls* (New York: Random House, 1997); and Jane H. Hunter, *How Young Ladies Became Girls: The Victorian Origins of American Girlhood* (New Haven: Yale University Press, 2002).

3 Brumberg, *The Body Project*, esp. 100–104. On new forms of culture in the early twentieth century, including movies, see Kathy Peiss, *Cheap Amusements: Working Women and Leisure in Turn-of-the-Century New York* (Philadelphia: Temple University Press, 1986); and Nan Enstad, *Ladies of Labor, Girls of Adventure: Working Women, Popular Culture, and Labor Politics at the Turn of the Twentieth Century* (New York: Columbia University Press, 1999).

4   Robert S. Lynd and Helen Merrell Lynd, *Middletown: A Study in Modern American Culture* (1919; reprint, New York: Harcourt Brace Jovanovich, 1956), 229–36, quotation on 232. Attending lectures, a once-popular activity that combined education and sociability, also declined, while movie attendance increased.

5   On the backlash against the clubs, see Andrew C. Rieser, *The Chautauqua Moment: Protestants, Progressives, and the Culture of Modern Liberalism* (New York: Columbia University Press, 2003), 169–74. On changing professional requirements and values, see Margaret W. Rossiter, *Women Scientists in America: Struggles and Strategies to 1940* (Baltimore: Johns Hopkins University Press, 1982); Regina Markell Morantz-Sanchez, *Sympathy and Science: Women Physicians in American Medicine* (New York: Oxford University Press, 1985); and Kirsten Swinth, *Painting Professionals: Women Artists and the Development of Modern American Art, 1870–1930* (Chapel Hill: University of North Carolina Press, 2001).

6   Jane Addams, *The Second Twenty Years at Hull-House: September 1909 to September 1929* (New York: Macmillan, 1930).

7   Jonathan Yardley, "The real readers of literature do not fit the stereotype of tweedy male," *Trenton Times*, Sept. 3, 1989. The author reflects on the widely publicized research of Nicholas Zill and Marianne Winglee, summed up in "Literature Reading in the United States: Data from National Surveys and Their Policy Implications," *Book Research Quarterly* 5 (Spring 1989): 24–58.

8   D. T. Max, "The Oprah Effect," *New York Times Magazine* (Dec. 26, 1999): 41.

9   Ibid., 37, 36. My comments apply to the club in its first incarnation, from September 1996 to April 2002, when it was disbanded. In its second phase, between 2003 and the fall of 2005, Oprah's Book Club featured books by William Faulkner and other classic writers before shifting back to contemporary works.

10 Sales estimates come from Kathleen Rooney, *Reading with Oprah: The Book Club That Changed America* (Fayetteville: University of Arkansas Press, 2005), 169. There is already an extensive literature on Oprah's Book Club. See, in addition to Rooney, Cecilia Konchar Farr, *Reading Oprah: How Oprah's Book Club Changed the Way America Reads* (Albany: State University of New York Press, 2005); Mary R. Lamb, "The 'Talking Life' of Books: Women Readers in Oprah's Book Club," in *Reading Women: Literary Figures and Cultural Icons from the Victorian Age to the Present*, ed. Janet Badia and Jennifer Phegley, 255–80 (Toronto: University of Toronto Press, 2005); and Trysh Travis, "'It Will Change the World If Everybody Reads This Book': New Thought Religion in Oprah's Book Club," *American Quarterly* 59 (Sept. 2007): 1017–41.

11 [Paula Chin], "Touched by an Oprah," *People Weekly*, Dec. 20, 1999, [113].

12 "Oprah on 'The Fire for Reading,'" *Publishers Weekly*, Mar. 10, 2003, 16; Marilyn Johnson, "Oprah Winfrey: A Life in Books," *Life*, September 1997, 48.

13 Max, "The Oprah Effect," 37; discussion of Malika Oufkir's "Stolen Lives," on Oprah's Book Club, June 20, 2001.

14 Lynette Clemetson, "Oprah at a Crossroads," *Newsweek*, Jan. 8, 2001, 44 (cover story). Readers' exchanges about book selections may be found on Oprah.com.

15 Addams, "Democracy and Education," *Chautauqua Assembly Herald* 25 (Aug. 9, 1900): 2.

16 Bob Lamm, "Reading Groups: Where Are All the Men?" *Publishers Weekly*, Nov. 18, 1996, 48.

17 Quotations from Robin N. Neidorf, "Feminist Book Groups: The New C.R.?" *Ms.*, Jan./Feb. 1995, 64–67 (an excellent overview of the psychological and social impact of groups); Pat Neblett, *Circles of Sisterhood: A Book Discussion Group Guide for Women of Color* (New York: Harlem River Press, 1997), 17–18; and Carol Huber, "Once Begun, We Are Mighty," and Ellie Becker "Talking as Quilting," in *The Book Group Book: A Thoughtful Guide to Forming and Enjoying a Stimulating Book Discussion Group*, ed. Ellen Slezak (Chicago: Chicago Review Press, 1993), 5 and 95.

18 Neidorf, "Feminist Book Groups," 65. See also Dorian Burden, "Reading Groups: A Working Woman's Retreat," *Executive Female* 17 (July/August 1994): 76–77; and Shireen Dodson, *The Mother-Daughter Book Club: How Ten Busy Mothers and Daughters Came Together to Talk, Laugh and Learn through Their Love of Reading* (New York: HarperCollins, 1996).

19 Elizabeth Long, *Book Clubs: Women and the Uses of Reading in Everyday Life* (Chicago: University of Chicago Press, 2003), esp. 59–73. Many groups are long-lived. Some founded in the nineteenth century still survive. Among more recent groups, some that started when housewives with young children sought outside stimulation have continued as members went back to school or work, got divorced, remarried, came out as lesbians, or survived cancer.

SELECTED BIBLIOGRAPHY

ARCHIVAL SOURCES
Atlanta, Georgia
    Robert W. Woodruff Library, Atlanta University Center
        The Chautauqua Circle Collection
Bryn Mawr, Pennsylvania
    Bryn Mawr College Archives
        Mary Elizabeth Garrett Papers
        M. Carey Thomas Papers
Cambridge, Massachusetts
    Houghton Library, Harvard University
        Louisa May Alcott Papers: bMS Am 1130.8 and bMS Am 800.23
        Little, Brown & Co. Papers: *87M-113
    Schlesinger Library, Radcliffe Institute, Harvard University
        Alice Hamilton Papers
        Hamilton Family Papers
Chicago, Illinois
    Chicago Historical Society
        Irene McCoy Gaines Papers
    Special Collections Research Center, University of Chicago Library
        Edith and Grace Abbott Papers
        Ida B. Wells Papers
    Special Collections, University of Illinois at Chicago Library
        Jane Addams Memorial Collection
Farmington, Connecticut
    Hill-Stead Archives, Hill-Stead Museum
    Miss Porter's School Archives
New York, New York
    Manuscripts and Archives Division, The New York Public Library, Astor, Lenox
        and Tilden Foundations

Free Circulating Libraries Records, RG 4
Superintendent of Work with Schools Records, RG 8
Schomburg Center for Research in Black Culture, New York Public Library
Harry A. Williamson Collection
Northampton, Massachusetts
Sophia Smith Collection, Smith College
Ellen Gates Starr Papers
Philadelphia, Pennsylvania
American Philosophical Society Library
Simon Flexner Papers
Princeton, New Jersey
Manuscripts Division, Rare Books and Special Collections Department, Princeton
University Library
Alfred and Mary Gwinn Hodder Papers
Swarthmore, Pennsylvania
Swarthmore College Peace Collection, Swarthmore College
Jane Addams Collection
Washington, D.C.
Library of Congress, Manuscript Division
Blackwell Family Papers
Mary Church Terrell Papers
Moorland-Spingarn Research Center, Howard University
Bethel Literary and Historical Association Records
Anna J. Cooper Papers
Mary Church Terrell Papers

MANUSCRIPT COLLECTIONS ON MICROFILM

The Jane Addams Papers. Edited by Mary Lynn McCree Bryan. Ann Arbor: University
Microfilms International, 1984.
The Papers of M. Carey Thomas in the Bryn Mawr College Archives. Edited by Lucy
Fisher West. Woodbridge, Conn.: Research Publications, 1982.
Papers of the Women's Trade Union League and Its Principal Leaders. Edited by
Edward T. James. Woodbridge, Conn.: Research Publications, 1974.

SERIAL PUBLICATIONS

Chicago Broad Ax
Chicago Defender
Colored American Magazine (Boston, Mass.)
Hull-House Bulletin
Hull-House Year Book
Woman's Era (Boston, Mass.)

BOOKS AND ARTICLES

Abbott, Lyman, ed. *Hints for Home Reading: A Series of Papers on Books and Their Use.* New York: G. P. Putnam's Sons, 1880.

Addams, Jane. "A Book That Changed My Life." *Christian Century* 44 (Oct. 13, 1927): 1196–98.

———. *Democracy and Social Ethics.* 1902. Edited by Anne Firor Scott. Cambridge, Mass.: Harvard University Press, 1964.

———. *The Second Twenty Years at Hull-House: September 1909 to September 1929.* New York: Macmillan, 1930.

———. *Twenty Years at Hull-House.* New York: Macmillan, 1910.

Alberghene, Janice M., and Beverly Lyon Clark, eds. *Little Women and the Feminist Imagination: Criticism, Controversy, Personal Essays.* New York: Garland, 1999.

Alcott, Louisa May. *Little Women.* Edited by Madelon Bedell. New York: Modern Library, 1983.

Amory, Hugh, and David D. Hall, eds. *The Colonial Book in the Atlantic World.* A History of the Book in America, vol. 1. Cambridge: Cambridge University Press, 2000.

Anderson, Benedict. *Imagined Communities: Reflections on the Origin and Spread of Nationalism.* London: Verso, 1983.

Antin, Mary. *The Promised Land.* Boston: Houghton Mifflin, 1912.

Antler, Joyce. *The Journey Home: Jewish Women and the American Century.* New York: Free Press, 1997.

Appleyard, J. A. *Becoming a Reader: The Experience of Fiction from Childhood to Adulthood.* Cambridge: Cambridge University Press, 1990.

Armstrong, Nancy. *Desire and Domestic Fiction: A Political History of the Novel.* New York: Oxford University Press, 1987.

Augst, Thomas. *The Clerk's Tale: Young Men and Moral Life in Nineteenth-Century America.* Chicago: University of Chicago Press, 2003.

Austin, Mary. *Earth Horizon: Autobiography.* Boston: Houghton Mifflin, 1932.

Baker, S. Josephine. *Fighting for Life.* New York: Macmillan, 1939.

Bakhtin, M. M. *The Dialogic Imagination: Four Essays.* Edited by Michael Holquist. Translated by Caryl Emerson and Michael Holquist. Austin: University of Texas Press, 1981.

Baym, Nina. *American Women Writers and the Work of History, 1790–1860.* New Brunswick, N.J.: Rutgers University Press, 1995.

———. *Novels, Readers, and Reviewers: Responses to Fiction in Antebellum America.* Ithaca, N.Y.: Cornell University Press, 1984.

———. *Woman's Fiction: A Guide to Novels by and about Women in America, 1820–1870.* Ithaca, N.Y.: Cornell University Press, 1978.

Beauvoir, Simone de. *Memoirs of a Dutiful Daughter.* Translated by James Kirkup. Cleveland: World, 1959.

Bederman, Gail. *Manliness and Civilization: A Cultural History of Gender and Race in the United States, 1880–1917.* Chicago: University of Chicago Press, 1995.

"The Best Hundred Books By the Best Judges." *Pall Mall Gazette.* Extra issue 24 (1886).

Bisno, Abraham. *Abraham Bisno: Union Pioneer.* Madison: University of Wisconsin Press, 1967.

Bjorklund, Diane. *Interpreting the Self: Two Hundred Years of American Autobiography.* Chicago: University of Chicago Press, 1998.

Blair, Karen J. *The Clubwoman as Feminist: True Womanhood Redefined, 1868–1914.* New York: Holmes and Meier, 1980.

Bledstein, Burton J. *The Culture of Professionalism: The Middle Class and the Development of Higher Education in America.* New York: W. W. Norton, 1976.

Blumin, Stuart M. *The Emergence of the Middle Class: Social Experience in the American City, 1760–1900.* Cambridge: Cambridge University Press, 1989.

Boris, Eileen. *Art and Labor: Ruskin, Morris, and the Craftsman Ideal in America.* Philadelphia: Temple University Press, 1986.

Bourdieu, Pierre. *Distinction: A Social Critique of the Judgement of Taste.* Translated by Richard Nice. Cambridge, Mass.: Harvard University Press, 1984.

Boyarin, Jonathan, ed. *The Ethnography of Reading.* Berkeley and Los Angeles: University of California Press, 1992.

Brandt, Deborah. *Literacy in American Lives.* Cambridge: Cambridge University Press, 2001.

Braxton, Joanne M. *Black Women Writing Autobiography: A Tradition within a Tradition.* Philadelphia: Temple University Press, 1989.

Britton, James. *Language and Learning.* London: Allen Lane, 1970.

Brodhead, Richard H. *Cultures of Letters: Scenes of Reading and Writing in Nineteenth-Century America.* Chicago: University of Chicago Press, 1993.

Brown, Candy Gunther. *The Word in the World: Evangelical Writing, Publishing, and Reading in America, 1789–1880.* Chapel Hill: University of North Carolina Press, 2004.

Brown, Elsa Barkley. "Negotiating and Transforming the Public Sphere: African American Political Life in the Transition from Slavery to Freedom." *Public Culture* 7 (1994): 107–46.

Brown, Lois. *Pauline Elizabeth Hopkins: Black Daughter of the Revolution.* Chapel Hill: University of North Carolina Press, 2008.

Brown, Victoria Bissell. *The Education of Jane Addams.* Philadelphia: University of Pennsylvania Press, 2004.

Brownstein, Rachel M. *Becoming a Heroine: Reading about Women in Novels.* New York: Penguin, 1984.

Bruce, Dickson D., Jr. *Black American Writing from the Nadir: The Evolution of a Literary Tradition, 1877–1915.* Baton Rouge: Louisiana State University Press, 1989.

Brumberg, Joan Jacobs. *The Body Project: An Intimate History of American Girls.* New York: Random House, 1997.

———. "The 'Me' of Me: Voices of Jewish Girls in Adolescent Diaries of the 1920s and 1950s." In *Talking Back: Images of Jewish Women in American Popular Culture*, edited by Joyce Antler, 53–67. Hanover, N.H.: Brandeis University Press, 1998.

Brumberg, Stephan F. *Going to America, Going to School: The Jewish Immigrant Public School Encounter in Turn-of-the-Century New York City.* New York: Praeger, 1986.

Bruner, Jerome. *The Culture of Education.* Cambridge, Mass.: Harvard University Press, 1996.

Bryan, Mary Lynn McCree, Barbara Bair, and Maree De Angury, eds. *The Selected Papers of Jane Addams.* Vol. 1. *Preparing to Lead, 1860–81.* Urbana: University of Illinois Press, 2003.

Cahan, Abraham. *The Education of Abraham Cahan.* Translated by Leon Stein. Philadelphia: Jewish Publication Society of America, 1969.

Calinescu, Matei. *Rereading.* New Haven: Yale University Press, 1993.

Canby, Henry Seidel. *American Memoir.* Boston: Houghton Mifflin, 1947.

Carby, Hazel V. *Reconstructing Womanhood: The Emergence of the Afro-American Woman Novelist.* New York: Oxford University Press, 1987.

Carrier, Esther Jane. *Fiction in Public Libraries, 1876–1900.* New York: Scarecrow Press, 1965.

Carson, Mina J. "Agnes Hamilton of Fort Wayne: The Education of a Christian Settlement Worker." *Indiana Magazine of History* 80 (March 1984): 1–34.

———. *Settlement Folk: Social Thought and the American Settlement Movement, 1885–1930.* Chicago: University of Chicago Press, 1990.

Carter, Paul A. *The Spiritual Crisis of the Gilded Age.* DeKalb: Northern Illinois University Press, 1971.

Casper, Scott E. "Biographical Mania: The Transformation of Biographical Theory in Nineteenth-Century America." *Nineteenth-Century Prose* 22 (Fall 1995): 39–62.

———. *Constructing American Lives: Biography and Culture in Nineteenth-Century America.* Chapel Hill: University of North Carolina Press, 1999.

Casper, Scott E., Jeffrey D. Groves, Stephen W. Nissenbaum, and Michael Winship, eds. *The Industrial Book, 1840–1880.* A History of the Book in America, vol. 3. Chapel Hill: University of North Carolina Press, 2007.

Cavallo, Guglielmo, and Roger Chartier, eds. *A History of Reading in the West.* Translated by Lydia G. Cochrane. Amherst: University of Massachusetts Press, 1995.

Certeau, Michel de. "Reading as Poaching." In *The Practice of Everyday Life,* translated by Steven F. Rendall, 165–76. Berkeley and Los Angeles: University of California Press, 1984.

Chambers-Schiller, Lee Virginia. *Liberty, a Better Husband: Single Women in America; The Generations of 1780–1840.* New Haven: Yale University Press, 1984.

Chartier, Roger. "Intellectual History or Sociocultural History?: The French Trajectories." In *Modern European Intellectual History: Reappraisals and New Perspectives,* edited by Dominick LaCapra and Steven L. Kaplan, 13–46. Ithaca, N.Y.: Cornell University Press, 1982.

———. *The Order of Books: Readers, Authors, and Libraries in Europe between the Fourteenth and Eighteenth Centuries.* Translated by Lydia G. Cochrane. Stanford, Calif.: Stanford University Press, 1994.

———. "Texts, Printing, Readings." In *The New Cultural History,* edited by Lynn Hunt, 154–75. Berkeley and Los Angeles: University of California Press, 1989.

Chodorow, Nancy J. *The Power of Feelings: Personal Meaning in Psychoanalysis, Gender, and Culture.* New Haven: Yale University Press, 1999.

Clark, Gregory, and S. Michael Halloran, eds. *Oratorical Culture in Nineteenth-Century America: Transformations in the Theory and Practice of Rhetoric.* Carbondale: Southern Illinois University Press, 1993.

Cmiel, Kenneth. *Democratic Eloquence: The Fight over Popular Speech in Nineteenth-Century America.* Berkeley and Los Angeles: University of California Press, 1990.

Cohen, Hagit. "The Demands of Integration—The Challenges of Ethnicization: Jewish

Women's Yiddish Reading Circles in North America between the Two World Wars."
NASHIM: A Journal of Jewish Women's Studies and Gender Issues 16 (2008): 98–129.

Cohen, Rose. "The Books I Knew as a Child." *Bookman* 49 (March 1919): 15–19.

———. *Out of the Shadow.* 1918. Reprint, Ithaca, N.Y.: Cornell University Press, 1995.

———. "To the Friends of 'Out of the Shadow.'" *Bookman* 55 (March 1922): 36–40.

Cooper, Anna Julia. *A Voice from the South: By a Black Woman of the South.* 1892. Reprint, New York: Oxford University Press, 1988.

Cornelius, Janet Duitsman. *"When I Can Read My Title Clear": Literacy, Slavery, and Religion in the Antebellum South.* Columbia: University of South Carolina Press, 1991.

Costin, Lela B. *Two Sisters for Social Justice: A Biography of Grace and Edith Abbott.* Urbana: University of Illinois Press, 1983.

Cott, Nancy F. "Passionlessness: An Interpretation of Victorian Sexual Ideology, 1790–1850." *Signs* 4 (Winter 1978): 219–36.

Coultrap-McQuin, Susan. *Doing Literary Business: American Women Writers in the Nineteenth Century.* Chapel Hill: University of North Carolina Press, 1990.

Danky, James P., and Wayne A. Wiegand, eds. *Print Culture in a Diverse America.* Urbana: University of Illinois Press, 1998.

———. *Women in Print: Essays on the Print Culture of American Women from the Nineteenth and Twentieth Centuries.* Madison: University of Wisconsin Press, 2006.

Darling, Richard L. *The Rise of Children's Book Reviewing in America, 1865–1881.* New York: Bowker, 1968.

Darnton, Robert. "What Is the History of Books?" *Daedalus* 111 (Summer 1982): 65–83.

Davidson, Cathy N. *Revolution and the Word: The Rise of the Novel in America.* New York: Oxford University Press, 1986.

———, ed. *Reading in America: Literature and Social History.* Baltimore: Johns Hopkins University Press, 1989.

Davidson, James West. *"They Say": Ida B. Wells and the Reconstruction of Race.* New York: Oxford University Press, 2007.

Davis, Allen F. *American Heroine: The Life and Legend of Jane Addams.* New York: Oxford University Press, 1973.

———. *Spearheads for Reform: The Social Settlements and the Progressive Movement, 1890–1914.* New York: Oxford University Press, 1967.

Davis, Philip. *And Crown Thy Good.* New York: Philosophical Library, 1952.

Dearborn, Mary V. *Pocahontas's Daughters: Gender and Ethnicity in American Culture.* New York: Oxford University Press, 1986.

DeCosta-Willis, Miriam, ed. *The Memphis Diary of Ida B. Wells.* Boston: Beacon Press, 1995.

Delamar, Gloria T. *Louisa May Alcott and "Little Women": Biography, Critique, Publications, Poems, Songs and Contemporary Relevance.* Jefferson, N.C.: McFarland, 1990.

Denning, Michael. *Mechanic Accents: Dime Novels and Working-Class Culture in America.* London: Verso, 1987.

Dobkin, Marjorie Housepian, ed. *The Making of a Feminist: Early Journals and Letters of M. Carey Thomas.* Kent, Ohio: Kent State University Press, 1979.

Docherty, Linda J. "Women as Readers: Visual Interpretations." *Proceedings of the American Antiquarian Society* 107, part 2 (1997): 335–88.

Dodson, Shireen. *The Mother-Daughter Book Club: How Ten Busy Mothers and Daughters Came Together to Talk, Laugh and Learn through Their Love of Reading.* New York: HarperCollins, 1996.

Dougherty, James. "Jane Addams: Culture and Imagination." *Yale Review* 71 (Spring 1982): 363–79.

Dray, Philip. *At the Hands of Persons Unknown: The Lynching of Black America.* New York: Random House, 2002.

Drucker, Sally Ann. "'It Doesn't Say So in Mother's Prayerbook': Autobiographies in English by Immigrant Jewish Women." *American Jewish History* 74 (Autumn 1989): 55–71.

Dublin, Thomas. "Critical Essay." In *Rose Cohen. Reading Series: A Place in History.* Brookline, Mass.: Jewish Women's Archive, 2003. http://jwa.org/discover/inthepast/readingseries/cohen/criticalessay.html (accessed August 19, 2009).

————. Introduction to the 1995 edition, *Out of the Shadow*, by Rose Cohen, ix–xxi. Ithaca, N.Y.: Cornell University Press, 1995.

DuPlessis, Rachel Blau. *Writing beyond the Ending: Narrative Strategies of Twentieth-Century Women Writers.* Bloomington: Indiana University Press, 1985.

Duster, Alfreda M., ed. *Crusade for Justice: The Autobiography of Ida B. Wells.* Chicago: University of Chicago Press, 1970.

Dye, Nancy Schrom. *As Equals and as Sisters: Feminism, the Labor Movement, and the Women's Trade Union League of New York.* Columbia: University of Missouri Press, 1980.

Elshtain, Jean Bethke. *Jane Addams and the Dream of American Democracy.* New York: Basic Books, 2002.

Enstad, Nan. *Ladies of Labor, Girls of Adventure: Working Women, Popular Culture, and Labor Politics at the Turn of the Twentieth Century.* New York: Columbia University Press, 1999.

Erikson, Erik H. *Identity: Youth and Crisis.* New York: W. W. Norton, 1968.

Faderman, Lillian. *Odd Girls and Twilight Lovers: A History of Lesbian Life in Twentieth-Century America.* New York: Columbia University Press, 1991.

Faragher, John Mack, and Florence Howe, eds. *Women and Higher Education in American History.* New York: W. W. Norton, 1988.

Farrell, John C. *Beloved Lady: A History of Jane Addams' Ideas on Reform and Peace.* Baltimore: Johns Hopkins University Press, 1967.

Feffer, Andrew. *The Chicago Pragmatists and American Progressivism.* Ithaca, N.Y.: Cornell University Press, 1993.

Feimster, Crystal N. *Southern Horrors: Women and the Politics of Rape and Lynching.* Cambridge, Mass.: Harvard University Press, 2009.

Fetterley, Judith. *The Resisting Reader: A Feminist Approach to American Fiction.* Bloomington: Indiana University Press, 1978.

Fish, Stanley. *Is There a Text in This Class?: The Authority of Interpretive Communities.* Cambridge, Mass.: Harvard University Press, 1980.

Flint, Kate. *The Woman Reader, 1837–1914.* New York: Oxford University Press, 1993.

Flynn, Elizabeth A., and Patrocinio P. Schweickart, eds. *Gender and Reading: Essays on Readers, Texts, and Contexts*. Baltimore: Johns Hopkins University Press, 1986.

Foster, Frances Smith. *Written by Herself: Literary Production by African American Women, 1746–1892*. Bloomington: Indiana University Press, 1993.

Foster, Shirley, and Judy Simons. *What Katy Read: Feminist Re-Readings of "Classic" Stories for Girls*. Iowa City: University of Iowa Press, 1995.

Frankel, Noralee, and Nancy S. Dye, eds. *Gender, Class, Race, and Reform in the Progressive Era*. Lexington: University Press of Kentucky, 1991.

Gagnier, Regenia. "Social Atoms: Working-Class Autobiography, Subjectivity, and Gender." *Victorian Studies* 30 (Spring 1987): 335–63.

Gaines, Kevin K. *Uplifting the Race: Black Leadership, Politics, and Culture in the Twentieth Century*. Chapel Hill: University of North Carolina Press, 1996.

Garland, Hamlin. *A Son of the Middle Border*. 1917. Reprint, New York: Macmillan, 1956.

Garvey, Ellen Gruber. *The Adman in the Parlor: Magazines and the Gendering of Consumer Culture, 1880s to 1910s*. New York: Oxford University Press, 1996.

Geertz, Clifford. *The Interpretation of Cultures: Selected Essays*. New York: Basic Books, 1973.

Gere, Anne Ruggles. *Intimate Practices: Literacy and Cultural Work in U.S. Women's Clubs, 1880–1920*. Urbana: University of Illinois Press, 1997.

Gere, Anne Ruggles, and Sarah R. Robbins. "Gendered Literacy in Black and White: Turn-of-the-Century African-American and European-American Club Women's Printed Texts." *Signs* 21 (Spring 1996): 643–78.

Gernes, Todd Steven. "Recasting the Culture of Ephemera: Young Women's Literary Culture in Nineteenth-Century America." Ph.D. diss., Brown University, 1992.

Giddings, Paula. *Ida: A Sword among Lions: Ida B. Wells and the Campaign against Lynching*. New York: Amistad, 2008.

———. *When and Where I Enter: The Impact of Black Women on Race and Sex in America*. New York: Bantam Books, 1984.

Gilman, Charlotte Perkins. *The Living of Charlotte Perkins Gilman*. 1935. Reprint, New York: Harper & Row, 1975.

Gilmore, Glenda Elizabeth. *Gender and Jim Crow: Women and the Politics of White Supremacy in North Carolina, 1896–1920*. Chapel Hill: University of North Carolina Press, 1996.

Golden, Catherine J. *Images of the Woman Reader in Victorian British and American Fiction*. Gainesville: University Press of Florida, 2003.

Goldman, Emma. *Living My Life*. 2 vols. 1931. Reprint, New York: Dover Publications, 1970.

Goldsby, Jacqueline. *A Spectacular Secret: Lynching in American Life and Literature*. Chicago: University of Chicago Press, 2006.

Graff, Harvey J. *The Literacy Myth: Literacy and Social Structure in the Nineteenth-Century City*. New York: Academic Press, 1979.

Green, Martin. *Dreams of Adventure, Deeds of Empire*. New York: Basic Books, 1979.

Hall, David D. *Cultures of Print: Essays in the History of the Book*. Amherst: University of Massachusetts Press, 1996.

———. "The Uses of Literacy in New England, 1600–1850." In *Printing and Society in*

Early America, edited by William L. Joyce et al., 1–47. Worcester, Mass.: American Antiquarian Society, 1983.

Hallett, Judith P. "Edith Hamilton (1867–1963)." *Classical World* 90 (November/ December 1996–January/February 1997): 107–47.

Hamilton, Alice. *Exploring the Dangerous Trades*. Boston: Little, Brown, 1943.

Harding, D. H. "Psychological Processes in the Reading of Fiction." In *The Cool Web: The Pattern of Children's Reading*, edited by Margaret Meek, Aidan Warlow, and Griselda Barton, 58–72. London: Bodley Head, 1977.

Harris, Trudier, comp. *Selected Works of Ida B. Wells-Barnett*. New York: Oxford University Press, 1991.

Hart, James D. *The Popular Book: A History of America's Literary Taste*. Berkeley and Los Angeles: University of California Press, n.d.

Hasanovitz, Elizabeth. *One of Them: Chapters from a Passionate Autobiography*. Boston: Houghton Mifflin, 1918.

Hedrick, Joan D. *Harriet Beecher Stowe: A Life*. New York: Oxford University Press, 1994.

———. "Parlor Literature: Harriet Beecher Stowe and the Question of 'Great Women Artists.'" *Signs* 17 (Winter 1992): 275–303.

Heilbrun, Carolyn G. *Writing a Woman's Life*. New York: W. W. Norton, 1988.

Heininger, Mary Lynn Stevens. *At Home with a Book: Reading in America, 1840–1940*. Rochester, N.Y.: Strong Museum, 1986.

Hendricks, Wanda A. *Gender, Race, and Politics in the Midwest: Black Club Women in Illinois*. Bloomington: Indiana University Press, 1998.

Henriksen, Louise Levitas. *Anzia Yezierska: A Writer's Life*. New Brunswick, N.J.: Rutgers University Press, 1988.

Higginbotham, Evelyn Brooks. *Righteous Discontent: The Women's Movement in the Black Baptist Church, 1880–1920*. Cambridge, Mass.: Harvard University Press, 1993.

Higham, John. "The Reorientation of American Culture in the 1890s." In *Writing American History: Essays on Modern Scholarship*. Bloomington: Indiana University Press, 1970.

Hill, Mary A. *Charlotte Perkins Gilman: The Making of a Radical Feminist, 1860–1896*. Philadelphia: Temple University Press, 1980.

A History of the Club Movement among the Colored Women of the United States of America. 1902. Reprint, Washington, D.C.: National Association of Colored Women's Clubs, 1978.

Hobbs, Catherine, ed. *Nineteenth-Century Women Learn to Write*. Charlottesville: University Press of Virginia, 1995.

Hodes, Martha. *White Women, Black Men: Illicit Sex in the Nineteenth-Century South*. New Haven: Yale University Press, 1997.

Holland, Norman. *The Dynamics of Literary Response*. New York: W. W. Norton, 1975.

Horowitz, Helen Lefkowitz. *Alma Mater: Design and Experience in the Women's Colleges from Their Nineteenth-Century Beginnings to the 1930s*. New York: Alfred A. Knopf, 1984.

———. *Culture and the City: Cultural Philanthropy in Chicago from the 1880s to 1917*. Lexington: University Press of Kentucky, 1976.

———. "'Nous Autres': Reading, Passion, and the Creation of M. Carey Thomas." *Journal of American History* 79 (June 1992): 68–95.

———. *The Power and Passion of M. Carey Thomas.* New York: Alfred A. Knopf, 1994.

Howe, Daniel Walker, ed. *Victorian America.* Philadelphia: University of Pennsylvania Press, 1976.

Hunt, Lynn. *Inventing Human Rights: A History.* New York: W. W. Norton, 2007.

Hunter, Jane H. *How Young Ladies Became Girls: The Victorian Origins of American Girlhood.* New Haven: Yale University Press, 2002.

Hyman, Paula E. *Gender and Assimilation in Modern Jewish History: The Roles and Representation of Women.* Seattle: University of Washington Press, 1995.

———. "Gender and the Immigrant Jewish Experience in the United States." In *Jewish Women in Historical Perspective*, edited by Judith R. Baskin, 222–42. Detroit: Wayne State University Press, 1991.

Iyengar, Sunil, and Don Ball. *To Read or Not to Read: A Question of National Conscience.* Washington, D.C.: National Endowment for the Arts, 2007.

Jackson, Shannon. *Lines of Activity: Performance, Historiography, Hull-House Domesticity.* Ann Arbor: University of Michigan Press, 2001.

Jauss, Hans Robert. "Literary History as a Challenge to Literary Theory." In *New Directions in Literary History*, edited by Ralph Cohen, 11–41. Baltimore: Johns Hopkins University Press, 1974.

Jelinek, Estelle C., ed. *Women's Autobiography: Essays in Criticism.* Bloomington: Indiana University Press, 1980.

John, Arthur. *The Best Years of the* Century: *Richard Watson Gilder,* Scribner's Monthly, *and the* Century Magazine, *1870–1909.* Urbana: University of Illinois Press, 1981.

Johnson, James Weldon. *Along This Way: The Autobiography of James Weldon Johnson.* New York: Viking Press, 1933.

Johnson, Marilyn. "Oprah Winfrey: A Life in Books." *Life*, September 1997, 48.

Jones, Beverly Washington. *Quest for Equality: The Life and Writings of Mary Eliza Church Terrell.* Brooklyn: Carlson, 1990.

———. *Stanford L. Warren Branch Library: 77 Years of Public Service: A Phoenix in the Durham Community.* Durham, N.C.: Durham County Library, 1990.

Jones, Jacqueline. *Labor of Love, Labor of Sorrow: Black Women, Work, and the Family from Slavery to the Present.* New York: Basic Books, 1985.

Jordan, John O., and Robert L. Patten, eds. *Literature in the Marketplace: Nineteenth-Century British Publishing and Reading Practices.* Cambridge: Cambridge University Press, 1995.

Joselit, Jenna Weissman. "Reading, Writing, and a Library Card: New York Jews and the New York Public Library." *Biblion: The Bulletin of the New York Public Library* 5 (Fall 1996): 97–117.

Juhasz, Suzanne. *Reading from the Heart: Women, Literature, and the Search for True Love.* New York: Penguin, 1994.

Kaestle, Carl F., et al. *Literacy in the United States: Readers and Reading since 1880.* New Haven: Yale University Press, 1991.

Kaestle, Carl F., and Janice Radway, eds. *Print in Motion: The Expansion of Publishing and Reading in the United States, 1880–1940.* A History of the Book in America, vol. 4. Chapel Hill: University of North Carolina Press, 2009.

Kaplan, Cora. "*The Thorn Birds*: Fiction, Fantasy, Femininity." In *Sea Changes: Feminism and Culture*. London: Verso, 1986.

Katz, Harriet Averbuch. "Cathedral of Humanity: A Study of Jane Addams' Ideas on Art and Culture." D.S.W. diss., Yeshiva University, 1975.

Kelley, Mary. *Learning to Stand and Speak: Women, Education, and Public Life in America's Republic*. Chapel Hill: University of North Carolina Press, 2006.

———. *Private Woman, Public Stage: Literary Domesticity in Nineteenth-Century America*. New York: Oxford University Press, 1984.

———. "Reading Women/Women Reading: The Making of Learned Women in Antebellum America." *Journal of American History* 83 (September 1996): 401–24.

Kellman, Ellen. "Women as Readers of Sacred and Secular [Yiddish] Literature: An Historical Overview." In *Conference Proceedings, Di froyen: Women and Yiddish, Tribute to the Past, Directions for the Future*, 18–21. New York: National Council of Jewish Women, New York Section, Jewish Women's Resource Center, 1997.

Kelly, R. Gordon. *Mother Was a Lady: Self and Society in Selected American Children's Periodicals, 1865–1890*. Westport, Conn.: Greenwood, 1974.

———, ed. *Children's Periodicals of the United States*. Westport, Conn.: Greenwood, 1984.

Kerber, Linda K. "Can a Woman Be an Individual?: The Limits of Puritan Tradition in the Early Republic." *Texas Studies in Literature and Language* 25 (Spring 1983): 165–78.

———. "Separate Spheres, Female Worlds, Woman's Place: The Rhetoric of Women's History." *Journal of American History* 75 (June 1988): 9–39.

———. *Women of the Republic: Intellect and Ideology in Revolutionary America*. Chapel Hill: University of North Carolina Press, 1980.

Kett, Joseph F. *The Pursuit of Knowledge under Difficulties: From Self-Improvement to Adult Education in America, 1750–1990*. Stanford, Calif.: Stanford University Press, 1994.

———. *Rites of Passage: Adolescence in America, 1790 to the Present*. New York: Basic Books, 1977.

Klapper, Melissa R. *Jewish Girls Coming of Age in America, 1860–1920*. New York: New York University Press, 2005.

Knight, Denise D., ed. *The Diaries of Charlotte Perkins Gilman*. 2 vols. Charlottesville: University Press of Virginia, 1994.

Knight, Louise W. *Citizen: Jane Addams and the Struggle for Democracy*. Chicago: University of Chicago Press, 2005.

Knupfer, Anne Meis. *Toward a Tenderer Humanity and a Nobler Womanhood: African American Women's Clubs in Turn-of-the-Century Chicago*. New York: New York University Press, 1996.

Kohut, Rebekah. *My Portion (An Autobiography)*. New York: Thomas Seltzer, 1925.

Kramer, Sydelle, and Jenny Masur, eds. *Jewish Grandmothers*. Boston: Beacon Press, 1976.

Krause, Corinne Azen. *Grandmothers, Mothers, and Daughters: Oral Histories of Three Generations of Ethnic American Women*. Boston: Twayne, 1991.

Lamb, Mary R. "The 'Talking Life' of Books: Women Readers in Oprah's Book Club." In *Reading Women: Literary Figures and Cultural Icons from the Victorian Age to the*

Present, edited by Janet Badia and Jennifer Phlegley, 255–80. Toronto: University of Toronto Press, 2005.

Lamm, Bob. "Reading Groups: Where Are All the Men?" *Publishers Weekly*, November 18, 1996, 48.

Lane, Ann J. *To Herland and Beyond: The Life and Work of Charlotte Perkins Gilman.* New York: Pantheon, 1990.

Larson, Kate Clifford. "The Saturday Evening Girls: A Progressive Era Literary Club and the Intellectual Life of Working Class and Immigrant Girls in Turn-of-the-Century Boston." *Library Quarterly* 71 (April 2001): 195–230.

Lasch, Christopher. *The New Radicalism in America, 1889–1963: The Intellectual as a Social Type.* New York: Alfred A. Knopf, 1965.

Levine, Lawrence W. *Highbrow/Lowbrow: The Emergence of Cultural Hierarchy in America.* Cambridge, Mass.: Harvard University Press, 1988.

Leypoldt, Augusta H., and George Iles, eds. *List of Books for Girls and Women and Their Clubs.* Boston: Library Bureau, 1895.

Lilienthal, Meta. *Dear Remembered World: Childhood Memories of an Old New Yorker.* New York: Richard R. Smith, 1947.

Linn, James Weber. *Jane Addams: A Biography.* New York: D. Appleton-Century, 1935.

Lissak, Rivka Shpak. *Pluralism and Progressives: Hull House and the New Immigrants, 1890–1919.* Chicago: University of Chicago Press, 1989.

Logan, Shirley Wilson. *"We Are Coming": The Persuasive Discourse of Nineteenth-Century Black Women.* Carbondale: Southern Illinois University Press, 1999.

Long, Elizabeth. *Book Clubs: Women and the Uses of Reading in Everyday Life.* Chicago: University of Chicago Press, 2003.

———. "Textual Interpretation as Collective Action." In *The Ethnography of Reading*, edited by Jonathan Boyarin, 180–211. Berkeley and Los Angeles: University of California Press, 1993.

Lovett, Robert Morss. *All Our Years: The Autobiography of Robert Morss Lovett.* New York: Viking, 1948.

———. "A Boy's Reading Fifty Years Ago." *New Republic*, November 17, 1926, 335–36.

Lundin, Anne H. "Victorian Horizons: The Reception of Children's Books in England and America, 1880–1900." *Library Quarterly* 64 (January 1994): 30–59.

Lynd, Robert S., and Helen Merrell Lynd. *Middletown: A Study in Modern American Culture.* 1929. Reprint, New York: Harcourt Brace Jovanovich, 1956.

Lyons, Martyn. "New Readers in the Nineteenth Century: Women, Children, Workers." In *A History of Reading in the West*, edited by Guglielmo Cavallo and Roger Chartier, translated by Lydia G. Cochrane, 313–44. Amherst: University of Massachusetts Press, 1999.

Lytle, Susan L. "Living Literacy: Rethinking Development in Adulthood." In *Literacy: A Critical Sourcebook*, edited by Ellen Cushman et al., 376–401. Boston: Bedford/St. Martin's, 2001.

Machor, James L., ed. *Readers in History: Nineteenth-Century American Literature and the Contexts of Response.* Baltimore: Johns Hopkins University Press, 1993.

MacLeod, Anne Scott. *American Childhood: Essays on Children's Literature of the Nineteenth and Twentieth Centuries.* Athens: University of Georgia Press, 1994.

Martin, Theodora Penny. *The Sound of Our Own Voices: Women's Study Clubs, 1860–1910*. Boston: Beacon Press, 1987.

Matthews, Victoria Earle. "The Value of Race Literature: An Address." *Massachusetts Review* 27 (Summer 1986): 170–85.

Maynes, Mary Jo. "Gender and Narrative Form in French and German Working-Class Autobiographies." In *Interpreting Women's Lives: Feminist Theory and Personal Narratives*, edited by the Personal Narratives Group, 103–17. Bloomington: Indiana University Press, 1989.

McCarthy, Kathleen D. *Women's Culture: American Philanthropy and Art, 1830–1930*. Chicago: University of Chicago Press, 1991.

McCauley, Elfrieda B. "The New England Mill Girls: Feminine Influence in the Development of Public Libraries in New England, 1820–1860." D.L.S. diss., Columbia University, 1971.

McCree, Mary Lynn. "The First Year of Hull-House, 1889–1890, in Letters by Jane Addams and Ellen Gates Starr." *Chicago History* 1 (1970): 101–14.

McHenry, Elizabeth. *Forgotten Readers: Recovering the Lost History of African American Literary Societies*. Durham, N.C.: Duke University Press, 2002.

McHenry, Elizabeth, and Shirley Brice Heath. "The Literate and the Literary: African Americans as Writers and Readers—1830–1940." *Written Communication* 11 (October 1994): 419–44.

McMurry, Linda O. *To Keep the Waters Troubled: The Life of Ida B. Wells*. New York: Oxford University Press, 1998.

Meacham, Standish. *Toynbee Hall and Social Reform, 1880–1914: The Search for Community*. New Haven: Yale University Press, 1987.

Meehan, Jeannette Porter. *The Lady of the Limberlost: The Life and Letters of Gene Stratton-Porter*. Garden City, N.Y.: Doubleday, Doran, 1928.

Menand, Louis. *The Metaphysical Club*. New York: Farrar, Straus and Giroux, 2001.

Merrill, Marlene Deahl, ed. *Growing Up in Boston's Gilded Age: The Journal of Alice Stone Blackwell, 1872–1874*. New Haven: Yale University Press, 1990.

Meyer, Annie Nathan. *It's Been Fun: An Autobiography*. New York: Henry Schuman, 1951.

Mitchell, Sally. *The New Girl: Girls' Culture in England, 1880–1915*. New York: Columbia University Press, 1995.

Modell, John. "Dating Becomes the Way of American Youth." In *Essays on the Family and Historical Change*, edited by Leslie Page Moch and Gary D. Stark, 91–126. College Station: Texas A&M University Press, 1983.

Monaghan, E. Jennifer. *Learning to Read and Write in Colonial America*. Amherst: University of Massachusetts Press, 2005.

Morantz-Sanchez, Regina Markell. *Sympathy and Science: Women Physicians in American Medicine*. New York: Oxford University Press, 1985.

Motz, Marilyn Ferris. *True Sisterhood: Michigan Women and Their Kin, 1820–1920*. Albany: State University of New York Press, 1983.

Moylan, Michele, and Lane Stiles, eds. *Reading Books: Essays on the Material Text and Literature in America*. Amherst: University of Massachusetts Press, 1996.

Muncy, Robyn. *Creating a Female Dominion in American Reform, 1890–1935*. New York: Oxford University Press, 1991.

Myerson, Joel, Daniel Shealy, and Madeleine B. Stern, eds. *The Journals of Louisa May Alcott*. Boston: Little, Brown, 1989.

———. *The Selected Letters of Louisa May Alcott*. Boston: Little, Brown, 1987.

Nathan, Maud. *Once upon a Time and Today*. New York: G. P. Putnam's Sons, 1933.

National Endowment for the Arts. *Reading at Risk: A Survey of Literary Reading in America*. Washington, D.C.: National Endowment for the Arts, 2004.

Neblett, Pat. *Circles of Sisterhood: A Book Discussion Group Guide for Women of Color*. New York: Harlem River Press, 1997.

Neidorf, Robin N. "Feminist Book Groups: The New C.R.?" *Ms.*, January/February 1995, 64–67.

Nell, Victor. *Lost in a Book: The Psychology of Reading for Pleasure*. New Haven: Yale University Press, 1988.

Nord, David Paul. *Faith in Reading: Religious Publishing and the Birth of Mass Media in America*. New York: Oxford University Press, 2004.

———. "Working-Class Readers: Family, Community, and Reading in Late-Nineteenth-Century America." *Communication Research* 13 (April 1986): 156–81.

Oatley, Keith. "Emotions and the Story Worlds of Fiction." In *Narrative Impact: Social and Cognitive Foundations*, edited by Melanie C. Green et al., 39–70. Mahwah, N.J.: Lawrence Erlbaum, 2002.

O'Brien, Sharon. "Tomboyism and Adolescent Conflict: Three Nineteenth-Century Case Studies." In *Woman's Being, Woman's Place: Female Identity and Vocation in American History*, edited by Mary Kelley, 351–72. Boston: G. K. Hall, 1979.

———. *Willa Cather: The Emerging Voice*. New York: Oxford University Press, 1987.

O'Connor, Thomas F. "American Catholic Reading Circles, 1886–1909." *Libraries and Culture* 26 (Spring 1991): 334–47.

Okker, Patricia. *Our Sister Editors: Sarah J. Hale and the Tradition of Nineteenth-Century American Women Editors*. Athens: University of Georgia Press, 1995.

Orleck, Annelise. *Common Sense and a Little Fire: Women and Working-Class Politics in the United States, 1900–1965*. Chapel Hill: University of North Carolina Press, 1995.

Ovington, Mary White. *The Walls Came Tumbling Down*. 1947. Reprint, New York: Arno Press, 1969.

Palmieri, Patricia Ann. *In Adamless Eden: The Community of Women Faculty at Wellesley*. New Haven: Yale University Press, 1995.

Parush, Iris. *Reading Jewish Women: Marginality and Modernization in Nineteenth-Century Eastern European Jewish Society*. Hanover, N.H.: University Press of New England, 2004.

Pawley, Christine. *Reading on the Middle Border: The Culture of Print in Late-Nineteenth-Century Osage, Iowa*. Amherst: University of Massachusetts Press, 2001.

———. "What to Read and How to Read: The Social Infrastructure of Young People's Reading, Osage, Iowa, 1870–1900." *Library Quarterly* 68 (July 1998): 276–97.

Peiss, Kathy. *Cheap Amusements: Working Women and Leisure in Turn-of-the-Century New York*. Philadelphia: Temple University Press, 1986.

Perkins, Frederic Beecher. *The Best Reading: Hints on the Selection of Books; on the Formation of Libraries, Public and Private; on Courses of Reading, Etc.* 4th ed. New York: G. P. Putnam's Sons, 1877.

Perkins, Margo V. *Autobiography as Activism: Three Black Women of the Sixties.* Jackson: University Press of Mississippi, 2000.

Personal Narratives Group, eds. *Interpreting Women's Lives: Feminist Theory and Personal Narratives.* Bloomington: Indiana University Press, 1989.

Pesotta, Rose. *Days of Our Lives.* Boston: Excelsior, 1958.

Peterson, Carla L. *"Doers of the Word": African-American Women Speakers and Writers in the North (1830–1880).* New York: Oxford University Press, 1995.

Peterson, Joyce Shaw. "Working Girls and Millionaires: The Melodramatic Romances of Laura Jean Libbey." *American Studies* 24 (Spring 1983): 19–35.

Philpott, Thomas Lee. *The Slum and the Ghetto: Neighborhood Deterioration and Middle-Class Reform, Chicago, 1880–1930.* New York: Oxford University Press, 1978.

Polacheck, Hilda Satt. *I Came a Stranger: The Story of a Hull-House Girl.* Edited by Dena J. Polacheck Epstein. Urbana: University of Illinois Press, 1991.

Porter, Noah. *Books and Reading; or, What Books Shall I Read and How Shall I Read Them?* 1870. Reprint, New York: Charles Scribner's Sons, 1883.

Quindlen, Anna. *How Reading Changed My Life.* New York: Ballantine, 1998.

Radway, Janice A. "Beyond Mary Bailey and Old Maid Librarians: Reimagining Readers and Rethinking Reading." *Journal of Education for Library and Information Science* 35 (Fall 1994): 1–21.

———. *A Feeling for Books: The Book-of-the-Month Club, Literary Taste, and Middle-Class Desire.* Chapel Hill: University of North Carolina Press, 1997.

———. "Interpretive Communities and Variable Literacies: The Functions of Romance Reading." *Daedalus* 113 (Summer 1984): 49–73.

———. *Reading the Romance: Women, Patriarchy, and Popular Literature.* Chapel Hill: University of North Carolina Press, 1984.

Raleigh, John Henry. "What Scott Meant to the Victorians." In *Time, Place, and Idea: Essays on the Novel,* 96–125. Carbondale: Southern Illinois University Press, 1968.

Randall, Mercedes M. *Improper Bostonian: Emily Greene Balch.* New York: Twayne, 1964.

Ravage, M. E. *An American in the Making: The Life Story of an Immigrant.* 1917. Reprint, New York: Dover Publications, 1971.

Reed, Christopher Robert. *"All the World Is Here!": The Black Presence at White City.* Bloomington: Indiana University Press, 2000.

Reid, Doris Fielding. *Edith Hamilton: An Intimate Portrait.* New York: W. W. Norton, 1967.

Reinhold, Meyer. *Classica Americana: The Greek and Roman Heritage in the United States.* Detroit: Wayne State University Press, 1984.

Residents of Hull-House. *Hull-House Maps and Papers.* New York: Thomas Y. Crowell, 1895.

Reynolds, Kimberley. *Girls Only?: Gender and Popular Children's Fiction in Britain, 1880–1910.* Philadelphia: Temple University Press, 1990.

Richardson, Dorothy. *The Long Day: The Story of a New York Working Girl.* 1905. Reprint, New York: Quadrangle Books, 1972.

Richmond, Mary E. "Books and Reading" and "An Outline for Readers of Biography." In *The Long View: Papers and Addresses,* edited by J. C. Colcord and R. Z. S. Mann, 19–28 and 593–601. New York: Russell Sage Foundation, 1930.

Rieser, Andrew C. *The Chautauqua Moment: Protestants, Progressives, and the Culture of Modern Liberalism.* New York: Columbia University Press, 2003.

Rischin, Moses. *The Promised City: New York's Jews, 1870–1914.* New York: Corinth, 1962.

Rodgers, Daniel T. *The Work Ethic in Industrial America, 1850–1920.* Chicago: University of Chicago Press, 1978.

Rooney, Kathleen. *Reading with Oprah: The Book Club That Changed America.* Fayetteville: University of Arkansas Press, 2005.

Roosevelt, Theodore. *An Autobiography.* 1913. Reprint, New York: De Capo Press, 1985.

Rose, Jonathan. *The Intellectual Life of the British Working Classes.* New Haven: Yale University Press, 2001.

———. "Rereading the English Common Reader: A Preface to a History of Audiences." *Journal of the History of Ideas* 53 (January–March 1992): 47–70.

Rosenberg, Rosalind. *Beyond Separate Spheres: Intellectual Roots of Modern Feminism.* New Haven: Yale University Press, 1982.

Rosenblatt, Louise M. *Literature as Exploration.* New York: D. Appleton-Century, 1938.

Rosenfeld, Alvin H. "Inventing the Jew: Notes on Jewish Autobiography." *Midstream* 21 (April 1975): 54–67.

Roskies, David G. "Yiddish Popular Literature and the Female Reader." *Journal of Popular Culture* 10 (Spring 1977): 852–58.

Ross, Dorothy. "Gendered Social Knowledge: Domestic Discourse, Jane Addams, and the Possibilities of Social Science." In *Gender and American Social Science: The Formative Years,* edited by Helene Silverberg, 235–64. Princeton, N.J.: Princeton University Press, 1998.

Ross, Edward A. *Seventy Years of It: An Autobiography.* New York: D. Appleton-Century, 1936.

Rossiter, Margaret W. *Women Scientists in America: Struggles and Strategies to 1940.* Baltimore: Johns Hopkins University Press, 1982.

Royster, Jacqueline Jones. "To Call a Thing by Its True Name: The Rhetoric of Ida B. Wells." In *Reclaiming Rhetorica: Women in the Rhetorical Tradition,* edited by Andrea A. Lunsford, 167–84. Pittsburgh: University of Pittsburgh Press, 1995.

———. *Traces of a Stream: Literacy and Social Change among African American Women.* Pittsburgh: University of Pittsburgh Press, 2000.

———, ed. *Southern Horrors and Other Writings: The Anti-Lynching Campaign of Ida B. Wells, 1892–1900.* Boston: Bedford Books, 1997.

Rubin, Joan Shelley. *The Making of Middlebrow Culture.* Chapel Hill: University of North Carolina Press, 1992.

———. *Songs of Ourselves: The Uses of Poetry in America.* Cambridge, Mass.: Harvard University Press, 2007.

———. "What Is the History of the History of Books?" *Journal of American History* 90 (September 2003): 555–75.

Ruskay, Sophie. *Horsecars and Cobblestones.* New York: Beechhurst Press, 1948.

Ryan, Barbara, and Amy M. Thomas, eds. *Reading Acts: U.S. Readers' Interactions with Literature, 1800–1950.* Knoxville: University of Tennessee Press, 2002.

Ryan, Mary P. *The Empire of the Mother: American Writing about Domesticity, 1830–1860.* New York: Institute for Research in History and Haworth Press, 1982.

Salem, Dorothy. *To Better Our World: Black Women in Organized Reform, 1890–1920*. Brooklyn: Carlson, 1990.

Salmon, Edward G. *Juvenile Literature as It Is*. London: Henry J. Drane, 1888.

———. "What Girls Read." *Nineteenth Century* 20 (October 1886): 515–27.

Sanger, Margaret. *An Autobiography*. 1938. Reprint, New York: Dover Publications, 1971.

Sayre, Robert F. "The Proper Study—Autobiographies in American Studies." *American Quarterly* 29 (1977): 241–62.

Schechter, Patricia A. *Ida B. Wells-Barnett and American Reform, 1880–1930*. Chapel Hill: University of North Carolina Press, 2001.

Schneiderman, Rose, with Lucy Goldthwaite. *All for One*. New York: Paul S. Eriksson, 1967.

Schwager, Sally. "Educating Women in America." *Signs* 12 (Winter 1987): 333–72.

Schwartz, Lynne Sharon. *Ruined by Reading: A Life in Books*. Boston: Beacon Press, 1996.

Scott, Anne Firor. *Making the Invisible Woman Visible*. Urbana: University of Illinois Press, 1984.

———. *Natural Allies: Women's Associations in American History*. Urbana: University of Illinois Press, 1991.

———. "Women and Libraries." *Journal of Library History* 21 (Spring 1986): 400–405.

Scott, Donald M. "Print and the Public Lecture System, 1840–60." In *Printing and Society in Early America*, edited by William L. Joyce et al., 278–99. Worcester, Mass.: American Antiquarian Society, 1983.

Scudder, Vida Dutton. *On Journey*. New York: E. P. Dutton, 1937.

Seigfried, Charlene Haddock. *Pragmatism and Feminism: Reweaving the Social Fabric*. Chicago: University of Chicago Press, 1996.

Shapiro, Herbert, and David L. Sterling, eds. *"I Belong to the Working Class": The Unfinished Autobiography of Rose Pastor Stokes*. Athens: University of Georgia Press, 1992.

Shaw, Stephanie J. "Black Club Women and the Creation of the National Association of Colored Women." *Journal of Women's History* 3 (Fall 1991): 10–25.

Showalter, Elaine. *Sister's Choice: Tradition and Change in Women's Writing*. Oxford: Clarendon Press, 1991.

Sicherman, Barbara. *Alice Hamilton: A Life in Letters*. Cambridge, Mass.: Harvard University Press, 1984.

———. "Connecting Lives: Women and Reading, Then and Now." In *Women in Print: Essays on the Print Culture of American Women from the Nineteenth and Twentieth Centuries*, edited by James P. Danky and Wayne A. Wiegand, 3–24. Madison: University of Wisconsin Press, 2006.

———. "Ideologies and Practices of Reading." In *The Industrial Book, 1840–1880*, edited by Scott E. Casper et al., A History of the Book in America, 3:279–302. Chapel Hill: University of North Carolina Press, 2007.

———. "Reading and Ambition: M. Carey Thomas and Female Heroism." *American Quarterly* 45 (March 1993): 73–103.

———. "Reading and Middle-Class Identity in Victorian America: Cultural Consumption, Conspicuous and Otherwise." In *Reading Acts: U.S. Readers'*

Interactions with Literature, 1800–1950, edited by Barbara Ryan and Amy M.
Thomas, 137–60. Knoxville: University of Tennessee Press, 2002.

———. "Reading *Little Women*: The Many Lives of a Text." In *U.S. History as Women's
History: New Feminist Essays*, edited by Linda K. Kerber et al., 245–66. Chapel Hill:
University of North Carolina Press, 1995.

———. "Sense and Sensibility: A Case Study of Women's Reading in Late-Victorian
America." In *Reading in America: Literature and Social History*, edited by Cathy N.
Davidson, 201–25. Baltimore: Johns Hopkins University Press, 1989.

Simkhovitch, Mary Kingsbury. *Neighborhood: My Story of Greenwich House*. New York:
W. W. Norton, 1938.

Singer, Jerome L. *Daydreaming: An Introduction to the Experimental Study of Inner
Experience*. New York: Random House, 1966.

Sink, Robert. "Democratic Images: Children in the Library; Lewis Hine's Photographs
for the Child Welfare Exhibit of 1911." *Biblion: The Bulletin of the New York Public
Library* 1 (Spring 1993): 21–24.

Sklar, Kathryn Kish. *Florence Kelley and the Nation's Work: The Rise of Women's Political
Culture, 1830–1900*. New Haven: Yale University Press, 1995.

———. "Hull House in the 1890s: A Community of Women Reformers." *Signs* 10
(Summer 1985): 658–77.

———, ed. *Notes of Sixty Years: The Autobiography of Florence Kelley*. Chicago: Charles
H. Kerr, 1986.

Slezak, Ellen, ed. *The Book Group Book: A Thoughtful Guide to Forming and Enjoying a
Stimulating Book Discussion Group*. Chicago: Chicago Review Press, 1993.

Smith, David E. *John Bunyan in America*. Bloomington: Indiana University Press, 1966.

Smith, Nila Banton. *American Reading Instruction*. Newark, Del.: International
Reading Association, 1986.

Smith-Rosenberg, Carroll. *Disorderly Conduct: Visions of Gender in Victorian America*.
New York: Alfred A. Knopf, 1985.

Sollors, Werner. Introduction to *The Promised Land*, by Mary Antin. New York:
Penguin Books, 1997.

Solomon, Barbara Miller. *In the Company of Educated Women: A History of Women
and Higher Education in America*. New Haven: Yale University Press, 1985.

Soltow, Lee, and Edward Stevens. *The Rise of Literacy and the Common School in the
United States: A Socioeconomic Analysis to 1870*. Chicago: University of Chicago
Press, 1981.

Spewack, Bella. *Streets: A Memoir of the Lower East Side*. New York: Feminist Press, 1995.

Stampfer, Shaul. "Gender Differentiation and Education of the Jewish Woman in
Nineteenth-Century Eastern Europe." *Polin: A Journal of Polish-Jewish Studies* 7
(1992): 63–87.

Stern, Elizabeth G. *My Mother and I*. New York: Macmillan, 1917.

Stern, Madeleine B., ed. *Critical Essays on Louisa May Alcott*. Boston: G. K. Hall, 1984.

Stevenson, Louise L. "Sarah Porter Educates Useful Ladies, 1847–1900." *Winterthur
Portfolio* 18 (Spring 1983): 39–59.

———. *The Victorian Homefront: American Thought and Culture, 1860–1880*. New
York: Twayne, 1991.

Suleiman, Susan R., and Inge Crosman, eds. *The Reader in the Text: Essays on Audience and Interpretation*. Princeton, N.J.: Princeton University Press, 1980.

Swinth, Kirsten. *Painting Professionals: Women Artists and the Development of Modern American Art, 1870–1930*. Chapel Hill: University of North Carolina Press, 2001.

Tarbell, Ida M. *All in the Day's Work: An Autobiography*. New York: Macmillan, 1939.

Terman, Lewis M., and Margaret Lima. *Children's Reading: A Guide for Parents and Teachers*. 2nd ed. New York: D. Appleton & Co., 1931.

Terrell, Mary Church. *A Colored Woman in a White World*. Washington, D.C.: Ransdell, 1940.

Thompson, Mildred I. *Ida B. Wells-Barnett: An Exploratory Study of an American Black Woman, 1893–1930*. Brooklyn: Carlson, 1990.

Tompkins, Jane. *Sensational Designs: The Cultural Work of American Fiction, 1790–1860*. New York: Oxford University Press, 1985.

———, ed. *Reader-Response Criticism: From Formalism to Post-Structuralism*. Baltimore: Johns Hopkins University Press, 1980.

Townsend, Lucy Forsyth. "Anna Peck Sill and the Rise of Women's Collegiate Curriculum." Ph.D. diss., Loyola University of Chicago, 1985.

Trachtenberg, Alan. *The Incorporation of America: Culture and Society in the Gilded Age*. New York: Hill and Wang, 1982.

Travis, Trysh. "'It Will Change the World if Everybody Reads This Book': New Thought Religion in Oprah's Book Club." *American Quarterly* 59 (September 2007): 1017–41.

Turner, James. "Secularization and Sacralization: Speculations on Some Religious Origins of the Secular Humanities Curriculum, 1850–1900." In *The Secularization of the Academy*, edited by George Marsden and Bradley J. Longfield, 74–106. New York: Oxford University Press, 1992.

Vicinus, Martha. "What Makes a Heroine?: Nineteenth-Century Girls' Biographies." *Genre* 20 (Summer 1987): 171–88.

Vincent, David. *Literacy and Popular Culture: England, 1750–1914*. Cambridge: Cambridge University Press, 1989.

Wald, Lillian D. *The House on Henry Street*. New York: Henry Holt, 1915.

Weimann, Jeanne M. *The Fair Women*. Chicago: Academy Chicago, 1981.

Weinberg, Sydney Stahl. *The World of Our Mothers: The Lives of Jewish Immigrant Women*. New York: Schocken Books, 1988.

Weissler, Chava. "'For Women and for Men Who Are Like Women': The Construction of Gender in Yiddish Devotional Literature." *Journal of Feminist Studies in Religion* 5 (1989): 7–24.

———. "Prayers in Yiddish and the Religious World of Ashkenazic Women." In *Jewish Women in Historical Perspective*, edited by Judith R. Baskin, 159–81. Detroit: Wayne State University Press, 1991.

Westbrook, Robert B. *John Dewey and American Democracy*. Ithaca, N.Y.: Cornell University Press, 1991.

Wharton, Edith. *A Backward Glance*. New York: D. Appleton-Century, 1934.

White, Deborah Gray. *Too Heavy a Load: Black Women in Defense of Themselves, 1894–1994*. New York: W. W. Norton, 1999.

White, William Allen. *The Autobiography of William Allen White*. New York: Macmillan, 1946.

Williams, Heather Andrea. *Self-Taught: African American Education in Slavery and Freedom*. Chapel Hill: University of North Carolina Press, 2005.

Williams, Raymond. *Culture and Society, 1780–1950*. New York: Columbia University Press, 1983.

———. *Keywords: A Vocabulary of Culture and Society*. Rev. ed. New York: Oxford University Press, 1983.

Wilson, Christopher P. "The Rhetoric of Consumption: Mass-Market Magazines and the Demise of the Gentle Reader, 1880–1920." In *The Culture of Consumption: Critical Essays in American History, 1880–1980*, edited by Richard Wightman Fox and T. J. Jackson Lears, 39–64. New York: Pantheon, 1983.

Winterer, Caroline. *The Culture of Classicism: Ancient Greece and Rome in American Intellectual Life, 1780–1910*. Baltimore: Johns Hopkins University Press, 2002.

———. *The Mirror of Antiquity: American Women and the Classical Tradition, 1750–1900*. Ithaca, N.Y.: Cornell University Press, 2007.

Wolff, Robert Lee. *Gains and Losses: Novels of Faith and Doubt in Victorian England*. New York: Garland, 1977.

Wright, T. R. *The Religion of Humanity: The Impact of Comtean Positivism on Victorian Britain*. Cambridge: Cambridge University Press, 1986.

Zaborowska, Magdalena J. *How We Found America: Reading Gender through East European Immigrant Narratives*. Chapel Hill: University of North Carolina Press, 1995.

Zboray, Ronald J. *A Fictive People: Antebellum Economic Development and the Reading Public*. New York: Oxford University Press, 1993.

Zboray, Ronald J., and Mary Saracino Zboray. *Everyday Ideas: Socioliterary Experience among Antebellum New Englanders*. Knoxville: University of Tennessee Press, 2006.

———. "Political News and Female Readership in Antebellum Boston and Its Region." *Journalism History* 22 (Spring 1966): 2–14.

Zipser, Arthur, and Pearl Zipser. *Fire and Grace: The Life of Rose Pastor Stokes*. Athens: University of Georgia Press, 1989.

ACKNOWLEDGMENTS

It is a great pleasure to acknowledge the institutions and individuals who have provided me with such exceptional support during the many years in which I have been immersed in this book. Although it is not possible to thank by name everyone who responded to a pesky query or directed me to the latest book, theorist, or cache of letters, each encounter in its own way helped along a process that began as a germ of an idea and gradually took shape as a book.

Fellowships from the John Simon Guggenheim Memorial Foundation and the National Endowment for the Humanities brought important material support and professional validation. Residencies at the Bellagio Study and Conference Center and the Rutgers Center for Historical Analysis provided congenial surroundings and colleagues who relieved the isolation that is so much a part of a scholar's life. I am grateful to several deans at Trinity College for their unwavering support of my work and to the William R. Kenan Jr. Charitable Trust for its generous contributions to my academic life and research. These institutional supports gave me the extended periods of time necessary for reading, writing, and reflection.

Of the many archivists, librarians, and administrators who responded to my requests for assistance, Mary Lynn McCree Bryan, editor of the Jane Addams Papers Project, is in a class by herself. Ever since I began research on Alice Hamilton many years ago, she has shared her unsurpassed knowledge of everything connected with Hull-House without expecting anything in return. The Schlesinger Library of the Radcliffe Institute was for a time a second home. Its staff, and notably the late Patricia Miller King, were always quick to assist, as were Peggy Glowacki of the University of Illinois at Chicago, Wendy Chmielewski of the Swarthmore College Peace Collection, and Caroline Rittenhouse of the Bryn Mawr College Archives. Among Trinity College's unfailingly helpful library and instructional staff, Patricia Bunker and Mary Curry deserve special mention for assistance with research and interlibrary loan. Erin Valentino drew on her exemplary knowledge of *The Chicago Manual of Style* to create a full-fledged bibliography out of disparate notes, going well beyond any professional obligation to do so; she also helped with visual images. Dave Tatem provided technical know-how as well as the calm assurance that kept at bay the panic of a historian confronted with the vagaries of computer programs.

I am grateful also to the research assistants, near and far, who provided help when I needed it most: Lise Bettinger, Carmen Britt, Ann Brown, Alexandra Edsall, Rebecca Edwards, and Ellen Holtzman. Tammy Banks-Spooner, Ann Morrissey, Janet Thurman Murphy, and Elizabeth Young deserve special thanks for the length as well as the quality of their service, as does Susan Hoffman Fishman, whose eye for detail and enthusiasm for the project greatly eased the burden of final preparation of the manuscript.

Many individuals shared ideas and information or offered encouragement. Some are acknowledged in the notes. Here I want to thank Joyce Antler, Inge Aures, Rima Brauer, Lois Brown, Scott Casper, Joanne Cunard, Cathy Davidson, Jane De Hart, Booker DeVaughn, Leonard Dinnerstein, Crystal Feimster, Ellen Fitzpatrick, John Gillis, Catherine Golden, Harvey Graff, Dolores Greenberg, Robert Gross, David Hall, Barbara Hochman, Carl Kaestle, Mary Kelley, Brad Klein, Helen Lang, James Miller, Patricia Palmieri, Judith Perkins, Sarah Robbins, Charlene Haddock Seigfried, Robert Sink, Louise Stevenson, Scott D. Taylor, Trysh Travis, Martha Vicinus, Wayne Wiegand, Michael Winship, and the late Marlene Fisher. Dolores Kreisman heard about the project endlessly and provided important feedback, especially early on. Elizabeth Long shared insights into women's reading in many stimulating conversations over the years. I am especially grateful to Mardges Bacon who not only put her knowledge of visual materials at my disposal, but provided much-needed encouragement to a novice in this area. Mary Ellen White offered advice about readers and images of a more contemporary kind. Late in the day, with members of my book group, Catherine Bermon, Susan Hoffman Fishman, Roberta Prescott, Lena Stein, and Anne Wolfson, I finally learned firsthand what the collective enterprise of reading was all about.

Comments by colleagues and friends who read portions of the manuscript helped sharpen my ideas and hone my prose. Louise W. Knight, Jacqueline Goldsby, Norman Miller, Ellen Kellman, and Stephanie Kuduk Weiner brought to bear their scholarly expertise on specific chapters, as did Kenneth Moss and other members of the Johns Hopkins History Seminar. Relatively early in the project, I enjoyed lively exchanges, along with celebratory food and drink, with members of two feminist writers' groups. Ann duCille, Farah Jasmine Griffin, Joan Hedrick, Gertrude Hughes, Indira Karamcheti, Jane Nadel-Klein, Margo Perkins, and Laura Wexler, colleagues from several disciplines, did much to extend my intellectual reach.

Other friends and colleagues not only read a number of chapters, but provided invaluable support at critical junctures. Joan Hedrick read the entire manuscript, much of it more than once. Her substantive knowledge and keen eye for nailing an argument have improved this book in more ways than I can say. Linda Kerber and Dorothy Ross helped me frame my arguments in the larger contexts of women's and intellectual history, while Joan Jacobs Brumberg not only shared her wealth of knowledge about nineteenth-century girls but kept me generously supplied with visual images and archival finds. Jerry Watts tutored me in African American intellectual and cultural history and spurred me on with his admonition to "keep going." The comments of Janice Radway and Joan Shelley Rubin, readers for the University of North Carolina Press, clarified what needed to be done to turn a manuscript into a book. Their own work on the history of reading has been exemplary. Jan's scholarship in particular has been an inspiration ever since I read *Reading the Romance* and understood how I could adapt her ethnographic approach to contemporary reading practices to my nineteenth-century subjects. She has been extraordinarily generous in commenting, always astutely, on several incarnations of this book.

I am grateful as well to Kate Douglas Torrey, my editor at the University of North Carolina Press who steered this book through its many stages. Not only were her comments on the manuscript and on the publication process always on the mark, but her faith in the project from its earliest beginnings helped get me through the rough patches. Other staff members of the press have been invariably helpful, and it has been a great pleasure working with them as well. Vicky Wells and especially Ron Maner merit individual mention for going well beyond the call of duty. John Wilson proved to be a model copyeditor, at once sensitive to nuance and meticulous in spotting infelicities of various kinds. Thanks also to Kay Banning for preparing such an imaginative and generous index.

Finally, I owe a debt of long standing to two teachers and mentors that can never be repaid: Jeannette Bailey Cheek, my high school history teacher who inspired me to become a historian, and Janet Wilson James, from whom I learned a great deal about women's history. I dedicate this book to their memories.

INDEX

De Quincey, Thomas: *Confessions of an English Opium-Eater*, 138–39. *See also* Addams, Jane

Dewey, John, 184, 185, 186, 190, 313 (n. 91)

Diaries: and female subjectivity, 52, 53, 275 (n. 60; and Agnes Hamilton, 96–97, 101, 102; and M. Carey Thomas, 111, 114, 126, 290 (n. 27); and Jane Addams, 143, 155, 169, 170, 171, 300 (n. 25), 305 (n. 104); and Rose Gollup Cohen, 203; and Ida B. Wells, 225, 226, 231, 235, 249

Dickens, Charles, 58, 86, 261 (n. 2); Alcott influenced by, 20; and Ida B. Wells, 29, 224–25, 226; *A Child's History of England*, 48; young women's reading of, 50; and family literary culture, 51; *Bleak House*, 116; *The Old Curiosity Shop*, 143; *The Pickwick Papers*, 143; *David Copperfield*, 177, 202, 207, 317 (n. 35); *Oliver Twist*, 207. *See also* Addams, Jane; Cohen, Rose Gollup

Dickinson, Emily, 16

Dik, A. M., 196–97

Dime novels, 62–63

Dixon, Thomas, Jr., 247–48

Dodge, Mary Mapes: *Hans Brinker; or, The Silver Skates*, 17

Domesticity: and cultural contradictions of gender, 2; and *Little Women*, 16, 26, 32, 33; and girls' stories, 18; and women's socialization, 55; Edith Hamilton on, 89; and true womanhood, 100

Domestic novels, 39, 85

Douglass, Frederick, 119, 234, 237, 239, 241, 245

Drummond, Henry: *Natural Law in the Spiritual World*, 287 (n. 93)

Dublin, Thomas, 319 (n. 59)

Du Bois, W. E. B.: *The Souls of Black Folk*, 244

Duffey, Eliza: *What Women Should Know*, 125

Dunbar, Paul Laurence, 244, 245

DuPlessis, Rachel Blau, 292 (n. 49)

Dürer, Albrecht, 160, 161, 305 (n. 107)

Duster, Alfreda, 250

Ederle, Gertrude, 252

Edgeworth, Maria, 86, 118

Education: discrimination against women in, 2, 121, 130–31, 293 (n. 54); expansion of, for women, 38–39, 75, 252, 268–69 (n. 4), 269 (n. 6); public, 39, 43, 210, 212, 215, 217, 223, 283 (n. 37), 320 (n. 65); and African American women, 39, 221–22, 223, 224, 226, 244; and Hamilton family, 87–90, 107, 283 (n. 37); and Hull-House, 166–69, 172, 173, 175, 176, 179–83; and Jewish immigrant women, 195–96, 197, 209, 210–11, 212, 314–15 (n. 6), 315 (n. 8), 320 (n. 65). *See also* Higher education

Eliot, Charles W., 132

Eliot, George: and Hamilton family, 86, 95; heroines of, 117; and M. Carey Thomas, 117; *Romola*, 147, 156, 169–72, 173, 179, 180; *Felix Holt, the Radical*, 173; *Silas Marner*, 206; Pastor's recommendation of, 261 (n. 2). *See also* Addams, Jane

Ely, Richard, 103

Emerine J. Hamilton Library, 84

Emerson, Ralph Waldo: Alcott's admiration for, 18; and family literary culture, 49; and Florence Kelley, 58; and Hamilton family, 87; and M. Carey Thomas, 109, 117; on Goethe, 146, 301 (n. 50); and Hull-House classes, 173; and Plutarch, 299 (n. 18). *See also* Addams, Jane

Engels, Friedrich, 59

Enslaved African Americans, 38, 157, 223

Erasmus, 160

Erikson, Erik, 67, 90, 277 (n. 28)

Evans, Augusta Jane: *Vashti*, 230

Evening Star (Memphis), 229, 326 (n. 33)

Ewing, Juliana, 92, 285–86 (n. 73)

Expressive literacy: African American women's claiming of, 7, 8, 222; Jewish immigrant women's attainment of, 7, 178, 198, 199, 203, 219

Family literary culture: and middle class, 3, 17, 24, 37, 41–42, 48, 51, 52; and *Little*

Gender norms: and propriety, 2, 42; and *Little Women*, 35; and division of labor, 40; and culture of reading, 42; and favorite authors, 50–51, 274 (n. 51); and autobiographies, 55; and formality of gender relationships, 68, 252; and division of cultural labor, 73, 74; and women's ambitions, 136, 137; and Jane Addams, 153; and feminism, 212; and Ida B. Wells, 233, 234. *See also* Victorian culture

General Federation of Women's Clubs, 71

Gernes, Todd Steven, 278 (n. 37)

Gibbon, Edward, 94

Gilded Age: public achievement of women in, 1; literacy in, 3, 40–41; cultural ideology in, 43; and general circulation magazines, 45, 47; reading advice literature in, 45–46

Gildersleeve, Basil, 121

Gilman, Charlotte Perkins: and family literary culture, 6; on Alcott, 25; and poetry, 53, 74; collaborative literary endeavors of, 68–70; education of, 69; adolescent reading of, 69–70, 278 (n. 37); "The Yellow Wallpaper," 74

Godey's Lady's Book, 39

Godwin, William, 58, 123–24, 127, 128, 294 (n. 64)

Goethe, Johann Wolfgang von, 18, 146, 147, 148, 158

Golden, Harry, 317 (n. 35)

Goldsmith, Oliver, 58

Gollomb, Joseph, 207, 319 (n. 52)

Grant, Ulysses S.: *Memoirs*, 51

Gray, Louisa M.: *The Children of Abbotsmuir Manse*, 92, 97, 285 (n. 54)

Gray, Maxwell (Mary Gleed Tuttiet), 283 (n. 34)

Greek immigrants, 184

Greenaway, Kate, 48

Griffith, D. W.: *The Birth of a Nation*, 248

Guttmann, Oskar: *Aesthetic Physical Culture*, 228

Gwinn, Charles, 121

Gwinn, Mamie: and reading circle, 121, 123, 293 (n. 58); and Godwin, 123, 124; M. Carey Thomas's relationship with, 125, 130, 297 (n. 100); and Swinburne, 127; essay on intellectual women, 295 (n. 71); and Malthus, 295 (n. 69)

Haggard, H. Rider: *She*, 230

Haldeman, George, 143, 157, 300 (n. 25)

Hale, Sarah Josepha, 39

Hall, David D., 272 (n. 29)

Hamilton, Agnes: passion for reading, 79, 98, 101–2, 286 (n. 81), 287 (n. 88); and Lighthouse settlement, 81, 104; as art teacher, 84; and Jessie Hamilton, 85, 93, 94, 96, 102, 104; and Scott, 86; and Jane Austen, 86–87, 97, 101; and "forbidden" books, 87; self-directed education of, 90, 91, 283 (n. 37); and rereading, 91–92, 284 (n. 52); and family narratives, 93–94; diary of, 96–97, 101, 102; and Christian service, 101, 102, 103, 104, 105; ambitions of, 101, 103, 118; and biography, 102–3; on diversionary reading, 283 (n. 33)

Hamilton, A. Holman, 83, 84, 106, 283 (n. 35)

Hamilton, Alice: as writer, 6, 74, 81, 105; and letter writing, 53; *Exploring the Dangerous Trades*, 54, 105; access to books, 79, 81; self-directed education of, 79, 87, 90; and Hull-House, 81; on Emerine Hamilton, 82–83; as "reluctant reader," 85, 105; and Edith Hamilton, 85, 107–8, 282 (n. 20); on Hamilton family reading, 85, 282 (n. 21); and Scott, 88; and Miss Porter's School, 89; and Allen Hamilton Williams, 97–98; single status of, 98, 286 (n. 82); aspirations of, 103; and literary inspiration, 104–5; awareness of social problems, 104–5, 287–88 (n. 102); on parents' reading, 283 (n. 30)

Hamilton, Allen (grandfather), 81, 82

Hamilton, Allen (grandson), 84

Hamilton, Arthur, 280 (n. 7)

Hamilton, Edith: as writer, 6, 74, 81,
88–89; and Jessie Hamilton, 79, 80,
81, 88–89, 97, 284 (n. 43), 285 (n. 59);
access to books, 79, 81; self-directed
education of, 79, 88, 90; and Greek language, 80, 90, 105; passion for reading,
85, 106, 107–8; and Alice Hamilton, 85,
107–8, 282 (n. 20); and Scott, 86, 88; on
diversionary reading, 87, 283 (n. 34);
The Greek Way, 89; and literary circle,
94; and higher education, 105, 107; aspirations of, 105–6
Hamilton, Emerine Jane (Holman), 81,
82–83, 84, 85, 86, 103
Hamilton, Gertrude Pond, 83–84, 107, 288
(n. 109)
Hamilton, Jessie: and Edith Hamilton,
79, 80, 81, 88–89, 97, 284 (n. 43), 285
(n. 59); as artist, 81, 90, 95; as art
teacher, 84; and Agnes Hamilton, 85,
93, 94, 96, 102, 104; on serious versus
pleasure reading, 86, 172; and magazines, 87; and literary circle, 94; on
Carlyle, 94, 95; education of, 96, 97
Hamilton, Katherine: aspirations of, 81;
education of, 89, 90; and literary circle,
94; illness of, 101; and Fort Wayne Public Library, 281 (n. 18); and Margaret
Vance Hamilton, 282 (n. 24); and "forbidden" books, 283 (n. 36)
Hamilton, Margaret, 81, 85
Hamilton, Margaret Vance: and Fort
Wayne Public Library, 84; and Free
Reading Room for Women, 84; and
Scott, 86, 282 (n. 24); cottage of, 95, 286
(n. 84); and literary allusions, 97; and
bookbinding, 281 (n. 19)
Hamilton, Montgomery: early reading
of, 83; family library of, 83–84, 88, 283
(n. 35); and daughters' careers, 84–85;
and Scott, 86; and American literature,
87; and daughters' education, 88; on
romance plots, 98, 100
Hamilton, Norah, 81, 84, 85, 286 (n. 84)
Hamilton family: and family literary
culture, 6, 79–83, 84, 85, 90, 94–95,

106–8; ambitions of, 80, 81, 88–89, 90,
98, 106–7; antimarriage ethic of, 80, 98,
100, 286 (nn. 82, 84); and Scott, 83, 86,
88, 283–84 (n. 38); private libraries of,
83–84, 281 (n. 12); and reading clubs,
85, 90, 94–95; and juvenile literature,
85–86, 91–92, 285 (n. 54) ; and self-
directed reading, 86; inward nature
of, 86, 106–7; range of books enjoyed
by, 86–87, 94–95, 100; and diversionary reading, 87, 88, 283 (n. 33); and
"forbidden" books, 87, 283 (nn. 35, 36);
and education, 87–90, 107, 283 (n. 37);
and religious practices, 88, 89, 92, 101,
102, 103, 288 (n. 107); and social reading, 90–91, 94–95, 107; and rereading,
91–92; and family narratives, 93–94,
101; and literary circle, 94; and life
related to fiction, 95–98, 100, 102, 104;
and romance, 98, 100
Hare, Maria Leycester, 93, 103, 104
Harper, Frances Ellen Watkins, 75, 327–28
(n. 54)
Harper, William A., 247
Harper's Monthly, 45, 70, 87, 111, 131
Harrington, Helen, 303 (n. 74)
Hart, James S., 24
Hasanovitz, Elizabeth, 213
Hawthorne, Nathaniel, 23, 24, 39, 87, 169,
173
Haymarket Affair, 165
Hazard, Caroline, 70
Hedrick, Joan D., 275 (n. 63)
Heilbrun, Carolyn G., 117, 267 (n. 87), 292
(n. 44)
Heine, Heinrich, 47
Henry Street Settlement (formerly
Nurses' Settlement), 194, 204, 206
Henty, G. A., 18
Higginson, Thomas Wentworth, 73
Higher education: opportunities for
women in, 1, 37, 39–40, 252, 269 (n. 10);
and Florence Kelley, 59; and Chautau-
qua Literary and Scientific Circle, 71;
and reading clubs and circles, 72; and
Edith Hamilton, 105, 107; and M. Carey

Thomas, 110, 116, 120–21, 126, 130–31, 132, 133; and Progressive generation of women, 118; and Jane Addams, 137, 143–45, 300 (n. 31); curricular approaches to, 144

Hildreth, Richard, 86

Hill, Mabel, 70

Hillside Register (Providence), 69

Hine, Lewis, 321 (n. 72)

Holman, Jesse Lynch, 81–82; *The Prisoners of Niagara*, 82, 281 (n. 9)

Holman, William Steele, 81

Homer, 144, 145

Homer, Winslow: *The New Novel*, 63, 64

Horton, Edith: *A Group of Famous Women*, 212

Howells, Williams Dean, 51, 97, 117

Hughes, Thomas: *Tom Brown at Oxford*, 61, 62, 112; *Tom Brown's School Days*, 276 (n. 7)

Hugo, Victor: *Les Misérables*, 64, 173, 230–31, 317 (n. 35)

Hull-House: founding of, 7, 136, 137, 153, 162, 165; and literacy, 7, 166, 174, 182–83, 307 (n. 5), 311 (n. 72); Polacheck's participation in, 7, 175, 176–78; democratic credentials of, 142; Toynbee Hall compared to, 165; cultural mission of, 166, 167–69, 173, 182–83, 185–86, 190, 306–7 (n. 4), 311 (n. 64); and Shakespeare, 166, 169, 172, 173, 176, 179–81, 183, 310 (nn. 53, 55); and education, 166–69, 172, 173, 175, 176, 179–83; clubs of, 168–69, 173–74, 175, 177, 179–81; and reading clubs and circles, 169, 171, 173–74, 309 (n. 35); Home Library Association, 169, 307 (n. 13); reading parties of, 169–71, 172–73, 174, 179, 254, 308 (n. 28), 309 (n. 31); Florentine photographs for, 170, 173, 307 (n. 17); College Extension Classes, 172, 308 (n. 25); and visual arts, 173, 308 (n. 30); social setting of, 175, 176, 179, 184, 190, 203; Labor Museum, 176, 183, 184–86, 309 (n. 40); and vocational classes, 179, 183, 310 (n. 49); theater program of, 183–84, 190, 311

(nn. 68, 72); and local ethnic groups, 184, 185, 186; mass entertainment competing with, 191

Huxley, T. H., 150, 151, 173

Immigrants. *See* Jewish immigrant women; Russian Jewish immigrants

Individualism: and social class, 55; and self-expression through reading, 67; in men, 68, 74; and Emerson, 87; and Hamilton family, 105, 107, 288 (n. 110); and Jane Addams, 136, 146, 147–48, 152, 156, 158, 301 (n. 46), 302 (n. 55)

Ingraham, J. H.: *The Prince of the House of David*, 112

Interpretive community, 260 (n. 9)

Irving, Washington, 83, 141

Jackson, Shannon, 306 (n. 3), 307 (n. 10)

James, Henry, 17, 19, 123, 171

Jauss, Hans Robert, 16, 262 (n. 16)

Jewish Daily Forward, 210

Jewish immigrant women: and *Little Women*, 6, 31–33; literacy of, 7–8, 178, 193, 194, 196, 197–98, 203, 219, 315–16 (n. 16), 316 (n. 17), 322 (n. 91); and autobiographies, 8, 194, 198, 209–10, 320 (n. 63); identity of, 8–9; and Pastor's recommended reading, 13–14, 261 (n. 2); reading practices of, 31–32, 194, 218–19; and access to books, 193, 218; and education, 195–96, 197, 209, 210–11, 212, 314–15 (n. 6), 315 (n. 8), 320 (n. 65); and secular reading, 196–97, 219; and English language, 198, 203, 204, 206, 318 (nn. 41, 43). *See also* Antin, Mary; Cohen, Rose Gollup; Pesotta, Rose; Polacheck, Hilda Satt

Jewish men: and importance of literacy, 194–95; and Hebrew language, 195, 196, 197, 198; and secular reading, 196, 197

Jewish women: and Yiddish language, 8, 195, 196–204, 212, 219, 317 (n. 31); reading clubs of, 71, 196; and Hebrew language, 195, 198, 199–200, 201, 212, 314 (nn. 3, 4), 316 (n. 26); access to

Lincoln, Abraham, 141–42

Literacy: of white women, 6, 37, 38; expressive, 7, 8, 178, 198, 199, 203, 219, 222; and Hull-House, 7, 166, 174, 182–83, 307 (n. 5), 311 (n. 72); and African Americans, 7–8, 38, 222, 223, 224, 323 (n. 3); of Jewish immigrant women, 7–8, 178, 193, 194, 196, 197–99, 200, 203, 204–5, 206, 208, 219, 222, 315–16 (n. 16), 316 (nn. 17, 26), 322 (n. 91); and gender, 37, 38, 268 (n. 1); Bible, 38, 43; and aggregate literacy rates, 38, 268 (n. 1); in Britain, 38, 268 (n. 2); and economic opportunities, 39, 40–41; civic uses of, 255

Literary culture: white women's oversight of, 6; and theater, 7; and *Little Women*, 35, 37; and middle-class aspirations, 40, 41, 46; and Jane Addams, 106–7, 135, 136, 137, 138–39, 140, 142, 144, 151, 153, 186–87, 189; and Hull-House, 174; decline in importance, 251, 254, 334 (n. 1). *See also* Family literary culture

Literature: role in construction of female identity, 2, 3, 5, 8–9; and race, 8, 222, 242–44, 246; and classics, 17, 24, 30, 48–49, 87, 90, 94, 95, 112, 115, 144–45, 158, 177; American, 24, 87, 123, 144; women's financial success in, 39; advice, 45–46; as women's province, 57; British, 64, 87, 123; and history, 65, 70, 86; and reading clubs and circles, 73; as source of experience, 135, 187; and self-improvement, 222; parlor, 275 (n. 63). *See also* Juvenile literature; Poetry

"Little Things," 22–23, 264 (n. 47)

Little Women (Alcott): and "girls' stories" market, 5, 14, 17–18, 263 (n. 24); family literary culture in, 5, 35–36; diverse responses to, 5–6, 30–32, 35; and women's ambitions, 6, 15–16, 26, 28, 29, 33–34, 36, 50, 114; and Jewish immigrant women, 6, 31–33; as recommended reading, 13–14; and readers' identification with Jo March, 14, 15, 21, 22, 23, 25,

26–27, 28–29, 30, 35, 114; publishing history of, 14, 22, 23, 28, 261 (n. 3), 264 (n. 45); adaptations to other media, 14, 34, 261 (n. 9); influence of, 14–15, 26, 29, 34–35, 267–68 (n. 87); romance plot of, 16, 21, 22, 27, 28, 34, 115, 264 (n. 38); quest plot of, 16, 22, 26, 28, 29, 34–35, 115; readers' interaction with, 16–17, 20–21, 22, 23, 25, 28, 34–35, 266 (n. 72); critics of, 18–19, 20, 29, 34; tone of, 19, 34; and tomboy as literary type, 20, 30, 101; home theatricals in, 20, 52, 263 (n. 32); and Jo's marriage, 20–21, 28, 29; autobiographical status of, 21, 22, 23, 27, 264–65 (n. 48), 265 (n. 50); as female bildungsroman, 26, 29, 34–35; and female creativity in Jo, 26–27, 29, 35; and libraries, 30, 32, 216, 261 (n. 3); and Rose Gollup Cohen, 204; and Spewack, 217

Logan, Shirley Wilson, 324 (n. 15), 330 (n. 86)

Long, Elizabeth, 256–57, 284 (n. 46)

Longfellow, Henry Wadsworth, 48, 51, 53, 143, 183, 205

Lott, Theodore W., 229

Lovett, Robert Morss, 62–63

Lowell, James Russell, 173

Lukens sisters, 22, 23, 264 (n. 47)

Luther, Martin, 92, 159, 160, 161

Lynd, Helen Merrell, 252

Lynd, Robert, 252

Lyons, Maritcha, 237, 329 (n. 85)

Macaulay, Thomas Babington, 53, 86, 87, 88, 112

MacDonald, George, 60

Madison, James, 58

Magazines: market for, 39, 45; for young people, 50, 54; and letter writing, 275 (n. 61)

Mahogany Tree (Boston), 93

Malthus, Thomas, 295 (n. 69)

Manhattan Trade School for Girls, 206

Mann, Horace, 43

Marlitt, E. (Eugenie John), 87, 283 (n. 36)

Marlowe, Julia, 180

Marriage: and women's careers, 2, 27; and antimarriage ethic of Hamilton family, 80, 98, 100, 286 (nn. 82, 84); and M. Carey Thomas's reading circle, 123, 125; George Sand on, 148; and heterosexual culture, 252; and twentieth-century careers, 253

Marryat, Frederick, 18

Masons' reading rooms, 49

Matthews, Victoria Earle, 237, 242, 243–46

May, Sophie (Rebecca Clarke): "Susy and Prudy" stories, 85

Mazzini, Giuseppe, 141, 142, 157, 166–67, 174

McCarthy, Kathleen D., 270 (n. 12)

McHenry, Elizabeth, 72, 244

Men: real-life mentors and models for, 2; reading of, compared to women, 2, 5, 50, 57, 67, 256, 259 (n. 3), 334 (n. 1); and family literary culture, 3, 6; and access to literacy, 8, 37; as Alcott readers, 25, 267 (n. 81); education of, 38; and newspaper reading, 45; and letter writing, 52, 275 (n. 61); and dime novels, 62–63; joint cultural activities of, 68; criticism of reading clubs, 74; and Hull-House, 178, 180; Jewish, 194–98

Meyer, Annie Nathan, 266 (n. 75)

Michelangelo, 157, 305 (n. 107)

Middle class: and family literary culture, 3, 17, 24, 37, 41–42, 48, 51, 52; and Hull-House classes, 7, 166, 178; and *Little Women*, 16, 19–20, 22, 23, 27, 29–31, 32, 33, 34, 35; and leisure, 17, 20, 25, 27; culture of reading, 40, 41–42, 44, 46; working class distinguished from, 41, 46, 270 (nn. 13, 14); status indicators of, 41, 270 (n. 14); and dime novels, 62; and protected childhood, 67; and Chautauqua Society, 71; changing youth culture of, 252; and education and professional training, 270 (n. 13)

Middle-class women: careers of, 2–3;

and literary culture, 6; charitable and reform activities of, 38–39; and magazines, 39, 45; as carriers of literacy, 40, 251; and reading clubs, 71; ambitions of, 118; everyday practices incorporated into Hull-House, 174; and gender disparities, 255

Miller, Hugh: *The Old Red Sandstone*, 67

Milton, John, 58

Miss Porter's School, 89–90, 93, 96, 101, 102

Monroe, Harriet, 180

Moore, George, 181

Morris, Charles, 231

Morris, William, 173, 184

Moses, Belle, 33

Motherhood, 2, 38, 51

Motley, John Lothrop: *The Rise of the Dutch Republic*, 92

Motz, Marilyn Ferris, 275 (n. 61)

Movies, 3, 119, 183, 190, 191, 252, 311 (n. 68)

Ms. (magazine), 14

Murray, Daniel, 243

Nation, 17, 130

National Association for the Advancement of Colored People (NAACP), 241, 331 (n. 96)

National Association of Colored Women (NACW), 71, 240, 241, 242, 243, 244, 330 (n. 93), 333 (n. 114)

National Colored Press Association, 234, 236

Negro Fellowship League (NFL), 246–48, 333 (n. 120), 334 (n. 131)

Nell, Victor, 287 (n. 88)

New England Journal of Education, 70

Newspapers, 45, 48, 221

New York Age, 236–37, 238

New York Call, 207

New York Ledger, 63–64

New York Public Library, 216, 217; Seward Park Children's Room, 214, 215, 216, 321 (n. 72)

Niagara Movement, 241

Nightingale, Florence, 100

Niles, Thomas, Jr., 18, 20, 22, 23, 263 (nn. 24, 28, 32)

The Nineteenth Century, 50

Norris, William Edward: *A Bachelor's Blunder*, 95

North American Review, 47

North Bennet Street Industrial School (Boston), 181–82

Nurses' Settlement. *See* Henry Street Settlement

Oatley, Keith, 5, 260 (n. 11), 290 (n. 26), 292 (n. 47)

O'Donovan, Edmond: *The Merv Oasis*, 105

Oliphant, Margaret, 60

Oprah's Book Club, 254–55, 335 (n. 9)

Optic, Oliver (William Oliver Adams), 29, 50, 224

O'Reilly, Leonora, 194, 206, 208, 318–19 (n. 50), 319 (n. 59)

Otis, James: *Toby Tyler*, 40

Ouida: "Afternoon," 281 (n. 19); *Pascarel*, 296 (n. 86)

Our Young Folks, 54

Outlook, 207

Ovington, Mary White, 118–19, 292 (n. 50)

Ozick, Cynthia, 14–15, 16, 28

Pacifism, 160, 161

Pansy (Isabella Alden), 50

Parkman, Francis, 58

Pastor (Stokes), Rose, 13, 16, 33, 260 (n. 1), 261 (n. 2)

Pawley, Christine, 50, 278 (n. 30)

Penn, I. Garland, 243

Perkins, Frederic Beecher, 69

Pesotta, Rose, 196, 318 (n. 41)

Petry, Ann, 30

Phelps, Elizabeth: *The Gates Ajar*, 143

Pickford, Mary, 252

Pinchback, P. B. S., 227

Plato: *Dialogues*, 173

Pleasure reading: and family literary culture, 3, 57; and Alcott, 13; favorable attitudes toward, 37, 60, 67; serious

reading compared to, 86–87, 95–96, 172, 284 (n. 47); and M. Carey Thomas, 110, 128, 129, 132, 133; and Jane Addams, 140, 151; and Rose Gollup Cohen, 199; and Mary Antin, 215; and Agnes Hamilton, 287 (n. 88)

Plutarch, 49, 65, 141, 277 (n. 21), 299 (n. 18)

Poe, Edgar Allan, 87, 266 (n. 77)

Poetry: women as authors of, 39, 53–54, 69, 70, 74; and reading instruction, 47; memorizing and reciting of, 51, 53, 62, 86, 88, 143, 274 (n. 56); and family literary culture, 52; and Scott, 53, 86, 88; and young women's reading, 58, 59, 62; and M. Carey Thomas, 110, 111, 124; and Jane Addams, 143, 301 (n. 38)

Polacheck, Hilda Satt: and Hull-House classes, 7, 175, 176–78; on Jane Addams, 170; *I Came a Stranger*, 175, 178, 309 (n. 39); education of, 175–76; writing of, 176, 177–78; and Labor Museum, 176, 309 (n. 40); reading of, 176–77; and Americanization, 177, 178, 182, 190

Pope, Alexander, 87

Porter, Cole, 218

Porter, Jane: *Thaddeus of Warsaw*, 48; *Scottish Chiefs*, 65

Porter, Noah, 45–46, 89

Porter, Sarah, 89–90, 93

Positivism, 156, 158, 159–60, 304 (n. 88), 305 (n. 104)

Pragmatism, 157, 189–90

Pratt, Anna, 265 (n. 50)

Prentiss, Elizabeth Payson: *Stepping Heavenward*, 102, 103, 285 (n. 71), 287 (n. 93)

Prescott, William H., 58

Priestley, Joseph, 58

Private activities/public sphere relationship: and women's ambitions, 3–4, 55, 84, 150, 153, 253; and women's role in culture, 40; and autobiographies, 54; and family literary culture, 57; and young women's reading, 68; and reading clubs and circles, 72; and World's

educational role of, 252; re-emergence in twentieth century, 254, 255–57, 336 (n. 19); and female bonding, 256

Reading and self-culture: and *Little Women*, 5; and literary culture, 6; and M. Carey Thomas, 7, 109, 110, 113, 121, 123, 125, 133; and Jane Addams, 7, 135–36, 137, 151–52; and young women's reading, 58–59, 68, 69, 70–71; and Hamilton family, 86–88, 95, 96, 107

Reading communities: and women's ambitions, 3, 51; and meanings, 4, 259 (n. 6); case studies of, 4–5; defining of, 260 (n. 9)

Reading practices: Chartier on, 4; and book history, 5; of African American women, 8, 29, 219; of working-class women, 13, 30, 31, 171, 267 (n. 79); social class as influence on, 29, 30–31; of Jewish immigrant women, 31–32, 194, 218–19; cultural norms as influence on, 31–33; and reading aloud, 50, 51–52, 53, 64, 68, 85, 94, 95, 169, 173–74, 180, 200, 284 (n. 52), 309 (n. 31); and family literary culture, 51–52, 68, 273 (n. 42); and literary allusions, 57, 96, 97–98; and rereading, 91–92, 96, 284 (n. 52)

Reid, Mayne, 18, 83

Religion: and African American women, 8, 219; and *Little Women*, 19, 263 (n. 32); and reading instruction, 43; and culture of reading, 43–44; and Chautauqua Society, 71; and Jewish literacy, 194–95, 196, 197, 198; and Ida B. Wells, 224, 225. *See also* Addams, Jane; Hamilton family; Thomas, M. Carey

Richardson, Dorothy, 30–31, 266–67 (n. 78)

Richardson, W. L., 311 (n. 64)

Riley, James Whitcomb, 218

Rockford Female Seminary (later Rockford College), 24, 137, 143–44, 158, 178, 300 (n. 30), 308 (n. 28)

Rogers, Julia, 121, 130, 293 (nn. 57, 58)

Romance: and Laura Jean Libbey, 13; views on reading, 13, 260 (n. 7), 291 (n. 37); in *Little Women*, 16, 21, 22, 27, 28, 34, 115, 264 (n. 38); and Alice Stone Blackwell, 61–62, 65, 67, 276 (n. 7); and Hamilton family, 98, 100; and quest plot, 118, 119; and Rose Gollup Cohen, 201–2; Radway on, 260 (n. 7); Kaplan on, 291 (n. 37)

Roosevelt, Theodore, 25, 273 (n. 40)

Rosa, Salvator, 161

Rosenfeld, Morris, 185

Ross, Dorothy, 313 (n. 86)

Ross, Edward A., 48–49, 291 (n. 32)

Rossetti, Gabriel Dante, 124, 133

Roth, Philip, 193, 215

Rubin, Joan Shelley, 271 (nn. 19, 27), 274 (n. 56), 278 (n. 31)

Rubinow, Isaac M., 315 (n. 10)

Ruskin, John: and Hamilton family, 90; and M. Carey Thomas, 112; Mary E. Garrett on, 121, 123, 293 (n. 57); *Modern Painters*, 157, 161; and Hull-House classes, 173, 184; *Bible of Amiens*, 305 (n. 104). *See also* Addams, Jane

Russell, Bertrand, 96

Russian Jewish immigrants: and libraries, 8, 193; and *Little Women*, 16; and women's education, 195–96, 197, 314–15 (n. 6), 315 (n. 8)

St. Nicholas (magazine), 22, 50, 54

Salmon, Edward G.: "What Girls Read," 50, 274 (n. 51)

Sand, George, 148, 283 (n. 35)

Santayana, George, 310 (n. 53)

Savonarola, 147, 148, 156–57, 171

Schechter, Patricia A., 324–25 (n. 15), 331 (n. 96)

Schliemann, Heinrich, 302 (n. 58)

Schreiner, Olive: *Dreams*, 205

Scott, Leroy: *The Walking Delegate*, 177

Scott, Walter, 48, 58; and Stowe, 44; popularity of, 50, 86; poetry of, 53, 86, 88; and Alice Stone Blackwell, 64; *The Lady of the Lake*, 86, 88, 283–84 (n. 38);

Wollstonecraft, Mary, 124, 294 (n. 64)

Woman's Christian Temperance Union (WCTU), 49, 54

Woman's Congress, 24

Woman's Journal, 54, 60, 63

Woman's Loyal Union (WLU), 245, 331 (n. 102)

Woman suffrage movement, 75, 82, 130, 133

Women: subordinate position of, 2; reading of, compared to men, 2, 5, 50, 57, 67, 256, 259 (n. 3), 334 (n. 1); literary accomplishments of, 3; as teachers of reading, 47. *See also* African American women; Jewish immigrant women; Jewish women; Middle-class women; Progressive generation of women; White women; Working-class women; Young women's reading

Women's ambitions: role of reading in, 1, 2–3, 32, 42, 46, 51, 55, 57, 59, 120; and role of narratives, 3, 15–16, 53, 65, 80, 259 (n. 4); and private activities/public sphere relationship, 3–4, 55, 84, 150, 153, 253; and *Little Women*, 6, 15–16, 26, 28, 29, 33–34, 36, 50, 114; and higher education, 40; and autobiographies, 55, 100; and support of peers, 55, 125; and self-culture, 59; and young women's reading, 68, 114, 120, 133; and marriage, 98; and gender norms, 136, 137; and Hull-House, 182. *See also* Addams, Jane; Hamilton family; Thomas, M. Carey

Women's reading of fiction: and advice literature, 46; and favorite authors, 50, 274 (n. 51); and young women, 63, 65; Bakhtin on, 66; and identification with characters, 66–67, 98, 104, 257; and agency, 80, 101, 125, 129, 257; and control, 133; medical advice against, 293–94 (n. 59)

Women's Trade Union League, 207

Woodhull, Victoria, 117

Woodson, Carter G., 249

Working class: middle class distinguished from, 41, 46, 270 (nn. 13, 14); and culture of reading, 45; and newspapers, 45; and theater, 183, 252

Working-class women: literacy of, 7; reading practices of, 13, 30, 31, 171, 267 (n. 79); reading clubs of, 71; relationship with patrons, 170

World's Columbian Exposition (Chicago), 73–75; Woman's Building, 73

World's Congress of Representative Women, 75

World War I, 160, 320 (n. 63)

Writers and writing: as corollary to reading, 3, 53, 57; and *Little Women*, 5, 23, 24, 26–27, 30, 33–34, 114; and women's place in literary culture, 24; valorization of, 38; women earning money from, 39, 54, 70, 75, 114; and culture of reading, 42; and family literary culture, 52; and diaries, 52, 53, 275 (n. 60); and letter writing, 52–53, 93, 94–95, 96, 275 (n. 61); and poetry, 62; and young women's collaborative writing, 70, 123; and reading clubs and circles, 73; and parlor literature, 275 (n. 63). *See also* Autobiographical writings

Yezierska, Anzia, 170

Yiddishes Tageblatt, 13

Yonge, Charlotte Mary: popularity of, 50; Hamilton family's reading of, 85, 92, 105; *The Daisy Chain*, 101, 282 (n. 21); heroines of, 118

Young women's reading: and *Little Women*, 13–22, 25, 35, 36; recommendations for, 45–46; and girls' books, 50–51; and socialization, 57, 60, 66; and autobiographical writings, 58–59, 67, 278 (n. 31); as self-culture, 58–59, 68, 69, 70–71; and emotional connection, 60, 62, 63, 64, 66, 67, 251, 277 (n. 15); and male authors and characters, 61; and romance, 61–62, 65, 67, 68, 276 (n. 7); parents' supervision of, 62–65,